W9-AMY-408

The Only Jealousy of Emer and *Fighting the Waves*

Manuscript Materials

THE CORNELL YEATS

PLAYS

The Countess Cathleen, edited by Michael J. Sidnell and Wayne K. Chapman
The Land of Heart's Desire, edited by Jared Curtis
Diarmuid and Grania, edited by J. C. C. Mays
The Hour-Glass, edited by Catherine Phillips
Deirdre, edited by Virginia Bartholome Rohan
The Dreaming of the Bones and *Calvary*, edited by Wayne K. Chapman
The Only Jealousy of Emer and *Fighting the Waves*, edited by Steven Winnett
The Words Upon the Window Pane, edited by Mary FitzGerald
The Herne's Egg, edited by Alison Armstrong
Purgatory, edited by Sandra F. Siegel
The Death of Cuchulain, edited by Phillip L. Marcus

POEMS

The Early Poetry, Volume I: "Mosada" and "The Island of Statues," edited by George Bornstein
The Early Poetry, Volume II: "The Wanderings of Oisin" and Other Early Poems to 1895, edited by George Bornstein
The Wind Among the Reeds, edited by Carolyn Holdsworth
"In the Seven Woods" and "The Green Helmet and Other Poems," edited by David Holdeman
Responsibilities, edited by William H. O'Donnell
The Wild Swans at Coole, edited by Stephen Parrish
Michael Robartes and the Dancer, edited by Thomas Parkinson, with Anne Brannen
The Winding Stair (1929), edited by David R. Clark
Words for Music, Perhaps, edited by David R. Clark
"Parnell's Funeral and Other Poems" from "A Full Moon in March," edited by David R. Clark
New Poems, edited by J. C. C. Mays and Stephen Parrish
Last Poems, edited by James Pethica

The Only Jealousy of Emer and *Fighting the Waves*

Manuscript Materials

BY W. B. YEATS

EDITED BY

STEVEN WINNETT

Cornell University Press

ITHACA AND LONDON

The preparation of this volume was made possible in part
by a grant from The Atlantic Philanthropies.

First published 2004 by Cornell University Press

Printed in the United States of America

Library of Congress Cataloging-in-Publication Data

Yeats, W. B. (William Butler), 1865-1939.
The only jealousy of Emer : and, Fighting the waves : manuscript materials / by W.B. Yeats ; edited by Steven Winnett.
p. cm. -- (The Cornell Yeats)
Includes bibliographical references.
ISBN 0-8014-4293-1
1. Yeats, W. B. (William Butler), 1865-1939. Only jealousy of Emer--Criticism, Textual.
2. Yeats, W. B. (William Butler), 1865-1939. Fighting the waves--Criticism, Textual.
3. Yeats, W. B. (William Butler), 1865-1939--Manuscripts. I. Winnett, Steven. II. Yeats, W. B. (William Butler), 1865-1939. Fighting the waves. III. Title: Fighting the waves. IV. Title.

PR5904.O59 2004
821'.8--dc22

2004057717

Cornell University strives to utilize environmentally responsible suppliers and materials to the fullest extent possible in the publishing of its books. Such materials include vegetable-based, low-VOC inks and acid-free papers that are recycled, totally chlorine-free, or partly composed of non-wood fibers. For further information, visit our website at www.cornellpress.cornell.edu.

1 3 5 7 9 cloth printing 10 8 6 4 2

The Cornell Yeats

The volumes in this series present all available manuscripts, revised typescripts, proof sheets, and other materials that record the growth of Yeats's poems and plays from the earliest draftings through to the lifetime published texts. Most of the materials are from the archives of Senator Michael Yeats, now in the care of the National Library of Ireland, supplemented by materials held by the late Anne Yeats; the remainder are preserved in public collections and private hands in Ireland and around the world. The volumes of poems, with a few exceptions, follow the titles of Yeats's own collections; several volumes of plays in the series contain more than one play.

In all the volumes manuscripts are reproduced in photographs accompanied by transcriptions, in order to illuminate Yeats's creative process—to show the poet at work. The remaining materials—such as clean typescripts and printed versions—are generally recorded in collated form in an apparatus hung below a finished text. Each volume contains an Introduction describing the significance of the materials it includes, tracing the relation of the various texts to one another. There is also a census of manuscripts, with full descriptive detail, and appendixes are frequently used to present related materials, some of them unpublished.

As the editions seek to present, comprehensively and accurately, the various versions behind Yeats's published poems and plays, including versions he left unpublished, they will be of use to readers who seek to understand how great writing can be made, and to scholars and editors who seek to establish and verify authoritative final texts.

THE YEATS EDITORIAL BOARD

Contents

Acknowledgments

Senator Michael Butler Yeats has been most generous in allowing the use of manuscripts of W. B. Yeats, including those in the National Library of Ireland and elsewhere. I am grateful to the late Richard Ellmann, New College, Oxford, for sharing his knowledge and expertise in the study of Yeats manuscripts with me.

I owe thanks to many others who have assisted me in various capacities, especially to J. C. Buitelaar, New College, Oxford; David R. Clark, University of Massachusetts, Amherst; Jennifer L. Gentzyel, University of Massachusetts, Boston; George Harper, Florida State University; John Kelly, St. John's College, Oxford; E. G. MacKenzie, Lady Margaret Hall, Oxford; Daniel J. Murphy, Columbia University; and V. G. Ruys, Tonneelmuseum, Amsterdam. I also wish to acknowledge with deep gratitude the financial support provided by the Canada Council that made it possible for me to study at Oxford.

Transcriptions and photographs presented in this volume appear by the permission of their present keepers and through the courteous assistance of their respective staff members: the Manuscript Collections of the British Library; Special Collections and Archives, John J. Burns Library, Boston College; University of Chicago Library Special Collections Research Center; Special Collections and Archives, Robert W. Woodruff Library, Emory University; the Council of Trustees of the National Library of Ireland; the Henry W. and Albert A. Berg Collection, New York Public Library; Houghton Library, Harvard University; the H. Lytton Wilson Collection of William Butler Yeats, Special Collections, Morris Library, Southern Illinois University at Carbondale; W. B. Yeats Microfilmed Manuscripts Collection, Frank Melville Jr. Memorial Library, State University of New York at Stony Brook; and the Harry Ransom Humanities Research Center, University of Texas, Austin.

I am grateful to the members of the Yeats Editorial Board, especially to Stephen Parrish, Ann Saddlemyer, and Jared Curtis, for their efforts in reshaping the material I originally presented as my doctoral dissertation to New College, Oxford and their suggestions for revision.

STEVEN WINNETT

Boston, Massachusetts

Census of Manuscripts

The British Library, London:

Add. MS 55,878 Page proof of *Wheels and Butterflies* (London: Macmillan: 1934) with a typescript Preface dated "August 4" by Yeats. Contains *Fighting the Waves,* first page proof, marked "Revise" and "PRESS," dated August 7, 1934. The Introduction has only scattered revisions of punctuation and spelling, most made by the printer. Macmillan Archive, volume MXCIII.

Add. MS 55,879 Page proof of *The Only Jealousy of Emer* from *The Collected Plays of W. B. Yeats* (London: Macmillan, 1934), inscribed in pencil "Author's Marked Proofs" and stamped "5 July 1934" and "FIRST PROOF" by Clark of Edinburgh. All revisions incorporated in *Collected Plays*. Macmillan Archive, volume MXCIV.

Add. MS 55,884 Page proof of *The Only Jealousy of Emer* from *Four Plays for Dancers* (London: Macmillan, 1921), stamped "PRESS" by R. & R. Clark of Edinburgh with date "8 Feb [?]." All revisions incorporated in the text of *Collected Plays* (1934); see Russell K. Alspach, ed., *The Variorum Edition of the Plays of W. B. Yeats* (London: Macmillan, 1966). Macmillan Archive, volume MXCIX.

Add. MS 55,885 Page proof of "More Plays for Dancers," revised to *Wheels and Butterflies,* stamped by Clark of Edinburgh "8 Feb 1939"; text of *Fighting the Waves* runs on pages 289–308, revised to 16–26 with pencil note "Became vol V." Numerous revisions and corrections, mainly of spelling and punctuation, apparently made by the printer in broad blue pencil, along with a few changes of wording and additions designed to clarify the text. Macmillan Archive, volume MC.

Add. MS 55,891 Page proof of *The Only Jealousy of Emer* from the unpublished "Coole Edition." Macmillan Archive, volume MCVI.

Add. MS 55,892 Third page proof of *Fighting the Waves* in *Wheels and Butterflies,* stamped "12 July 1935" by R. & R. Clark, Edinburgh, bearing scattered revisions or suggestions made by the printer or Mrs. Yeats or at her direction. Part of the proof from the unpublished "Coole Edition." Macmillan Archive, volume MCVII.

LCP Ten-page typescript of *Fighting the Waves* submitted to the Lord Chamberlain's Office for licensing, March 30, 1930, for performance at the Lyric Theatre, Hammersmith. Under Crown copyright.[1]

Chicago Page proof of *The Only Jealousy of Emer* prior to the play's publication in *Poetry* (1919). In the University of Chicago Library Special Collections Research Center.

Emory Page proof of *The Only Jealousy of Emer* from *Two Plays for Dancers,* marked up toward *Four Plays for Dancers,* with four revisions of punctuation and one textual revision in ink, by Yeats, along with one penciled query, not Yeats's. In the Special Collections and Archives, Robert W. Woodruff Library, Emory University.

Harvard Earliest complete holograph of *The Only Jealousy of Emer*. Eighteen leaves of three-hole, lined loose-leaf paper, 19.0 by 24.0 cm, watermarked WALKER'S / LOOSE / LEAF, comprising the first version of the draft, with eighteen leaves of same paper interpolated, bearing revisions for insertion in the text. MS Eng 338.7; in the Houghton Library, Harvard University.

NLI 8773 Holograph and typescript notes on *Four Plays for Dancers* with page proof of a note on *The Only Jealousy of Emer* stamped "7 Oct 1920." Contains typescript Preface of three pages—signed "WBY July 1920"—and five manuscript pages toward the Preface.

NLI 8774(1–22) Twenty-two folders containing manuscript drafts of *The Only Jealousy of Emer* and *Fighting the Waves:*

NLI 8774(1) Seven-page carbon typescript, with pages 25.3 by 20.3 cm, watermarked SWIFT BROOK / BOND, containing revisions to Introduction to *Fighting the Waves.*

NLI 8774(2) Seven-page typescript, ribbon copy, of 8774(1), containing revisions to Introduction to *Fighting the Waves.*

NLI 8774(3) Five-page carbon typescript of 8774(2) with revisions, containing revisions to Introduction to *Fighting the Waves.*

NLI 8774(4) Two pages of carbon typescript of 8774(2) plus one page of manuscript, containing revisions to Introduction to *Fighting the Waves.*

NLI 8774(5) Seven pages of typescript, revisions of *Fighting the Waves*, here still called *The Only Jealousy of Emer,* two on typing paper 22.3 by 17.4 cm with no watermark, five on three-hole notebook paper, ruled, with no watermark, 24 by 19 cm. MS N.

NLI 8774(6) Thirteen-page typescript of *Fighting the Waves* (two front pages blank, followed by eleven numbered, 25.3 by 20.3 cm, watermarked SWIFT BROOK / SUPERFINE. Leaf

[1]An eight-page typescript of *The Only Jealousy of Emer*, submitted to the Lord Chamberlain's Office for licensing, was approved on August 19, 1955, for a production at a theater in Edinburgh. The late date precludes its readings from inclusion among the variants recorded below.

1 is foliated in pencil "30"; leaves 2–12 are foliated twice (the typewritten page 1 . . . 11 is crossed out and replaced by penciled numbers 42–52, presumably for *Wheels and Butterflies*. MS O.

NLI 8774(7) Two-page typescript of note to *The Only Jealousy of Emer,* with revisions, on 25.9 by 20 cm paper, without watermark, pin hole in upper-left corner.

NLI 8774(8) One-page draft of the opening chorus to *The Only Jealousy of Emer* on three-hole notebook paper, ruled, 24.0 by 19.0 cm, watermarked WALKER'S / LOOSE / LEAF; contributes to MS K.

NLI 8774(9) Ten leaves of holograph of *The Only Jealousy of Emer,* 22.7 by 18 cm, folded to make five bifolia, watermarked ORPHEUS / [harp design] / PARCHMENT. MS A.

NLI 8774(10) Two leaves of holograph of *The Only Jealousy of Emer*, on plain paper 22.6 by 17.5 cm, watermarked THE / WESTMINSTER / NOTE, folded down the middle. MS B.

NLI 8774(11) Blue book with "The / Big / Value / Exercise Book / [ornament] / 361 Pages / Ruled / Faint" on front cover, and "Arithmetical Tables" on outside back cover; notebook contains eighteen leaves, 20.1 by 16.2 cm, all sewn to cover. First thirteen leaves are paginated, in pencil, 1–36, with writing on rectos only, holograph draft of *The Only Jealousy of Emer.* MS C.

NLI 8774(12) Two leaves of holograph of *The Only Jealousy of Emer*, torn from an exercise book, 20.2 by 16.2 cm. MS D.

NLI 8774(13) Maroon notebook of holograph of *The Only Jealousy of Emer*; wavy design etched into front and back covers; contains forty-six leaves 20.2 by 16.2 cm paginated, in pencil, 1–92. MS E concludes on leaf 6, MS F on leaf 22, and MS G takes up the remainder of the notebook.

NLI 8774(14) Six leaves of holograph of *The Only Jealousy of Emer* on three-hole ruled notebook paper, numbered 11–16, 24 by 19 cm, watermarked WALKER'S / LOOSE / LEAF; contributes to MS K.

NLI 8774(15) Two leaves of holograph of *The Only Jealousy of Emer* on ruled tablet paper, 24.8 by 19.2 cm. MS I.

NLI 8774(16) Nine leaves of holograph of *The Only Jealousy of Emer* on ruled three-hole notebook paper, 24 by 19 cm, watermarked WALKER'S / LOOSE / LEAF with metal rings in each hole; contributes to MS K.

NLI 8774(17) Two and a half leaves of holograph of *The Only Jealousy of Emer* on ruled three-hole notebook paper, 20.2 by 17 cm, watermarked WALKER'S / LOOSE / LEAF; contributes to MS P.

NLI 8774(18) Three-page typescript of corrections to *The Only Jealousy of Emer,* bearing revisions, on 25.2 by 20.2 cm paper watermarked SWIFT BROOK / BOND; contributes to MS P.

NLI 8774(19) Two leaves of holograph of *The Only Jealousy of Emer*, one on typing paper, 25.2 by 20.2 cm, watermarked CAMERON BOND, the other on ruled tablet paper, 22.7 by 17.7 cm, with chain lines at intervals of 2.5 cm; no visible watermark; MS J.

NLI 8774(20) Four leaves of holograph of *The Only Jealousy of Emer* numbered 1, 2, 3, 6; the first two on typing paper, 25.2 by 20.2 cm, watermarked CAMERON BOND, the second two on ruled tablet paper, 27.0 by 21.0 cm, watermark illegible; MS H.

NLI 8774(21) The earliest typescript of *The Only Jealousy of Emer*, a twenty-page copy revised by Yeats on paper 25.5 by 20.3 cm with pin holes at top left, watermarked CHARLES MARTIN / EXTRA STRONG. The first six leaves are ribbon copy, the remainder carbons. Leaf 1 is unnumbered; all succeeding leaves are numbered 2–20; all versos are blank. MS L.

NLI 8774(22) Three pages of draft of the final song in *The Only Jealousy of Emer* on three-hole notebook paper, with rounded corners, 20.2 by 16.4 cm. In a folder with the second typescript of the play. MS M.

NLI 13,567 Thirteen-page autograph manuscript of revisions of the Introduction to *Fighting the Waves*; the numbered leaves are ruled three-hole notebook paper, 20.3 by 16.4 cm, watermarked WALKER'S / LOOSE / LEAF. Text begins with Part II and ends with a four-line squib.

NLI 13,574(1), (2) Two hard-back notebooks that Yeats kept in the 1880s and 1890s. The first contains references to Irish legends and myths in John Rhys's *Lectures on the Origin and Growth of Religion as Illustrated by Celtic Heathendom* (London; Edinburgh: Williams and Norgate, 1888), while the second is an alphabetical index of the Irish gods. Used as a reference tool by Yeats.

NLI 21,494 Twelve-page single-spaced typescript of *Fighting the Waves* with pin holes in upper-left corner. On cover is title and inscription "Prompt Copy"; visible burn marks from the Abbey Theatre fire. Title page has a pencil sketch of the stage. Paper is 26.2 by 20.2 cm, watermarked ALLANDER / BOND. Bears scattered revisions in ink and pencil, evidently not Yeats's.

NLI 30,003 Revised proof of the Introduction to *Fighting the Waves* in the *Dublin Magazine* (April–June 1932), pages 7–11.

NLI 30,007 Corrected page proof of the unpublished "Coole Edition," "Marked by author"; contains *Four Plays for Dancers,* including *The Only Jealousy of Emer* on pages 109–127, stamped by R. & R. Clark of Edinburgh "7 Dec 1931." Scattered revisions by Yeats in ink and by printer in pencil.

NLI 30,079 An envelope containing manuscript notes and fragments on ruled paper torn from an exercise book, 22.2 by 15 cm, for *The Only Jealousy of Emer,* beginning "While writing these plays, which are intended to be played before some fifty people in a drawing room or a studio, I have rejoiced in my freedom from the stupidity of an ordinary audience . . . ." Accompanied by "Contents" for *Four Plays for Dancers* and a note promising specimens of Edmond Dulac's designs of masks and costumes.

NLI 30,165 Four pages of single-spaced typescript of *Fighting the Waves* containing instructions to a typist and directions for staging and performance of the play. The first page, unnumbered, contains drafts toward the Prologue and Epilogue; the second page, numbered "2," and the remaining pages, unnumbered, contain drafts of text from l. 227 to the end, lightly revised.

NLI 30,185 First three pages of proof of *Fighting the Waves* for the "Coole Edition" stamped "7 Oct 1932" by Clark of Edinburgh, bearing printer's revisions only, followed by typescripts of the Introduction.

NLI 30,190 Three-page autograph draft of the Preface to *Plays and Controversies,* signed by Yeats: "Dublin Feb 1923."

NLI 30,492 Five-page autograph draft of *Fighting the Waves* (one page contains an entry on the verso), on ruled three-hole notebook paper, 24.2 by 19 cm, watermarked WALKER'S / LOOSE / LEAF.

NLI 30,600 Fifteen pages of revised typescript, some ribbon copies, some carbons, of the Introduction to *Wheels and Butterflies,* beginning with Section II.

NLI 30,602 The earliest full text of *Fighting the Waves.* Eight-page single-spaced typescript with scattered ink revisions and penciled stage directions; earlier than the texts in the Abbey Theatre prompt copy (21,494) and the Lord Chamberlain's copy (LCP 9598).

NLI 30,873 Five typewritten texts of *The Only Jealousy of Emer* evidently prepared as actors' texts:

(A) Twenty-page double-spaced typescript, carbon copy of C (below), lightly revised by Yeats, marked "Corrected" in upper-right corner, on paper measuring 25.4 by 20.3 cm, watermarked CHARLES MARTIN / EXTRA STRONG, speaker identifications and stage directions underlined in red, pin holes at upper-left corner.

(B) Another carbon copy of C on same paper, also marked "Corrected" with same revisions, and a few variants, entered by Yeats, and the same red underlining,

(C) Ribbon copy of A and B with inked note reading "Corrected. In this copy stage directions are corrected"; the note was then crossed out lightly. Bears most of the same revisions in ink, with a few others, and added in ink on page 20 (of two page 20s) a thirty-nine-line poem: "What makes her heart beat thus."

(D) Carbon copy of E (below), with same revisions entered in ink by Yeats.

(E) Ribbon copy of another typing, with same revisions entered in ink by Yeats.

Quinn(14), 4[v] Described in *The Wild Swans of Coole*, ed. Stephen Parrish, Cornell Yeats (Ithaca: Cornell University Press, 1994). Quinn(14) is a five-leaf holograph draft of "The Sad Shepherd," a lyric published in *The Wild Swans of Coole* (1919). On the verso of leaf 4 are ten draft lines for *The Only Jealousy of Emer*. The Quinn manuscripts are in the Henry W. and Albert A. Berg Collection, New York Public Library, Astor, Lennox and Tilden Foundation.

Southern Illinois University Eight-page revised typescript of the Introduction to *The Only Jealousy of Emer*, printer's copy for its appearance in the *Dublin Magazine*.

Texas Page proof of *The Only Jealousy of Emer* from the unpublished Scribner edition.

Introduction

I. Publishing and Performing History

The Only Jealousy of Emer marks one of the major turning points of Yeats's career, because in its final form it is a synthesis of two profound experiences that were to shape his later work. His marriage to Georgie Hyde Lees in 1917 brought him a certain degree of contentment with the joys of this world. His wife's automatic script brought him a philosophical framework for poems and plays.[1] The strange handwritten messages apparently from the spirit world gave Yeats, he believed, a certain insight into that "other world" of folklore, spirits, fairies, divinities, occult powers, and the figures of both mythology and history whose ways, deeds, and values provide a deep background of Yeatsian fact for his work. Yeats is as much a poet of fact as of feeling. Everything in his work has a source—be it from folklore, legend, mythology, the occult, or history—a source which for him had a definite objective reality.[2] The demands of this world and of that other world of Yeatsian spiritual reality are often in conflict, and *The Only Jealousy of Emer*, particularly in its early drafts, is a vivid portrayal of such a struggle.

The autobiographical foundation of *The Only Jealousy of Emer* has long been a commonplace of writings on Yeats and his work.[3] George Mills Harper provided direct insight on this in his critical text of the first edition (1925) of Yeats's *A Vision*:

> Throughout most of the time during which the AS [Automatic Script] and Sleeps were being recorded, Yeats was preoccupied with The Only Jealousy, in which he, George, Maud [Gonne], and Iseult [Gonne] were projected in the four main characters. In the AS for 20 November 1917 he was informed by the Control that "there is a symbolism of the growth of the soul" in the Cuchulain plays. On 21 December in a long Script he learned that his "own sin[s] exactly correspond to those of C[uchulain], and that George (Emer), Iseult (Eithne) and Maud (Woman of the Sidhe) represent race, passion, and love in that order. On 7 January 1918 Yeats

[1]See *Yeats's Vision Papers*, vols. 1–3, gen. ed. George Mills Harper (London: Macmillan, 1992; Iowa City: University of Iowa Press, 1992).

[2]Consider, as just one instance among many, Yeats's publicly stating as *fact*—in the pages of *The Speaker* in 1900—the existence of a "continual communion of the Irish country people with supernatural beings of all kinds. . . . Already some that have devoted themselves to the study of the visions and beliefs of such people are asking whether it is we, still but very few, or primitive and barbaric people, still a countless multitude, who are the exceptions in the order of nature, and whether the seer of visions and hearer of voices is not the normal and healthy man." (Colton Johnson, ed., *The Collected Works of W. B. Yeats*, vol. 10, *Later Articles and Reviews* [New York: Scribner, 2000], pp. 24–25.)

[3]See, for example, Birgit Bjersby, *The Interpretation of the Cuchulain Legend in the Works of W. B. Yeats* (Uppsala: Lundequistska, 1950), pp. 94–99.

> asked, "Who will C love?" The Control replied, "I cannot tell you till you know yourself and you do know I think but perhaps unconsciously." When he asked if it were Emer, the Control did not reply.[4]

The manuscripts of *The Only Jealousy of Emer* show Yeats's varying responses to the question "Who will Cuchulain love?"[5] In the early drafts, the answer was clearly Emer, as Cuchulain rejected with contempt the shadowy Platonic world embodied by the Woman of the Sidhe. The later drafts, however, show the increasing influence on Yeats of the new lunar worldview found in the automatic script. This outlook was very convenient artistically for Yeats, in that it gave him a vehicle for expressing the basic conflicts of life without needing to resolve them. Thus, as the drafts progress, Yeats's sympathies are divided between Emer and the Woman of the Sidhe. By the time of the final drafts, Yeats has so objectified the conflict portrayed that it is hard to say whose side he is on. The answer would seem to be that his complex vision could and did accommodate all three desires (race, passion, and love) without seeing any need to resolve the conflicts between them.

The success of his play *At the Hawk's Well* in April 1916 had led Yeats to the project of writing a similar dance play on the story of Cuchulain and Fand, the Woman of the Sidhe, as he wrote to Lady Gregory in that month:

> P.S. I want to follow The Hawk's Well with a play on The Only Jealousy of Emer but I cannot think who should be the changeling put in Cuchulain's place when he is taken to the other world. There would be two masks changed upon the stage. Who should it be – Cuchulain's grandfather, or some god or devil or woman?[6]

The shock of the Easter Rebellion presumably postponed this plan for the time being. The tragic events in Dublin found poetic expression in "Easter, 1916" and other poems, and dramatic embodiment in *The Dreaming of the Bones*, which Yeats worked on during the first half of 1917, completing the play by August.[7]

Having made a final proposal to the widowed Maud Gonne in July 1916, he now turned to her daughter Iseult, again a fruitless quest.[8] He then proposed to Georgie Hyde Lees, a family friend of six years and a fellow member of the Order of the Golden Dawn, with whom he had had an understanding for some time. They were married in October 1917.[9]

The newlyweds settled in at Oxford for the winter, and Yeats felt he now had a peaceful

---

[4]Notes 11 and 13–19 to 1:242 of George Mills Harper's critical text of the first edition of *A Vision*. A few weeks later, GY's Control assured Yeats his play was "a true dream" but that Cuchulain's love would be "an enigma," *Yeats's Vision Papers*, 1:220.

[5]See Helen Vendler's illuminating comments in *Yeats's "Vision" and the Later Plays* (Cambridge: Harvard University Press, 1963), pp. 230–234.

[6]Allan Wade, ed., *The Letters of W. B. Yeats* (London: Rupert Hart-Davis, 1954), p. 612. In the early drafts the substitue is called an "Evil Genius." The changeling was not in fact found in the original story of Cuchulain and Fand; for the origin of this motif in Yeats's interpretation of the story, see Appendix II below.

[7]For the history of the writing of this play, see Wayne K. Chapman's introduction to his edition, *"The Dreaming of the Bones" and "Calvary,"* Cornell Yeats (Ithaca: Cornell University Press, 2003).

[8]Gonne's estranged husband, John MacBride, was one of the ringleaders of the rebellion executed by the British (*Gonne-Yeats Letters, 1893–1938: Always Your Friend*, Anna MacBride White and A. Norman Jeffares, eds. [London: Pimlico, 1993], pp. 368–369).

[9]Georgie Hyde Lees was the stepdaughter of Olivia Shakespear's brother; for details of their courtship and marriage see Ann Saddlemyer, *Becoming George—The Life of Mrs. W. B. Yeats* (Oxford: Oxford University Press, 2002).

atmosphere in which he could get on with his work. He paid tribute to his wife in a letter to Lady Gregory of December 16, 1917, when he was busy with the first drafts of *The Only Jealousy of Emer*: "My wife is a perfect wife, kind, wise, and unselfish. I think you were such another young girl once. She has made my life serene and full of order."[10] On November 3 he had written to Lady Gregory, "I have just begun a new Cuchulain play on the Noh model—I think it very dramatic & strange. It is 'only jealousy of Emer' story & much that I have felt lately seems coming in to it."[11] On January 12, 1918, he announced that the new play was almost finished, and two days later wrote again, "Today I finished."[12]

At some point in 1918, Yeats decided that he would publish *The Dreaming of the Bones* and *The Only Jealousy of Emer* together at his Cuala Press as *Two Plays for Dancers*. That volume came out in January 1919, at which time the two plays appeared separately in two American periodicals to secure copyright in the United States.[13] By 1919 Yeats wrote his fourth dance play, *Calvary* (the first was *At the Hawk's Well*), and in 1921 all four plays were published in the Macmillan volume *Four Plays for Dancers*. For this book, Yeats made some minor textual revisions to *The Only Jealousy of Emer* and added a note on the play. He similarly introduced some slight changes into the play for its next printing in *Plays and Controversies* (1923).[14]

In his Preface to *Four Plays for Dancers*, Yeats had provided an explanation for the non-performance up until then[15] of three of the four dance plays:

> . . . the players must move a little stiffly and gravely like marionettes and, I think, to the accompaniment of drum taps. I felt, however, during the performance of "The Hawk's Well," the only one played up to this, that there was much to discover. Should I make a serious attempt, which I may not, being rather tired of the theatre, to arrange and supervise performances, the dancing will give me the most trouble, for I know but vaguely what I want. I do not want any existing form of stage dancing, but something with a similar gamut of expression, something more reserved, more self-controlled, as befits performers within arm's reach of their audience.[16]

The performance obstacles cited by Yeats did not stand in the way of a young Dutch actor,

---

[10]Wade, *Letters*, p. 634.

[11]Letter to Lady Gregory, Emory University, Wade, *Letters*, p. 644: "Before long I will send you the new Cuchulain play. I have written two good lyrics for it."

[12]Ibid., p. 645; however, on June 6 he wrote to Ezra Pound that "the 'Only Jealousy' . . . will be the better of two more lyrics" (Lilly Library, Indiana University).

[13]*The Dreaming of the Bones* appeared in *The Little Review*, and *The Only Jealousy of Emer* in *Poetry* (Chicago), both in January 1919.

[14]The reasons for Yeats publishing his play in three different collections within five years are to be found in Allan Wade, ed., *A Bibliography of the Writings of W. B. Yeats* (London: Rupert Hart-Davis, 1951; 3rd ed., revised by R. K. Alspach, 1968). *Two Plays for Dancers* was published in a limited edition of 400 copies (p. 129). *Four Plays for Dancers*, intended for the general market, was published in 1500 copies by Macmillan on October 28, 1921 (p. 134). In 1922, Macmillan began to publish a new *Collected Edition of the Works of W. B. Yeats*. Volumes 1 and 2 appeared on November 3, 1922, in editions of 1500 copies each: *Later Poems* and *Plays in Prose and Verse*. Presumably *Four Plays for Dancers* was still in print and on sale at this point, so it was not included in the new collected edition until volume 3, *Plays and Controversies* (pp. 142–143).

[15]However, the fact that he had completed several typescripts of *The Only Jealousy of Emer* before its first printing in January 1919 seems to suggest that he might have had a performance of some kind in mind.

[16]Russell K. Alspach, ed., *The Variorum Edition of the Plays of W. B. Yeats* (London: Macmillan, 1966), pp. 1304–1305.

Albert van Dalsum, who organized the first performance of *The Only Jealousy of Emer* in the Hollandsche Schouwburg in Amsterdam on April 2, 1922.[17] Van Dalsum, much influenced by the stage designer Gordon Craig, saw this performance as

> . . . an experiment in the use of the mask . . . and the style of acting that this imposed, the slow, grave, extended gestures and movements; he saw the adoption of the mask as an attempt to rediscover style, and as an act of "self-liberation", relevant in an age which realized the profound power of the irrational, the mystery behind the mask. He was helped by the dancer Lili Green. For the masks he turned to the sculptor Hildo Krop, whose art, developed from close connections with the Arts and Crafts movement, touched life at many points. These masks were of papier-mache, with woolen hair, painted basically in ivory, with deep shadows.[18]

Yeats, apparently ignorant of van Dalsum's performances in Holland, saw the first Irish production of the play at the Abbey Theatre on May 9, 1926, produced by Lennox Robinson for the Dublin Drama League's annual meeting. Joseph Holloway described the performance in his theater diary:

> Yeats made a speech of explanation before the Noh Plays or Plays for Dancers were performed. . . . The Only Jealousy of Emer . . . had J. Stephenson as the spokesman and chanter of the three "Musicians". Tom Moran and E. Leeming were the other two, the former playing a small drum and gong, and the latter the flute. Their getup was weirdly Japanese. Two carried in the bier on which the figure of "Cuchulain" lay, and the three drew a dark cloth with a strange device on gold across the stage, and when it was withdrawn the figures of "Emer" and the ghost of "Cuchulain" were discovered, and "The First Musician" told their story up to a certain point, and then the players took it up. "Eithne Inguba" came on and afterwards "The Woman of the Sidhe". . . . The two figures of "Cuchulain" wore masks, also, "The Woman", whose hands, arms and legs, and mask were gold. She tried to fascinate "The Ghost", till "Emer" called him back into his body, and then "The Musicians" again put the cloth across the front of the stage, and the players moved off, and two of them carried away the empty bier. . . .
>
> I liked Eileen Crowe's "Emer" . . . Norah McGuinness, who designed the costumes and masks, as well as playing the "Woman of the Sidhe", gave an interesting performance of a strange, uncanny character. The masking of the "Ghost" and the

---

[17]The play was performed in translation as *Vrouwe Emers Groote Strijd.* A Dutch reviewer commented, "Yeats's play, a work of divine and human life, a play in which the grief of life lasts as a profound echo, has qualities which are to be felt by being gleaned from what is hidden in the performance. This is, above all, Yeats's sphere, in which a darker nature breathes." The Dutch version of the play was revived in 1923 at The Hague and in 1924 at Utrecht. In 1926 it was again produced in Amsterdam, under the new title *Maskerspel Vrouwe Emer* and with a new score. See Liam Miller, *The Noble Drama of W. B. Yeats* (Dublin: Cuala Press, 1977), pp. 272–275. There had similarly been an unauthorized performance of *At the Hawk's Well* in New York in 1918 (Wade, *Letters*, p. 651). In addition, the text of Yeats's much earlier play *The Land of Heart's Desire* had been pirated many times in the United States in the early 1900s (Jared Curtis, ed., *The Land of Heart's Desire*, Cornell Yeats [Ithaca: Cornell University Press, 2002], p. xx, n. 12.)

[18]D. J. Gordon, *W. B. Yeats: Images of a Poet*, by D. J. Gordon, with contributions by Ian Fletcher, Frank Kermode, and Robin Skelton (Manchester: Manchester University Press, c1961, 1970 printing), p. 61.

> "Figure of Cuchulain" was not effective, and Shelah Richards's getup as "Eithne Inguba" was to my eyes ugly.
>
> All literary and artistic Dublin were present, and great stillness prevailed during the enactment of both pieces. The audience was all on the ground floor to get the proper effect intended for the stage.[19]

Norah McGuinness, cast at the last moment as the Woman of the Sidhe, recorded a somewhat different impression of this debut performance of *The Only Jealousy of Emer*:

> I can't remember now just why, but for some reason I was asked to take the part of the "Woman of the Sidhe". I hadn't to speak (I suppose the musicians or someone else spoke the words) – I was rehearsed to do a dance of seduction. F. J. MacCormick [*sic*], who played the Ghost of Cuchulain, was my victim.
>
> I had never been on a stage before, so I was extremely nervous, as I stood in the wings at the first performance. I had a gold and black mask – a very scanty gold and black costume (designed by me) – and my limbs were painted gold.
>
> Suddenly W. B. was beside me. He looked me up and down with approval – but, alas, then said: "There was a boy in the Middle Ages who was covered in gold – and he died!" At that moment I got my cue to go on the stage. F. J. MacCormick was waiting – on his knees, back to the audience – to be seduced by my dance. Every step and every gesture of my dance was a cue to what he had to say or do. I could only think of the boy in the Middle Ages; every step was forgotten and I flopped meaninglessly around the stage, while MacCormick hissed expletives at me.
>
> I spent the night at Lennox Robinson's house, and the hottest bath-water did not remove the gold. After a restless night a visit to the chemist reassured me.[20]

On November 27, 1926, the Dutch actor van Dalsum revived his production of *The Only Jealousy* for a single performance. "After this, a Dutch friend of Yeats showed him photographs of the bronzes that had appeared a year before in an *avant-garde* Dutch periodical."[21] Excited by the photographs of Hildo van Krop's masks, Yeats wrote to Sturge Moore later that year:

> I have got two fine Japanese Noh masks and am trying to get some magnificent masks made by the Dutch sculptor Van Krop for my Only Jealousy of Emer. With these masks I shall be able to give a series of Dance Plays here, as we have just added to the Abbey Theatre a small perfectly equipped theatre which holds a hundred people. I am hoping henceforth with the assistance of the Abbey School of Acting to make experiments for which the popular audience of a larger theatre is not ready. As the Young Players of the school will be comparatively inexperienced

---

[19]Robert Hogan and Michael J. O' Neill, eds., *Joseph Holloway's Irish Theatre* (Dixon, Calif.: Proscenium, 1968), I, pp. 13–14. The other play was *The Cat and the Moon*. At the last minute, Lennox Robinson replaced Leeming.

[20]*Irish Times*, June 13, 1965 (Yeats Centenary Issue). F. J. McCormick was one of the new generation of Abbey actors (see R. F. Foster, *W. B. Yeats: A Life / II: The Arch-Poet* [Oxford: Oxford University Press, 2003], p. 258). For a photograph of Norah McGuinness's costume design, see Miller, *The Noble Drama of W. B. Yeats*, plate XXIII, pp. 336–337.

[21]Gordon and Fletcher, *W. B. Yeats: Images of a Poet*, p. 61. The periodical was *Wendingen* (= "Turning Points"). Gordon and Fletcher have included photographs of Hildo van Krop's bronzes in their book.

> there will be some advantage in letting them appear before the public in a strange dramatic form, related rather to ritual than to the ordinary form of drama.[22]

Then, on May 21, 1927, on a visit to the Festival Theatre in Cambridge, he saw Ninette de Valois dance for the first time. Soon, he had persuaded the Irish-born dancer to assist in establishing a School of Dance at the Abbey, and to perform in his dance plays, rewriting *The Only Jealousy* so that the role of the Woman of the Sidhe could be interpreted through dance-mime alone.[23] The result was a radically new version called *Fighting the Waves* that Yeats began in late January 1928 while convalescing in Cannes. Besides dropping the Woman's speaking part, he changed the play from verse to prose, added dances, and greatly increased the scale of the production. He explained the reasons for this in his introduction to *Fighting the Waves*:

> I wrote *The Only Jealousy of Emer* for performance in a private house or studio, considering it, for reasons which I have explained, unsuited to a public stage. Then somebody put it on a public stage in Holland and Hildo van Krop made his powerful masks. Because the dramatist who can collaborate with a great sculptor is lucky, I rewrote the play not only to fit it for such a stage but to free it from abstraction and confusion.[24]

At first sight the connection between Krop's masks and the public stage is not clear; surely these masks could equally be used for a private performance? Yeats must have been given some of the details of the Amsterdam performances; if so, he would have known that the Dutch productions were not only played before a larger audience than he had envisaged but were also on a larger scale. For example, there had been an orchestra in Amsterdam instead of the few simple instruments Yeats had prescribed for the Musicians, who in the Dutch production had only acted as a Chorus. Yeats must therefore have concluded that, powerful as Krop's masks could be in an ordinary production, they would be far more powerful in a large-scale production with a much greater emphasis on music and dancing than the original *Only Jealousy*.

Freeing the play from "abstraction and confusion" would clearly be a necessary precondition for a production which would depend on masks, music, and dancing rather than words for its most powerful effects. The phrase also hints that Yeats must have been somewhat dissatisfied with his verse play, having now observed it in performance. He now applied the same principles of revision after a performance which he had outlined in a letter to John Quinn back in 1905:

> I have altogether re-written my Shadowy Waters. There is hardly a page of the old. The very temper of the thing is different. It is full of homely phrases and of the idiom of daily speech. I have made the sailors rough, as sailors should be, characterized all the people more or less, and yet not lost any of my lyrical moments. It has become a simple passionate play, or at any rate it has a simple passionate story for the common sightseer, though it keep back something for instructed eyes.[25]

---

[22]Ursula Bridge, ed., *W. B. Yeats and T. Sturge Moore: Their Correspondence* (London: Routledge & Kegan Paul, 1953), p. 110. This letter, misdated by the editor, was written about Sepetember 20, 1927.

[23]Ninette de Valois, *Come Dance With Me: A Memoir, 1898–1956* (London: H. Hamilton, 1957), pp. 88–89.

[24]Alspach, *Variorum Plays*, p. 567.

[25]Wade, *Letters*, p. 461.

Lennox Robinson's visit to the ailing poet in Cannes provided an opportunity to bring dancer and masks together, as Yeats explained to Lady Gregory:

> . . . when Lennox was here a few days ago, I dictated to George a vigorous new version in prose of "The Only Jealousy" arranged for stage dancing as we hope that Miss De Valois and her Dublin representative and pupils will be able soon to dance in those Dutch masks. Lennox will see Miss Valois in London then get a musician. The masks are our opportunity. I have seen pupils of Miss De Valois who had been under her only six months dance admirably.[26]

On his way back to Dublin, Robinson met the composer George Antheil in Paris. Antheil enthusiastically accepted the invitation to provide the music. However, it was not until March 1929, when the young musician and the Yeatses were in Rapallo, that composition began in earnest for "a musical setting for a trilogy consisting of *The Hawk's Well*, *On Baile's Strand* and . . . *Fighting the Waves*."[27] This ambitious project did not come to fruition, but Antheil did provide the music for *Fighting the Waves*, and, when Yeats heard some of it early in April 1929, he praised it as "the most dramatic music I have heard – a very strong beat, something heroic and powerful and strange."[28] Liam Miller provides the following description of Antheil's score:

> Antheil's music for the play, of which the vocal and piano parts were printed in *Wheels and Butterflies*, 1934, consists of an Overture to which the opening dance was performed, looking directly into the setting of the opening chorus and continuing into a brief movement to accompany the opening of the "wave" curtain which reveals the tableau on stage. There is a setting of the first Musician's brief lyric, "White shell, white wing!" and one of Fand's dance. The final chorus and Fand's last dance complete the score. The instrumentation, as described in a letter to me from Mrs. Antheil, dated September 3, 1974, is for "small chamber orchestra: flute, clarinet, trumpet, trombone, bass drum, piano, first and second violin, cello and contrabass." Mrs. Antheil has kindly allowed me to examine the manuscript of the score for *Fighting the Waves* and this reveals the complexity presented to the Abbey and the challenge to the resources of the theatre. In the setting for Fand's dance, Antheil makes such demands as:
>
> * Trombone should fit into its bell an enormous extension cardboard megaphone

---

[26]Bjersby, *Interpretation of the Cuchulain Legend*, p. 50; letter to Lady Gregory, February 10, 1928; quoted (but misdated January) in *Lady Gregory, The Journals*, vol. 2, *Books 30–44*, ed. Daniel J. Murphy (Gerrards Cross, Bucks: Colin Smythe, 1987).

[27]Wade, *Letters*, p. 760; for a description of the Yeatses, Antheil, and the Pounds in Rapallo, see Saddlemyer, *Becoming George*, pp. 416–417. To get the measure of the music of Antheil (1900–1959), consider this description of his 1923 work "Ballet Mecanique," which was "inspired by movies, Surrealism, Dadaism and mechanistic visions of mankind's future" and which was originally scored for "multiple synchronized player pianos along with bells, sirens, airplane propeller noise and all manner of percussion. Performed at Carnegie Hall in 1927 with a dozen pianists, including Aaron Copland, it resulted in scandal and riot" (*New York Times*, March 29, 2000, p. B1). For Antheil's amusing account in his autobiography, *Bad Boy of Music*, of his collaboration with Yeats, see Appendix I. Antheil's music for Yeats's play is available on a recording of several of his pieces by the Ensemble Modern, conducted by H. K. Gruber. The compact disc is called *Fighting the Waves: Music of George Antheil* (New York: BMG Music, 1996).

[28]Letter to Lady Gregory, April 10, 1929 (Wade, *Letters*, p. 761).

extending at least one yard from the end of the instrument.
* Actors on or behind scenes simply wailing along with the marked downward chromatic passage.[29]

Yeats had written to Sturge Moore on March 24 that the first performance was planned for Dublin on April 29, 1929;[30] since Miss de Valois could not prepare the ballet in time, the production was scheduled for August 13 at the Abbey Theatre to coincide with Horse Show week.[31] Yeats wrote to Olivia Shakespear about the production:

> My *Fighting the Waves* has been my greatest success on the stage since *Kathleen-ni-Houlihan*, and its production was a great event here, the politicians and the governor general and the American minister present – the masks by the Dutchman Krop magnificent and Antheil's music. Everyone here is as convinced as I am that I have discovered a new form by this combination of dance, speech and music. The dancing of the goddess in her abstract almost non-representative mask was extraordinarily exciting. . . . The waves are . . . dancers. I felt that the sea was eternity and that they were all upon its edge. The theatre was packed night after night, so the play will be revived.[32]

The reaction from the pit, however, was not all enthusiasm, as Joseph Holloway's colorful account shows:

> I met F. J. McCormack [*sic*] and Eileen Crowe as I came out of the Abbey at 11 o'clock after the ballet, Fighting the Waves, and Mac said to me, "I see you have survived it. Oh, what noise!"
>
> It is the first time I have ever heard Stephenson sing that I didn't enjoy his lovely, clear, carrying voice. Oh, the harsh, discordant notes he had to sing! I said when I heard that Yeats liked the music that was enough for me – as he has no ear for sound! Those on the stage worked hard against the braying . . . There was an augmented orchestra to interpret the noisy discords – drums, flutes, cornets, etc., and Miss Grey was at the piano. Dr. Larchet conducted and couldn't extract head or tail out of the score. The principles [*sic*] wore masks and also some of the dancers. It was a pity to waste such talent on such strange materials. In the balcony, people started to leave shortly after the ballet started. It was worse than the talkies. The steam whistle organ on the merry-go-round discourses heavenly music by comparison with the music shook out of a bag of notes anyhow by the American concoctor of this riot of discords.
>
> I had seen the play-part of the Ballet [i.e., *The Only Jealousy of Emer*] before at an At-Home held by the Drama League. . . . Those masks suggested the big-head of my early pantomime days, and conveyed nothing to me save a more or less obstruction to the spoken words. . . . The opening ballet of Cuchulain fighting the waves

---

[29]Miller, *Noble Drama of W. B. Yeats*, p. 281.
[30]Bridge, *W. B. Yeats and T. Sturge Moore*, p. 146.
[31]Lennox Robinson, *Ireland's Abbey Theatre: A History 1899–1951* (London: Sidgwick and Jackson, 1951), p. 143.
[32]Wade, *Letters*, p. 767.

> was decorative and beautiful to the eye, but the music that accompanied it was like the falling of a tin tray on the flags.[33]

The play was revived for a production at the Hammersmith Odeon, London, in April 1930,[34] but was never performed again. As Yeats noted in his Preface to *Wheels and Butterflies*, "Mr. George Antheil's most strange, most dramatic music requires a large expensive orchestra."[35] On November 17, 1930, *The Words Upon the Window-Pane* had its first production at the Abbey Theatre, and it was a great success. Yeats wrote to Olivia Shakespear on December 2, 1930, of his plans to publish this along with three other recent prose plays, *Fighting the Waves*, *The Cat and the Moon*, and *The Resurrection*, in a single volume:

> I want to bring out a book of four plays called My Wheels and Butterflies – the wheels are the four introductions. Dublin is said to be full of little societies meeting in cellars and garrets so I shall put this rhyme on a fly-leaf
>
> To cellar and garret
> A wheel I send
> But every butterfly
> To a friend.
>
> The "wheels" are addressed to Ireland mainly – a scheme of intellectual nationalisms.[36]

Yeats added that he was then at work on his "Commentary" on *The Words Upon the Window-Pane*, which he first published in two parts in the *Dublin Magazine* for October–December 1931 and January–March 1932. A similar introduction to *Fighting the Waves* was published in the *Dublin Magazine* for April–June 1932.[37] *Wheels and Butterflies* itself was not published until 1934; for this volume Yeats revised the introduction to *The Words Upon the Window-Pane* slightly and that to *Fighting the Waves* extensively.

In 1934, Yeats also published his final version of the verse play *The Only Jealousy of Emer*; the substantial changes made to the text show the unmistakable influence of the prose version. Hence, *Fighting the Waves* is itself an integral part of the history of Yeats's composition of and revision of *The Only Jealousy of Emer*, and its manuscript drafts are therefore shown in this volume as part of the direct sequence of the composition of *The Only Jealousy of Emer*, even

---

[33]Hogan and O' Neill, *Joseph Holloway's Irish Theatre*, I, pp. 50–51. Eileen Crowe, like F. J. McCormick, was one of the Abbey players; see n. 20 above.

[34]Bridge, *W. B. Yeats and T. Sturge Moore*, p. 195.

[35]Alspach, *Variorum Plays*, p. 1308.

[36]Wade, *Letters*, p. 779.

[37]Yeats's publication of the preface to the play in advance of that of the play itself might have been the result of his desire to take advantage of the intellectual excitement caused in Dublin by his two new plays. "I write very much for young men between twenty and thirty, as at that age, and younger, I wanted to feel that any poet I cared for—Shelley let us say—saw more than he told of, in some sense saw into the mystery" (Wade, *Letters*, p. 781; letter to Olivia Shakespear of February 1931). It may also have been the influence on Yeats of "this crowded Dublin life which always incites me to prose" (Wade, *Letters*, p. 814; letter to Olivia Shakespear, August 17, 1933).

Yeats had also published the Preface to *At the Hawk's Well* before the first English printing of the play. The Preface was published in *To-Day*, May 1917, and the play in the June issue of the same magazine.

though Yeats himself ultimately considered *Fighting the Waves* a lesser work than *The Only Jealousy of Emer*, writing in the Preface to the 1934 edition of his *Collected Plays*:

> I do not include in the present book *Fighting the Waves*, a prose version of *The Only Jealousy of Emer* so arranged as to admit of many dancers and to be immediately intelligible to an average theatrical audience; it can be found in *Wheels and Butterflies*.

II. Some Sources and the Early Drafts of *The Only Jealousy of Emer*

The early drafts of *The Only Jealousy of Emer* transcribed in this volume show the influence of many sources. Areas of special interest in examining the relationship between this source material and Yeats's early drafts are the origin of the changeling motif, differences between the sources and the play, and the possible influence of the only other play on the same subject—Wilfrid Blunt's *Fand of the Fair Cheek* (1904).

The Origin of the Changeling Motif

Yeats devoted a section of his compilation of *Irish Fairy and Folk Tales* (1892) to changelings, and included therein his own early poem "The Stolen Child." The folklore notions found in Yeats's introduction to this section are very close to those behind the earliest drafts of *The Only Jealousy of Emer*:

> Sometimes the fairies fancy mortals, and carry them away into their own country, leaving behind instead some sickly fairy child, or a log of wood so bewitched that it seems to be a mortal pining away, and dying, and being buried. Most commonly they steal children. . . .
>
> Those who are carried away are happy, according to some accounts, having plenty of good living and music and mirth. Others say, however, that they are continually longing for their earthly friends. Lady Wilde gives a gloomy tradition that there are two kinds of fairies – one kind merry and gentle, the other evil, and sacrificing every year a life to Satan, for which purpose they steal mortals.[39]

The strongly domestic imagery associated with Emer in the early drafts is likewise reminiscent of the language used in "The Stolen Child" included in this section of *Irish Fairy and Folk Tales* to describe the world left behind by the child carried away by the fairies:

> Away with us, he's going,
> The solemn-eyed;
> He'll hear no more the lowing
> Of the calves on the warm hill-side.
> Or the kettle on the hob

[38]*Collected Plays* (London: Macmillan, 1934), p. v.

[39]*Irish Fairy and Folk Tales* (London, 1892; repr. New York: Barnes and Noble Books, 1993), p. 65.

Sing peace into his breast;
Or see the brown mice bob
Round and round the oatmeal chest.

One of the many sources of the changeling motif in *The Only Jealousy of Emer* was John Rhys's *Lectures on the Origin and Growth of Religion as Illustrated by Celtic Heathendom.*[40] In the late 1880s and early 1890s Yeats was determined to acquire a detailed knowledge of the Irish gods and mythological heroes. The high regard in which Yeats held Rhys's book can be seen in a pair of hard-backed notebooks which he kept at the time.[41] Here Yeats tried to organize the somewhat confusing pantheon of the Irish divinities into a more coherent framework; for example, he attempted to relate them to the Sephiroth (emanations) of the Kabbala.[42] In the first notebook there is also a crossed-out passage on the god Manannan which mentions Fand's love for Cuchulain and refers to Rhys's version of the story.[43]

Rhys's book provided the factual information and scholarly parallels which Yeats needed to confirm for himself and for others that the ancient Irish myths and legends, till then despised in the educated circles of English-ruled Ireland as incoherent and insignificant, were as noble and deserving of study (and hence of literary interpretation) as the myths and legends of Greece and India. *Celtic Heathendom* consistently demonstrated parallels between the Celtic and the ancient Greek religions, which were not the conscious invention of poets and artists. Rather, they were the product of the animistic "religious germ" in primitive man, which produced strikingly similar myths when confronted with the unknown.[44] No fine line could be drawn between the abstractions of theology and the concrete embodiments of myth: "who is there to tell us where precisely theology and religion end, and where myth and fiction begin?"[45] Such notions were grist to Yeats's literary and Irish nationalist mill.[46]

One of the stories Rhys told of Cuchulain was that of his love for Fand. He drew a comparison between this tale and the Welsh story of Pwyll and Arawn. Pwyll, a mortal prince of Dyved, changes places with Arawn, a king of Hades, for a year and a day. As Yeats later wrote in the article "Away," published in 1902, "Pwyll overcomes Arawn's energy with one blow, and Arawn's rule in Dyved was a marvel because of his wisdom, for in all these stories strength comes from among men, and wisdom from among gods who are but 'shadows.'"[47] This interpretation would reappear in the early drafts of *The Only Jealousy of Emer*.

Yeats recounted Rhys's summary of "The Sick-Bed of Cuchulain and The Only Jealousy of Emer" almost word for word in "Away." In this article, one of a series on Irish folklore, Yeats demonstrated the underlying unity between the folk beliefs of his time in the West of Ireland and the ancient Irish legends, and showed how these folk beliefs could be used to explain the

---

[40]London; Edinburgh: Williams and Norgate, 1888. The lectures were delivered in 1886.

[41]NLI 13,574.

[42]NLI 13,574(1), 4^r.

[43]Ibid., 7^r. The second notebook, probably written up from the first one, is an alphabetical thumb index of the Irish gods.

[44]*Celtic Heathendom*, pp. 108, 114.

[45]Ibid., p. 107.

[46]Yeats could not, however, agree with Rhys's calling Cuchulain a "solar hero," i.e., a mortal who procured boons from the gods for mankind against the forces of darkness (ibid., pp. 671–672).

[47]"Away" is reproduced in *Uncollected Prose by W. B. Yeats* (London: Macmillan, 1975), ed. John P. Frayne and Colter Johnson; the passage quoted appears on 2:282. Part of Rhys's retelling of the story of Cuchulain and Fand is reproduced in Appendix II below.

mysteries of ancient mythology.

Yeats began his article with a discussion of several case histories of people who had been taken "away" by the fairies or "the Sidhe." "These men and women are said to be 'away', and for the most part go about their work in a dream, or lie all day in bed, awakening after the fall of night to a strange and hurried life."[48] People are taken "away" by the fairies "to help in their work, or their play, or to nurse their children, or to be their lovers." But they need not be physically away:

> The ancient peoples from whom the country people inherit their belief had to explain how, when you were "away", as it seemed to you, you seemed, it might be, to your neighbors or your family, to be lying in a faint upon the ground, or in your bed, or even going about your daily work. It was probably one who was himself "away" who explained, that somebody or something was put in your place, and this explanation was the only possible one to ancient peoples, who did not make our distinction between body and soul. The Irish country people always insist that something, a heap of shavings or a broomstick or a wooden image, or some dead person, "maybe some old warrior", or some relative or neighbor of your own, is put in your place.[49]

Yeats went on to quote an example of such substitution that he was given by a countryman: " 'There was one Tierney on the road to Kinvara, I knew him well, was away with them seven years. It was at night he used to be brought away, and when they called him he should go. They'd leave some sort of a likeness of him in his place.' "[50] In the same manner, an evil spirit would take Cuchulain's place later in *The Only Jealousy of Emer*.

Yeats then showed how a knowledge of folklore could illuminate ancient tales like that of Cuchulain's sickbed. He saw a continuum in Ireland between the mythological era of Cuchulain and the beliefs among the country Irish of his own time:

> Cuchulain wins the love of Fand just as young, handsome countrymen are believed to win the love of fair women of "the others" who can do little, being but "shadows" without a mortal among them, at the hurling and in the battle; and November Eve is still a season of great power among the spirits. Emer goes to the Yew at the Strand and just as the wife goes to meet her husband who is "away" or has been "taken", or the husband to meet his wife, at midnight, at the "custom gap" in the field where the fair is held, or at some other well known place; while the after madness of Cuchulain reminds me of the mystery the country people, like all primitive people, see in madness, and of the way they sometimes associate it with "the others", and of a saying of a woman in the Burren hills, "Those that are away among them never come back, or if they do are not the same as before." His great sorrow for the love of Fand reminds me of the woman told of in Arran, who has often been heard weeping on the hill-side for the children she had left among "the others". One finds nothing in this tale about any person or any thing being put in Cuchulain's place; but

[48]Frayne and Johnson, *Uncollected Prose*, 2:267.
[49]Ibid., 275.
[50]Ibid., 276.

> Professor Rhys has shown that in the original form of the story of Cuchulain and the Beetle of Forgetfulness, Cuchulain made the prince who had come to summon him to the other world take his place at the court of Uladh [Ulster]. There are many stories everywhere of people who have their places taken by Angels, or spirits, or gods, that they may live another life in some other place, and I believe all such stories were once stories of people "away".[51]

The story Yeats mentions, as narrated and interpreted by Rhys, has Cuchulain journeying to the underworld to free the three sons of Doel Dermait, whose name means the Beetle of Forgetfulness.[52] While away on this adventure, Cuchulain's place at the court of Emain Macha is taken by a substitute.

Yeats, then, saw the changeling motif as central to the story of "The Only Jealousy of Emer," many years before he wrote his play on the subject.

The Sources and Yeats's Early Drafts: Some Comparisons

Rhys's version of the "The Sick-bed of Cuchulain and the Only Jealousy of Emer" was not the only redaction of the tale which was familiar to Yeats. Rhys's narrative was founded on the first translation into English of the tale, by the 19th century Irish scholar Eugene O'Curry, a translation that Yeats probably knew.[53] There exists only one manuscript of the story, so little variation from the original was possible in the other versions known to Yeats, those of de Joubainville,[54] Sigerson,[55] and of course Lady Gregory.[56] There are several details in these other versions that were not mentioned in Rhys's retelling of the story and that were important in the composition of Yeats's play.

In the manuscript, Eithne Inguba is called Cuchulain's wife in the first half of the story (where Cuchulain is asked to hunt for the birds), but in the second part Emer is called his wife. The accepted explanation of this inconsistency is that the tale consists of two stories which have been combined, one from the ninth century and one from the eleventh century.[57] Lady Gregory simply called Eithne Cuchulain's mistress and Emer his wife, and Yeats did the same.

De Joubainville's narrative stands apart from the others because he attempts to explain the motivations of the characters. Rhys and Lady Gregory say that Cuchulain was reluctant to go to the underworld to fight for Labraid because the invitation had come from a woman. De Joubainville suggests a deeper reason for his reluctance to go to Mag Mell, the Happy Plain, the country of the dead: because it was not customary to return from there.[58] It may be possible to read into this suggestion the kind of motivation that Yeats was to give Cuchulain in the early drafts of *The Only Jealousy*, where he vigorously defended "the imperfect."

The sources give the character of Fand more depth than does Yeats's play. They emphasize

---

[51]Ibid., 281–282.

[52]"The name may be compared with the Norse *óminnis hegri*, or the Heron of Forgetfulness, said to hover over banquets and to steal away the minds of men" (Rhys, *Celtic Heathendom*, p. 345 n.).

[53]*Atlantis*, I (1858), 363–392, and II (1859), 98–124.

[54]*L'épopéé celtique en Irlande* (Paris, 1892), I, pp. 170–216.

[55]*Bards of the Gael and Gall* (London, 1897), pp. 381–385.

[56]*Cuchulain of Muirtheimne* (1902; Gerrards Cross, 1970), pp. 216–221.

[57]Bjersby, *Interpretation of the Cuchulain Legend*, p. 46.

[58]*L'épopéé celtique*, p. 171.

her beauty, her nobility, and her purity. There is an extraordinary song in which Loeg praises the beauty of Labraid's isle and of his sister-in-law Fand. He sings that he would give up all of Ireland to live in this land. Eithne Inguba is certainly a beautiful woman, "but the woman I am speaking of now takes away the wits of whole armies."[59] Fand's beauty is perhaps taken for granted in Yeats's play, which lacks the sense of allurement conveyed by the sources.[60] The sources also show the nobility of Fand when she accepts Cuchulain's choice of Emer and agrees to go with Manannan: " 'On my honor,' she replied, 'there is one of you to whom I would rather be attached as wife; but it is with you [Manannan] that I shall go. I shall not wait for Cuchulain, because he has abandoned me; moreover, there is no queen at your side worthy of you; there is one next to Cuchulain.' "[61] Fand does not offer this generous tribute to her rival Emer in Yeats's play.

Yeats's Emer is comparatively more self-controlled in the expression of her jealousy than the Emer of the sources, but in both cases Emer draws a knife to slay Fand. In Yeats's play, Emer fulfills the conditions of a hard bargain with the Figure of Cuchulain. In the sources, there is no such Figure and no such bargain; Cuchulain is moved by his wife's grief:

> "It is certain," said Emer, "that I will not refuse this woman if you follow her. But all the same, everything red is beautiful, everything new is fair, everything high is lovely, everything common is bitter, everything we are without is much thought of, everything we know is thought little of, till all knowledge is known. And O Cuchulain," she said, "I was at one time in esteem with you and I would be so again if it were pleasing to you."
>
> And grief came upon her, and overcame her. "By my word, now," said Cuchulain, "you are pleasing to me, and will be pleasing to me as long as I live."[62]

Such an expression of grief would probably have seemed undignified to Yeats within the rigorous Noh-based conventions of his dance plays. Yeats did, however, follow his sources in ascribing Cuchulain's reluctance to go off with the Woman of the Sidhe to his memories of when he and Emer were first married. In the early drafts of the play, these memories were particularly vivid.

The "renunciation combat" between Fand and Emer in the sources was the root of the Figure of Cuchulain's cruel bargain:

> "Let me be given up," said Fand. "It is better for me to be given up," said Emer. "Not so," said Fand, "it is I that will be given up in the end, and it is I that have been in danger of it all this time."[63]

But Yeats added an ironic twist to the result of this "combat": Cuchulain returns to his mistress, not to his wife.

---

[59]*Cuchulain of Muirtheimne*, p. 217.

[60]Of course, Yeats's dramatic conventions make such a construction of character difficult to achieve. He tries to convey Fand's attraction through her dance.

[61]Translated from de Joubainville, *L'épopéé celtique*, p. 214.

[62] *Cuchulain of Muirtheimne*, p. 220.

[63]Ibid.

The character of Cuchulain is very different in the sources and in the play. Yeats's character is split into three: the Ghost of Cuchulain, the Figure of Cuchulain, and (the body of) Cuchulain. The Cuchulain of the sources is not totally passive; although he lies for a long time on his sick-bed, he does in the end regain his strength and prove himself in his battle on Labraid's behalf. Yeats's Cuchulain and Ghost of Cuchulain are weak and passive figures in comparison. It becomes difficult to understand why the Woman of the Sidhe should love such a passive figure as the Ghost of Cuchulain. In the sources, Fand's love for Cuchulain is increased by his great victory over Labraid's foes. Yeats's Cuchulain is a middle-aged Cuchulain, no longer a "young and passionate man" as before. The Cuchulain of the sources gives a vigorous defense of his love for Fand, whom he finds pure, chaste, noble, intelligent, rich, and loyal.[64] Yeats's aging hero gives no such defense of his love. The love of the Woman of the Sidhe for Cuchulain is thus in this respect seriously unconvincing; biographical and metaphysical considerations have taken the place of a purer, simpler emotion in the sources. The love is anterior to the events of the play, rather than dramatically part of them.

Clearly, then, the relation between Yeats's play and his Irish sources is far from being one of imitation. Rather, his use of these legendary materials in middle age was consistent with what he had written in a letter to Katherine Tynan at the start of his career: "I do not mean that we should not go back to old ballads and poems for inspiration, but we should search them for new methods of expressing ourselves."[65]

A Possible Influence: Blunt's "Fand of the Fair Cheek"

F. A. C. Wilson noted the probable influence on Yeats's play of William Larminie's 1892 poem, *Fand*.[66] Another possible literary influence on *The Only Jealousy of Emer* was the only previous play on the subject, Wilfrid Blunt's *Fand of the Fair Cheek* (1904).[67]

Blunt, a vigorous supporter of Irish Home Rule, had met Sir William and Lady Gregory when Sir William had been stationed in Egypt; Lady Gregory, who for a short time had been Blunt's lover, introduced Yeats to Blunt on April 1, 1898.[68] Blunt later added the Irish Literary Society to his many interests, and he and Yeats spoke on the Cuchulain saga at one of its meetings in April 1902.[69] In June of that year Yeats spent a weekend at Blunt's country house, Ferneycroft. Yeats was then writing *On Baile's Strand*, and he urged Blunt to contribute to "his Cuchulain cycle of plays"[70] to be staged at the Abbey Theatre. Yeats wrote to Lady Gregory that Blunt agreed to take " 'The only jealousy of Emer' for his subject, which would fit into our plan very well."[71]

---

[64]De Joubainville, *L'épopée celtique*, p. 210.

[65]Wade, *Letters*, p. 98; letter of December 21, 1888.

[66]*Yeats's Iconography* (London: Gollancz, 1960), pp. 80–81.

[67]For another example of how Yeats made use of a previous bad play on the same subject as his, see Mary FitzGerald, ed., *The Words Upon the Window Pane*, Cornell Yeats (Ithaca: Cornell University Press, 2002), pp. xvii–xxiii; FitzGerald has shown how Yeats turned "a terrible play" (*Swift and Stella*, by Charles Edward Lawrence) into one of his most powerful creations for the theater.

[68]Wilfrid Scawen Blunt, *My Diaries: Being a Personal Narrative of Events, 1888–1914*, 2 vols. (London: M. Secker, 1919–1920), 2:358.

[69]Ibid., 2:23; diary entry for April 26, 1902.

[70]Ibid., 2:28; diary entry for June 15, 1902.

[71]Wade, *Letters*, p. 376.

Blunt, distracted by his many other interests,[72] did not finish *Fand of the Fair Cheek* until September 1904.[73] In January 1905 Yeats read the play to his Abbey company of players, and Blunt noted in his diary that the players were "anxious to act it, and perhaps it will be put on the stage in April." Blunt also noted that Lady Gregory told him that Yeats had "declared that if I [Blunt] had begun to write plays when I was thirty, I should now have a European reputation."[74] In May 1905, he wrote to Yeats about the play:

> Many thanks for your letter abt. the play, as to which I quite understand the difficulties there may be with your company in acting it, it being so much a woman's piece. But I have so little sympathy with the heroics of male courage, even in the heroic ages, that I cd. not have written it otherwise, and I chose that particular episode in the Cuchulain Legend because it was comparatively free from the bombast of fighting. As to the metre [modeled on the rhymed Alexandrines of Victor Hugo's tragedies] I equally cd. not have written it in blank verse.[75]

An amateur performance of Blunt's play was staged at his home, Newbuildings, on September 24, 1906,[76] and the play was performed at the Abbey Theatre on April 20, 1907.[77]

However, Blunt's play could hardly serve Yeats's purposes when, in 1915, fresh from his contact with Japanese Noh theory, he decided to revive his Cuchulain cycle. The rhymed verse of *Fand of the Fair Cheek* lumbers interminably on through three most undramatic acts. The stagecraft is, by Yeats's standards, very old-fashioned. The play lacks the unity, compactness, and poetic energy which Yeats sought in his own work, but there are some similarities in the treatment of subject matter.

The first act of Blunt's play is set in "a room of the Speckled House at Emain." Cuchulain has been in a trance for a year after killing his son at Baile's Strand. Lugaid and Laegaire have stayed beside him, along with his mistress Eithne (here Blunt is following Lady Gregory), but have failed to waken him. Laegaire has called for Conhor and Emer. Conhor likewise fails to waken Cuchulain. He praises Emer in a speech which is very close to the kind of heavily "domestic" imagery used by Yeats in the early drafts of *The Only Jealousy of Emer*:

---

[72]He went to Egypt and, having left behind his copy of *Cuchulain of Muirtheimne*, he wrote to Yeats from Egypt on January 4, 1903, that he was "rather at a loss how to finish" (Richard J. Finneran, George Mills Harper, William Murphy, eds., *Letters to W. B. Yeats*, 2 vols. (London: Macmillan, 1977), 1:115.

[73]Blunt, *My Diaries*, 2:109; entry for September 6, 1904.

[74]Ibid., 2:119; entry for February 19, 1905.

[75]Finneran, et al., *Letters to W. B. Yeats*, 1:148. Yeats was later to ascribe the revision of his play *The Golden Helmet* into the rhymed Alexandrines of *The Green Helmet* to Blunt's influence: "He told me that he had been converted to my use of the Alexandrine metre for plays in verse, but that he had such a difficulty in finding rhymes that a rhymed play would take him two years to write" (Blunt, *My Diaries*, 2:261; entry for June 9, 1909). See S. B. Bushrui, *Yeats's Verse Plays: The Revisions 1900–1910* (Oxford: Clarendon Press, 1965), p. 184.

[76] Blunt, *My Diaries*, 2:160; entry for September 27, 1906.

[77] The play was produced by Ben Iden Payne, and the lyric interludes were set to music by Arthur Darley (Miller, *Noble Drama of W. B. Yeats*, p. 138). Blunt noted a review of the performance in his diary which said the play had been "a great success" (*My Diaries*, 2:176; entry for April 23, 1907). But Willie Fay of the Abbey Players later recalled that the play "gave the company some excellent material on which to practice the speaking of verse, but it had a poor reception except from the faithful few who enjoyed good verse-speaking" (W. G. Fay and Catherine Carswell, *The Fays of the Abbey Theatre* [London: Rich & Cowan, 1935], p. 225). Blunt, rather like Yeats with *The Only Jealousy of Emer*, was not informed of this performance until after the fact. "It is only in Ireland, I suppose, that a play could be performed for the first time and the author know nothing of it" (*My Diaries*, 2:176).

Ay! A supreme fair woman,—yet his wife. Time was
She clung to him, his shadow. Whereso'er he went
She followed unreproved, beloved, obedient,
And yet commanding him. How often have I seen
The two in their first courting on the hurling green,
He godlike in his skiol, she rapt and watching him,
Intent upon his triumphs.[78]

Eithne flees when Emer arrives (perhaps the source of her flight from the awakened Figure of Cuchulain in Yeats's play). Emer also fails to revive Cuchulain, and is left alone with him. Fand now comes on the scene, improbably disguised as an old woman. Emer is hostile toward the gods (as in Yeats's play), who are indifferent to mortals: "They know not of our doings, and we know them not."[79] Fand argues that the Sidhe are Cuchulain's friends, but Emer, again as in Yeats's play, reminds Fand that the Sidhe always exact their price:

And their help's price? They prove
Their pleasure to what profit? They will hardly give
Their succour without payment.[80]

Blunt departs from his source to introduce a bargain as the dramatic device to resolve the problem caused by Cuchulain's trance, a lead which Yeats would later follow. Fand names her price for the liberation of Cuchulain from the enchantment: she will have Cuchulain to herself for forty days, for fighting and for loving. Emer agrees to meet her in forty days' time at Baile's Strand.

The second act of *Fand of the Fair Cheek* is set in the otherworld, at "the garden of Abrat in Magh Mell." Not much happens in this act, which illustrates the dramatic problems faced by both Blunt and Yeats in presenting supernatural characters, settings, and plots. Fand tells her sister Liban how a man's love is superior to that of a god. The forty days in the otherworld are now almost over. While Fand sings the praises of her mortal lover, the feast is most improbably joined by Eithne, disguised as a poet, and Manannan, disguised as a harper. The god of the sea imposes his order on the feast.

In the third and final act, Emer and her attendants await Cuchulain's return at Baile's Strand. Emer recalls Fand's words about the constancy and patience of wives, and their eventual victory over all temporary lovers (ideas which Eithne will voice in *The Only Jealousy*). Cuchulain and Fand now approach the tree, and Cuchulain does not want to leave his divine mistress, as in the sources. Emer, seized with jealousy, tries to kill Fand, but Cuchulain stops her from doing so. Nevertheless her actions wins back Cuchulain's heart. The victorious Emer is now in a position to forgive Fand, who disappears when called back to the otherworld by Manannan. Cuchulain now turns on Emer and blames her for the loss of Fand. Eithne arrives and waves the cloak of forgetfulness before Cuchulain, as in the sources, thus ensuring he will forget about Fand.

When Yeats wrote his play ten years after the performance of *Fand*, he may have recalled some of the dramatic possibilities and problems raised by Blunt's play and in its performance.

---

[78]Wilfrid Blunt, *Fand of the Fair Cheek* (London: privately printed, 1904), p. 9.

[79]Ibid., p. 14.

[80]Ibid., p. 15.

Like Blunt, Yeats began his play *in medias res*, with Cuchulain on his sickbed. Unlike Blunt, Yeats interpreted the story as one of fairy substitution, and the arrival and departure of the evil changeling could be simply depicted by a change of masks. Yeats improved on Blunt's dramatic device of the bargain by making it an agreement between Emer and the evil spirit; and where Blunt had offered Emer a "reasonable" choice (lose Cuchulain for forty days but get him back again), Yeats offered her an impossible choice (get Cuchulain back only by renouncing his love forever). This impossible bargain gave Yeats's play the sort of dramatic tension which *Fand of the Fair Cheek* could not generate.

III. Yeats at Work on *The Only Jealousy of Emer*

As Yeats reimagined the story, then, Fand, Emer, and Cuchulain enact an endlessly recurring ritual of impossible choice. The human condition was never a resolved unity or trinity for Yeats, only an endless and unresolved duality. Man is tragically caught between conflicting desires, but from that ceaseless struggle comes the meaning of his life. Fand, Emer, and Cuchulain all long for completion in their own ways, but tragically none of them can attain it. We are but spectators of the "bitter reward" they all share, one which they will share again and again, as the closing song reminds us, through "many a tragic tomb."

The early manuscripts of the play make no reference to the terminology of what would later become *A Vision*. The dominant theories here are Irish folklore tradition and Platonic allegory. The influence of primitive folklore is particularly marked in the first drafts of the play, and gives them a certain roughness which is in some ways preferable to the elegant polish of the finished product. Yeats's introduction to Ezra Pound's redaction of Ernest Fenellosa's Noh collection showed that primitive folklore was, for him, the proper source of great dramatic art: "I love all the arts that can still remind me of their origin among the common people."[81] Thus in the first draft Eithne Inguba (then called Etain) speaks of her feeling that there is an evil presence in the room:

~~There's something nearer than the sea~~
                    nearer to
There's something ~~near~~ the sea –
                              – its so ~~near~~   so near
That though I can but hear it in my flesh
It makes my hair stand up
~~There's something, standing between me & him~~
There's something stands between his bed & me
                         hear it, or see its shape
And though I cannot ~~see what shape it has~~
   ~~makes~~ There is
And it ~~has~~ no sound it makes my hair stand up (MS A: NLI 8774(9), 6^{r}, ll. 4–11)

The struggle for Cuchulain was at this stage one between the good and the evil Sidhe, and not some abstract battle between personified phases of the moon:

[81] "Certain Noble Plays of Japan," in W. B. Yeats, *Essays and Introductions* (London: Macmillan, 1961), p. 223.

Emer
my husband is bestir
~~No no for~~ look
~~My husband stirs~~ – ~~one of the friendly~~ sidhe
~~Has waked him from trance~~ has awaked him
Some friend among
~~One of the friendly~~ sidhe ~~awakes~~ him
And now he throws the covers from his face (MS A, 6^v, ll. 5–10)

The first draft was, then, very close in its atmosphere to Irish folklore; the Woman of the Sidhe was first called "Shape Changer." Her reasons for pursuing Cuchulain's love sprang, however, not so much from folklore stories of ethereal goddesses seeking mortal lovers,[82] as from Plato:

Cuchulain –
I know that face
~~You are she I saw~~
~~At the Hawks well, &~~
For you are she I met by the Hawks well
you have dropped your quills
Though ~~you have dropped your q~~
Shape Changer
I am that dream.
~~And~~ As man before he is born into the world
Is shaped as an egg; ~~There~~, a yellow yoke will is
About the white of egg, but when he is born
He's but the white, the yoke remains as a dream.
And both miserable, until they meet at death
substance
Is shaped as an egg, ~~made~~ has a double ~~nature~~
Like yoke & white, but when he has been born
One substance stays ~~behind~~ where the shape changers are
~~And both are miserable; one~~
~~For but one half~~
And both are miserable.
Cuchulain
I have heard this tale
From learned men –
~~From learned men, &~~ that
Among the learned, & the sublime
Among shape changers, when half of the cleft man
Is born, being ~~therefore~~ unborn & therefore perfect
~~Is his true~~

[82] F. A. C. Wilson draws an illuminating parallel between the story of *Emer* and Yeats's early short story about Red Hanrahan and the Sidhe-woman Cloona; see *Yeats's Iconography*, p. 90.

Is the true mistress, & that in all his loves
He can but find its image, or its symbol
Spirit.
~~And when he meets~~
And when at last he meets face to face
He is done all image & symbol.
(MS A, 9^{v}, ll. 1–12; MS A, 10^{v}, ll. 1–14; and MS B, 1^{r}, ll. 1–11)

The Spirit goes on to explain to Cuchulain in this draft how much she has sought him:

& yet this unborn half
~~Lacking, the~~
Being separate from the flesh is but a dream
And therefore miserable.
. . . .
All your life long
~~I have sought for you in many shapes~~
I have sought you out in many images. (MS B, 2^{r}, ll. 2–5, 14–16)

This is all much clearer than the explanations given in the final version of the play. The expansion of these lines in the next draft sheds even more light on what is happening and why it is happening:

Have you never heard that before a man is
born he is two in one, like ~~yo~~ yoke &
white in the one egg, & that ~~after his~~ birth
one half is in the flesh, & that half stays in
the will of the sidhe, & thus that always because
of this separation both are miserable
C.
I have indeed heard the learned say that
W S
And that always the half that has been born
seeks in many woman images of the half unborn
& because they are but images unhappily
only in (~~the unborn hafls death, or in~~
birth with that other self of dreams, where
lives hope or its end, that consummation can it find (MS D, 1^{r}, ll. 4–16)

In a later draft, Yeats used lunar imagery for the first time, likening the dancing Woman of the Sidhe to the moon. In his first full draft he kept the earlier combination of Plato and folklore and added on top of this the new language of the phases of the moon; the Woman of the Sidhe describes the Evil Genius as a creature of the last phases:

breath
. . . you are but the salty ~~wind~~ that blows

> Under the fishers door ~~a power that drops~~
> ~~Out of the crescent & that dreads the full~~. (MS G, 23^{r}, ll. 12–14)

The Evil Genius, like the Woman of the Sidhe, had been described in the earliest drafts in the language of Irish folklore; the Mistress had felt his presence as a weird premonition, and the evil spirit had introduced himself in simple terms:

> changed
> I am that evil spirit that has ~~followed~~ his
> Good luck to evil, & made his life accursed. (MS A, 8^{r}, ll. 1–2)

Yeats's cancellation of the word "followed" suggests that his original intention was a folklore conflict between Cuchulain's good and evil geniuses. The Woman of the Sidhe later spoke of having followed Cuchulain all of his life.

The final draft of the closing song does not mention the phases of the moon, but the opening and closing songs appended to one of the final drafts made use of Yeats's lunar system. It was in this draft that Yeats bade farewell to Plato's egg and cast the debate between Cuchulain and the Woman of the Sidhe into rhyming couplets using the imagery of the lunar phases. Although this change made his play less clear, and thus eliminated some of the simplicity of folklore much admired by Yeats, his reasons for introducing the lunar imagery were doubtless more than a mere desire to mystify. Although the dialogue in the early drafts was philosophically clear enough, dramatically it was dead. The function of the dialogue in the play was to provide some sort of explanation for what was going on, but at the same time the dialogue would have to contribute to the tightly unified imagery which was Yeats's aim, and would have to keep the play moving (without losing an impression of stillness) toward the climax of Emer's renunciation. The rhyming couplets gave a new energy to the play at a point where it had become bogged down in abstraction.

IV. The Making of *Fighting the Waves*

Although most critical attention has (deservedly) been devoted to *The Only Jealousy of Emer*, something should also be said at this stage about the play's prose counterpart, *Fighting the Waves*. Yeats himself did not include *Fighting the Waves* in the *Collected Plays* he published in 1934, dismissing it in the preface to that collection as "so arranged as to admit of many dancers and to be immediately intelligible to an average theatrical audience,"[83] a statement that some might dispute. Yeats simplified his vocabulary and stagecraft for the prose play, aspects of his work highlighted in the notes to transcriptions. *Fighting the Waves* presents itself as a much "flatter" piece than *The Only Jealousy*, and is of limited literary interest. Yeats himself dismissed the prose play as "in itself nothing, a mere occasion for sculptor and dancer, for the exciting dramatic music of George Antheil."[84] F. A. C. Wilson has praised some of the prose as having a "simple and dignified" quality, which one might call "Homeric."[85] But he does

[83]*Collected Plays*, p. v.
[84]Alspach, *Variorum Plays*, p. 567.
[85]*Yeats's Iconography*, pp. 81–82.

not argue that *Fighting the Waves* is in some way a better play than *The Only Jealousy*. Nevertheless, it might be of some interest to briefly examine *Fighting the Waves* along lines similar to those followed in the discussion of *The Only Jealousy*.

One's immediate impression is that the personal urgency that governed the creation of the play in 1917 seems to have vanished twelve years later, when Yeats dictated *Fighting the Waves* to his wife. Thus, the very flatness of the ballet's text seems to defeat any opportunity to identify a tragic hero, and Yeats seems far more concerned with the spectacle and with the chance of using Antheil's music than with the text. The extent and nature of the surviving manuscripts suggest that he spent far less time on the prose play than he had on the verse play. The ballet contains a final dance which was designed to attract sympathy to Fand, since it is called "Fand mourns among the waves"; but, since Fand has no lines to speak, it is difficult to see how she can be for long the object of our sympathies. Emer, as shown in notes to the transcriptions, is a much less noble figure in this play than in *The Only Jealousy*; indeed, there is even a hint that she has been jealous, in a passage from the first typescript draft:

E. I. A son of yours and his?

Emer So that is your first thought – his son and mine. (she laughs) Did you think that he belonged to you and me alone, ~~that we could keep him to ourselves. Do not look so strangely~~. The man he killed was the son of
has/ some woman he loved long ago, and I think he loved her better than he loved you or me.

He loved women before he heard our names, & he will love ~~women~~ women after he has forgotten us both. (MS N, 2^{r}, ll. 1–7)

The general loss of dignity in the tone of the text makes a search for a "tragic hero" a fruitless one in a piece where text is secondary to spectacle.

A knowledge of the esoteric system is unnecessary to an understanding of the play; Yeats carefully removed all references to the lunar mythology, with the exception of the opening and closing songs, which he retained merely for the purpose of "suggestion." The prose play reverts to the simple folklore of the earliest drafts of *The Only Jealousy*, but without the urgency, poetry, and passion that make those early drafts splendid things in their own right.

A biographical interpretation of *Fighting the Waves* is also of little point, for the same reasons: the sense of urgency is gone in this redaction. By eliminating the lunar imagery from the play, Yeats removed the mystery from the Woman of the Sidhe, a quality that had made her such a fascinating figure for him. Yeats's deep involvement in the drama of the verse play cannot be questioned; but one feels his detachment from the prose play. The meaning of the closing song has not of course changed in the prose play, but its context has; instead of providing a final comment on the misery and the mystery of Fand, it is instead a kind of chorus to a distracting dance by the Woman of the Sidhe, which in literary terms simply is not needed. Thus, the role of the closing song, and its power, are considerably weakened in the prose play.

Fighting the Waves, then, is an interesting curiosity (like its very curious preface), but both play and preface are mere shadows of the richness of *The Only Jealousy of Emer*, which retains its deeply moving quality both as read and as performed on stage.

V. The Logic of Revision

The manuscripts of *The Only Jealousy of Emer* help to elucidate some of the published play's mysteries. It now should be asked, in conclusion, what Yeats's original intentions in *The Only Jealousy* were, and whether his revisions constituted an improvement or not.

The earliest draft, MS A, shows that it was never Yeats's intention to strictly adhere to his sources: an Evil Spirit is in possession of Cuchulain's body. This was in line with Yeats's by then well-developed contention that the tale of Cuchulain and Fand was essentially one of possession. The presence of the changeling makes it virtually impossible for Cuchulain to choose Emer because he pities her, as in the sources; something must be done to get rid of the changeling, and clearly to get rid of him someone will have to pay a heavy price. But Emer is powerless against this evil spirit; the traditional remedies (such as fire) cannot prevail against a being who embodies the malignant fate that twists and confounds men's lives. It is the spirit who is in control of the situation, and not Emer. In addition, there is the formal constriction of the Noh structure working against the "happy ending" of the sources. This dramatic form was for Yeats a useful vehicle for the portrayal of frustrated and opposed rather than of satisfied and reconciled passions. An enriching bitterness had informed his two previous plays in this mode, *At the Hawk's Well* and *The Dreaming of the Bones*. In the first play, the Old Man and the young Cuchulain, unreconciled opposites, contend for the elusive waters of immortality; the water in turn ebbs and flows out of their reach, forever confounding their impossible desires; and the closing song calls them "idiots" and praises the domestic life, which can but be an impossibly nostalgic ideal for such as these, for "Wisdom must live a bitter life." And similarly all is bitterness and frustration in *The Dreaming of the Bones*: the lovers' lips can never meet; the bitter young man can never forgive them.

In *The Only Jealousy of Emer*, then, Cuchulain cannot be allowed a final choice; he must awake desiring the arms of his mistress, in which he can but find a temporary relief from the conflicting desires within. But Eithne's is not the love that satisfies opposing desires by reconciling them and subsuming them into itself; for Yeats, there are no satisfying trinities, only endless dualities. If we accept the dramatic logic of the situation, then the direction of the changes in the successive drafts seems almost inevitable.

Complicating this dramatic logic was the biographical factor. The early drafts, with their vigorous defense of man's love of "the imperfect," and with their generous tributes to Emer, show that Yeats clearly wanted the answer to the question, who will Cuchulain love, to be "Emer." But the very vigor of Cuchulain's defense, at the end of MS B, left Yeats an artistic dilemma: he could not easily proceed to a bitter ending after such a defense.

The bargain introduced in MS C offered a way out of this problem. It also solved the problem of getting rid of the changeling, whose controlling power had been acknowledged in the first draft: Emer had demanded Cuchulain from him (MS A, 7^{v}). The bargain made the bitter reward of the ending inevitable. The Mistress, at a minimum, would serve the dramatic function of being the object of Cuchulain's desires, for at the end the passive warrior would have to do or desire something to break the spell. Without the presence of the Mistress, Cuchulain might simply have awakened and rejected Emer, a conclusion that would have invited pathos (not the aim of the Noh) rather than leave us "astonished" and "dumb." Cuchulain's generous tributes to

Emer in the drafts now pass into the play's general atmosphere of bitterness, for upon awakening Cuchulain will have forgotten them completely.

In MS E, Cuchulain accepts the helmet to be rid of "regret and pity," Emer renounces his love, and "the curse" is complete; this is the world of *At the Hawk's Well*. The dramatic problem now was for Cuchulain to be attracted by the Woman of the Sidhe as forcefully as he had been by the well. There had been nothing alluring about the Woman of the Sidhe in the previous drafts; she had merely tried to entice Cuchulain to the land of the ever-living by reciting some worn-out Platonic philosophy to him. In addition, there was the biographical fact that Yeats came to realize he simply could not totally reject his love for Maud.

Thus in MS F Yeats introduced the Woman's dance to supplement her philosophy with seduction. Lunar imagery was used in tandem with the Platonic yolk and white of the egg. Such an amalgamation could hardly be sustained; and indeed the Platonic imagery had a fundamental dramatic weakness that the lunar imagery did not share. The flaw in the yolk/white image was that it invited Cuchulain's opposition. For the Woman of the Sidhe, love was desire for the perfect; for Cuchulain, scorning the doctrines of "the learned," love was pity for the imperfect. The yolk/white imagery could not bridge the gap between these two points of view.

The introduction of rhyming couplets using the lunar imagery into the dialogue between Cuchulain and the Woman of the Sidhe solved the artistic problem of how to nullify their opposed points of view. The esoteric lunar doctrine, by making the issues less clear, also made clear-cut opposition less possible. It also added to the aloof mysteriousness of the Woman, as did the opening and closing songs, both of which focused on the growing attraction of her beauty. Yeats at first wrote a closing song rejecting the Woman's beauty, but abandoned the attempt as its tenor was made impossible by the combined dramatic and biographical logic of the play.

Did all these revisions improve the play? We might regret the loss of many fine and vigorous lines from the early drafts, but the later revisions added an element of mysterious beauty that gives the play its peculiar attraction. Overall, the gain in richness and complexity must be said to outweigh the loss of simplicity. One can but marvel at the painstaking labors of Yeats to produce a small thing of beauty; the writing of *The Only Jealousy of Emer*, a play about the pursuit of perfection, was itself such a pursuit.

Order of Composition

Manuscripts of *The Only Jealousy of Emer*

The draft papers of *The Only Jealousy of Emer* can be divided into eleven groups. Though Curtis Bradford noted in his study of Yeats's manuscripts that Yeats usually began his plays with a prose scenario, "visions of a dramatic action, sometimes intense visions," if such a scenario ever existed for *The Only Jealousy of Emer*, it has not survived (*Yeats at Work* [Carbondale, 1965], p. 171).

MSS A and B (pp. 2–37 below) NLI 8774(9 and 10). The earliest surviving drafts of the play, from the Chorus's opening speech to Cuchulain's debate with the "Shape Changer" or "Spirit" (later the Woman of the Sidhe).

The play at this stage is very close, in atmosphere and imagery, to the rough but powerful vividness and simplicity of folklore. Thus, the struggle for Cuchulain's soul is very much one between the good and the evil Sidhe; there are no signs at this early stage of the more abstract personifications that came later. While the folklore atmosphere of this draft recalls the preceding dance plays, *At the Hawk's Well* and *The Dreaming of the Bones*, it is broken by a new metaphysical note that grows in importance in later drafts: the Woman of the Sidhe seeks Cuchulain's love, not because the shadowing gods pursue the affection of a strong mortal, but because before birth, man's body and soul were one and thus strain to be reunited.

MS C (pp. 38–61) NLI 8774(11). The draft revises and adds to some of the material in A, from the Mistress's awakening of Cuchulain through the Evil Genius (later the Figure of Cuchulain) enabling Emer to see the ghost of her husband. The Evil Genius strikes a bargain with Emer.

Speeches are switched between Emer and the Mistress ("Etain" in the first draft); the Mistress's kisses are reduced from two to one; the Ghost of Cuchulain crouches on stage from the beginning of the play.

MSS D and E (pp. 62–75) NLI 8774(12 and 13). Debate is resumed between Cuchulain and the Woman of the Sidhe from A and B; the Woman of the Sidhe offers Cuchulain a helmet of forgetfulness to blot out his memories of earthly life and love; Emer renounces the chance of regaining Cuchulain's love; the play is brought to a close for the first time as Cuchulain awakes, desiring his mistress and not his wife.

Both manuscripts are in prose.

MS F (pp. 76–107) NLI 8774(13). In this draft, lunar imagery and the dance by the Woman of the Sidhe are introduced; a final leaf of manuscript revises (then later cancels) the Evil Genius's explanation of how Cuchulain arrives at the house.

Dialogue is in blank verse.

MS G (pp. 108–161) NLI 8774(13). The first complete draft of the play, consolidating the previous drafts. Major changes are in unification of imagery and introduction of supernatural portents for Cuchulain's death.

MS H (pp. 162–169) NLI 8774(20). The first of three sets of papers (H, I, and J) that can be placed between the notebook draft G and the looseleaf draft K. This set contains a revision of the opening speech of the Chorus, and the mistress is now called Eithne Inguba.

MS I (pp. 170–175) NLI 8774(15). A revision of dialogue between Cuchulain and the Woman of the Sidhe. The kiss of forgetfulness replaces the somewhat clumsier helmet.

Debate is in prose.

MS J (pp. 176–179) NLI 8774(19). Fragment giving preliminary version, later discarded, of the closing song, cast in rhyming couplets.

MS K (pp. 180–263) NLI 8774(8 and 14) and Harvard. A single looseleaf draft reconstructed from fragments in collections in the National Library of Ireland and the Houghton Library, Harvard. This heavily revised second full draft includes the final version of the opening song and first version of the closing song. The diagram illustrates how the papers of this full draft have been assembled from the National Library of Ireland and the Houghton Library collections:

[NLI 8774(8)] + [H 338.7, fols. 1-12] + [NLI 8774(14)] + [H 338.7, fol. 20]
↓
[NLI 8774(16)]
↓
[H 338.7, fols. 13-19]

NLI 8774(8) is a draft of the opening song. The first twelve Houghton leaves are a draft (with substantial revisions incorporated) of the first half of the play. NLI 8774(14) contains the original continuation of this draft, with Houghton folio 20 as its original conclusion. NLI 8774(16) is a revision of NLI 8774(14), and Houghton folios 13–19 a revision in turn of NLI 8774(16). Houghton folio 20 contains the closing song of the play; Yeats altered its pagination when he combined the revised material with his original draft.

The complete dialogue between Cuchulain and the Woman of Sidhe has been rewritten in rhyming couplets, the imagery now fully esoteric and lunar.

More extensive stage directions are added to this version.

Quinn(14) (pp. 264–265) is a single sheet of revision subsequent to MS K.

MS L (pp. 268–310) The first typescript of the play, based on MS K, and corrected in ink. A few minor revisions to the text and additional stage directions; the False Cuchulain now called the Figure of Cuchulain.

MS M (pp. 312–326) NLI 8774(22) and Harvard. Holograph revisions of the closing song on several sheets of notebook paper.

A second typescript, one of a set apparently prepared for a performance that may never have taken place (NLI 30,873), contains this closing song in its revised state. See the collations to the *Poetry* text, pp. 308–310 below.

Manuscripts of *Fighting the Waves* and Revisions of *The Only Jealousy of Emer*

MS N (pp. 327–336) NLI 8774(5). The first draft of *Fighting the Waves*, still titled *The Only Jealousy of Emer*, with a nonspeaking role for the Woman of the Sidhe. There is one dance only.

This typescript includes corrections first in ink, then in pencil.

Further simplification of the language and structure of the play occur in a holograph fragment, NLI 30,492, pp. 338–349 below.

MS O (pp. 352–362) NLI 8774(6). A second typescript of *Fighting the Waves*. The Woman of the Sidhe is called Fand and has two additional dances (called "Prologue" and "Epilogue"); a new ending reveals Cuchulain about to mount into Fand's chariot.

MS P (pp. 364–367) NLI 8774(17 and 18). The 1934 revisions to *The Only Jealousy of Emer*, which follow many of the changes introduced in *Fighting the Waves*: Woman of the Sidhe is now named Fand and her argument with Cuchulain at the end of the play is dropped; Cuchulain is about to mount into Fand's chariot at the moment of Emer's renunciation of his love; Eithne boasts of her success at the play's end.

The first three leaves are holograph corrections, while the last two leaves are typescripts based on the first three.

Transcription Principles and Procedures

The conventions used in presenting the resultant readings are listed below. Beneath the first transcription of each manuscript or typescript are given two kinds of information:

1) Under *found in* are listed the manuscripts in the Census in which each draft appears.
2) Under *published in* are listed the separate publications to which the manuscript or typescript lead*s*.

The following typographical conventions are used to represent the various physical features of the texts:

roman type	ink
italic type	pencil
boldface type	typescript or print
italic boldface type	italic print

To transcribe Yeats's manuscripts with absolute fidelity is impossible. A glance at the photographs in this volume will show how difficult his hand is to read, especially when he is writing for his eye alone and with a carelessness reflecting the excitement of literary creation. He left the endings of many words unfinished or represented by a vague line, formed letters carelessly and inconsistently, was a poor and erratic speller, and punctuated unsystematically.

The photo-facsimiles will enable the interested reader to see what Yeats wrote. The task of an editor is to present a transcript in which the often obscure or illegible texts are *read*, and this inevitably requires a certain amount of interpretive "translation." The principles used in accordance with this process and the conventions used in presenting the resultant readings are given below.

A whole word is transcribed where a whole word seemed to be intended, even in cases where some of its letters are missing or represented only by Yeats's characteristic incompletely formed word endings, such as the "ing" and "ed" suffixes. If a precise spelling is not determinable the standard spelling is used, but where Yeats's misspelling is clear it is preserved. The various spellings of character names (for example, "Mananan" and "Manannan") have not been regularized (his final choice was "Manannan"). Where Yeats has begun to write the first letters of a word but finally left it unfinished, such as "cele" for "celebration," it has been transcribed as an incomplete word, with a conjectural reading sometimes supplied in a footnote. Yeats routinely abbreviated character names, an indication that he was composing in haste. Such obvious abbreviations are retained throughout; any obscure ones are expanded in the notes.

Yeats frequently broke words at unusual points or broke words not normally divided, such as "may be" for "maybe." Such spacing tends to indicate that he considered them to be either two separate words or words needing a hyphen, such as "wind blown" for "wind-blown" (though he rarely inserted hyphens in words that required them). In some cases the break may reflect the stress-pattern of his accentual-syllabic line. Such breaks are not represented in the transcriptions unless the width of the break approximates (or exceeds) the spacing that Yeats normally left *between* words. For example, Yeats often left a small gap between the two syllables in "Be cause"; this is always transcribed as "Because." Where Yeats left a space for an apostrophe but failed to insert it, the space is represented in the transcription without the missing apostrophe being supplied.

Ink blots and other accidental or obscure marks on the drafts are normally omitted silently. However, some ink blots, such as those left by heavily inked words found on some verso pages, are sometimes a revealing clue to the order in which unpaginated leaves were written. Such evidence has occasionally been utilized to confirm the compositional sequence.

Cancellation of single lines, or of individual words within a line, is indicated by single, horizontal straight cancel lines. These cancel lines are straight even when Yeats used multiple or erratic lines. Where Yeats intended to cancel an entire word but struck through only part of it, the cancel line in the transcript generally extends through the entire word. However, even when it seems likely that Yeats intended to cancel an entire phrase or line, no word that he did not at least partially cancel (or extend a cancellation mark under or over) is canceled in the transcriptions. Cancellation of an entire passage is indicated by a square bracket in the left margin. Yeats's "stet" marks are preserved, as are his underscorings to indicate italics or special emphasis. Where Yeats has canceled a part of a line, or a single word, and then the whole line, the transcription shows a second diagonal cancellation line, if appropriate, through the double cancel.

Overwritings are shown thus: ha{d / ve} = "have" changed to "had."

Spacing and relative positions of words and lines approximate the originals insofar as printed type can reproduce handwritten and typewritten material.

Yeats's use of caret and delete symbols is graphically represented. Caret symbols are raised to the line level even though Yeats usually placed them below the line. Circles, lines, and arrows used by Yeats to indicate the position on a page to which individual words, lines, or a block of text should be transposed or inserted are represented graphically and attempt to reproduce, as closely as possible, the actual disposition of such indicators.

In some manuscripts, foliation numbers and letters have been inscribed by a cataloguer. These are omitted from the transcriptions. Only Yeats's own (often inaccurate) pagination, or pagination included in typescripts prepared under his supervision, is included.

Line numbers are assigned to each line of dialogue, even if canceled, with the single exception of the Harvard manuscript section of MS K (see p. 182). However, if a line of verse is split between two speakers, the line number is not repeated unless the second portion appears on a new page, in which case the numbering convention of adding an "a" or "b" to the digit (for example, 12a or 12b) is used to identify each half of the line in commentary. In both verse and prose texts, speaker tags and stage directions, when they appear on a separate line or lines from dialogue, are not assigned line numbers.

In transcriptions of typescript material, minor and obvious typing errors such as strikeovers, or two separate words run together, are generally not recorded or are silently emended. All holograph revisions of typescript are recorded.

Illegible words and editorial conjectures are represented as follows:

[?]	an illegible or unintelligible word
[? ? ?]	several illegible or unintelligible words
[~~?~~]	a canceled illegible or unintelligible word
[?cauldron]	a conjectural reading
[?drowsing/drowsily]	equally possible conjectural readings

The following variants are not normally recorded in the *apparatus*:

1) variants of typeface, spacing, underlining, or punctuation in titles
2) variants involving the exchange of single and double quotation marks
3) variants involving the placement of punctuation inside or outside quotation marks
4) variants involving the exchange of "&" and "and"

In the *apparatus*, the following abbreviations are used:

del	deleted or deletion
rev	revised or revision
sd	stage direction

Part I

The Only Jealousy of Emer (1917–1919)

Manuscripts, with Transcriptions and Photographic Reproductions

[NLI 8774(9), 1r]

[NLI 8774(9), 1r]

1 Chorus.
2 ~~This is the great house~~
lie smoke dark
3 Above ~~lie~~ the ~~great~~^ beams of the roof
& yonder
4 ~~Through the open door comes in the wind of the~~
~~sea~~
the open door
5 Through ~~the great~~^ the shining of the sea
6 For this is the great ancient house
Dundalga,
7 Cuchullains famous house, & there upon
flags
the ~~stone~~
8 ~~The accursed majestical man in~~
~~deadly~~ swoon
9 The amorous violent man in deadly swoon
~~And here at his feet~~
10 ~~And at his feet, bowed down~~
11 And his neglected wife, bowed at his feet
12 And now his mistress comes, &
for a moment stands
13 ~~Behind, but ignorant~~
14 Ignorant why his wife has sent for her
being still ignorant
15 But in great trouble – ~~not knowing yet~~
16 If he is dead, or wounded, or but asleep
17 ~~And behind her through the open door the sea~~

---

6 Dundalga (today Dundalk), "Cuchulain's chief ancestral residence. It had its name from Dealga, a chieftain of the Firbolgs, who built it" (O'Curry, *Atlantis* I [1858], p. 376n.). In the sources Cuchulain asks not to be carried to Dundalga, where his wife, Emer, is, preferring the Speckled House at Emain Macha (*Cuchulain of Muirtheimne*, p. 211).

7 In the sources, Cuchulain lay on a bed; Yeats reverted to this in later manuscripts.

11 Yeats eliminated this pathos in later manuscripts. It is characteristic of the love of "the imperfect," which is more vehemently expressed here than in later drafts: for "at his feet" MS G has merely "watching"; in MS H, she is "at his side." Cf. previous note.

[NLI 8774(9), 1v]

[NLI 8774(9), 1[v]]

1 Far off, behind her through the open door
2 The shining bitter sea is crying out
3 ~~Emer~~
4 ~~I have called you hither~~
5 Etain.
6 Is it death.
7 Emer
8 I do not know what power
eyes &
9 Has shut his ~~ee~~ & ears but
it is not death
here house
10 An hour ago ~~here~~ in this very room
a while
11 He ~~fou~~ met with one, who seemed^most dear ~~in his eyes~~
12 And then, through sudden anger or hostility
13 He drove him out & killed him on the shore
was
14 Or so it is said, & he that so killed
15 Was his own son by some wild woman loved
16 ~~In early life~~ –
17 When he & she were young – or so it is said
18 And thereupon knowing what man he had killed
being
19 And^mad with sorrow he ran out

---

5 Etain] Eithne, in the sources. Perhaps Yeats was recalling the tale of Edain, like Cuchulain a mortal spirited off to the otherworld for love, who later wishes to return to her mortal love. See Lady Wilde, *Ancient Legends*, I, pp. 179–182.

10 "house" is changed to "the assembly house" in MS G, and "the house of the kings" in MS H, readings more in accord with *On Baile's Strand.*

11 For "fou" read "fought."

15 The "wild woman" is Aoife, a queen of Scotland.

[NLI 8774(9), 2r]

[NLI 8774(9), 2r]

And for a long while fought with the sea waves
~~The kings came down & watched but dared~~
~~The people watched, but none dared stay his~~
~~madness~~
The people watched, none spoke above his breath
And none dared speak to him or stay him
~~And when at last he fell out to sea~~
~~The wave~~
Until at last he had falled in sea.
His people took him up & laid him there
~~called~~
Not dead but in a trance: ~~in vain I have cried~~
In vain I have called his name in ~~to~~ his ears
see trance
I have kissed his lips in vain –
He is deaf – He is blind
But if call his name & kiss his lips
~~He will it may~~
The enchantment will it may be fall away
You are more dear than I
Etain
Being but
~~I am~~ his mistress
I am dearer than his wife but I am dear
But for a little while – He will love his wife

---

8 For "falled in sea" read "fallen in the sea."

10 With the first half of this line compare Yeats's note on the story in Lady Gregory's *Visions and Beliefs in the West of Ireland* (1922; Gerrards Cross, 1970), p. 364: "We have here certainly a story of trance and the soul leaving the body." In MS G, it is replaced by a less dramatically convincing explanation that Cuchulain is not dead because there have not been the necessary Shakespearean portents of his death.

11 Yeats scribbled an instruction to himself to "see trance" for the revisions; "trance" is found at the top of 3r.

12 The folklore motif of the kiss of disenchantment is of course well founded in tales like "Beauty and the Beast."

14 For "if call" read "if you call."

18–20 Repeated on p. 11 below to show continuation.

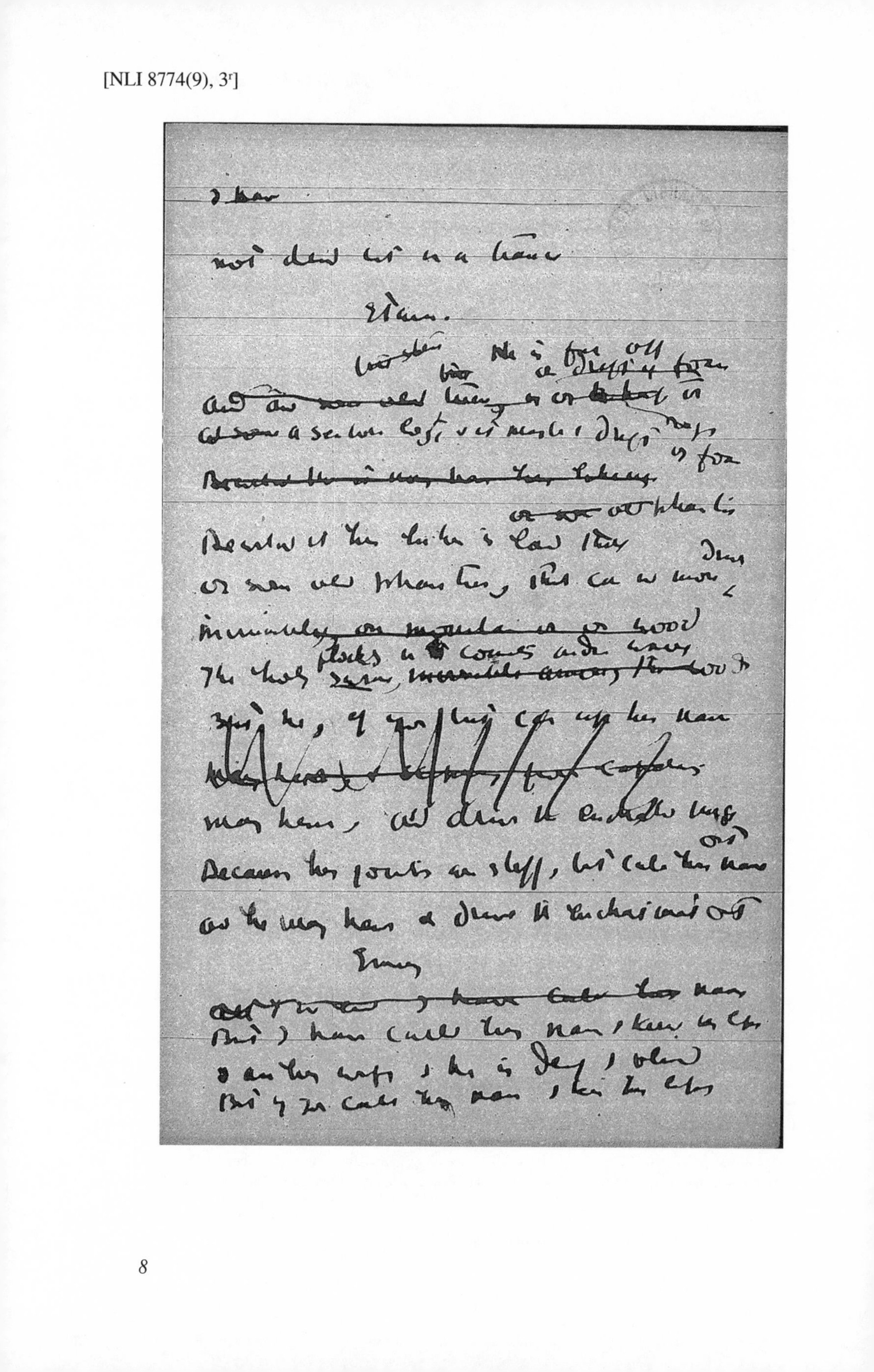

[NLI 8774(9), 3[r]]

[NLI 8774(9), 3^{r}]

1 ~~I have~~
2 Not dead but in a trance
3 Etain
4 He is far off
~~tree stem~~
tree ~~a drift of foam~~
5 ~~And and some old tree, is or a hat or~~
~~rags~~
6 ~~And some~~ a sea born log, & it may be a drift of foam
7 ~~Bewitched that it may have his likeness~~
~~or some old~~ phantom
8 Bewitched it his likeness is laid there
drive
9 Or some old phantom, that can no more ^
10 ~~Invisibly, on mountain or in wood~~
flocks in the country under waves
11 The holy ~~swine, invisible among the woods~~

12 But he, if you but cry up his name
13 ~~May hear, & escaping from captivity~~
14 May hear, and drive the enchanted beings out
15 Because his joints are stiff, but call his name
16 And he may hear & drive the enchantment out
17 Emer
18 ~~All to no end I have called his name~~
19 But I have called his name & kissed his lips
20 I am his wife & he is deaf & blind
21 But if you call his name & kiss his lips

This leaf and the following one were inserted into the original sequence. It seems likely that Yeats wrote as far as 6^{v}, then functioning as 3^{r}, left a line there, and revised 2^{r}, beginning with 2^{v}, and introducing the changeling motif.

5 For "and" read "as."

6 With "sea born log" compare Lady Wilde, *Ancient Legends, Mystic Charms, and Superstitions of Ireland* (London, 2 vols., 1887–1888), 1:52: "The evil influence of the fairy glance does not kill, but it throws the object into a death-like trance, in which the real body is carried off to some fairy mansion, while a log of wood, or some ugly deformed creature, is left in its place, clothed with the shadow of the stolen form." Cf. also Yeats's note on changelings in *Visions and Beliefs*: "This thing may be some old person who was taken years ago and having come near his allotted time is put back to get the rites of the church, or a substitute for some more youthful and more helpful person. The old man may have grown too infirm even to drive cattle. On the other hand, the thing may be a broomstick or a heap of shavings" (p. 359)

8 For "it" read "in."

10 The line refers to "Tir-fa-tonn (Tir-fo-thoinn), one of the old Irish conceptions of the Other World" (Jeffares and Knowland, *A Commentary on the Collected Plays*, p. 15). Country-under-Waves was described by John A. MacCullough in Louis H. Grey, ed., *The Mythology of All Races*, vol. 3, *Celtic* (Boston, 1918), p. 113. Its king sits "on a golden throne; a year spent there feasting seems but a few days." Submarine cattle were part of the folklore of the West of Ireland. Lady Gregory quotes a fisherman at Kilronan Pier in the Aran Islands: "They are in the sea as well as on the land. That is well known by those that are out fishing on the coast. When the weather is calm, they can look down sometimes and see cattle and pigs and all such things as we have ourselves" (*Visions and Beliefs*, p. 22)

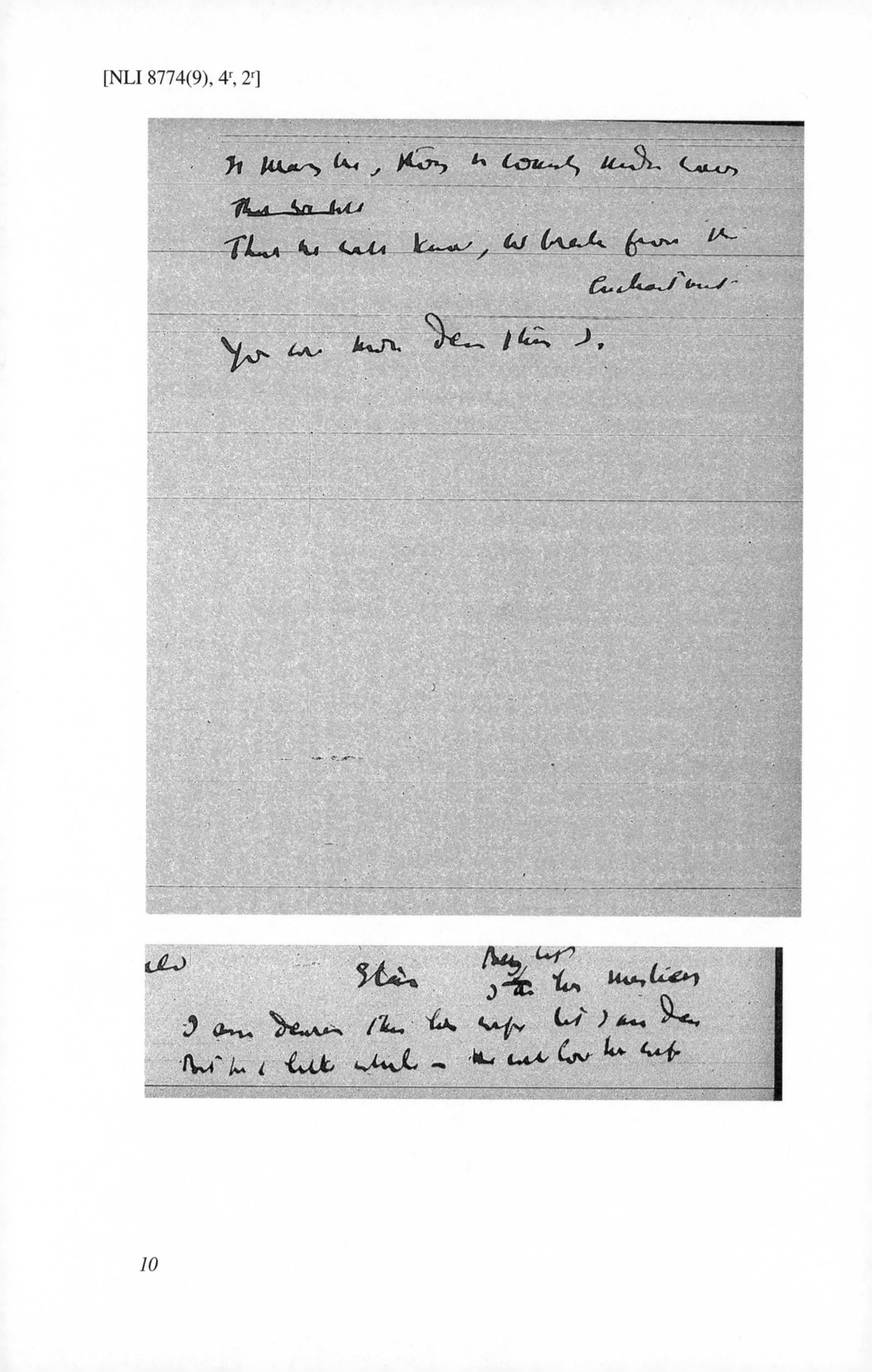

[NLI 8774(9), 4^{r}, 2^{r}]

[NLI 8774(9), 4^{r}]

1 It may be, there in country under waves
2 ~~That he will~~
3 That he will know, and break from the
enchantment
4 You are more dear than I.

[NLI 8774(9), 2^{r}]

18 Etain
Being but
19 ~~I am~~ his mistress
20 I am dearer than his wife but I am dear
21 But for a little while – He will love his wife

4^{r}, ll. 1–4 These lines revise l. 11ff. on 3^{r} and pick up l. 17 on 2^{r}.

2^{r}, ll. 18–20 Repeated here to show continuation. For an illustration of the full page, see p. 6.

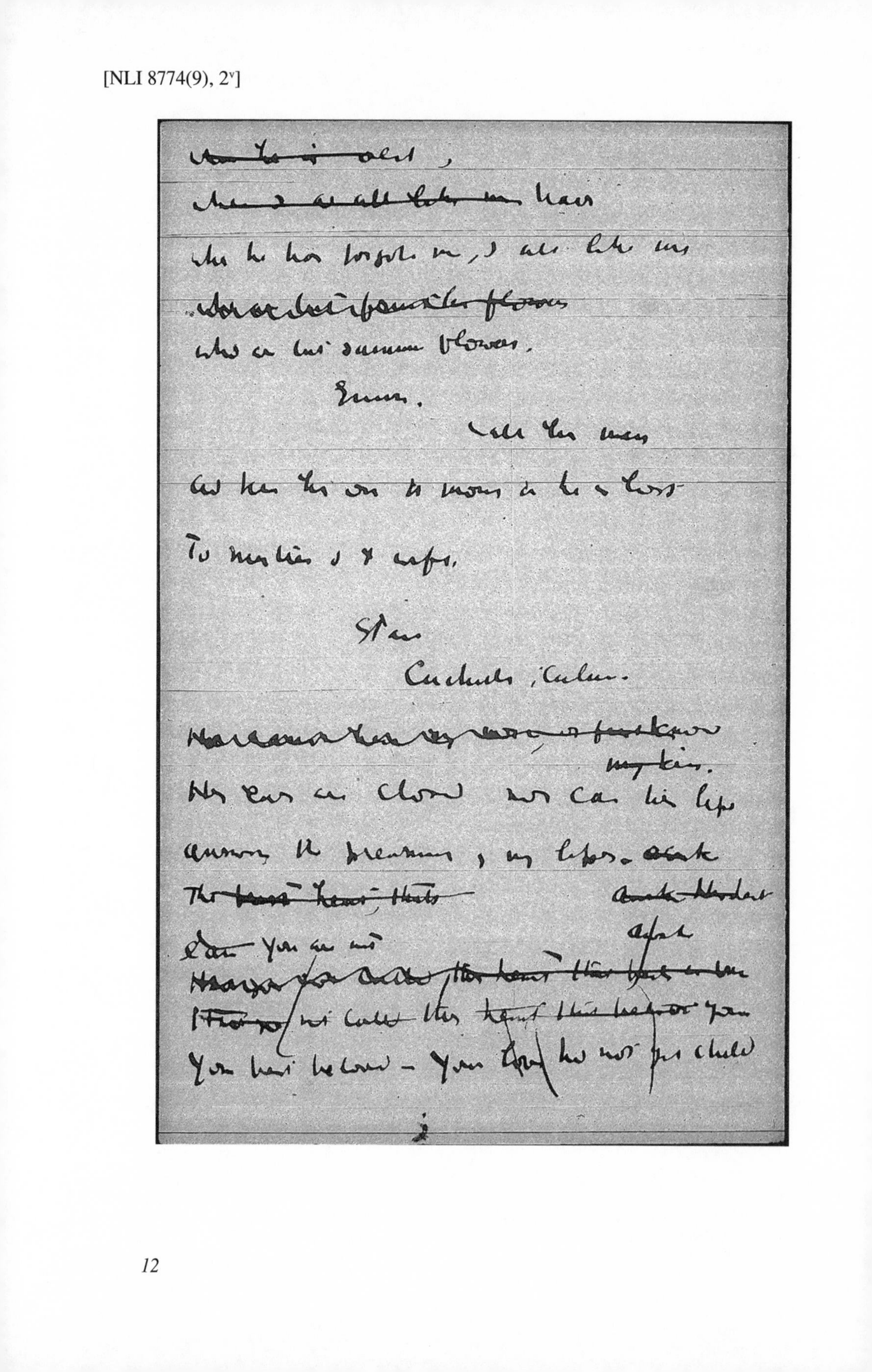

[NLI 8774(9), 2v]

[NLI 8774(9), 2^{v}]

~~When he is old,~~
~~When I and all like me have~~
When he has forgotten me, & all like me
~~Who are but countless flowers~~
Who are but summer flowers.
Emer.
Call his name
And kiss him on the mouth or he is lost
To mistress & to wife.
Etain
Cuchulain, Cuchulain.
~~He cannot hear my voice, or feel know~~
~~my kiss~~.
His ears are closed nor can his lips
Answer the pressure of my lips. ~~Awake~~
~~The breast heart, that's~~ ~~Awake his heart~~
~~I am~~ You are not ~~Awake~~
~~Have you not called this heart that beats in vain~~
~~Have you not called this heart that beats on you~~
Your best beloved – Your love had not yet chilled

2^{v} Yeats used the verso of 2 to revise and supplement its recto.

4, 5 The "flower" image is replaced by "sea-pinks" in MS C, "the foam upon the sailor's beard" in MS G, and finally by "Are flung into some corner like an old nut-shell" in MS H.

19 Completed, with the paper reversed, on 6^{v}, l. 17.

[NLI 8774(9), 5r]

[NLI 8774(9), 5r]

1 Awake
2 When ever did Cuchulain mope in such
3 ~~when his beloved~~
4 At a
5 Awake
6 You've never moped in silence when I have cried
7 Your name aloud – Your love had not yet chilled
8 when we were parted by the dawn of day
9 And therefore let my voice prevail against
imbittered
10 The enchantments of the cold ~~embittered~~ sea.
11 ~~I cry the~~
12 ~~Eyes ears & lips shut fast~~
13 All to no end for eyes & lips & ears
for eye and lip & ears
14 All to no end, ~~because eyes, ears & lips~~
Are me greater power
15 ~~All~~ held shut against ~~us~~ by some great power
16 ~~Than the brief passion I have awaked in~~
~~him~~
17 ~~Than the brief that a woman~~
~~he~~ has felt for
18 Than the brief passion, he ~~has given to~~ me
I
19 O how can who perish in his dream
mastery
20 ~~Tremble & perish prevail the might~~
21 ~~All those that never pass away.~~

---

17 For "brief that" read "brief passion."
20 For "prevail the might" read "prevail against the might of."

[NLI 8774(9), 5v]

[NLI 8774(9), 5v]

~~Tremble, tremble & perish, prevail in might~~
~~When matched with those that never pass away~~
Tremble & perish, equal myself in might
With those who can never pass away – ~~Take Cover~~
~~His eyes & ears, that may neither hear~~
~~lay cloak~~
~~Or shield upon his face & hide the sea~~
and yet
~~But cover up his face & hide the sea~~
~~And I will cry to him again~~
~~(They cover up his face)~~
or
But cover up his face, or turn it away
~~From that~~
*
From where the sea cries out, and I will cry
Cuchulain again and cry it while I have breath
And may be he will hear.
(They cover up his face & turn him away)
he it may be and it may be
* That when he can no longer hear or see
That enemy, he will awake by himself

3 For "equal" read "be equal."
7 In MS G, it is Emer who suggests this.

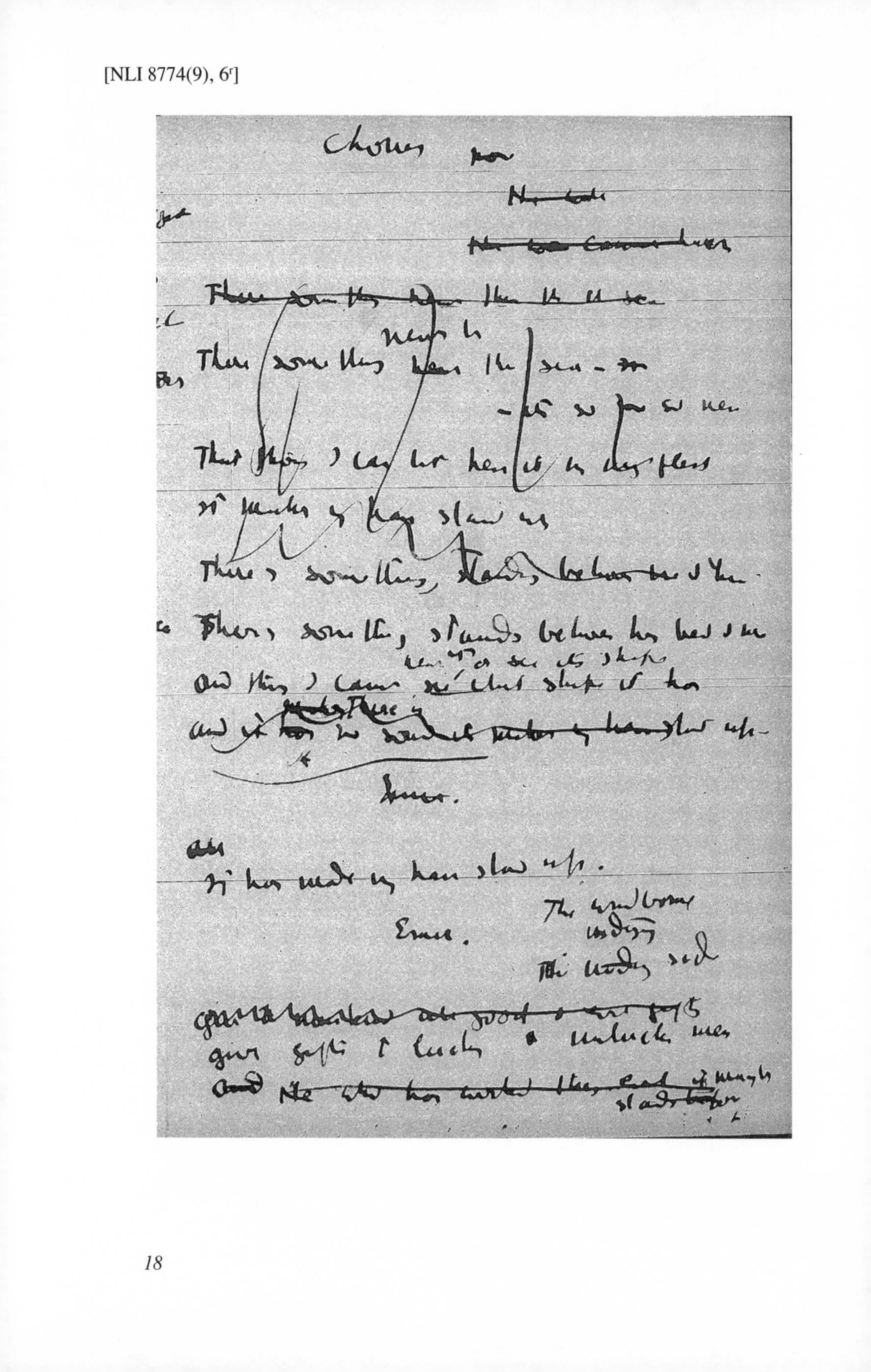

[NLI 8774(9), 6^{r}]

[NLI 8774(9), 6[r]]

Chorus
now
~~He wakes~~
~~He was cannot hear~~
~~There's something nearer there than the sea~~
nearer to
There's something ~~near~~ the sea –
– its so near so near
That though I can but hear it in my flesh
It makes my hair stand up
There's something, standing between me & him
{T / S}here's something stands between his bed & me
hear it, or see its shape
And though I cannot ~~see what shape it has~~
~~make~~s There is
And it ~~has~~ no sound it makes my hair stand up
*
~~Emer.~~
~~All~~
It has made my hair stand up.
Emer.
The windborne
~~undying~~
~~The undy~~ sidhe
~~Give to mankind all good & evil gifts~~
Give gifts to lucky & unlucky men
~~And He who has worked this evil it may be~~
~~stands before~~

---

5 This premonition, which accurately reflects the primitive folklore influence felt so strongly in this draft, is not repeated in later manuscripts. The "something" is the evil spirit coming to possess the body of Cuchulain.

12 The asterisk cues the insertion of now canceled text on 5[v]. Yeats drew the rule to indicate a pause in his labors or to mark a new beginning point (see l. 11).

[NLI 8774(9), 6v]

[NLI 8774(9), 6^{v}]

~~Between us & the bed~~
Etain
He who has worked this evil stands it may be
Between me & the bed
Emer
my husband is bestir
~~No no more~~ look
~~My husband stirs~~ – ~~one of the friendly~~ sidhe
~~Has waked him from trance has awaked him~~
Some friend among
~~One of the friendly~~ sidhe ~~awakes~~ him
And now he throws the covers from his face
(Cuchulain sits up but with his face
away)
Turn round Cuchulain turn to life again
(Cuchulain turns but shows an old
contorted face – a pause during which
Etain ~~comes back. Chorus sing~~)

When we were parted by the dawn of day

---

5 For "bestir" read "bestirring."

16 Yeats pauses here, halfway down the page. Eithne, presumably, has not left the stage, but has moved away while Emer speaks. There is no draft extant of any song to be inserted here, and after MS G there is no mention of a song accompanying Eithne's return.

17 This line immediately follows the last line on 2^{v}. Yeats wrote this line, then revised 2^{r}, then continued on 6^{r}, after turning the card over and upside down.

[NLI 8774(9), 7r]

[NLI 8774(9), 7[r]]

1 Emer
2 My husband stirs
3 It was no evil spirit but some friend
4 Come to awaken him – welcome welcome
5 Welcome, husband to your wife & house
6 (He sits up & shows an old
7 face – he shows a contorted
8 face of an evil spirit to . Etain
9 slowly moves back. Chorus
10 sing half a dozen lines – ~~during~~
11 ~~which Etain goes out~~).
12 Emer.
who have
13 Who are you^dare to take my husband's place
14 And something of his image – what spirit
15 ~~Has dared, to~~
16 Has dared so to offend this ancient
house.
17 False Cuchullain –

8 For "to ." read "to Etain."
17 Also called "Evil Spirit" and "Evil Genius" in this draft

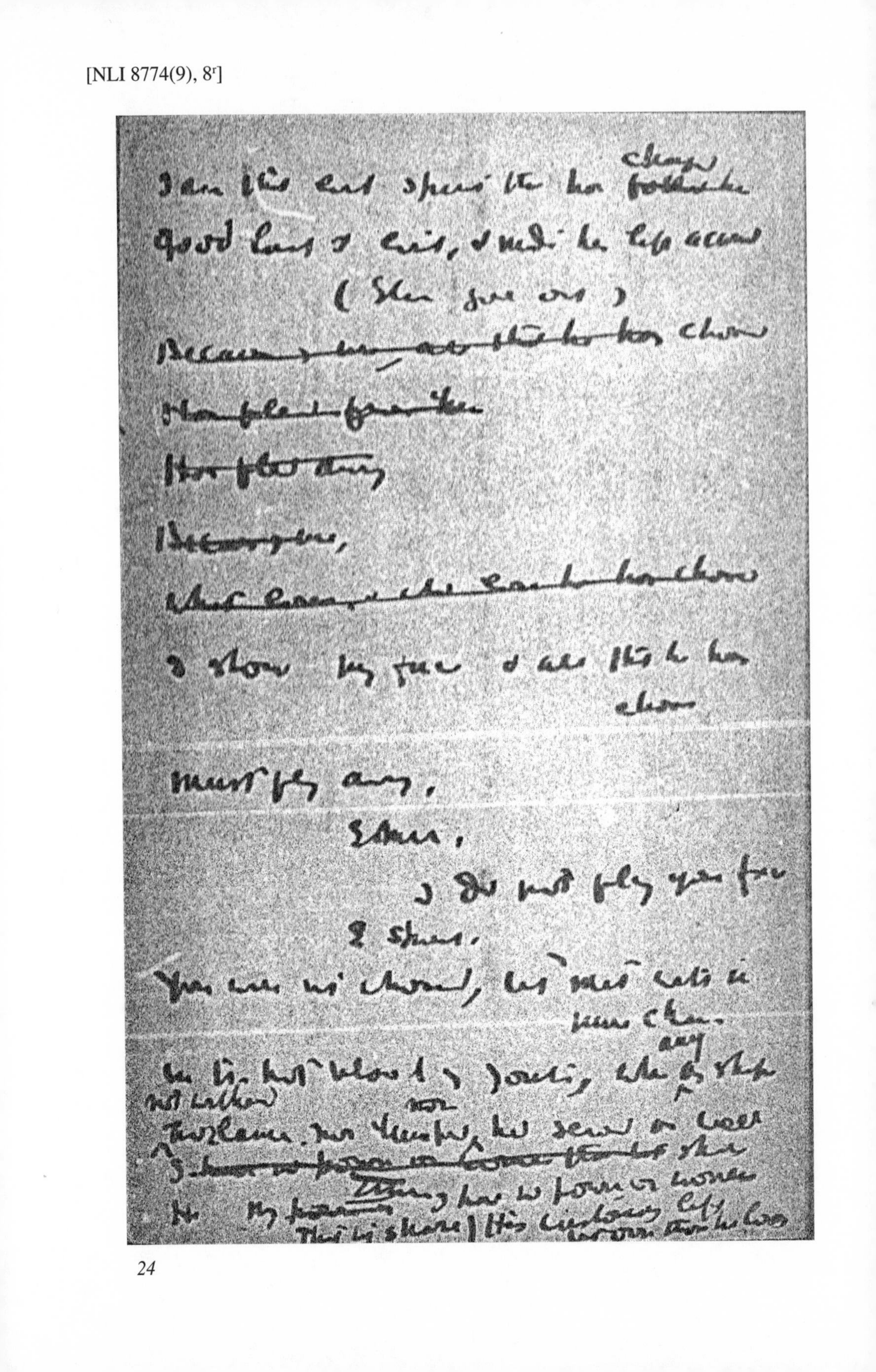

[NLI 8774(9), 8^{r}]

[NLI 8774(9), 8^r]

changed
I am that evil spirit that has ~~followed~~ his
Good luck to evil, & made his life accursed
(Etain goes out)
~~Because of me, all that he has chosen~~
~~Has fled from him~~
~~Has fled away~~
~~Because of me~~,
~~What ever, and who ever he has chosen~~
I show my face & all that he has
chosen
Must fly away.
Emer.
I do not fly your face
E Spirit
You were not chosen, but met with in
pure chance
any
In the hot blood of youth, when^any shape
not withered ~~nor~~
^Turned lame nor humped^had seemed as well[22]
I ~~have no power on women that but~~ share
Emer
~~His~~ My ~~power is~~ I have no power on women
That but share/ His customary life
but over those he loves

16 This withering insult is replaced in MS C by the blunt statement “Not being loved you are not in my power.”

[NLI 8774(9), 7^v, 8^v]

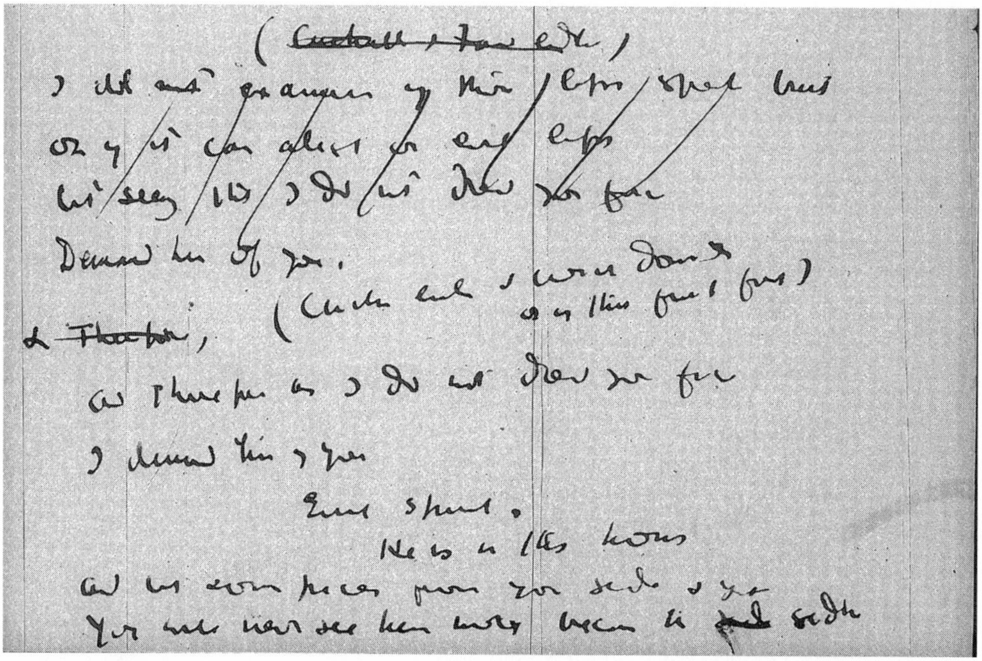

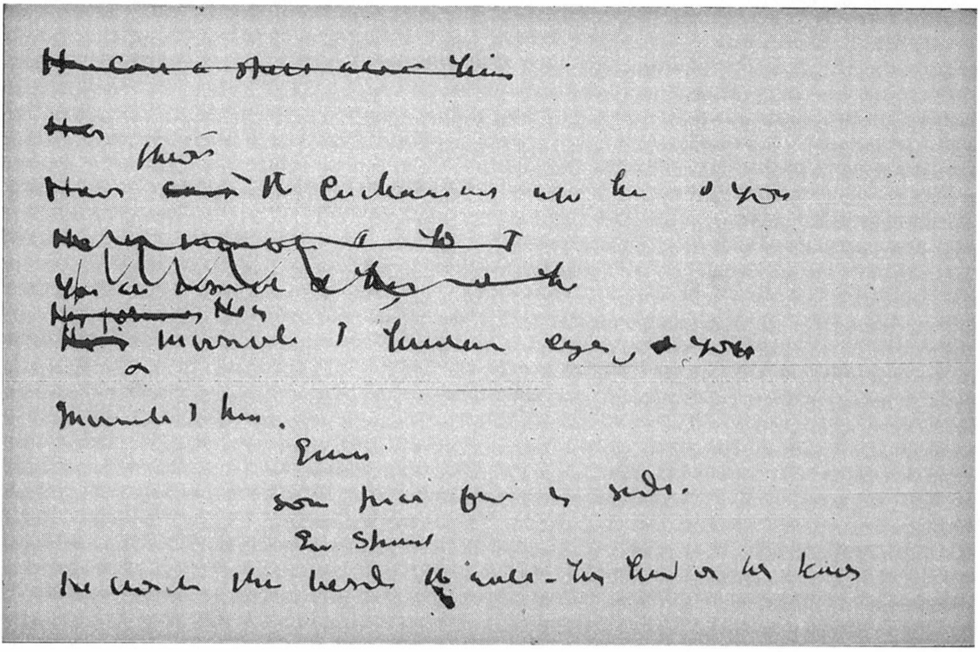

[NLI 8774(9), 7^{v}]

1 (Cuchullain & Fand enter)
2 I shall not examine if those lips speak truth
3 Or if it can alight on evil lips
4 But seeing that I do not dread your face
5 Demand him of you.
6 (Cuchulain enters & crouches down
7 or is thus face to feet)
8 & ~~Therefore~~,
9 And Therefore as I do not dread your face
10 I demand him of you
11 Evil Spirit
12 He is in this house
13 And but some few paces from your side & yet
14 You will never see him more because the ~~sidhe~~ sidhe

[NLI 8774(9), 8^{v}]

1 ~~Have cast a spell about him~~
2 ~~Have~~
thrown
3 Have ~~cast~~ the enchantment upon him & you
4 ~~He is invisible and you to [?him]~~
5 ~~You are invisible to him & he~~
~~His form is~~ He is
6 ~~He is~~^ invisible to human eyes, & you
7 Invisible to him.
8 Emer
9 Some paces from my side.
10 Evil Spirit
11 He crouches there beside the wall – his head on his knees

With the paper turned sideways, Yeats composed continuous lines on the versos of 7 and 8, presented together here.

7^{v}, l. 1 This is the only time the Woman of the Sidhe (obviously intended to be a more general figure than the Fand of the sources) is so called in the manuscripts of *The Only Jealousy*; she is not so named again until the drafts of *Fighting the Waves*. Emer speaks the lines that follow.

7 For "or" read "and"?

[NLI 8774(9), 9r]

[NLI 8774(9), 9[r]]

5 ~~6~~
Have thrown their enchantment on your eyes
& lips.
Emer.
You say he's but some few paces from my side
Evil G
against
There, there ~~at~~ the wall crouched head on knees
The the
~~Your~~ longing and ~~your~~ cries have drawn him here
in to the form
And made him dream himself ~~in to old form~~
That is familiar to him – for after death
~~When the heart is stirred it calls upon the old~~
~~When the heart is stirred with memory, the form~~
When memory stirs the man, &
when ever
That form recurs when the heart is stirred
That form awakes when ever the heart is stirred
Emer
Cuchulain come to me.
Evil Gen
You call in vain
Your voice can never reach him nor can hers
That he loves better than his wife – Sidhe
~~Have sent a messenger to lead him hence~~

---

1 This line resumes the draft from the last line of 7[v]. Yeats revises what he had written on 8[v].

4, 16 Read "Evil Genius."

[NLI 8774(9), 10r]

[NLI 8774(9), 10r]

A messenger from country under waves
To lead him hence, &
~~Shape changer of the country under waves~~
Have sent a messenger to lead him hence.
~~That messenger~~
~~And~~
the
A shape changer of^country under waves
To dream herself into his dream, & now
~~He but the blind man~~
He is but the blind man & she the dog
Emer.
O should she stand I will find some
way
Although she seem but air to pierce her breast
I ~~'ve~~ never have been jelous of a woman
But I'll not give him up to her
Ev Gen.
Be silent
For love I have heard every day
A shape changer pleading with a man
And it will be soon over, for soon enough

[NLI 8774(9), 9^v, 10^v]

[NLI 8774(9) 9ᵛ]

She'll lead him to the country under waves
[?any]
And keep him ever, ~~far from wheat & May flowers that fade~~
~~To a~~
For never was there man
But longed for fadeless flowers.
Cuchulain –
I know that face
~~You are she I saw~~
~~At the Hawks well, &~~
For you are she I met by the Hawks well
you have dropped your quills
Though ~~you have dropped your q~~
Shape Changer
I am that dream

[NLI 8774(9), 10ᵛ]

~~And~~ As man before he is born into the world
Is shaped as an egg; ~~There~~, a yellow yoke will is
About the white of egg, but when he is born
He's but the white, the yoke remains as a dream.
And both miserable, until they meet at death
substance
Is shaped as an egg, ~~made~~ has a double ~~nature~~
Like yoke & white, but when he has been born
One substance stays ~~behind,~~ where the shape changers are
~~And both are miserable: one~~
~~For but one half~~
And both are miserable /
Cuchulain
I have heard this tale
From learned men –

After rotating the paper, Yeats entered continuous lines on the versos of 9 and 10, presented together here.

9ᵛ, l. 5 fadeless] Unfading; *OED* quotes Coleridge, "To the Author of Poems" (Joseph Cottle), 1796: "May your fame fadeless live."

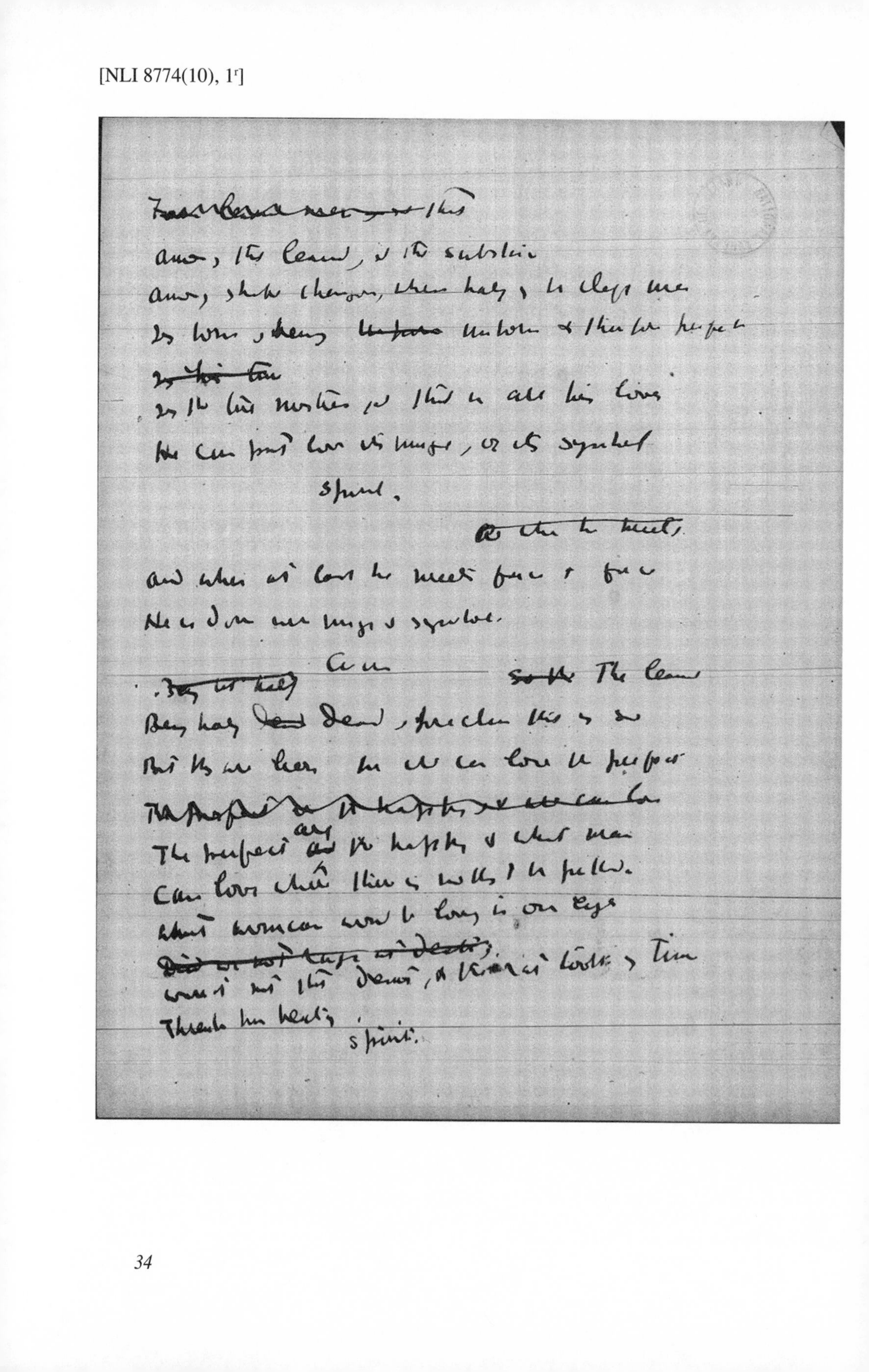

[NLI 8774(10), 1[r]]

[NLI 8774(10), 1r]

~~From learned men, &~~ that
Among the learned, & the sublime
Among shape changers, when half of the cleft man
Is born, being ~~therefore~~ unborn & therefore perfect
~~Is his true~~
Is the true mistress, & that in all his loves
He can but find its image, or its symbol
Spirit.
~~And when he meets~~
And when at last he meets face to face
He is done all image & symbol.
Cuchulain
~~So the~~ The learned
~~Being but half~~
Being half ~~dead~~ dead, proclaim this is so
But they are liars for who can love the perfect
~~The perfect is the happy, & who can love~~
are
The perfect ~~and~~ the happy & what man
^
Can love where there is nothing to be pitied
What woman would be long in our eye
~~Did we not rage at death;~~
Were it not that death, and the rat tooth of time
Threaten her beauty.
Spirit.

1–6 Cf. the completion after the round of incarnations symbolized by the 13th Cone of *A Vision*.

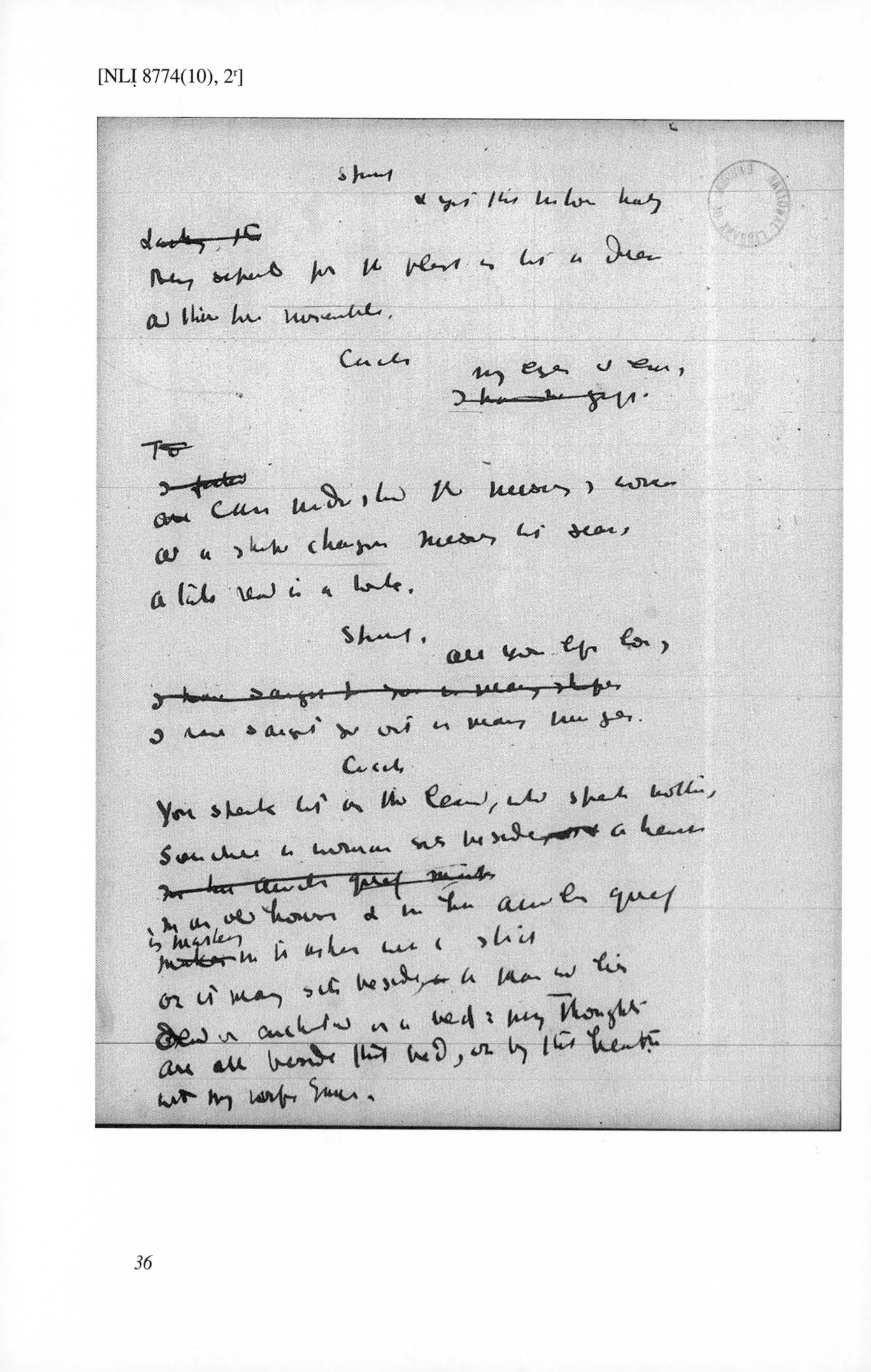

[NLI 8774(10), 2r]

[NLI 8774(10), 2[r]]

Spirit
& yet this unborn half
~~Lacking, the~~
Being separate from the flesh is but a dream
And therefore miserable.
Cuchulain
My eyes and ears
~~I have no gift~~
~~To~~
~~I failed~~
~~Are~~ Can understand the misery of woman
And a shape changers misery but seems
A tale read in a book.
Spirit.
All your life long
~~I have caught for you in many shapes~~
I have sought you out in many images.
Cuchulain
You speak but as the learned, who speak nothing
Somewhere a woman sits beside ~~peat &~~ a hearth
~~In her aimless grief marks~~
In an old house & in her aimless grief
is marking
~~Makes~~ in the ashes with a stick
Or it may sits beside ~~a~~ a man who lies
Dead or enchanted on a bed: my thoughts
Are all beside that bed, or by that hearth
With my wife Emer.

---

12 Cuchulain's defense of man's love of the imperfect is much more forceful in this draft than in later manuscripts.

18–26 These lines, not repeated in later drafts, vividly show how Cuchulain has been drawn back by "the longing and the cries," as the Evil Genius claims in MS A, 9[r], l. 6 above.

19–24 Cuhulain imagines two different scenes for Emer's expression of grief: "a woman sits beside a hearth / . . . marking in the ashes with a stick[,]" or, it "may [be,] sits beside a man who lies / Dead or enchanted on a bed."

[NLI 8774(11), 1r]

[NLI 8774(11), 1r]

All like me
~~Are but the sea pink in the rocky holed~~
Are but as the sea pink on the rocks
Where the tired sailor, rests beside his oars
are
Who ^ as the sea pink in the grassy place
Between two rocks where the tired sailor lies
Emer
Call out his name & kiss him on the mouth
Or he is lost to mistress & to wife
Mistress
Cuchullain – Cuchullain – eyes & ears are closed
Nor can he feel the pressure of my lips
~~Wh~~ Awake – When ever have I called your name
And got no answer – passion had not chilled
When we were parted at the dawn of day
fore
And there let my voice & lips put down
The enchantments etc.

Revision of MS A, 2v above. Mistress is speaking.
5 Yeats first wrote "grass," then added the "y" with a lighter stroke.
15 Refers back to MS A, 5r above.

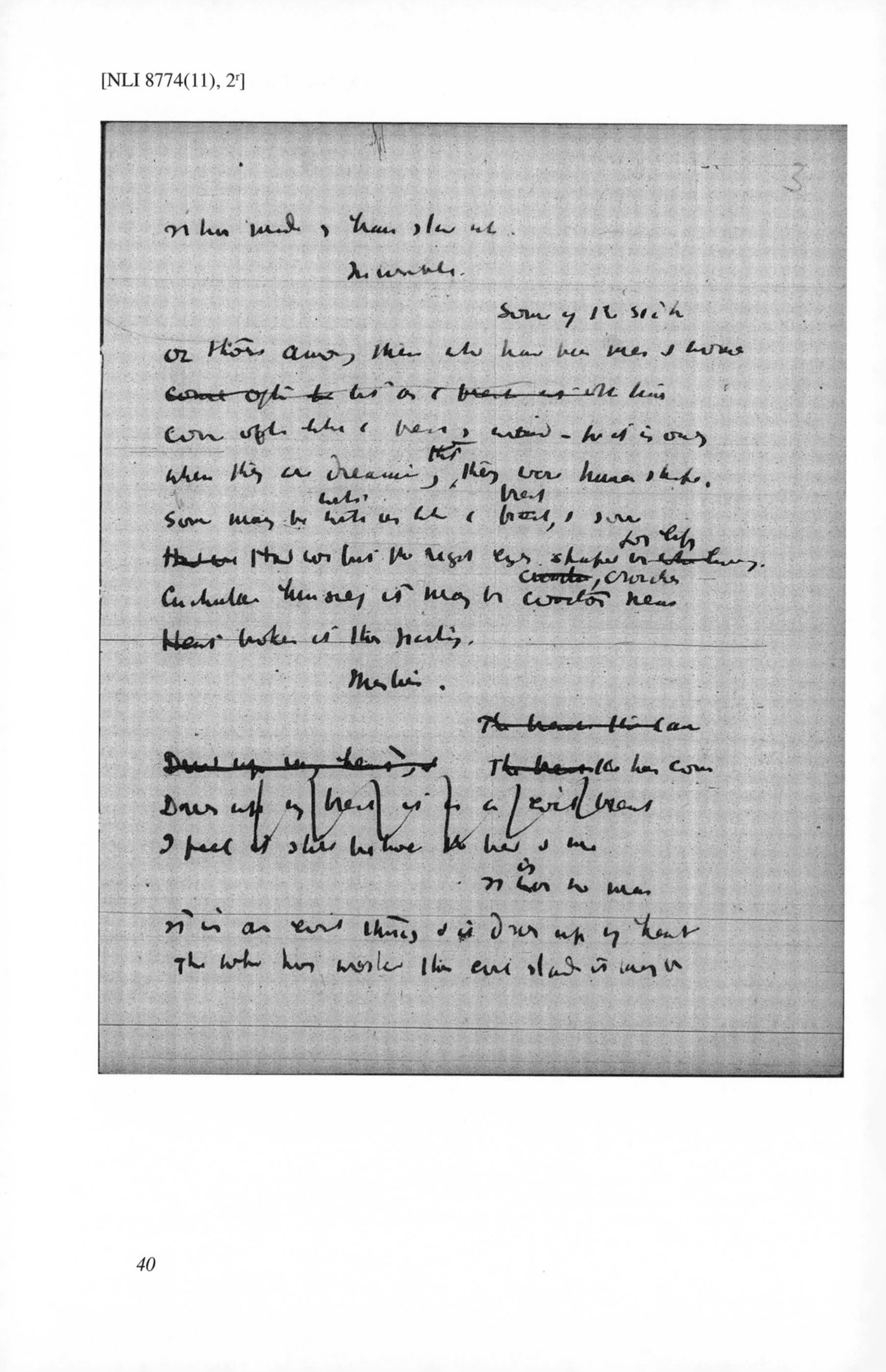

[NLI 8774(11), 2r]

[NLI 8774(11), 2^{r}]

1 It has made my hair stand up
Invisible.
Some of the sidhe
2 Or those among them who have been men & women
3 ~~Come often but but as a breath at other times~~
4 Come often like a breath of wind – for it is only
that
5 When they are dreaming, ^ they wear human shape
with breath
6 Some may be ~~with~~ us like a ~~breath~~, & some
for life
7 ~~Had we~~ Had we but the right eyes shaped ~~as when living~~
~~crouches~~, crouches
8 Cuchullain himself it may be ~~crouches~~ near
9 Heart broken at this parting.
Mistress.
~~The breath that came~~
10 ~~Dried up my heart, &~~ ~~The breath~~ that has come
11 Dries up my breath it is an evil breath
12 I feel it still between the bed & me
is
13 it ~~was~~ no man
14 It is an evil thing & it dries up my heart
15 The who has worked this evil stands it may be

Revision of MS A, 6^{r} above. Mistress speaks.

1*sd* This is perhaps a note to himself that the ghost of Cuchulain is on stage, invisible to Emer, who begins speaking at l. 1b.

15 For "The" read "He".

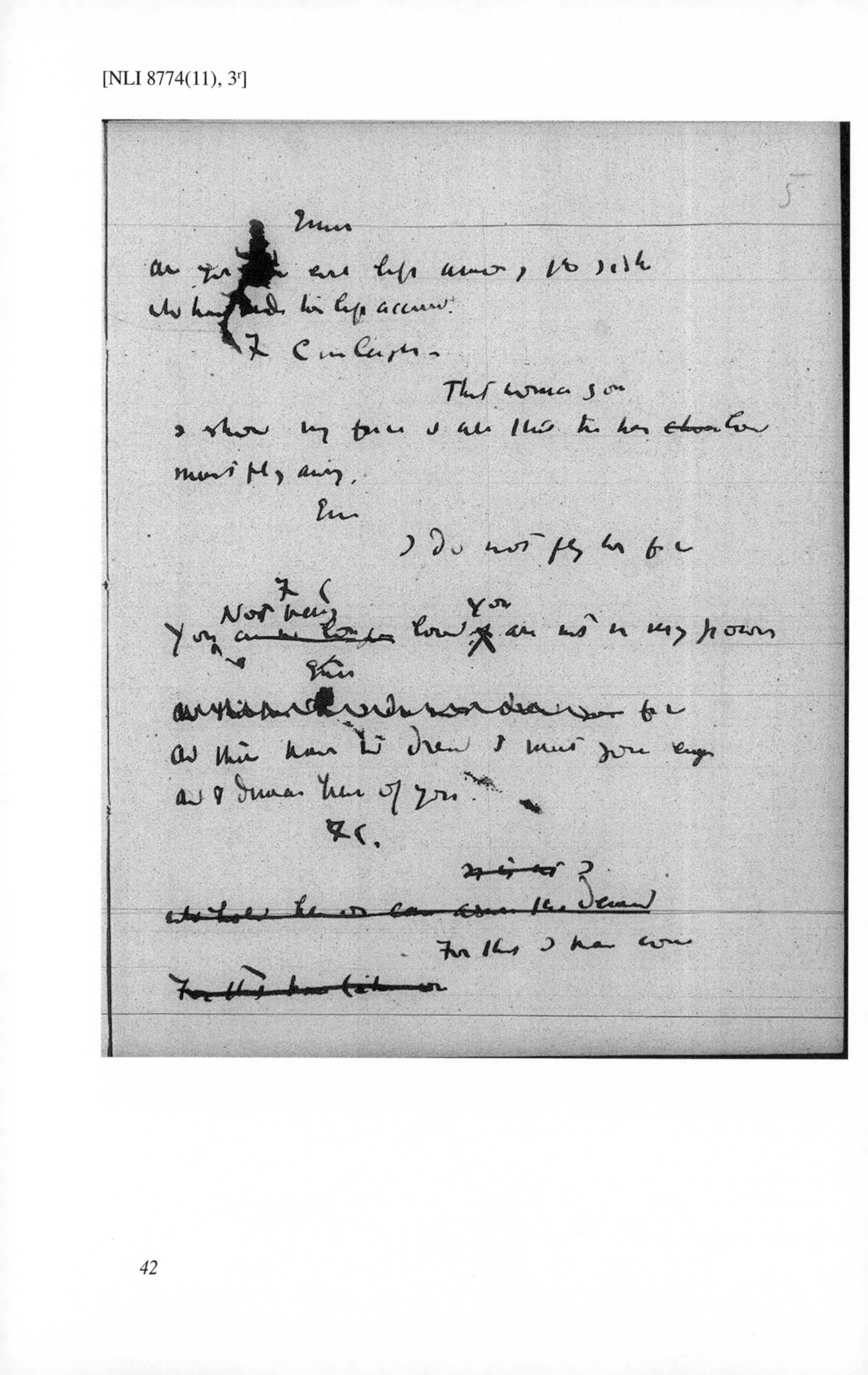

[NLI 8774(11), 3r]

[NLI 8774(11), 3^r]

Emer

Are you some evil life among the sidhe
Who have made his life accursed.

F Cuchulain laughs –

That woman gone

I show my face & all that he has ~~chosen~~ loved
Must fly away

Emer

I do not fly your face

F C

Not being   you
You^ ~~are no longer~~ loved ~~&~~^ are not in my power

Emer

And therefore as I do not dread your face
And thus have no dread to meet your eyes
And to demand him of you.

FC.

~~It is not I~~
~~Who hold him or can answer the demand~~
For that I have come
~~For that have taken on~~

Revision of MS A, 7^r above. The passage in which the False Cuchulain shows his face, and Etain goes out, has been omitted between MS C, 2^r, 3^r.

2b For "gone" read "has gone."

5 This passage was followed by a stage direction on MS A, 7^v for Cuchulain's entrance. The ghost of Cuchulain now is crouching on stage from the beginning of the play; cf. Emer's ironic reference on MS C, 2^r above.

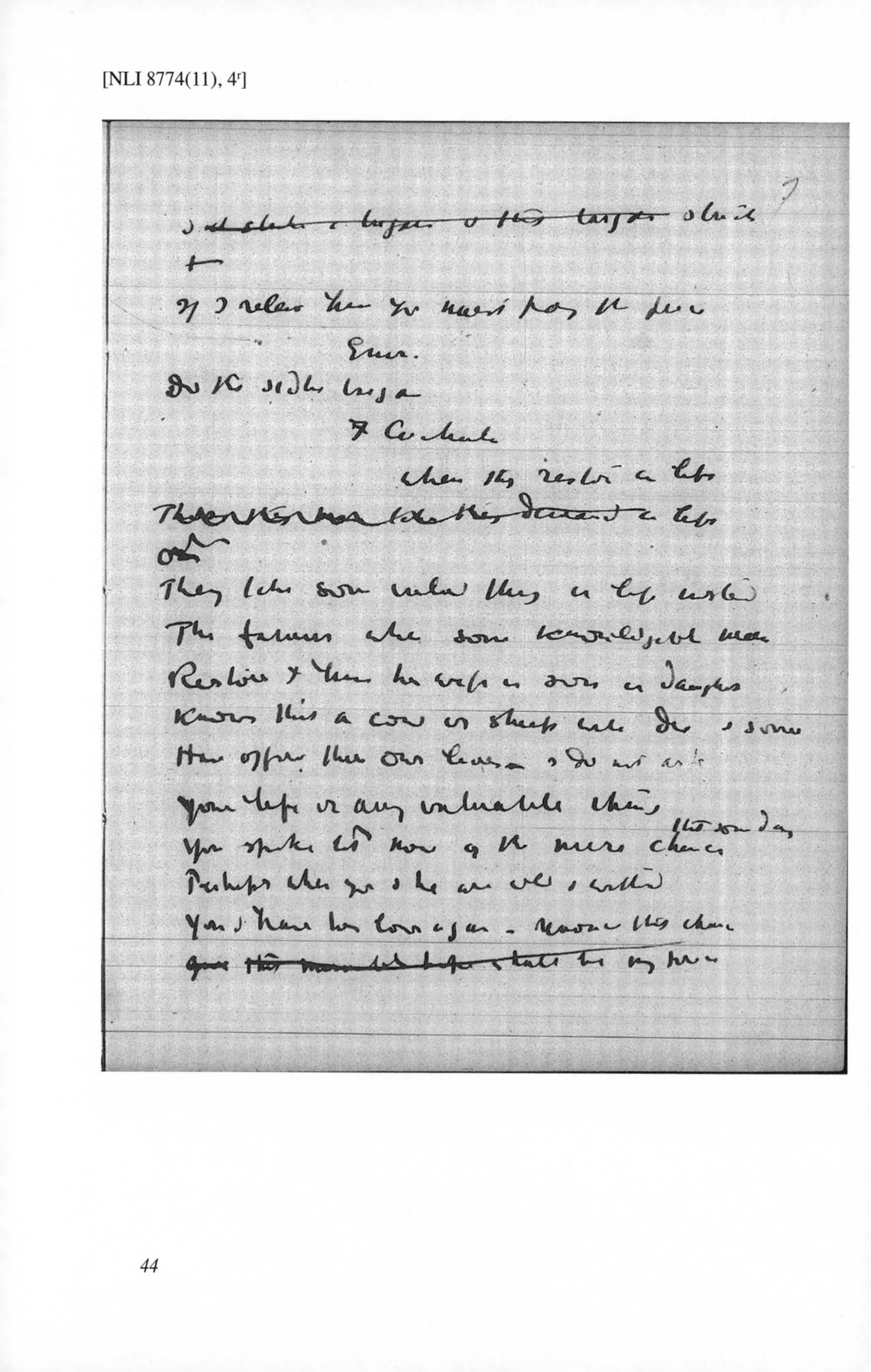

[NLI 8774(11), 4r]

[NLI 8774(11), 4^r]

I ~~ch stake a bargain & that bargain~~ sticks
&
If I release him you must pay the price
Emer.
Do the sidhe bargain
F Cuchulain
When they restore a life
~~Thus, they may later they demand a life~~
~~Or~~,
They like some valued thing or life instead
The farmer when some knowledgeable man
Restores to him his wife or son or daughter
Knows that a cow or sheep will die & some
Have offered their own lives – I do not ask
Your life or any valuable thing
that some day
You spoke but now of the mere chance
Perhaps when you & he are old & withered
You'd have his love again – renounce that chance
~~Give that miserable hope shall be my price~~

11 Refers to Etain's speech on MS A, 2^r above. Emer voices her hope on MS C, 6^r below; the inconsistency was corrected in MS K.

14 For "Give that" read "Give up that."

Pay me this miserable ~~[illegible]~~ hope the hope
that he shall live again.

Emer.

Oh me alone of all
~~who [illegible] given their love~~
of all who has loved, of all who has given her love
~~who have given their love, or have been loved~~ by him
You have no honour, & [illegible] [illegible] [illegible]

Fig Cuchulain

Have less
If you, [illegible] yourself [illegible] of honour
If you care [illegible], and [illegible] [illegible] [illegible]
that he shall live again.

~~Fig Cuchulain~~ Emer

Never never

Fig Cu.

~~You dare not be accursed & yet of all~~
~~[illegible]~~
~~You dare not be accursed~~, and
~~you [illegible]~~ ?
~~you do not dare [illegible]~~
You dare not be accursed yet he has dared

[NLI 8774(11), 5^{r}]

1 Pay me that miserable ~~hope~~ hopeless hope
2 And he shall live again.

Emer.

On me alone ~~of all~~
3 ~~Who have given him love~~
4 Of all he has loved, of all who have given him love
5 ~~Who have given him love, or have been loved by him~~
6 You have no power, & therefore you would bargain

False Cuchulain

have but
7 If you ^ put yourself into my power
8 Of your own will, & in this matter only
9 And he shall live again.

~~False Cuchulain~~ Emer

Never never

False Cuchulain

10 ~~You dare not be accursed, & yet of all~~
11 You dare not be accursed, &
12 ~~You will not d~~
13 ~~You do not dare to be accursed~~
14 You dare not be accursed yet he has dared

---

7 For "but" read "but to."

10 Cf. "The accursed majestical man" on MS A, 1^{r} above.

12 The letter "d" is the start of "dare."

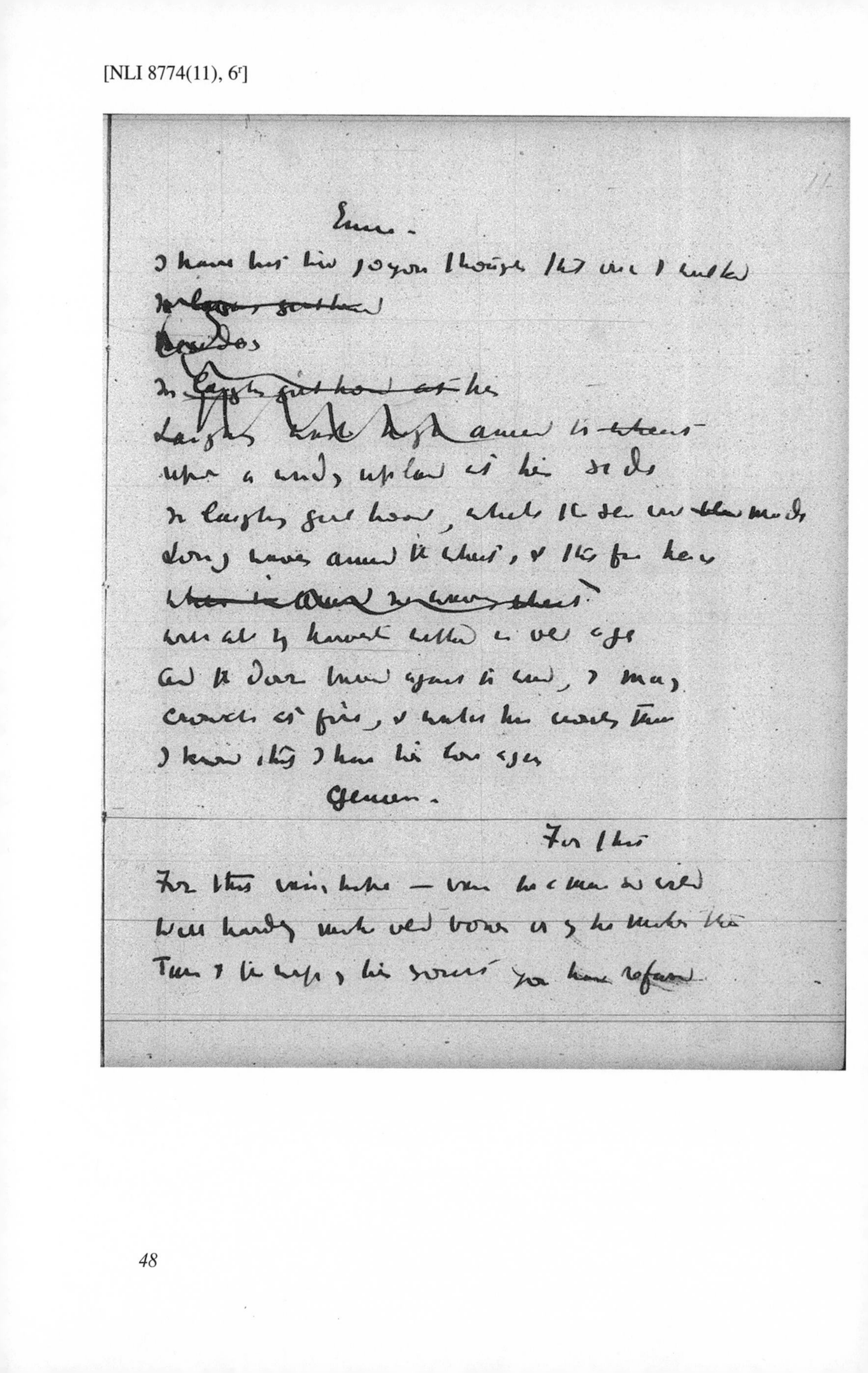

[NLI 8774(11), 6r]

[NLI 8774(11), 6^{r}]

Emer.
I have but two joyous thoughts that once I walked
~~In laughing girlhood~~
~~Besides~~
~~In laughing girlhood at his~~
Laughing waste high amid the wheat
Upon a windy upland at his side
In laughing girlhood, while the sea wind ~~blew~~ made
Long waves amid the wheat, & that far hence
~~When in amid no waving wheat~~
When all my harvests withered in old age
And the door barred against the wind, I may
Crouch at fire, & watch him crouching there
& know that I have his love again.
Genius
For that
For this vain hope – vain for a man so wild
Will hardly make old bones or if he makes them
Turn to the wife of his youth you have refused

---

1 The lovely "domestic" imagery that forms these "two joyous thoughts" in this draft and in MS G will be compressed into the less emphatic "A memory & a hope" in MS K, 10^{r}, l. 180.

3 Probably "Beside" is meant, a false start to the following line, which lacks the final word "side."

[NLI 8774(11), 7r]

[NLI 8774(11), 7^{r}]

Emer
~~I will not give up this one hope~~
~~I will not~~
Yes I for this can hope.
F Cuchulain
You watched this love
For many women, & have not been jelous
Knowing that he would tire of this love
But those that love the sidhe do not grow tired
And therefore dream & look.
Emer
My husband is ~~flat~~ there
F Cuchulain
Hush or the enchantment will be sealed again
That hid him from you,
Hush
darkness had
The ~~enchantment~~ that ^ hid him from your eyes
Hush been dissolved, but not ~~the~~ that other
That has hidden you from him.
Emer
~~Cuchulain Cuchulain~~ Cuchulain

4 This declaration was put in Emer's mouth on MS A, 10^{r} above.
12 For "Hush been" read "Hush has been."

[NLI 8774(11), 8r]

[NLI 8774(11), 8r]

FC

~~Hush for~~
Be silent – he can neither hear nor see
Our sound is silence, & our light but darkness
To those eyes now
Be silent – he is but a phantom now
He is not sollid to the touch nor can he hear
Or see for all your light is darkness to him
The longing & the cries have drawn him hither
He heard no sound, heard no articulate words
They could but banish rest and make him dream
~~He dreamed himself into the form~~
And in that dream he has taken on the form

He

That is most familiar to him, ~~&~~ crouches there
Not knowing at whose side or in what house

Emer

~~Who is she who~~
Who is that woman

F C

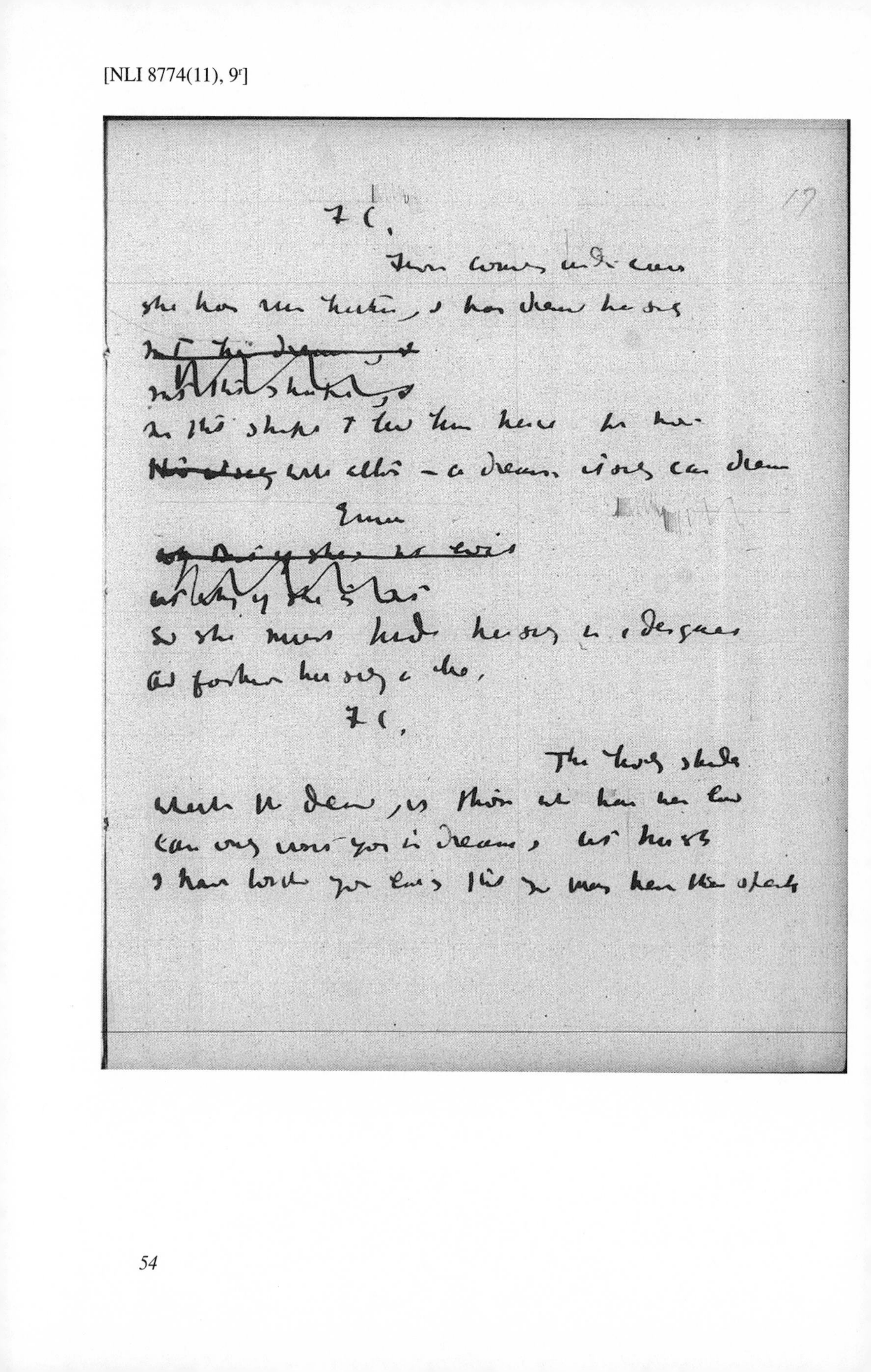

[NLI 8774(11), 9r]

[NLI 8774(11), 9^{r}]

F C.

From country under waves
She has run hither, & has dreamed herself
~~Into his dream, &~~
Into that shape, &
In that shape to lead him hence for now
~~His itself~~ will alter – a dream itself can dream

Emer

~~Why~~ ~~But if she's not evil~~
~~But why if she is not~~
So she must hide herself in a disguise
And fashion herself a lie.

F C.

The holy shades
Which the dead, or those who have never lived
Can only visit you in dreams, but hush
I have touched your ears that you may hear them speak

9^{r}, l. 6 For "His itself" read "His dream itself"?

11 For "Which the" read "Which are the."

13 In MS G, touching eyes and ears is combined into one deed.

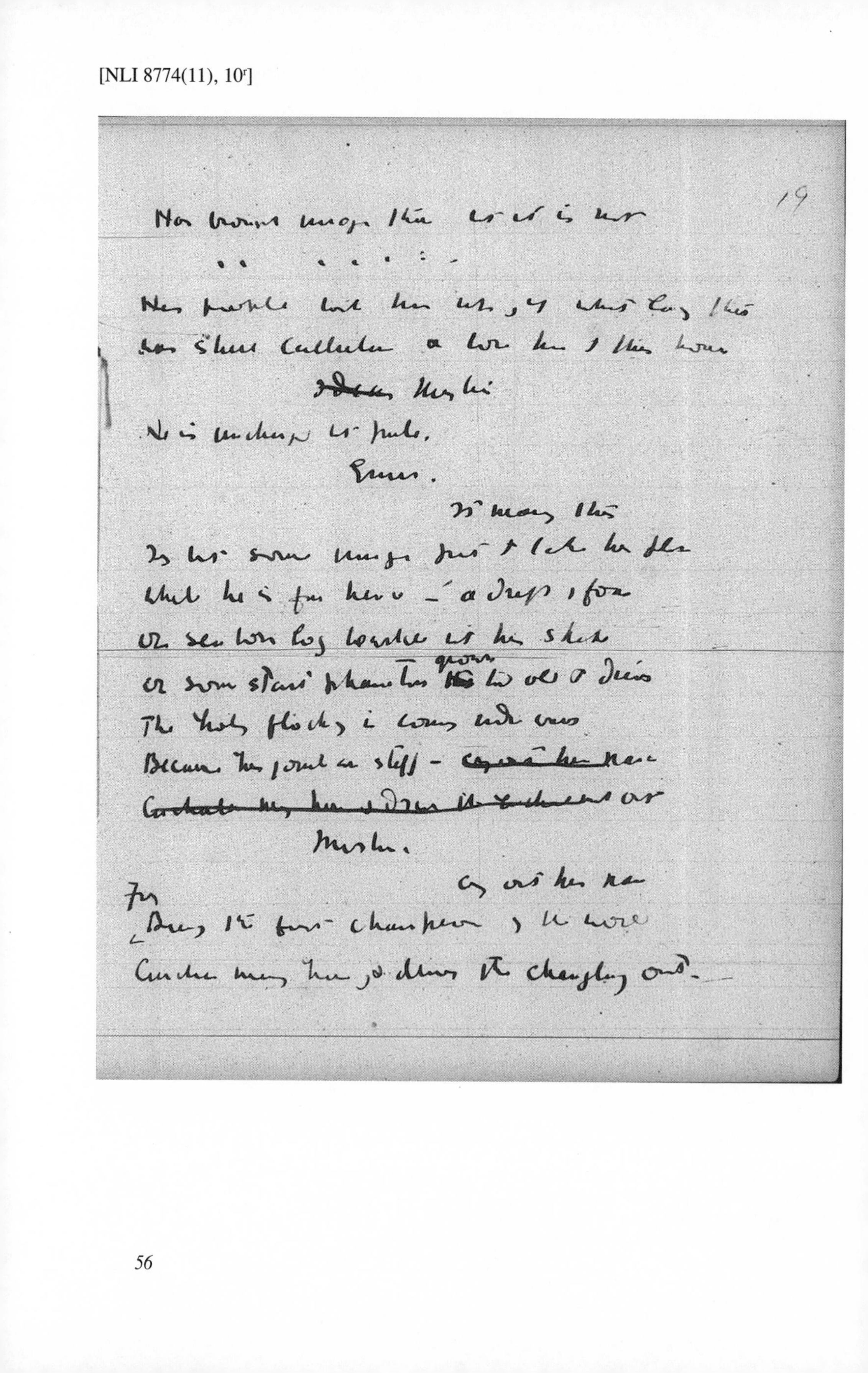

[NLI 8774(11), 10r]

[NLI 8774(11), 10r]

1 Has brought image there but it is not

. . . .

2 His people took him up, if what lay thus
3 Was still Cuchullain & bore him to this house

~~Idea~~ Mistress

4 He is unchanged but pale

Emer.

It may this

5 Is but some image put to take his place
6 While he is far hence – a drift of foam
7 Or sea born log bewitched into his shape

grown

8 Or some stark phantom ~~that~~ too old to drive
9 The holy flocks in country under waves
10 Because his joints are stiff – ~~cry out his name~~
11 ~~Cuchulain may hear & drive the changeling out~~

Mistress

12 Cry out his name

For

13 ^Being the first champion of the world
14 Cuchulain may hear, & drive the changeling out

---

1 Revision of MS A, 2r above. For "image" read "an image".

3/ The canceled word before "Mistress" may be a slip for "Etain."

4b–11 This speech was Etain's on MS A, 3r above, but it is more suited to Emer, the older and therefore more worldly-wise woman. In l. 4b, for "may" read "may be."

8 For "that" read "that's."

12 Resumes Etain's speech on MS A, 3r above.

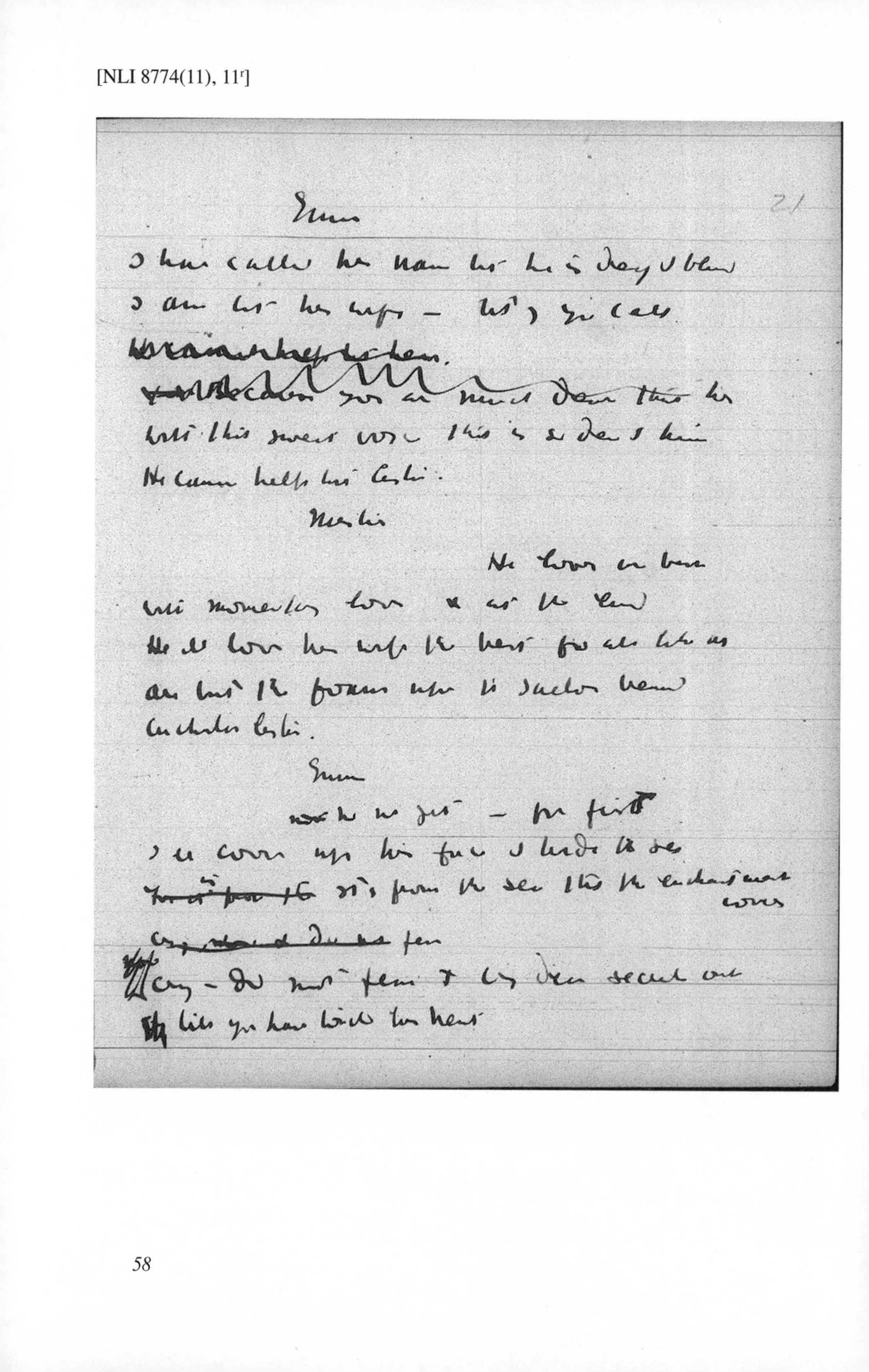

[NLI 8774(11), 11r]

[NLI 8774(11), 11r]

Emer
I have called his name but he is deaf & blind
I am but his wife – but if you call
~~He cannot help but hear.~~
~~You~~ – ~~Because you are much dearer than her~~
With that sweet voice that is so dear to him
He cannot help but listen.
Mistress
He loves me but
With momentary love & at the end
He'll love his wife the best for all like us
Are but the foam upon the sailor's beard
Cuchulain listen.
Emer
~~Not~~ No not yet – for first
I'll cover up his face & hide the sea
is
~~For it from the~~ It's from the sea that enchantment
comes
~~Cry aloud & do not fear~~
~~now~~
Cry – do not fear to cry dear secrets out
Etc till you have touched his heart

10b–15 This speech was Etain's on MS A, 5v above.

15 Etc] Yeats omits the Mistress's speech on how husbands always return to their wives and abandon their mistresses; cf. MS C, 1r above.

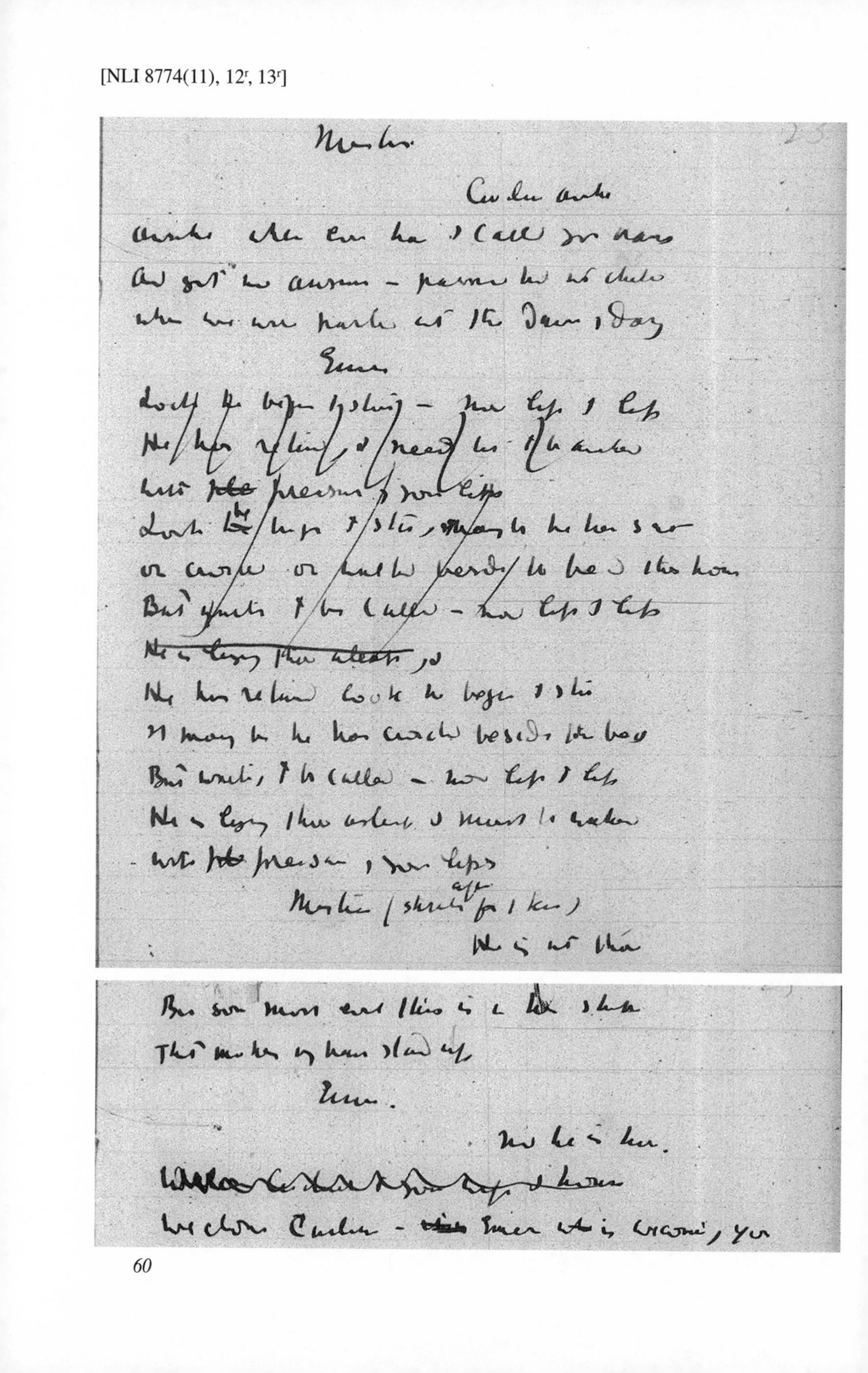

[NLI 8774(11), 12r, 13r]

[NLI 8774(11), 12[r]]

Mistress
Cuchulain awake
Awake when ever have I called your name
And got no answer – passion had not chilled
When we were parted at the dawn of the day
Emer
Look he begins to stir – Now lip to lip
He has returned, & needs but to be awaked
With ~~ple~~ pressure of your lips
he
Look ~~he~~ begins to stir, may be he has sat
Or crouched or walked beside the bed this hour
But waits to be called – Now lip to lip
~~He is lying there asleep, &~~
He has returned look he begins to stir
It may be he has crouched beside the bed
But waiting to be called – now lip to lip
He is lying there asleep & must be wakened
With ~~ple~~ pressure of your lips
after
Mistress (shrieks ~~from~~ 1 kiss)
He is not there

[NLI 8774(11), 13[r]]

But some most evil thing is in his shape
That makes my hair stand up
Emer.
No he is here.
~~Welcome Cuchulain to your wife & house~~
Welcome Cuchulain – ~~it is~~ Emer ~~who~~ is welcoming you

[NLI 8774(12), 1r]

[NLI 8774(12), 1^r]

When you & I were one being
C.
Not in all my life, I never in all my life been
& seen that beautiful body
W S.
Have you never heard that before a man is
born he is two in one, like ~~yo~~ yoke &
white in the one egg, & that ~~after his~~ birth
one half is in the flesh, & that half stays in
the will of the sidhe, & thus that always because
of this separation both are miserable
C.
I have indeed heard the learned say that
W S
And that always the half that has been born
seeks in many woman images of the half unborn
& because they are but images unhappily
only in (~~the unborn hafls death, or in~~
birth will that other self of dreams, where
lives hope or its end, that consummation can it find

---

1 Revision of MS A, 10^v above. Woman of the Sidhe speaks first.

2 For "life been" read "life have been."

10 Cf. MS A, 10^v above: "I have heard this tale / From learned men." Cuchulain is less rough-hewn in his defense of the imperfect here than he was in MSS A and B. This trend continues in future drafts.

12 For "many" read "many a."

14 For "hafls" read "half's."

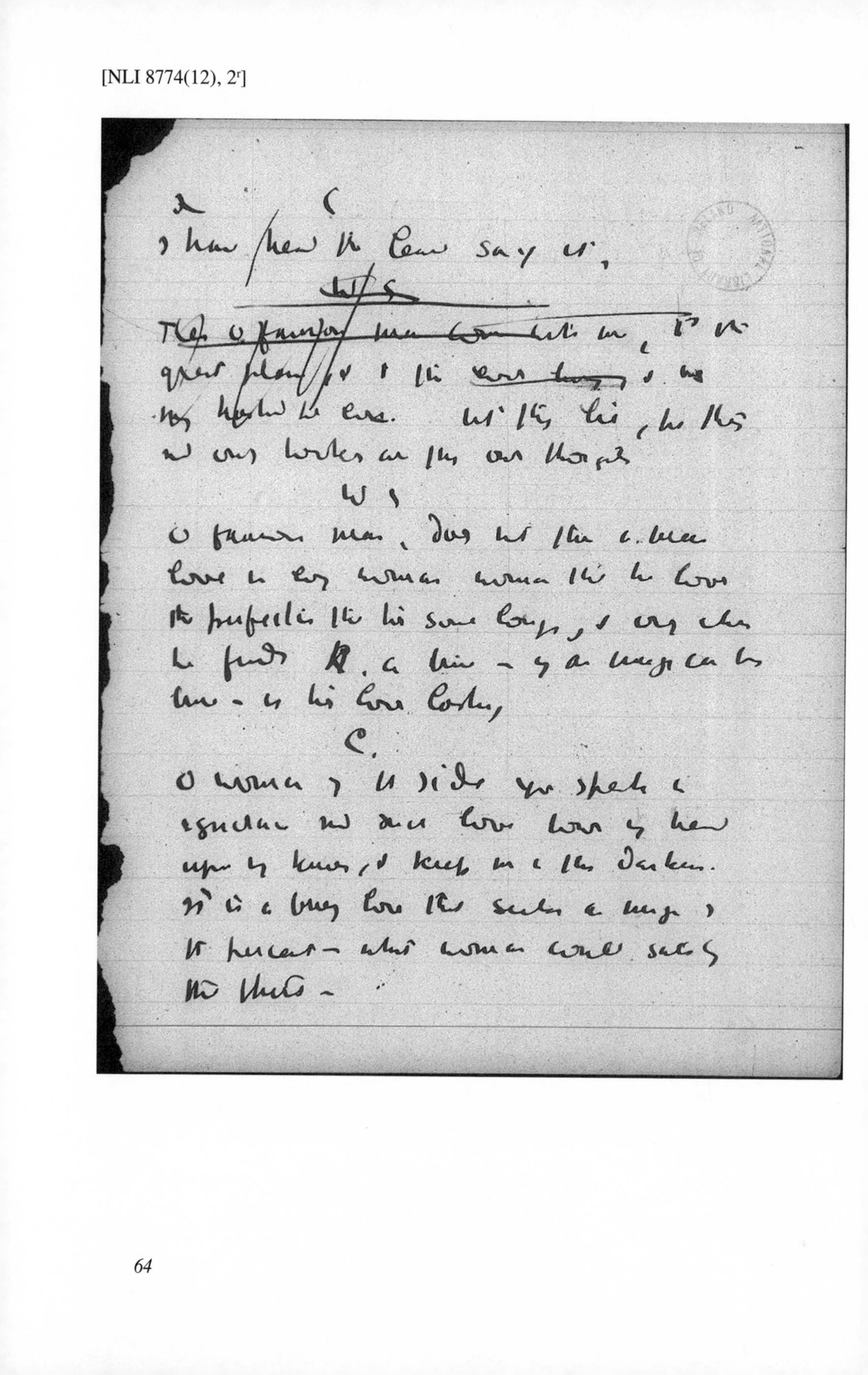

[NLI 8774(12), 2r]

[NLI 8774(12), 2r]

~~I~~ C
I have/heard the learned say it.
~~W S~~
~~Then o famous man come with~~ me, to the
great place, & to the ~~ever living~~, & be
my husband for ever. But they lie, he they
and our looks are thus our thoughts
W S
O famous man, does not then a man
love in every woman woman that he loves
the perfection that his soul longs, & only when
he finds a true – if an image can be
true – is his love lasting
C.
O woman of the sidhe you speak in
ignorance no such love bows my head
upon my knees, & keeps me in this darkness.
It is a brief love that seeks an image of
the perfect – what woman could satisfy
that thirst –

1–5 Yeats apparently meant to cancel ll. 2–4a, making Cuchulain's speech in l. 1 continuous with l. 4b: "I have heard the learned say it. But they lie . . . ." The slash in l. 1 and the lines above l. 2 may be intended to mark this change.

8 For "longs" read "longs for."

9 For "a true" read "a true image."

[NLI 8774(13), 1r]

[NLI 8774(13), 1^{r}]

W.S
Have you not then loved beauty.
C.
I have loved & begotten it many times – but it
not beauty that bows my head – o woman of the sidhe
it is the imperfect that we love – strength
will love weakness, that it may will over it
and weakness strength, that it may be willed over
W S
To love that o famous man is to be bound
to some tragic life, & to be oneself
amid tragedy & seeking help – that is the
love of the evil stained
C
O beautiful woman of the sidhe, that is the
love of man & woman. I see clear now
because I am no longer living. How can I
love o ~~woman~~ immortal woman when I look at
you I do not weep for pity.
W.S.

The next draft, on MS F, 5^{r} below, shows that this page is a direct continuation of MS D.

2 For "it" read "it is."

6 These abstractions are replaced by the imagery of the horn and the flame in the next draft, MS F.

12 For "clear" read "clearly."

[NLI 8774(13), 2r]

[NLI 8774(13), 2^{r}]

W Sidhe
The sidhe do not ~~to~~ seek the pity of men – they
give themselves as a gift
C.
O Emer.
W S.
So then it for her that you turn away from
me – for her whom when you lived you
treated so badly – giving your love here & there
C.
It is of Emer that I think who her her
W S.
Vain anguish – but in my love you find only
happiness, ~~for I am happy~~ for if you but
look at me as full of happiness as the horn
is full.
C.
~~What is that strength~~ D
Always a strength sitting beside the fire,
firm of will, calm of mind without jealousy

4 For "it" read "it is."

7 The space after the word "think" in the manuscript probably indicates that Yeats wrote "who her her" (read "who but her") somewhat later, perhaps after he had written and then canceled the next passage.

13–14 Cuchulain repeats this tribute to his wife, in slightly different terms, on MS F, 7^{r} below.

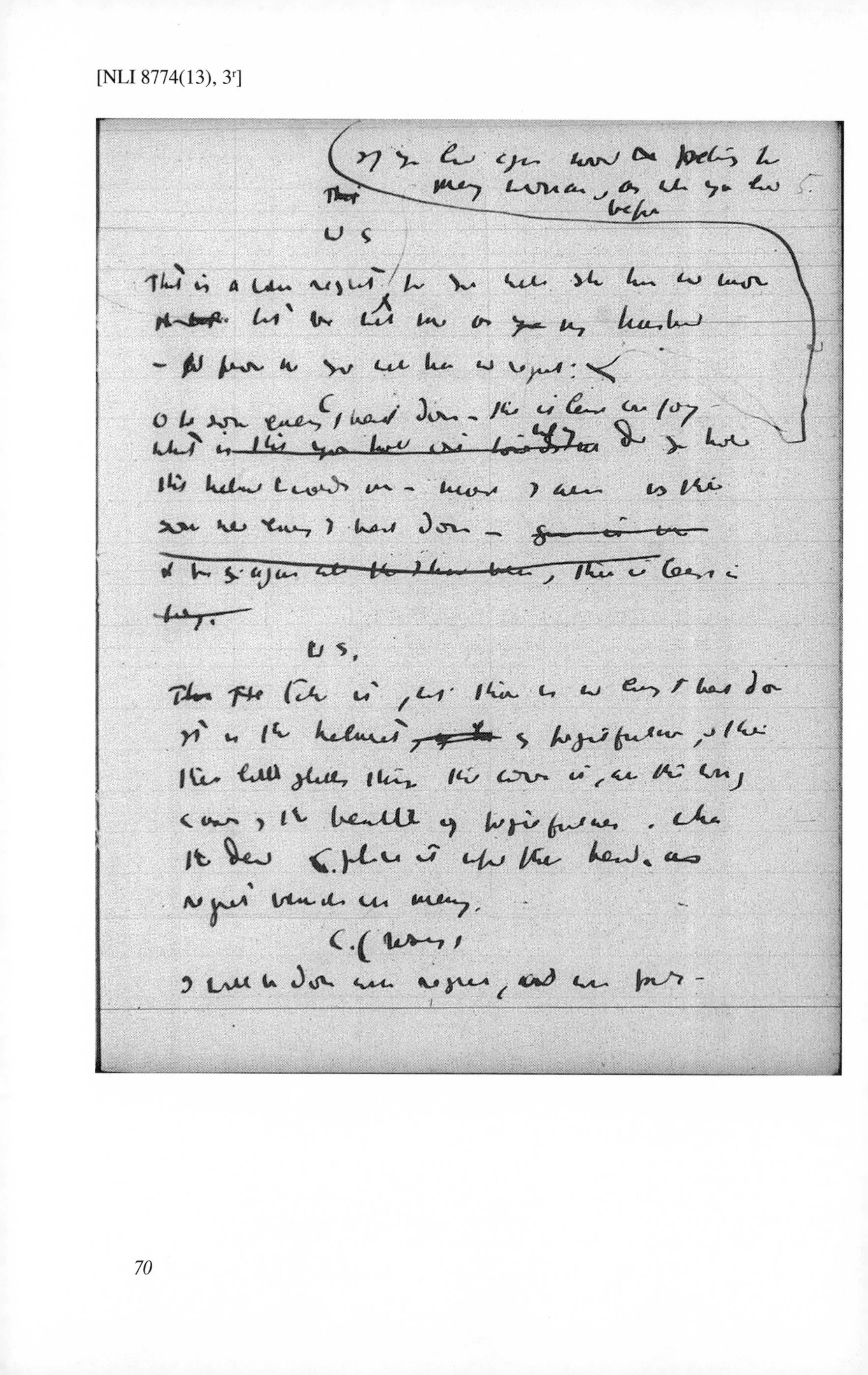

[NLI 8774(13), 3r]

[NLI 8774(13), 3^{r}]

If you lived again would ~~her~~ betray for
many woman, as when you lived
That before
W
That is a vain regret for you will still live as [?before]
~~E but~~ but be with me as ~~your~~ my husband
– And from me you will have no regret:
C
O for some enemy to beat down – thus at least one joy
Why
~~What is this you hold out towards me~~ do you hold
that helmet towards me – must I arm is this
some new enemy to beat down – ~~give it me~~
~~& be so again all that I have been, this at least is~~
~~joy.~~
W S.
~~Then The~~ take it, but there is no enemy to beat down
It is the helmet, ~~of lies~~ of forgetfulness, & these
these little shelly things that cover it, are the wing
cases of the beatle of forgetfulness. When
the dead place it upon their head, any
regret vanishes with memory.
C. (rising)
I will be done with regret, and with pity –

1, 3 The line leading from the revision above l. 1 to the caret in l. 1 is crossed by the darker line leading to the point at the end of l. 3; but no final preference for position is indicated. The revision should be read as "If you lived again you would betray her for many a woman . . . "

4 This belligerence is closer to the Cuchulain of the sources than that of the published play.

6 helmet] A Yeatsian invention; no such helmet is found in his sources or is recorded in world folk literature (Stith Thompson, *Motif-Index of Folk Literature* [Bloomington, 1935; rev. 1958]).

13 Again, a Yeatsian invention, here perhaps founded on Rhys's *drink* of forgetfulness; see Appendix II below.

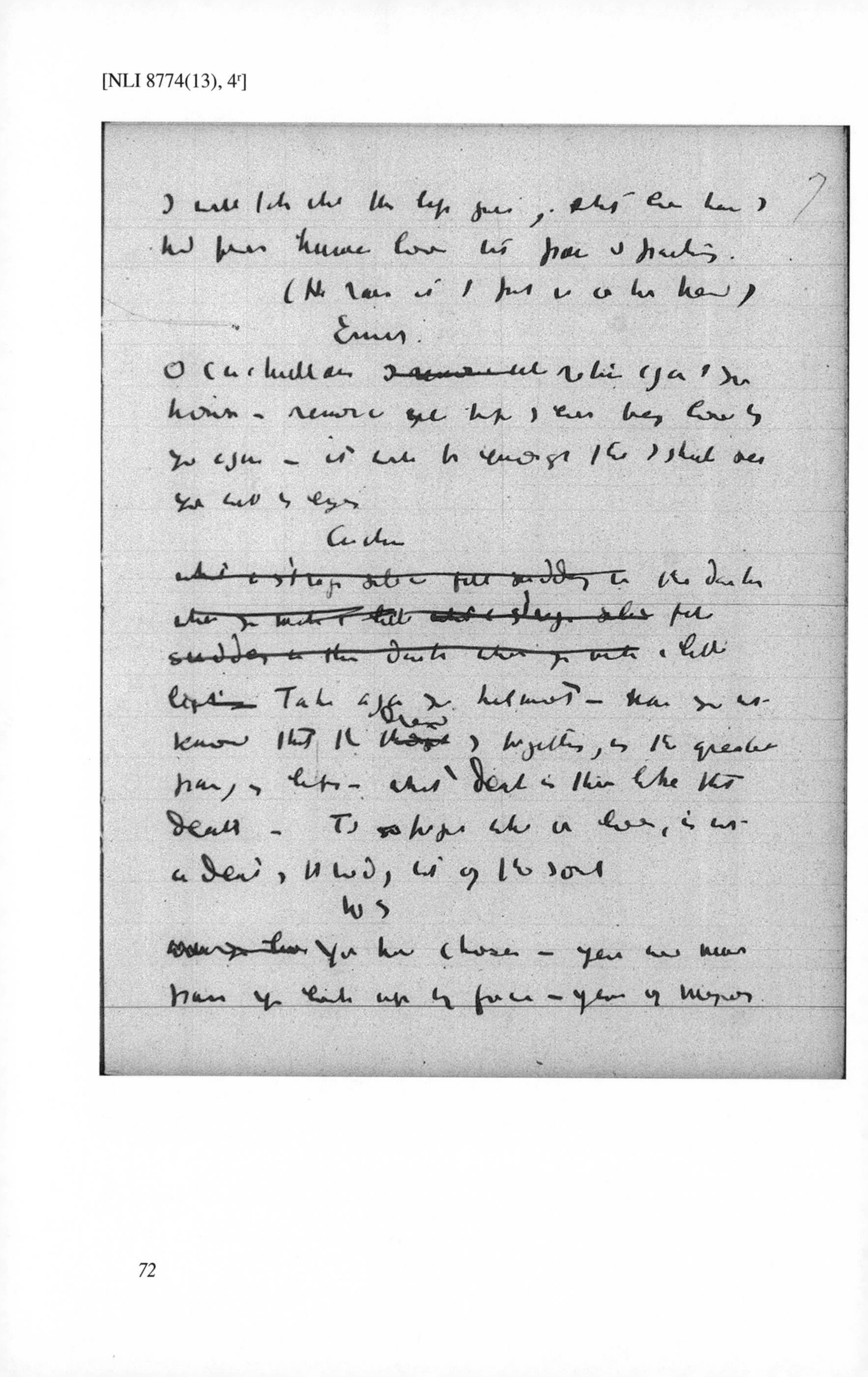

[NLI 8774(13), 4r]

[NLI 8774(13), 4r]

1 I will take what this life gave; what ever have I
2 had from human love but pain & parting.
(He takes it to put it on his head)
Emer.
3 O Cuchullain ~~I renounce all~~ return again to your
4 house – renounce all hope of ever being loved by
5 you again – it will be enough that I shall see
6 you with my eyes
Cuchulain
7 ~~What a strange silence fell suddenly in the darkness~~
8 ~~where you make a little what a strange silence fill~~
9 ~~sudden in the dark where you make a little~~
10 ~~light~~ – Take again your helmet – have you not
dread
11 known that the ~~thought~~ of forgetting, is the greatest
12 pang of life – what death is there like that
13 death – To so forget who one loves, is not
14 a death of the body but of the soul
W S
15 ~~Will you live~~ You have chosen – years are near
16 pain You look upon my face – years of misery

---

4 For "renounce" read "I renounce."

8 For "little" read "little light."

9 For "sudden" read "suddenly."

14 These abstractions are given more force in the next draft with the addition of the imagery of the cornfields; see MS F, 9r below.

15 For "near" read "near of."

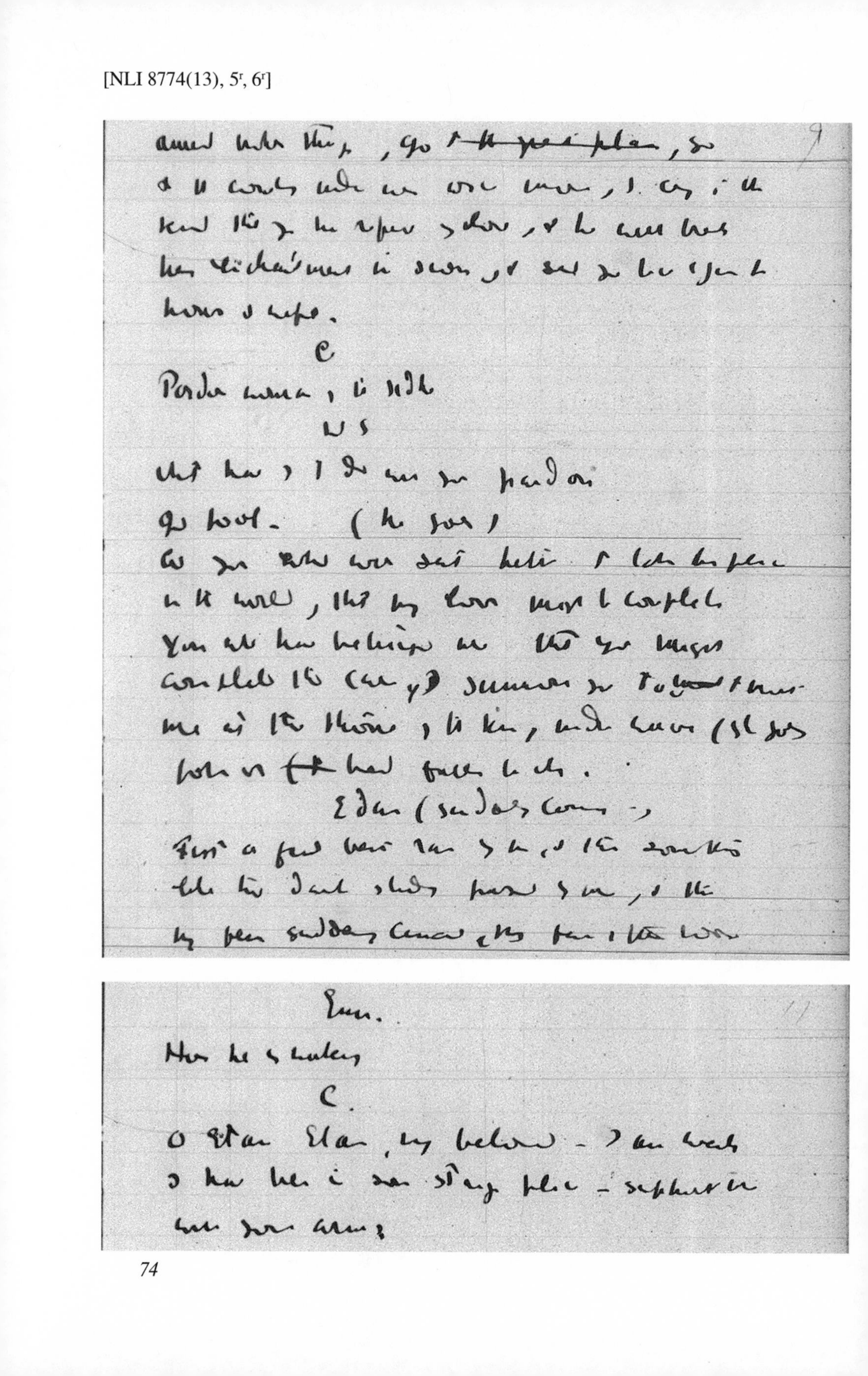

[NLI 8774(13), 5[r], 6[r]]

[NLI 8774(13), 5^{r}]

1 amid broken things. ~~Go to the great place~~, go
2 to the country under waves once more, & cry to the
3 kind that you have refused my love, & he will break
4 his enchantment in scorn, & send you back again to
5 house & wife

C

6 Pardon woman of the sidhe

W S

7 What have I to do with your pardon
8 Go fool. (he goes)
9 And you who were sent hither to take his place
10 in the world, that my love might be complete
11 You also have betrayed me that you might
12 complete the curse. I summon you to ~~meet~~ to meet
13 me at the throne of the king under wave (she goes
14 [?forth] as ~~(~~ the bed falls to etc.

Edain (suddenly comes)

15 First a faint breath ran by me, & then something
16 like two dark shades passed by me, & then
17 my fear suddenly ceased, my fear of the room.

[NLI 8774(13), 6^{r}]

Emer.

1 Hush he is waking

C.

2 O Etain Etain, my beloved – I am weak
3 I have been in some strange place – support me
4 with your arms

5^{r}, l. 3 For "kind" read "king."

6 In subsequent manuscripts, Cuchulain does not ask pardon of the Woman of the Sidhe; instead, he calls her a fool.

9 The nature of the evil spirit's mission changes throughout the manuscripts, becoming less and less capable of any "rational" explanation to accord with this Até-like temperament. Here he has been sent by the King-Under-Wave to assist the Woman in securing Cuchulain for the Sidhe, but has thwarted her for his own ends. His claims become even more twisted later in MS K, where he says he "took pity" on the Woman to help her—only to hinder her.

14 Yeats's abbreviated stage directions for the Figure of Cuchulain to fall back on the bed and change his mask.

[NLI 8774(13), 1r]

[NLI 8774(13), 1r]

C
1 Why do you turn about me like a moon
2 ~~You are you~~, that move ~~about slowly~~ about me in a dance
You that
3 Circling slowly, ~~&~~ ^ with smiling lips
shaking
4 ~~And from your hair, & from your limbs~~
5 Shake a faint light ~~out of your hair~~ from limb & hair
~~W of S~~ : ~~long since~~
if indeed
6 ~~You are that woman that I danced with once~~
7 You are that woman that I followed once
8 At the Hawks well, where have you dropped your ~~guil~~ quills
now
9 Why are you eyes ~~so~~ smiling
W. S
Look well at me
10 And judge if I be friend or enemy.
C.
11 ~~Where is your kind,~~
What is your name & country
11 ~~Where were you born~~
W.
~~I am of the~~
~~I have been since you were born~~

Revision (with much alteration) of MS A, 9v above.

2 For "You are" read "Who are."

5 Perhaps "faint light" was suggested by the "little light" of MS E, 4r above.

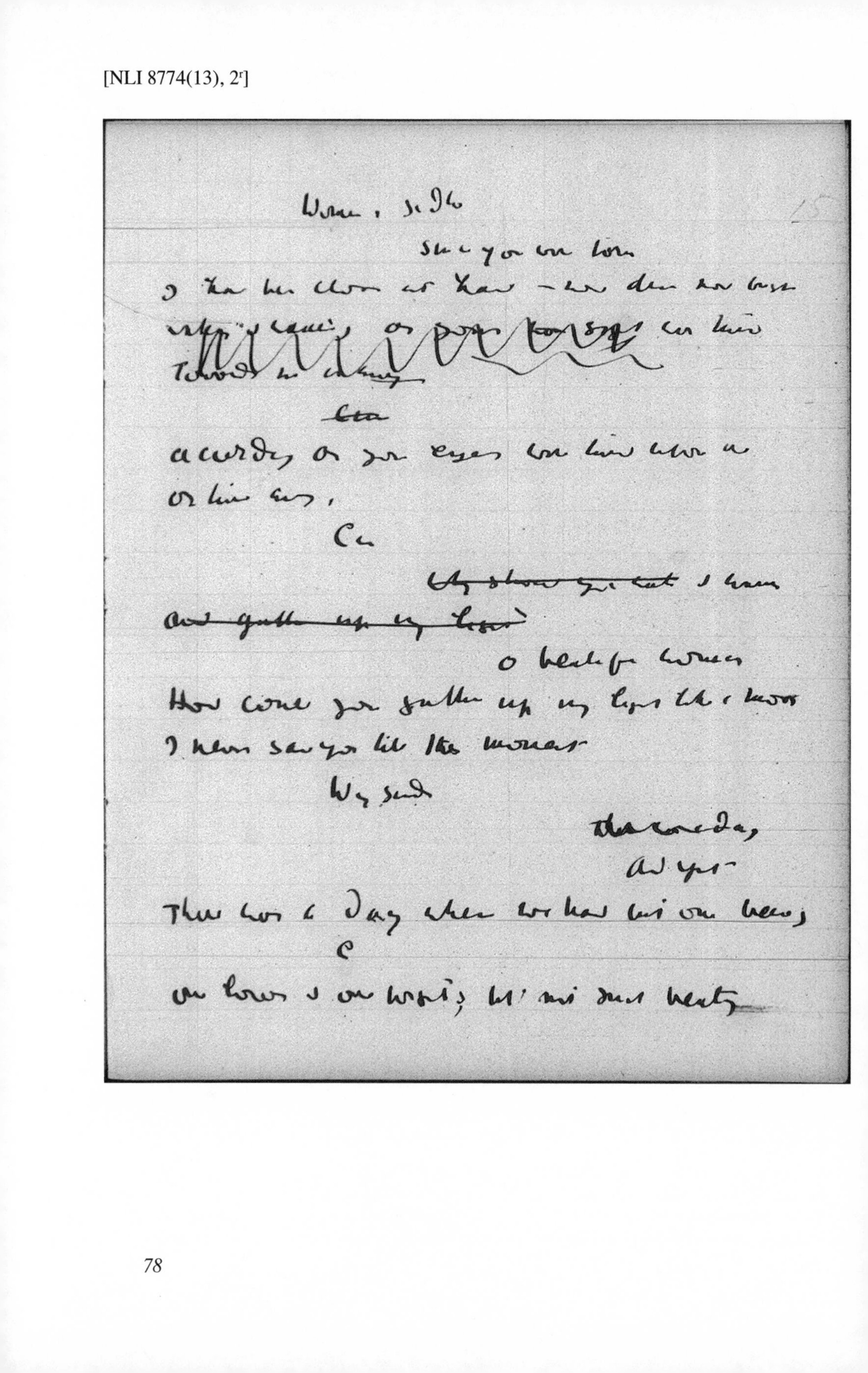

[NLI 8774(13), 2r]

[NLI 8774(13), 2^{r}]

Woman of Sidhe

Since you were born
I have been close at hand – now dim now bright
Waxing & waning as your [?~~look~~] sight was turned
Towards me or away

~~Cu~~

According as your eyes were turned upon me
Or turned away

Cu

~~Why should you wax & wain~~
~~And gather up my light~~
O beautiful woman
How could you gather up my light like a moon
I never saw you like this moment

W of Sidhe

~~There was a day~~
And yet
There was a day when we had but one being

C

One loves & one forgets, but not such beauty

2 There is a change of emphasis here from MS B, 2^{r}, l. 16 above: "I have sought you out in many images." Instead, the Woman portrays herself as the hunted: she has always been Cuchulain's goal.

[NLI 8774(13), 3r]

[NLI 8774(13), 3^{r}]

W of Sidhe
But did you never hear that man before his birth
Is two in one – the yoke & the white of the egg
~~And that one half is born into the flesh~~
~~And when~~
And that one half is born to wretched life
While the other half remains among the sidhe

C
I have heard the learned say so

W of S.
And have they told you
that's born in
That the half born ~~here~~ to flesh must seek
Through many women broken images
Of the unborn half
That the half born in the flesh must seek
~~For the half that waits in among the sidhe~~
For the half it can but find amid the sidhe
Women, that are its image in a glass
~~Each man, loves those women in the flesh~~
~~That are seen~~ And loves the more, the clearer the image is

14 This important detail in the analogy (later to be developed in the image of women's beauty approaching that of Phase 15 in *A Vision*) was not found on MS D, 1^{r} above.

[NLI 8774(13), 4r]

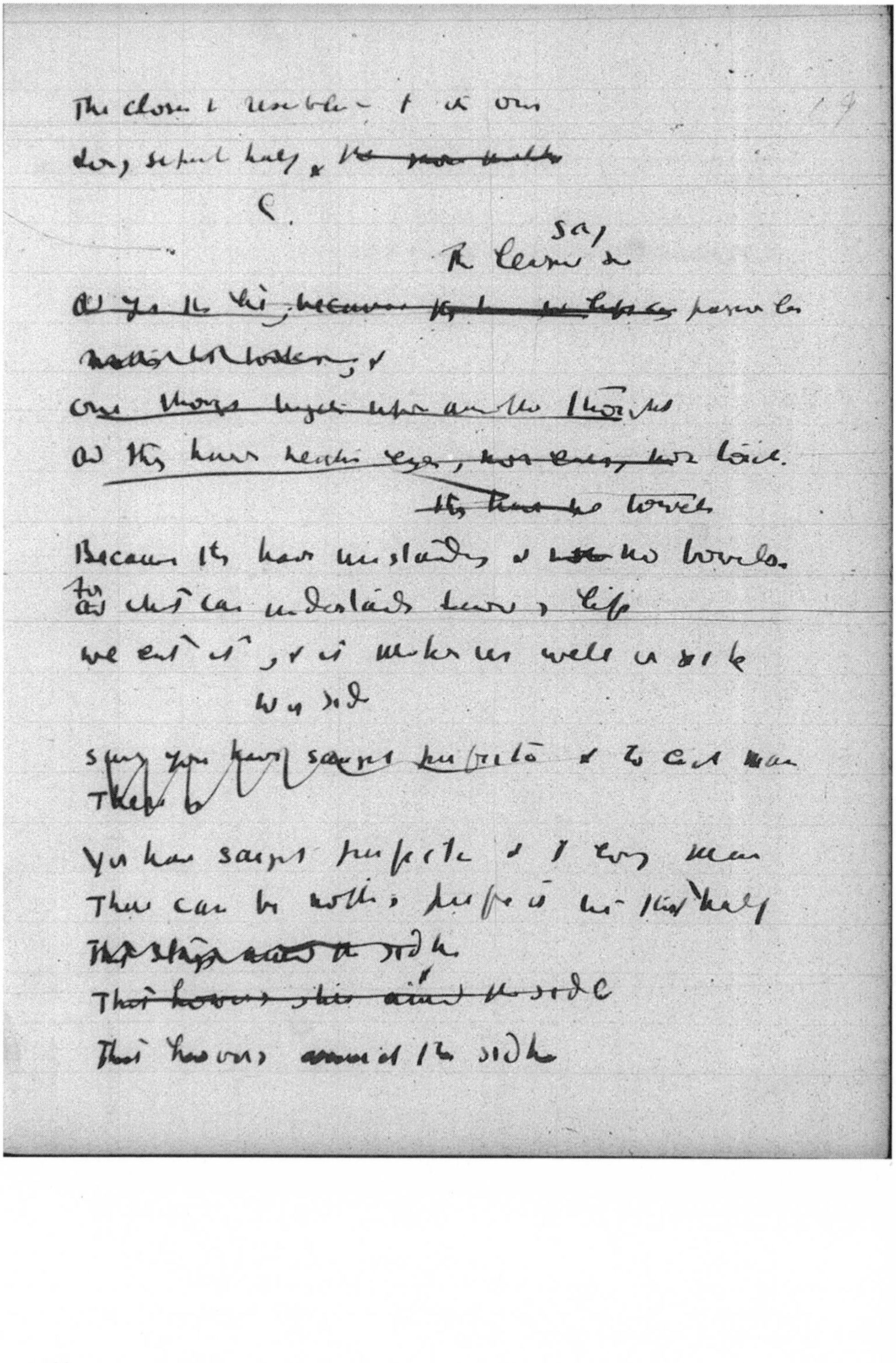

[NLI 8774(13), 4^{r}]

1 The closer the resemblance to its own
2 Long separate half, ~~the more [?unlike]~~
C.
say
The learned so
3 ~~And yet they lie, because they have our lips are~~ passionless
4 ~~Nothing but books, &~~
5 ~~One thought begets upon another thought~~
6 ~~And they have neither eyes, nor ears, nor touch.~~
~~they have no bowels~~
7 Because they have understanding & ~~neither~~ no bowels.
For
8 ~~And~~ what can understanding know of life
9 We eat it, & it makes us well or sick
W of Sidhe
10 Surely you have sought perfection & to each man
11 There is
12 You have sought perfection & to every man
13 There can be nothing perfect but that half
14 ~~That stays amid the sidhe~~
15 ~~That hovers still amid the sidhe~~
16 That hovers amid the sidhe

3 For "have our" read "have it our."

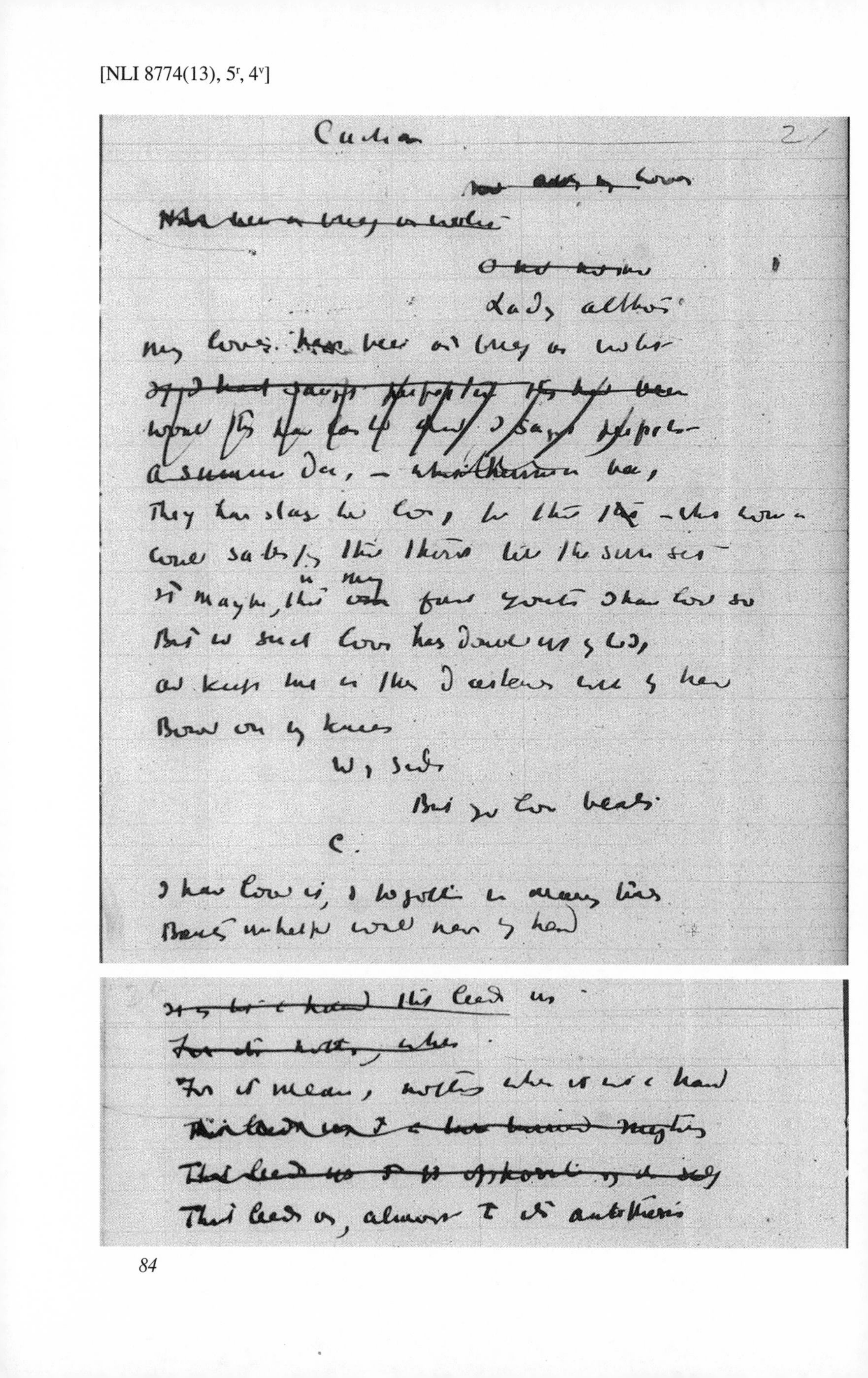

[NLI 8774(13), 5^{r}, 4^{v}]

[NLI 8774(13), 5^{r}]

Cuchulain

1 ~~No all my loves~~
~~Have been as brief as violets~~
~~O no no~~ no
Lady although
2 My loves have been as brief as violets
3 ~~If I had sought perfection they had been~~
4 Would they have lasted had I sought perfection
5 ~~A summer~~ day – ~~what human~~ being
6 They have stayed too long for that ~~that~~ – what woman
7 Could satisfy that thirst till the sun set
in my
8 It may be, that ~~our~~ first youth I have loved so
9 But no such love has doubled up my body
10 And keeps me in this darkness with my head
11 Bowed on my knees

W of Sidhe

But you love beauty.

C.

12 I have loved it, & begotten it many times
13 Beauty unhelped would never my head

[NLI 8774(13), 4^{v}]

1 ~~It is but a hand that leads us~~
2 ~~For its nothing, when~~
3 For it means nothing when it but a hand
4 ~~That leads us to a half buried mystery~~
5 ~~That leads us to the opposite of it self~~
6 That leads us, almost to its antithesis

5^{r}, l. 13 For "never my head" read "never bow my head."
4^{v}, l. 3 For "it but" read "it is but."

[NLI 8774(13), 6r, 5v]

[NLI 8774(13), 6ʳ]

~~You never have been loved nor~~
You never have known love unless you know
It is the imperfect that we love – man loves
        weaker   { e
Some ~~weaker~~ ~~h{is~~ protects as the horn lantern
~~Protects a flame, &~~
~~Protects the candle~~
The candle flame & beauty is but the horn
That lets the weaker things
  Protects the candle flame
                W of Sidhe.
                        Is love but pity
                Cuchulain
                        into
~~I think that love is pity raised to frenzy~~
                W of Sidhe
Which do you pity most – the wife you have left
The mistress that you will leave
                Cuchulain
                        Are the sidhe so bitter
                        ~~O Beautiful bitter woman~~
I pity most that woman I imagine
Now sitting by my body and my bed
                W of Sidhe

[NLI 8774(13), 5ᵛ]

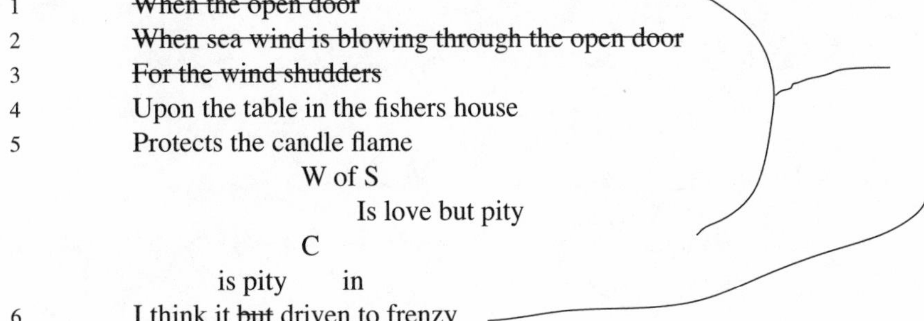

~~When the open door~~
~~When sea wind is blowing through the open door~~
~~For the wind shudders~~
Upon the table in the fishers house
Protects the candle flame
                W of S
                    Is love but pity
                C
        is pity   in
I think it ~~but~~ driven to frenzy

6ʳ, l. 7 horn] "The side of a lantern" (*OED*).

12–13 Cf. MS B, 2ʳ above: Cuchulain's memories gradually return him to the scene of the play.

5ᵛ Revises ll. 5–9 on facing 6ʳ.

2 For "When sea wind" read "When the sea wind."

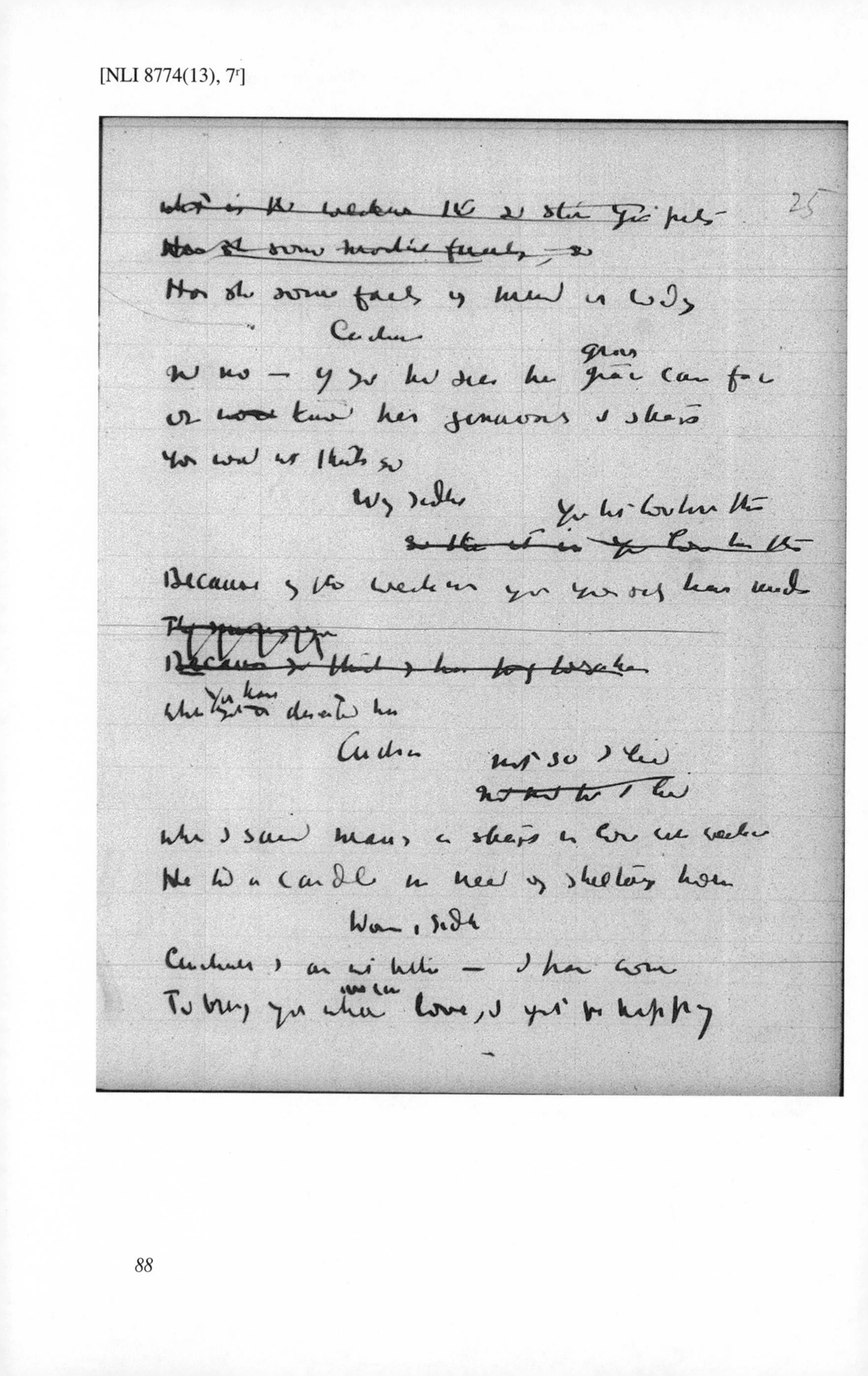

[NLI 8774(13), 7r]

[NLI 8774(13), 7r]

1 ~~What is that weakness that so stirs your pity~~
2 ~~Has she some mental failing, so~~
3 Has she some failing of mind or body
Cuchulain
grave
4 No no – if you had seen her ~~grave~~ calm face
5 Or ~~would~~ know her generosity and strength
6 You would not think so
W of Sidhe
You but love her then
~~So then it is~~ ~~You love her then~~
7 Because of the weakness you yourself have made
8 ~~The misery you~~
9 ~~Because you think of her long forsaken~~
you have
10 When ~~you've~~ deserted her
Cuchulain
Not so I lied
~~No no for I lied~~
11 When I said man's a strength in love with weakness
12 He but a candle in need of sheltering horn
Woman of Sidhe
13 Cuchulain I am not bitter – I have come
one can
14 To bring you where love, & yet be happy

---

3 For the woman of absolute beauty, love can only be founded on absolute desire. Just as Cuchulain is unable to understand her ("It means nothing when it is but a hand / That leads us, almost to its antithesis" [4v]), so she in turn is unable to understand what he means by "pity" (see MS F, 6r, n. 3).

12 For "He but" read "He is but."

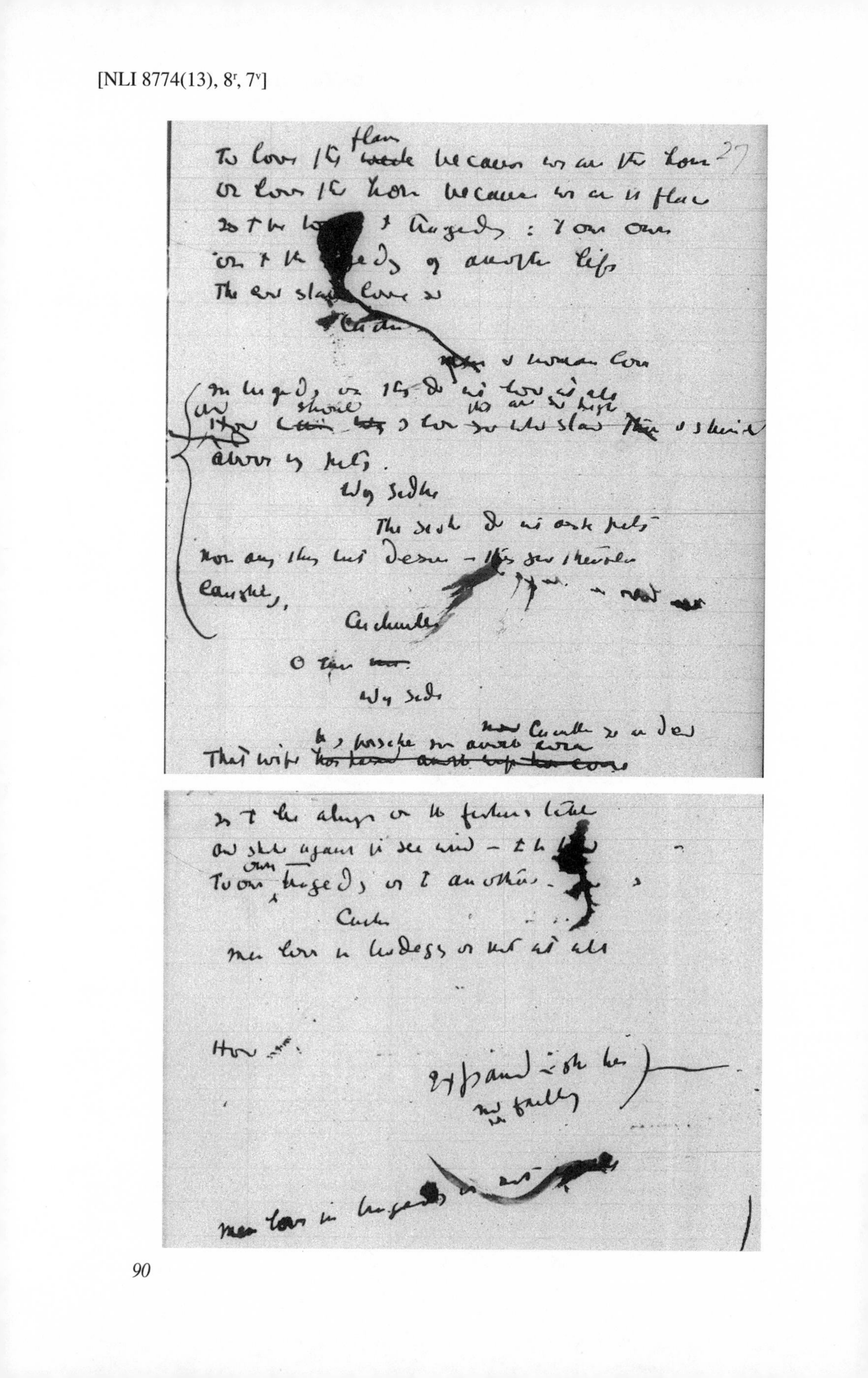

[NLI 8774(13), 8r, 7v]

[NLI 8774(13), 8r]

flame
1 To love the ~~weak~~ because we are the horn
2 Or love the horn because we are the flame
3 Is to be loved to tragedy: your own
4 Or to the tragedy of another life
5 The evil stained love so

Cuchulain
Men & women love
6 In tragedy or they do not love at all
And should that are so high
7 ^How ~~can~~ ~~W of~~ I love ~~you who stand there & shine~~
8 Above my pity.

W of Sidhe
The sidhe do not ask pity
9 Nor any thing but desire – they give themselves
10 Laughing.

Cuchullin
11 O Emer ~~Emer.~~

W of Sidhe
~~New~~ Cuchullain you are dead
~~b~~ & forsake for another wife
12 That wife ~~has parted another wife has come~~

[NLI 8774(13), 7v]

1 Is to lie always on the fishers table
2 And shake against the sea wind – to be loved
own
3 To our ^ tragedy or to anothers –

Cuchulain
4 Men love in tradegy or not at all

5 How
6 Expand – she has
7 no failling
8 no

8r, l. 11b The Woman of the Sidhe is trying to trick Cuchulain into submission, it seems, as she informs him below (MS F, 13r, l. 8) that he is *not* dead.

7v The expansion indicated at ll. 6–8 is effected in the place indicated in the text on MS G, 19r below. Yeats wrote this instruction on the revision page facing 8r, where a brace indicates the lines to be expanded. He probably wrote "Men love in tragedy or not at all" as a first revision of Cuchulain's speech, but quickly, hence at an angle, so as not to forget this later. Yeats probably wrote the other revisions on 7v when he had finished MS F; cf. the revisions on MS F, 13v below.

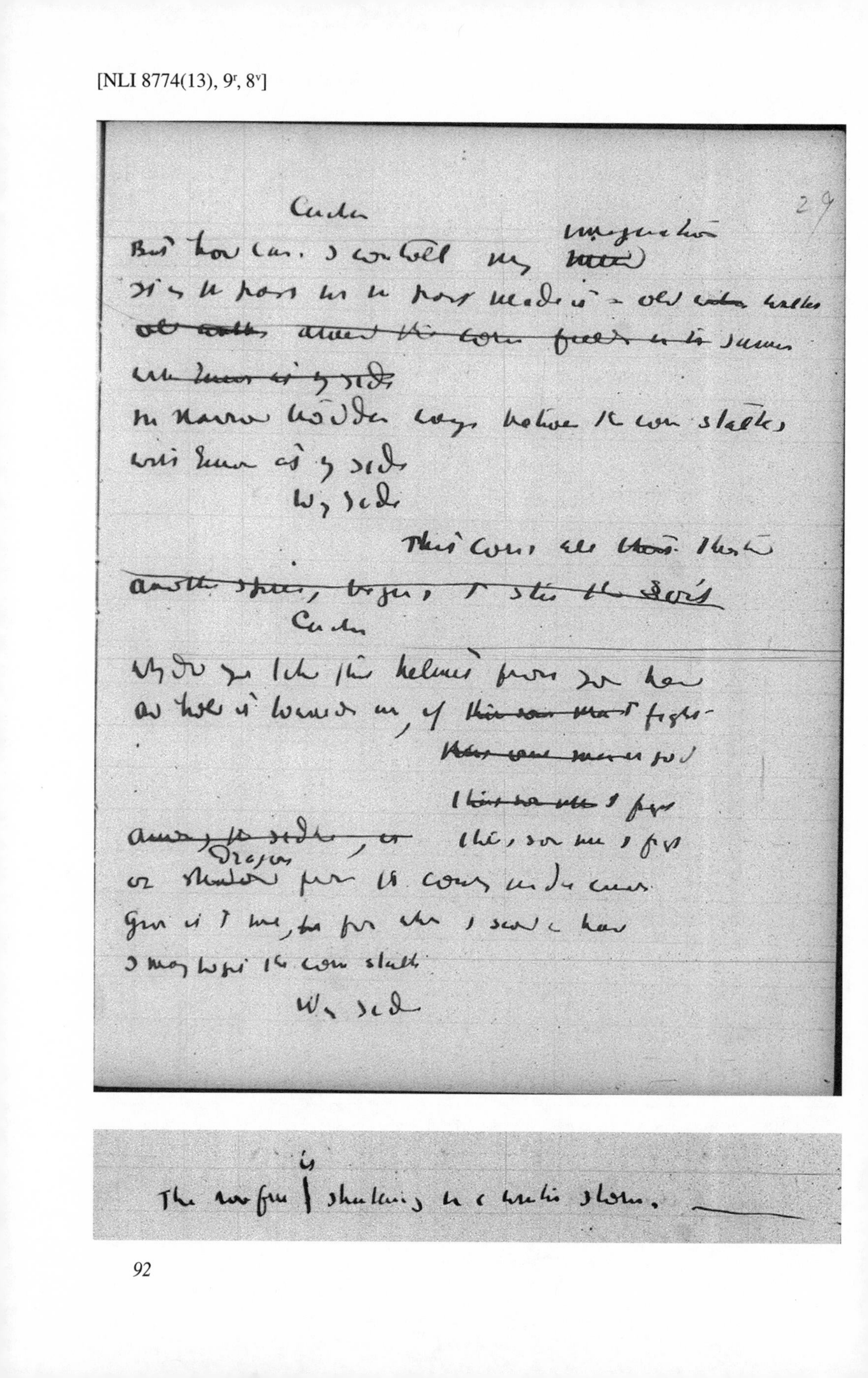

[NLI 8774(13), 9r, 8v]

[NLI 8774(13), 9r]

Cuchulain

imagination

1 But how can I controll my ~~mind~~
2 It is the past for the past made it – old ~~walking~~ walks
3 ~~Old walks around the corn fields in the summer~~
4 ~~With Emer at my side~~
5 In narrow trodden ways between the corn stalks
6 With Emer at my side

W of Sidhe

That corn's all ~~three~~ threshed

7 ~~Another spirit begins to stir the soil~~

Cuchulain

8 Why do you take that helmet from your head
9 And hold it towards me, if ~~there's some man to~~ fight
~~there's some man or~~ god
~~there's some other~~ to fight
10 ~~Among the sidhe, or~~ there's some man to fight
dragon
11 Or ~~shadow~~ from the country under waves
12 Give it to me, ~~for~~ for with sword in hand
13 I may forget the corn stalks

W of Sidhe

[NLI 8774(13), 8v]

is

1 The rooftree~~'s~~ shaking in a winter storm.

9r, l. 2 For "is" read "is in."

8 Cf. MS E, 3r above: Cuchulain wished for "some enemy to beat down" before the helmet was offered him. The new draft resolves a staging problem not touched upon in MS E—the Woman is *wearing* the helmet.

8v The line is arrowed to replace l. 7 on the facing 9r.

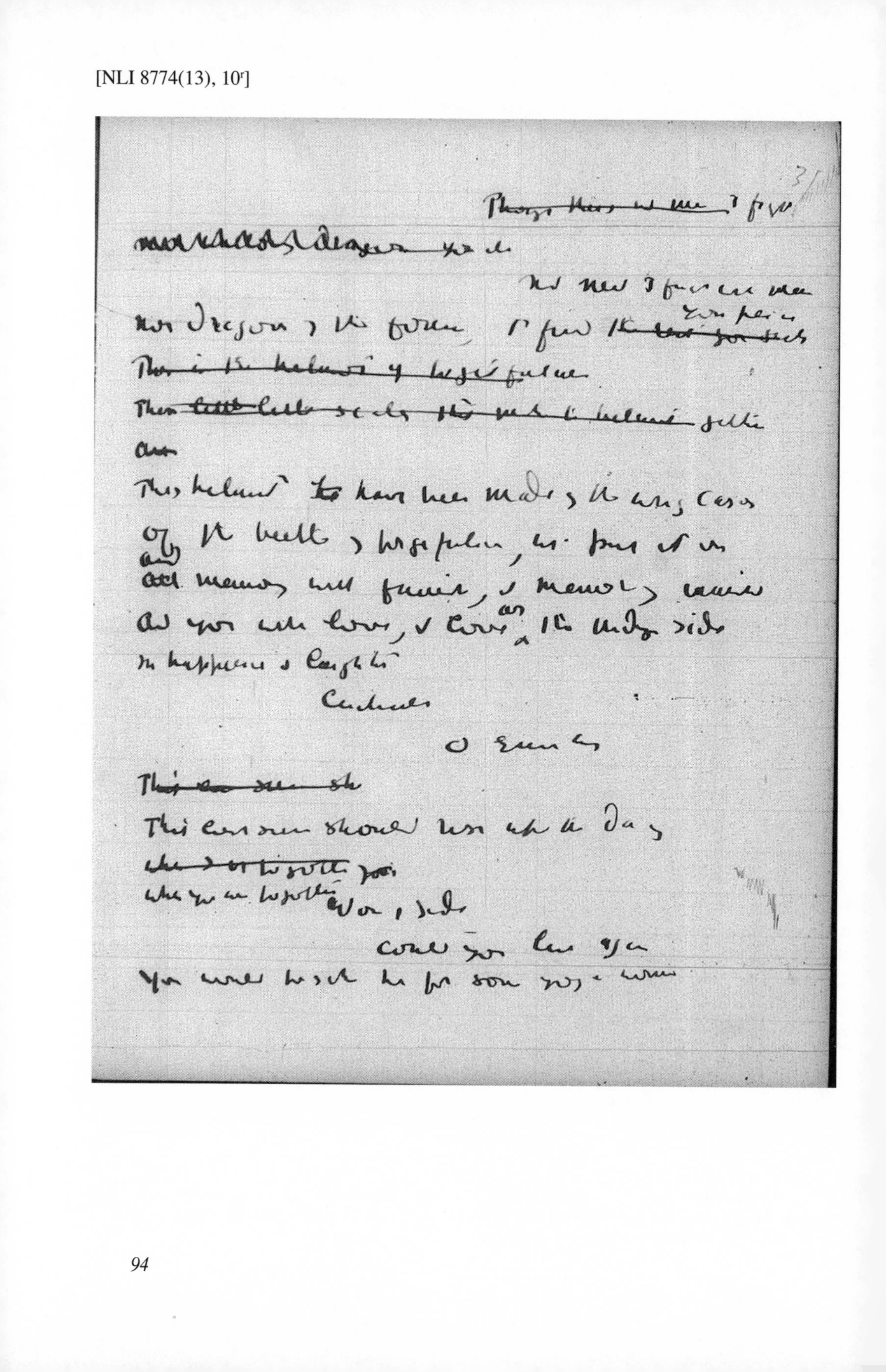

[NLI 8774(13), 10r]

[NLI 8774(13), 10r]

~~Though there's no man to fight~~
~~Nor wallowing dragon you etc~~
No need to fight with man
your peace
Nor dragon of the foam, to find ~~the rest you seek~~
~~This is the helmet of forgetfulness~~
~~These little little scales that make the helmet glitter~~
~~Are~~
This helmet ~~has~~ have been made of the wing cases
Of the beetle of forgetfulness, but put it on
And
~~All~~ memory will [?falter], & memory vanish
as
And you will love, & love ^ the undying sidhe
In happiness & laughter
Cuchulain
O Emer Emer
~~That last sun sh~~
That last sun should rise upon the day
~~When I have forgotten you.~~
When you are forgotten
Woman of Sidhe
Could you live again
You would forsake her for some younger woman.

10 For "will love" read "will live"?

[NLI 8774(13), 11r]

[NLI 8774(13), 11[r]]

Cuchulain
1 Give me the helmet.
Emer.
I will pay the price.
2 I am content to lose his love for ever
3 So that I may but see him in this house
4 In ~~sickness~~ weariness, or sickness or old age
where
5 Let him love ~~who~~ he will, & turn upon me
6 ~~Grey eyes that hold the [?bidding] of the sea~~
7 ~~Eyes harsh~~
8 ~~Harsh eyes, or~~
sea's
9 Eyes that the harsh 's made indifferent
10 If I but see him – I am content with that
Cuchulain
11 What a strange silence ~~betimes~~ has fallen in this dark
12 And a wise silence for I know you now
are
13 And know that you ignorant – What dread has love
14 So great as to forget the least poor ~~star~~ straw
15 Once seen in the incredible clear light
16 ~~She made She cast She threw about her some lost~~
17 She cast on some forlorn lost afternoon

1b This simple, dignified assertion replaces the somewhat more passionate renunciation on MS E, 4[r] above. Emer's speech is then expanded, the new lines using the unifying imagery of the sea.

17 A splendid development of the abstract language of MS E, 4[r]: "the dread of forgetting, is the greatest pang of life." The new imagery also helps to unify the play. The yellow straw links up beautifully with the cornstalks, and Emer's "incredible clear light" (the prosaic but life-giving, human light) of the sun, of the day, is set against the harsh, unreal light of the moon, of the night, cast by the Woman of the Sidhe.

[NLI 8774(13), 12r]

[NLI 8774(13), 12r]

had
1 Before the stars grown unkind – that face
2 Although it fair enough is a fools face.
3 ~~Woman there is wind t~~
For ~~no~~ has a
4 ~~No~~^wind has ~~ever~~ blown out of the north
5 ~~So bitter, so~~ as these words ‘You can forget’
6 ~~That kill the soul & not the body~~
7 That kill the intimate secret of the heart
8 So bitter as those words that you have spoken
that
9 ~~So~~ If I but put ~~this~~ helmet on my head
10 ~~I will forget the~~
11 ~~You I will forget, you~~
12 ~~I will forget, you have said, my hearts secret~~
heart’s
13 You say that my ~~heart’s secret is forgotten~~ forgot
14 You say that if I would wear this helmet
15 I would forget the secret of my heart
W of S.
16 ~~You have refused~~ (He makes a gesture)
I have offered you the peace
17 Of those that have no memory being happy
18 ~~You are not dead – go to king under wave~~

---

2 For “it” read “it’s.”

3 For “is wind t” read “is no wind that.”

16 This gesture seems to be a second, half-hearted request for the helmet; the gesture was dropped in the next draft.

18 For “to king” read “to the king.”

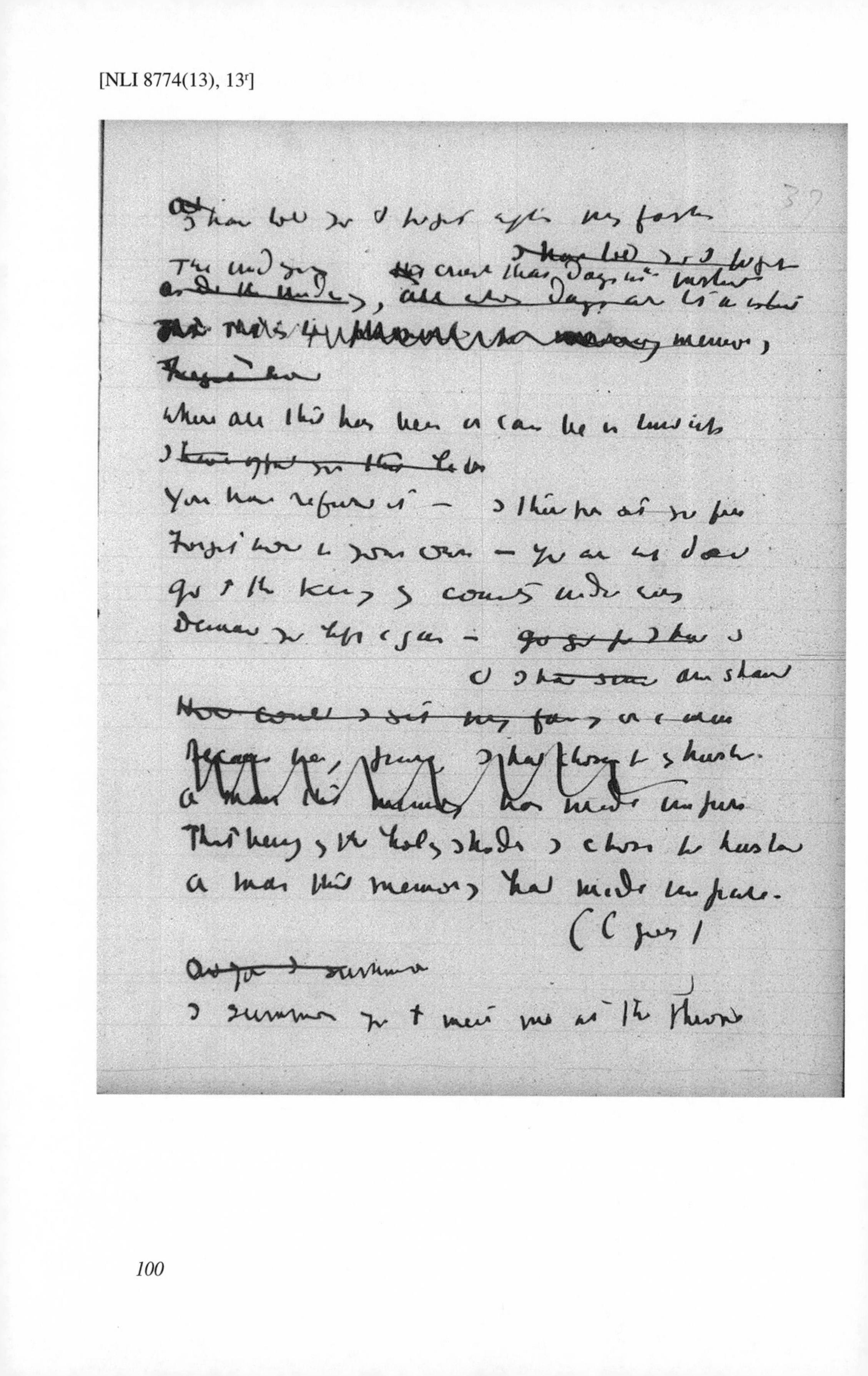

[NLI 8774(13), 13^{r}]

[NLI 8774(13), 13r]

~~And~~
1 I have told you to forget after my fashion
~~I have told you to forget~~
an
The undying that count their days in instant
2 ~~As do the undying, all whose days are but an instant~~
3 ~~That~~ ~~That is their pleasure for for memory memory~~
4 ~~Forget now~~
5 Where all that has been or can be is turned up
6 ~~I have offered you that life~~
7 You have refused it – I therefore set you free
8 Forget now in your own – You are not dead
9 Go to the king of country under waves
10 Demand your life again – ~~Go go for I have~~ I
O I ~~have [?scorned]~~ am shamed
11 ~~How could I set my fancy on a man~~
12 [Because here, freely, I had chosen for my husband
13 [A man that memory has made impure
14 That being of the holy shades I chose for husband
15 A man that memory had made impure.
(C goes)
16 ~~And you I summon~~
17 I summon you to meet me at the throne

---

8 For "your own" read "your own fashion"?

10b Perhaps the first revision was meant to be "I have been scorned."

13 For "has made" read "had made."

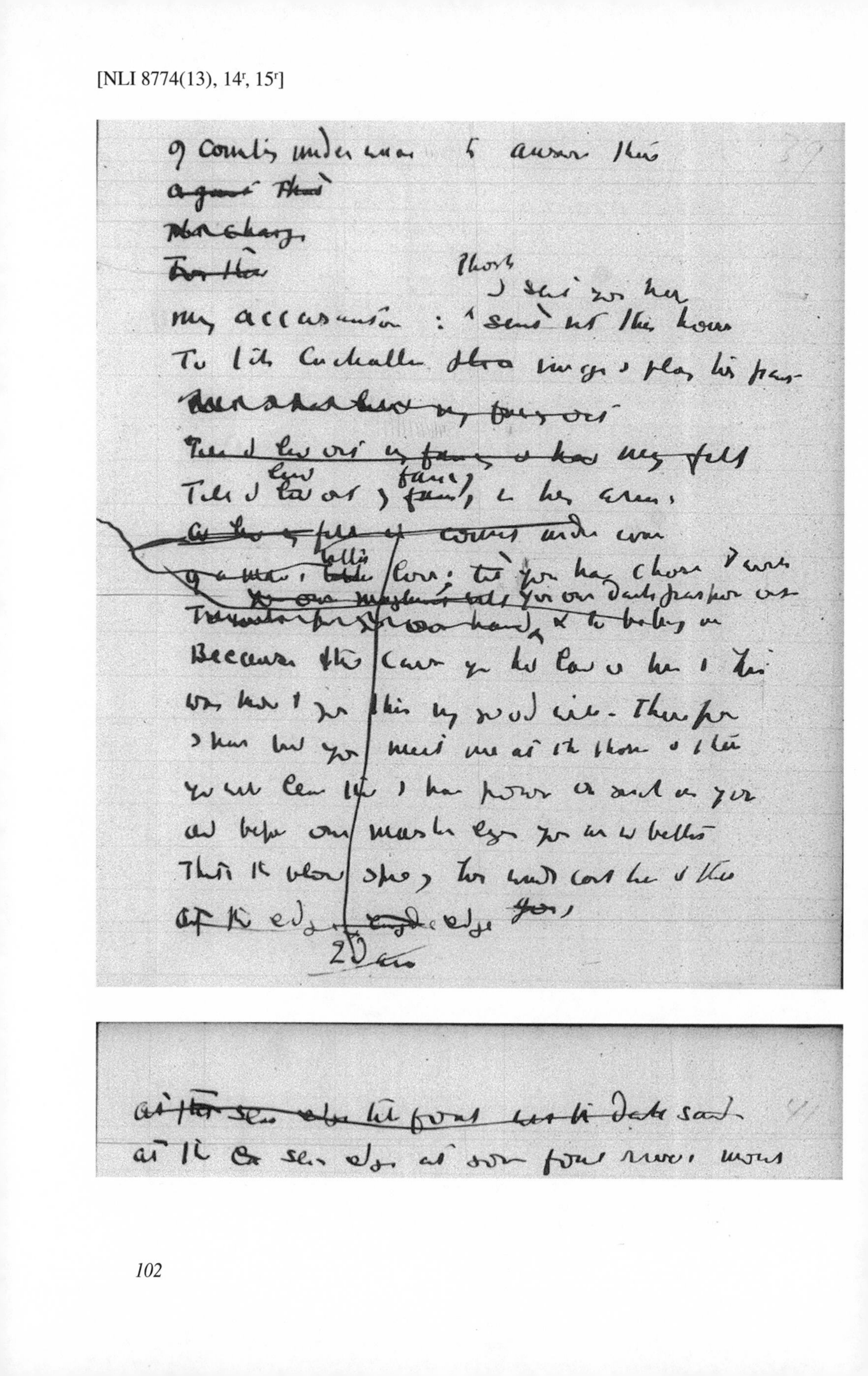

[NLI 8774(13), 14r, 15r]

[NLI 8774(13), 14^{r}]

1 Of country under wave to answer there
2 ~~Against~~ ~~That~~
3 ~~The charge~~
4 ~~For there~~
Though
^I sent you here
5 My accusation : sent into this house
6 To take Cuchullain's ~~place~~ image & play his part
7 ~~Till I had lived my fancy out~~
8 ~~Till I had lived out my fancy & had my fill~~
lived fancy
9 Till I ~~lived~~ out my ~~fancy~~ in his arms
10 ~~And had my fill in country under wave~~
bitter
11 Of a man's ~~bitter~~ love; but you have chosen to work
~~Your own malignant will~~ Your own dark purpose out
12 ~~Treacherously for your own hand~~^ & to betray me
13 Because the curse you had laid on her & him
14 Was more to you than my good will – Therefore
15 I have bid you meet me at the throne & there
16 You will learn that I have power over such as you
17 And before our masters eyes you are no better
18 Than the blown spray his winds cast here & there
~~goes~~
19 ~~At the edge, [?engde] edge~~
~~Edain~~

[NLI 8774(13), 15^{r}]

1 ~~At that seas edge till foul with the dark sand~~
2 At the ~~edge~~ seas edge at some foul river mouth

14^{r}, l. 13 curse] The curse briefly mentioned on MS E, 5^{r}; this speech is an expansion of the prose draft there.
15^{r} These two lines were entered at the top of the page; they revise l. 19 on 14^{r}.

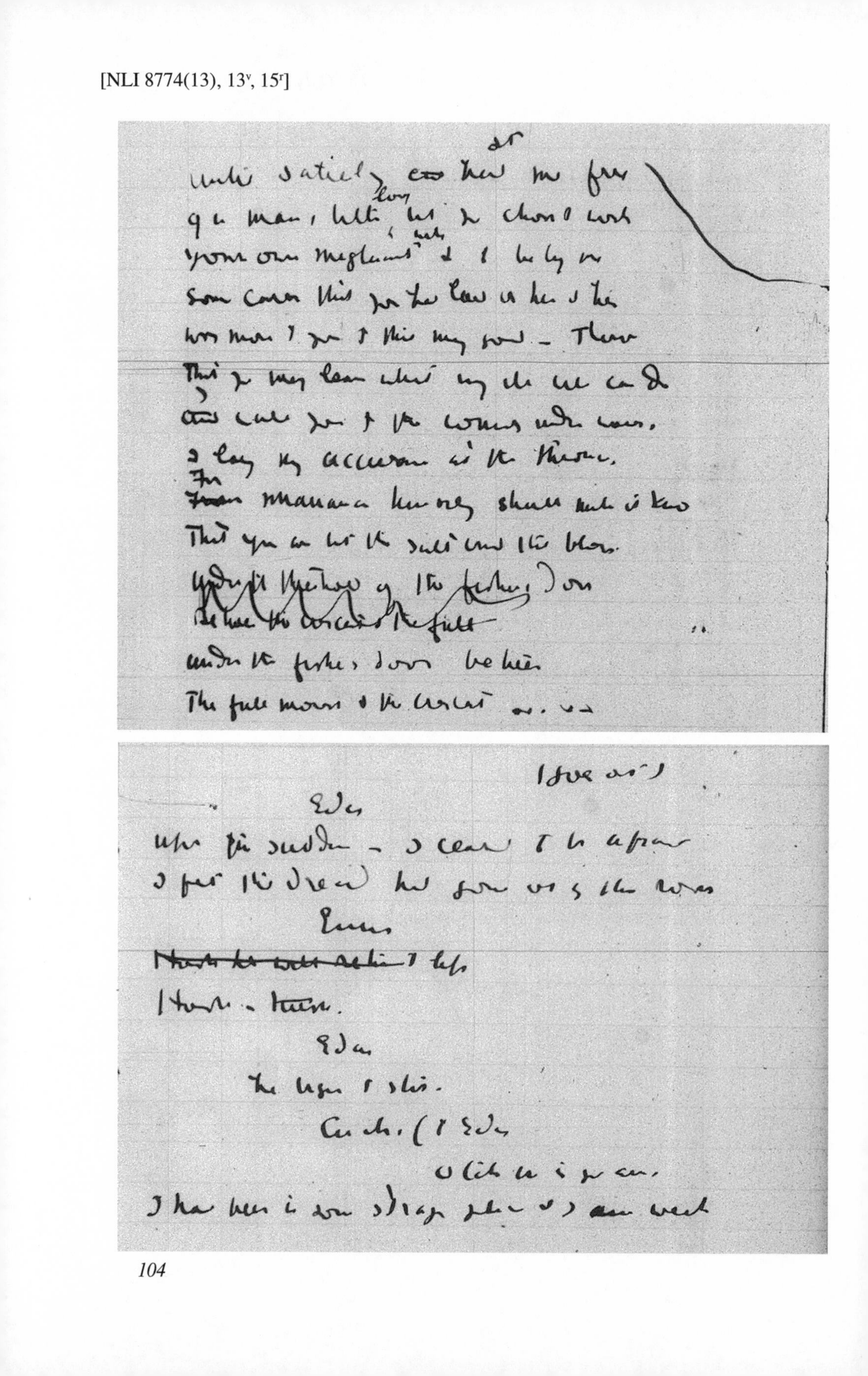

[NLI 8774(13), 13^{v}, 15^{r}]

[NLI 8774(13), 13^{v}]

set
Until satiety ~~had~~ had me free
love
Of a man's bitter but you chose to work
will
Your own malignant^& to betray me
Some curse that you had laid on her & him
Was more to you than my good – Therefore
That you may learn what my ill will can do
I
~~And~~ call you to the country under waves,
I lay my accusations at the throne,
For
~~From~~ Mananan himself shall make it known
That you are but the salt wind that blows
Under the threshold of the fishers door
Between the crescent & the full
Under the fishers door between
The full moon & the crescent . . . .

[NLI 8774(13), 15^{r}]

(goes out)
Edain
Upon the sudden – I ceased to be afraid
I felt the dread had gone out of the room
Emer
~~Hush he will return to life~~
Hush – Hush
Edain
he begins to stir.
Cuchulain (to Edain)
O take me in your arms
I have been in some strange place & I am weak

13^{v} The arrow points to the canceled passage on the facing 14^{r}. This revision was probably written after Yeats had completed his draft (the passage revised stops only a few lines from the end); cf. MS G, 23^{r} below.

5 For "my good" read "my good will."

10–14 The evil spirit's position among the phases will be fixed with increasing precision in subsequent manuscripts. This particular "salt wind," then, is a bitter wind of harsh spirits. Again Yeats uses a consistent imagery to hammer his play into unity.

15^{r} These lines follow on from the revision on 13^{v}.

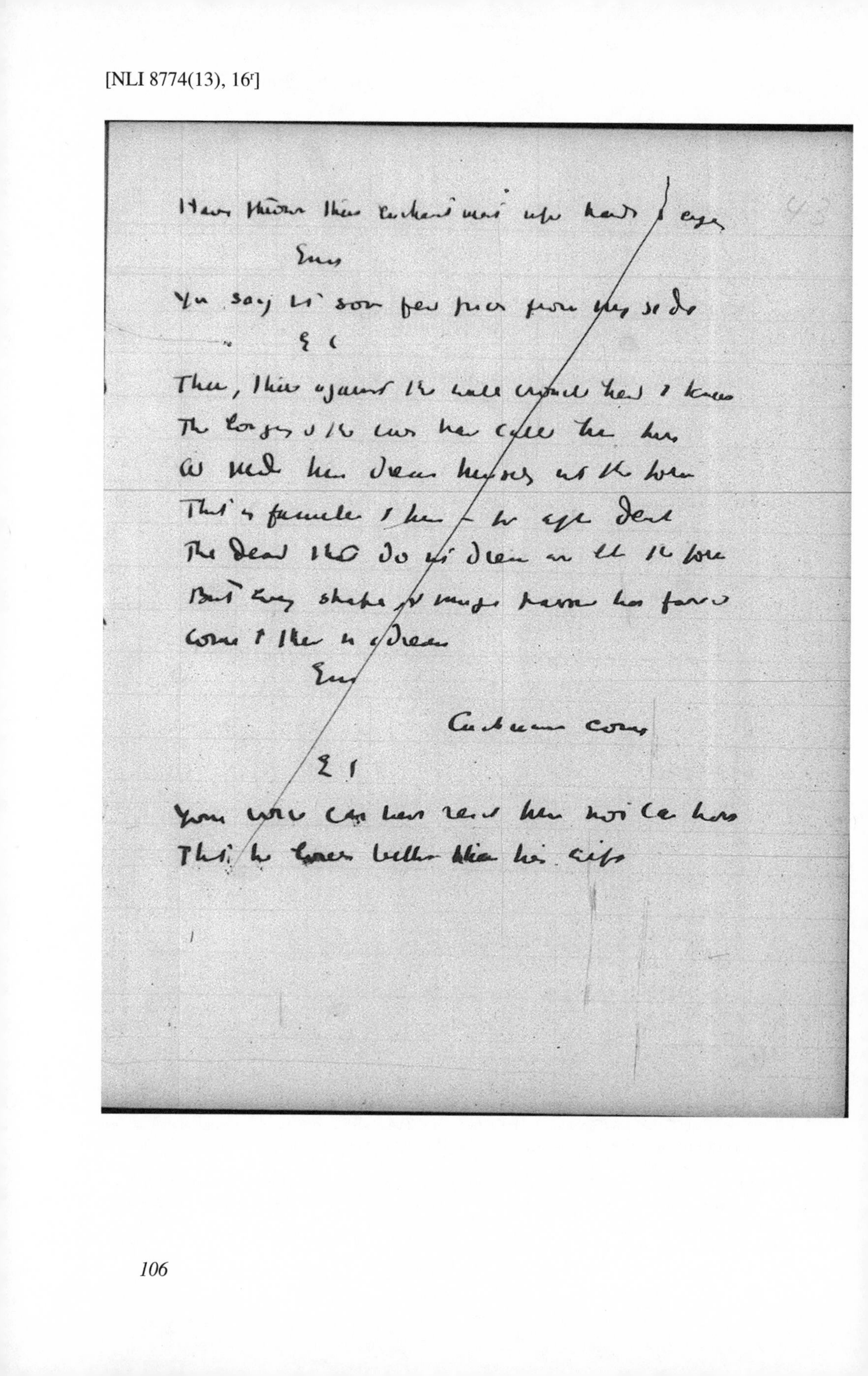

[NLI 8774(13), 16r]

[NLI 8774(13), 16^{r}]

Have thrown their enchantment upon hands & eyes
Emer
You say but some few paces from my side
E G
There, there against the wall crouched head to knees
The longing & the cries have called him here
And made him dream himself into the form
That is familiar to him – for after death
The dead that do not dream are like the [?former]
But living shape, & image passion has formed
Come to them in a dream
Emer
Cuchulain come
E G
Your voice can never reach him nor can hers
That he loves better than his wife

16^{r} Revision of MS A, 9^{r} above; in MS G, rejected in favor of the reading in MS C, 7^{r}.
8 For "image" read "images."

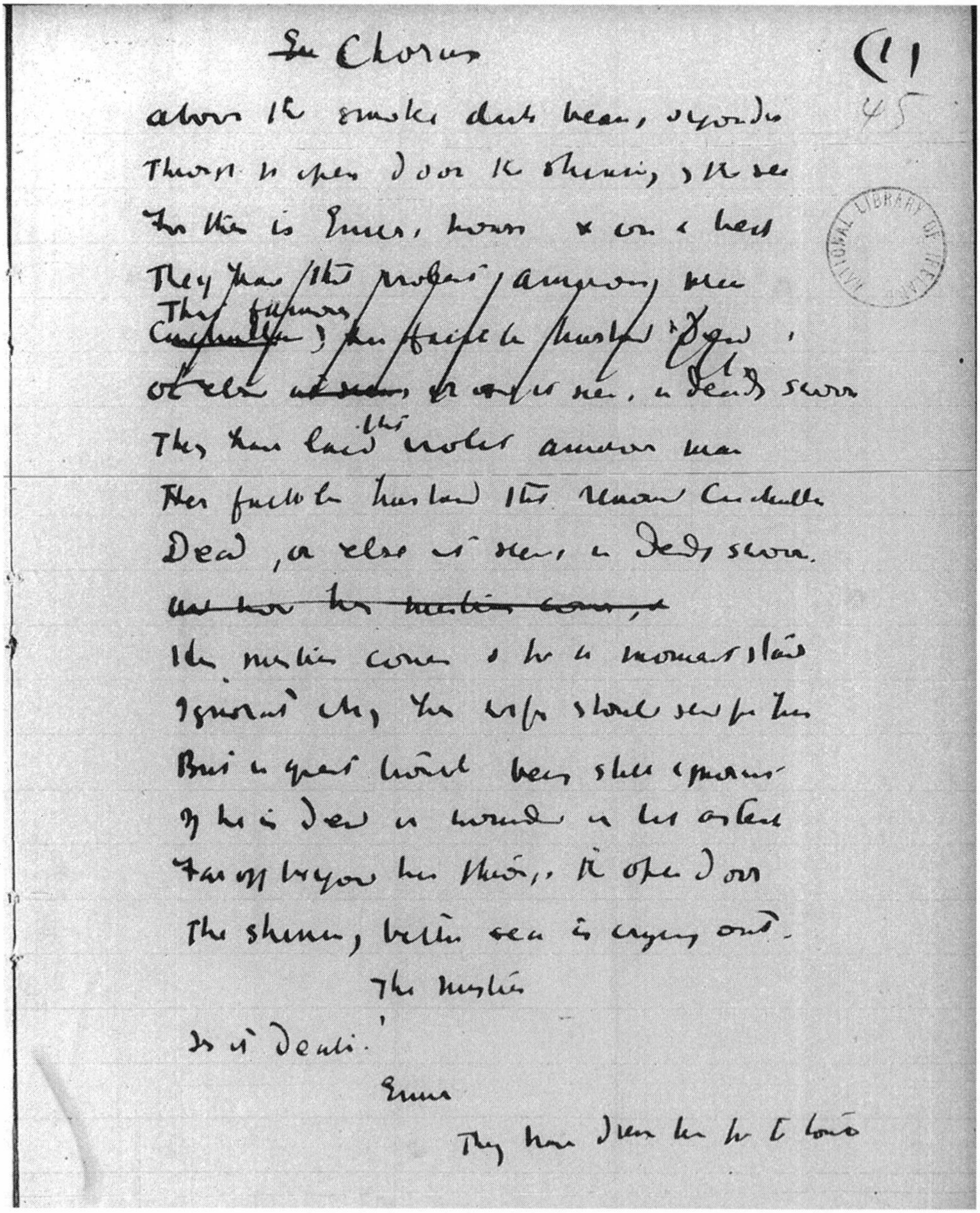

[NLI 8774(13), 1r, 1v]

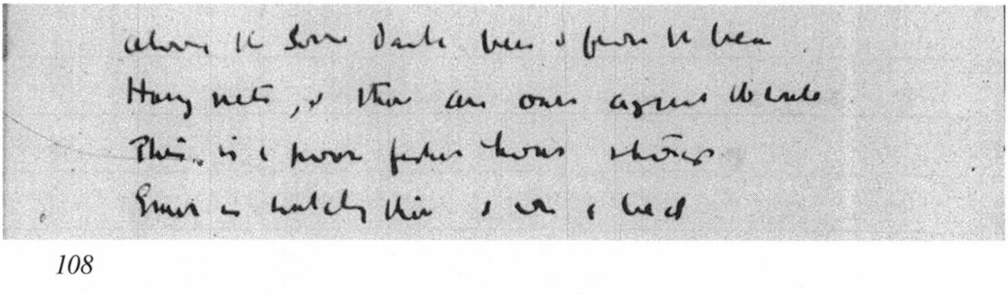

[NLI 8774(13), 1[r]]

~~En~~ Chorus (1)
Above the smoke dark beams & yonder
Through the open door the shining of the sea
For this is Emers house & on a bed
They have that violent amorous man
That famous
Cuchullain, her faithless husband dead
~~Or else it seems~~ or as it seems in deadly swoon
that
They have laid violent amorous man
Her faithless husband renowned Cuchullain
Dead, or else it seems in deadly swoon.
~~And now his mistress comes, &~~
His mistress comes & for a moment stands
Ignorant why his wife should send for her
But in great trouble being still ignorant
If he is dead or wounded or but asleep
Far off beyond her through the open door
The shining bitter sea is crying out.
The Mistress
Is it death.
Emer
They have drawn him from the tomb

[NLI 8774(13), 1[v]]

Above the smoke dark beams & from the beams
Hang nets, & there are oars against the wall
This is a poor fishers house though
Emer is watching there & on a bed

1[r] Revision of MS A, 1[r] above. For "En" above l. 1, read "Enter."

17b Simplifies MS C, 10[r]: "His people took him up, if what lay thus / Was still Cuchulain & bore him to this house."

1[v], l. 3 Cf. MS A, 1[r], "the great ancient house Dundalga." The alteration of the setting (it is *any* fisherman's house) gives it a feeling of isolation and dispossession; here men are held in the hostile grip of the gods (whose agent is the sea).

[NLI 8774(13), 2r]

[NLI 8774(13), 2ʳ]

2

But never could Cuchulain meet his ~~end~~ death
And   not   can
^I ^know, ~~the~~ it, nor ~~do~~ men like him
~~Pass with signs~~
Pass with omens
out   heaven
Pass with marvels, for the very ~~heavens itself~~
~~End~~ So that this end may not lack ceremony
Break out in fires &
But never could Cuchulain meet his death
~~And men not know that it coming~~
And not a man forsee it – the heavens themselves
So that his death might not lack ceremony
Would throw out fires & marvels – There would not be
A scullion but would know it like the world's end
That is no dead mans face.

Mistress

Who bore him here
What has ~~befallen~~
~~What brought him here – who drew him from the tomb~~

Emer

Towards middle day
~~An hour age~~ In the assembly house
He met with one who seemed a while most dear

2ʳ, l. 5 The dramatic purpose of these portents here is to provide justification for Emer's assertion that Cuchulain is not dead.

9 For "it coming" read "it was coming."

16 Cf. MS A, 1ᵛ above: "here in this very room / house." The setting has been changed to accord with *On Baile's Strand*, which takes place at "a great hall at Dundealgan, not 'Cuchulain's great ancient house' but an assembly-house nearer to the sea" (Alspach, *Variorum Plays*, p. 459).

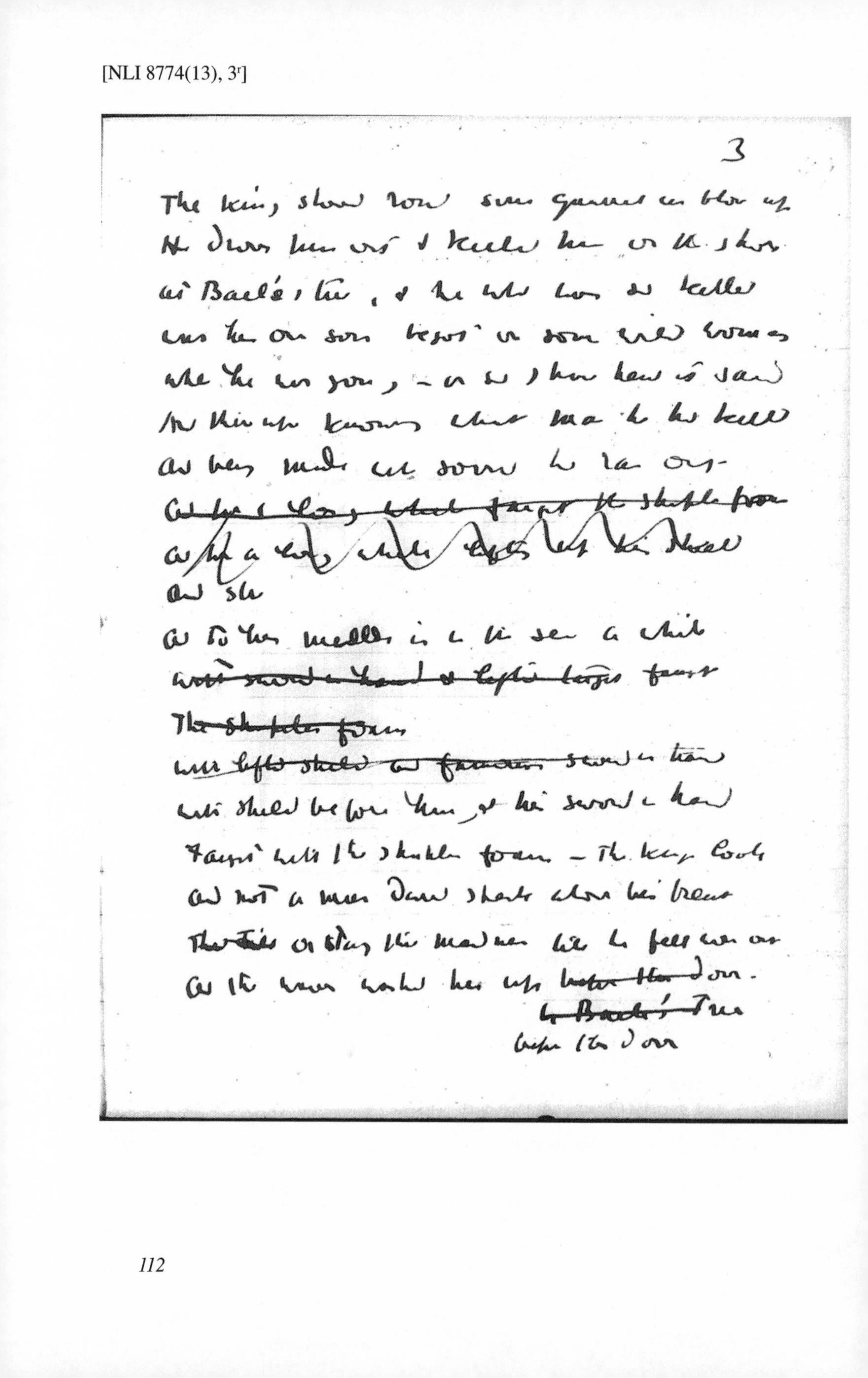

[NLI 8774(13), 3r]

3

[NLI 8774(13), 3^{r}]

3

The king stood round some quarrel was blow up
He drove him out & killed him on the shore
At Baile's tree, & he who was so killed
Was his own son begot on some wild woman
When he was young – or so I have heard it said
And thereupon knowing what man he had killed
And being mad with sorrow he ran out
And for a long while fought the shapeless foam
And for a long while lifting up his shield
And str
And to his middle is in the sea a while
~~With sword in hand & lifted larger~~ ~~fought~~
~~The shapeless foam~~
~~With lifted shield and fearless sword in hand~~
With shield before him, & his sword in hand
Fought with the shapeless foam – The kings look
And not a man dared speak above his breath
~~That~~ ~~Till~~ Or stay this madness till he fell worn out
And the waves washed him up ~~before this door~~.
~~by Baile's Tree~~
before this door

3^{r}, l. 1 For "king stood . . . blow up" read "kings stood . . . blown up."

3 Cf. MS G, 2^{r}, l. 16 and note; this detail has also been introduced to provide a link with *On Baile's Strand*. The tragic romance of Baile and Ailinn was the subject of a narrative poem by Yeats; for the original version, see *Cuchulain of Muirtheimne*, pp. 231–232. After Baile's death, a yew tree grew out of his grave on the strand near Dundealgan which afterward bore his name.

16 Cf. MS A, 2^{r} above: "fought with the sea waves." The revision carries a greater sense of the immensity of the gods' power, against which Cuchulain fought in vain. For "kings look" read "kings looked."

[NLI 8774(13), 4r]

4

The Master

Who dreams [illegible] the world & can [illegible]

Emer

The King

The Master

He is unchanged [illegible]

Emer.

No master

An image has been put at his place
A changeling, or the sea water
A sea-born log bewitched into his likeness
Or some stark phantom grown old & dried
The holy flocks in countries under sea
~~Because~~ now that his joints are stiff

The Master

Cry out his name
~~[illegible]~~ Because he is the first champion in the world
He may bring anger down the changeling [illegible]

Emer

I have called his name but he is deaf & blind

[NLI 8774(13), 4^{r}]

4

The Mistress
1 Who drew him from the tomb & laid him there
Emer
2 The kings
The Mistress
He is unchanged but pale
Emer.
It may be
3 An image has been put into his place
that
4 And^then he is far off, & that we watch
5 A seaborn log bewitched into his likeness
6 Or some stark phantom grown too old to drive
7 The holy flocks in country under wave
Now that
8 ~~Because~~ its joints are stiff
The Mistress
Cry out his name
Because he is
9 ~~For being the~~ the first champion in the world
10 He may being angry drive the changeling out
Emer
11 I have called his name but he is deaf & blind

[NLI 8774(13), 5[r]]

[NLI 8774(13), 5^{r}]

5

1 I am but his wife – but may be if you call
2 With that sweet voice that is so dear to him
3 He cannot help but listen.
The Mistress
He loves me best
4 Being his newest love but at the end
5 He'll love his wife the best, ~~for~~ women like me
6 Are but the foam upon the sailors beard
7 Cuchulain listen. ~~Emer~~
Emer
No no not yet – for first
8 I'll cover up his face & hide the sea
9 It's from the sea that the enchantment comes
Call
10 ~~Cry, & do not fear to call your dear secrets~~
(She covers face)
to
11 Call ~~on~~ him now, & call dear secrets out
12 Till you have touched his heart
The Mistress
Cuchulain ~~awake~~ come
13 ~~When ever have called, & you not answered~~
14 ~~When ever have I called did I call to you~~

[NLI 8774(13), 6r]

[NLI 8774(13), 6[r]]

~~4~~ 6.b

or

1 I have never called to you, sent a message
2 And had a wish that you would come
3 ~~But you have known & come~~,
4 And ~~hardly~~ scarce had a longing for your company
5 But you have known & come; ~~& to this hour~~
~~moped~~
6 ~~You have not moped in silence if I near~~
~~So do~~ And if indeed
7 ~~You're lying there awake, &~~
8 ~~You have come already, open your mouth & speak~~
9 ~~You have come already~~,
10 You're lying ~~there on~~ there, stretch out your wrist
for
11 ~~Open~~ Open your mouth & speak ~~for~~ to this hour
made you
12 My company has ~~made you talkative~~ talkative
13 You must not mope – Our passion was not chilled
14 When we were parted at the dawn of day.
hear me
15 He will not, ~~or he cannot~~, or his ears are shut
16 And no sound reaches him
Emer
Then kiss that image
~~Then kiss his mouth~~
17 The pressure of your mouth upon its mouth

6[r] Cf. MS C, 12[r] above; Yeats here attempts an expansion of the Mistress's speech in the earlier draft, then cancels it, probably seeing it as unnecessary.

6 For "if I" read "if I were."

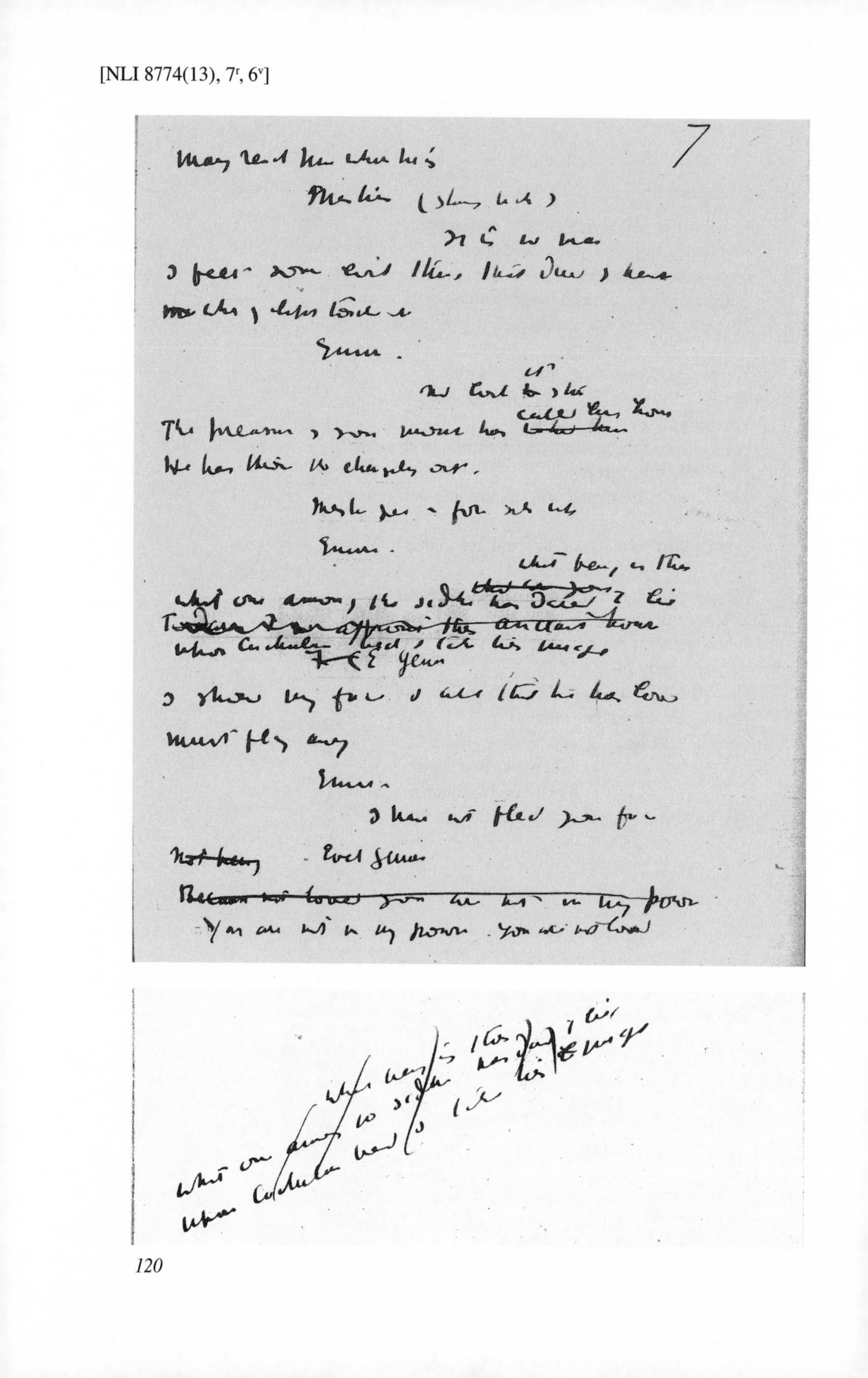

[NLI 8774(13), 7^r, 6^v]

[NLI 8774(13), 7^{r}]

7

1 May reach him where he is
Mistress (starting back)
It is no man
2 I felt some evil thing that dried my heart
3 ~~My~~ When my lips touched it
Emer.
it
No look ~~he~~ stirs
called him home
4 The pressure of your mouth has ~~waked him~~
5 He has thrown the changeling out.
Mistress goes – form sits up
Emer.
What being is this
~~Who are you~~
What one among the sidhe has dared to lie
6 ~~To dare to so affront this ancient house~~
Upon Cuchulain's bed & take his image

[NLI 8774(13), 6^{v}]

1 What being is this
2 What one among the sidhe has dared to lie
3 Upon Cuchulain's bed & take his ~~li~~ image

[NLI 8774(13), 7^{r} (continued)]

~~F C~~ E Genius
7 I show my face & all that he has loved
8 Must fly away
Emer
I have not fled your face
~~Not being~~ Evil Genius
9 Because not loved you are not in my power
10 You are not in my power. You are not loved

7^{r}, l. 3b Cf. MS C, 12^{r} above, where, as Emer says, Cuchulain "begins to stir," but is then wakened fully by the Mistress's kiss. Yeats has here simplified the action: the kiss causes him to stir and to wake.

5*sd* Yeats omitted the braces enclosing the stage direction.

6^{v} Illustrated at the foot of the facing page. First revision of immediately preceding lines on MS G, 7^{r}. Yeats wrote this first revision in his "tentative" style, i.e., diagonally across MS G, 6^{v}. He then incorporated the new material into the facing page, MS G, 7^{r}.

3 ~~li~~ image] Perhaps "living image" or "life image" was the original intent.

7^{r} (continued) Resumption of entry on this page.

[NLI 8774(13), 8r]

[NLI 8774(13), 8^{r}]

8

Emer
~~Be~~ And therefore have no dread to meet your eyes
And to demand him of you
E Genius
For this I have come
I ~~will~~ 'll set him free if you but pay the price
Emer
Do the sidhe bargain
E Genius
they
When ~~you we they~~ set free a captive
They like some valued thing of life instead
fisher
The ~~farmer~~ when some knowledgeable man
Restores to him his wife or son or daughter
~~Knows that a cow or sheep will die~~
Knows he will lose a boat or pot, or it may be
The cow that gives his children milk & some
Have offered their own lives – I do not ask
Your life or any valuable thing –
You spoke but now of the mere chance that some day
Perhaps when you & he are old & withered

8^{r}, l. 7 Yeats alters the imagery of MS C, 4^{r} above to make greater use of the unifying emblem of the sea.

[NLI 8774(13), 9r]

NLI 8774(13), 9ʳ]

You'll have his love again. Renounce that chance
~~Pay with me that miserable hopeless hope~~
And pay me with that miserable hope
And he shall live again.
Emer
On me alone
Or all that gave love to, or loved him
You have no power, & therefore you would bargain
E Genius
You have but to put yourself into my power
Of your own will & in that matter only
And he shall live again.
Emer
Never, never
E Genius
You dare not be accursed yet he has dared
Emer
~~I have but two things of price – the words~~
I have but two joyous thoughts two things of price
The words he spoke to me among the wheat-stalks
In laughing girlhood: And that somewhere someday

9ʳ, ll. 13–14 A condensation of MS C, 6ʳ above: "Upon a windy upland at his side / In laughing girlhood, while the sea wind made / Long waves amid the wheat."

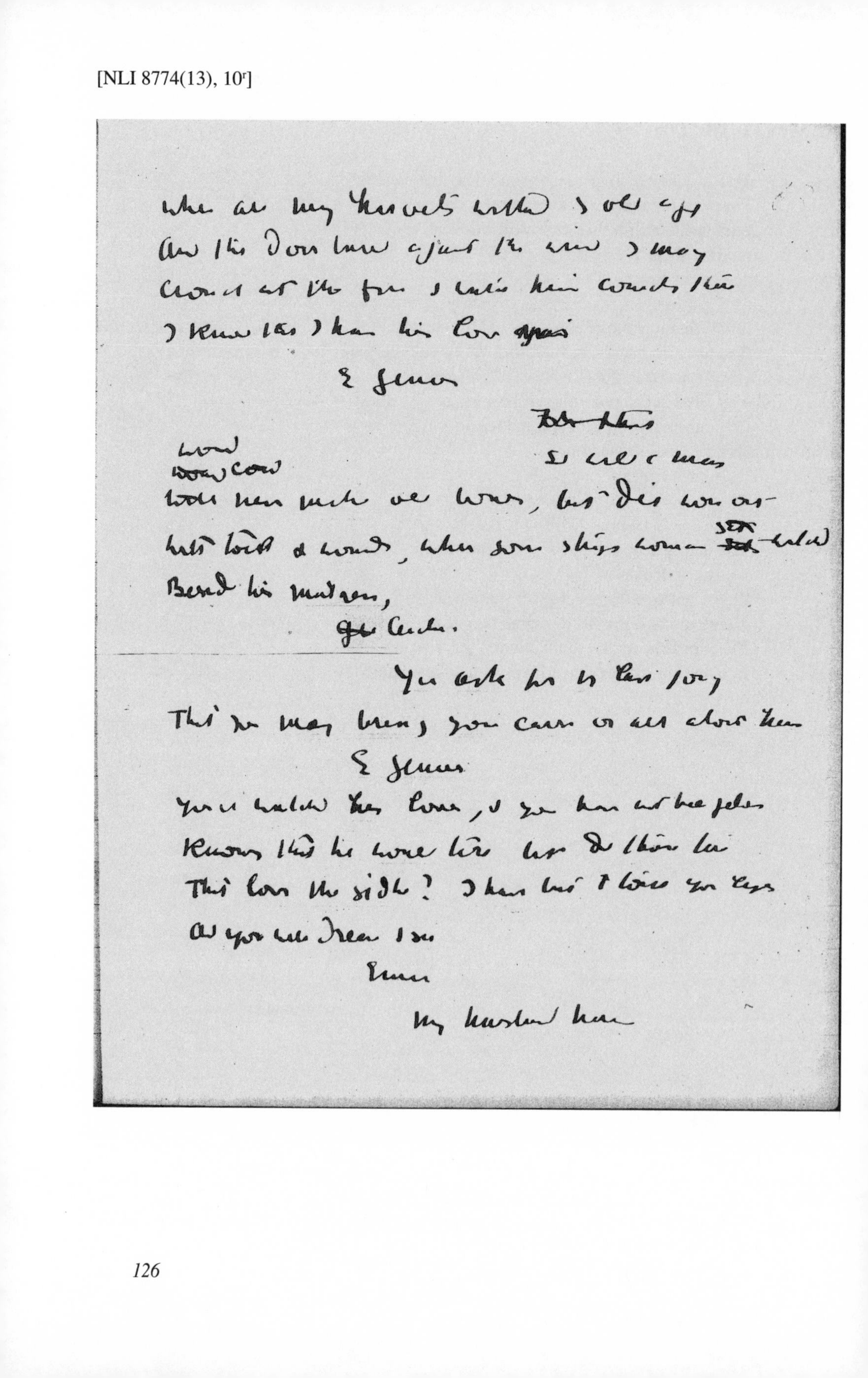

[NLI 8774(13), 10r]

[NLI 8774(13), 10r]

1 When all my harvests withered by old age
2 And the door barred against the wind I may
3 Crouch at the fire & watch him crouching there
4 & know that I have his love ~~again~~
E Genius
~~For that~~
So wild a man
Would
~~Would~~ ~~Could~~
5 ~~Will~~ never make old bones, but die worn out
set
6 With toils & wounds, where some strange woman ~~sits~~ watching
7 Beside his matress,
~~Gen~~ Cuchulain
You ask for the last joy
8 That you may bring your curse on all about him
E Genius
9 You've watched his loves, & you have not been jelous
10 Knowing that he would tire but do those tire
11 That love the sidhe? I have but to touch your eyes
12 And you will dream & see
Emer
My husband here

10r, ll. 6–7 This image replaces the abstraction of MS C, 6r above: "or if he makes them / Turn to the wife of his youth." The Evil Genius typically seizes on an image that is in ironic contrast to Emer's sickbed vigil over Cuchulain.

7b–8 Emer speaks these lines, not Cuchulain.

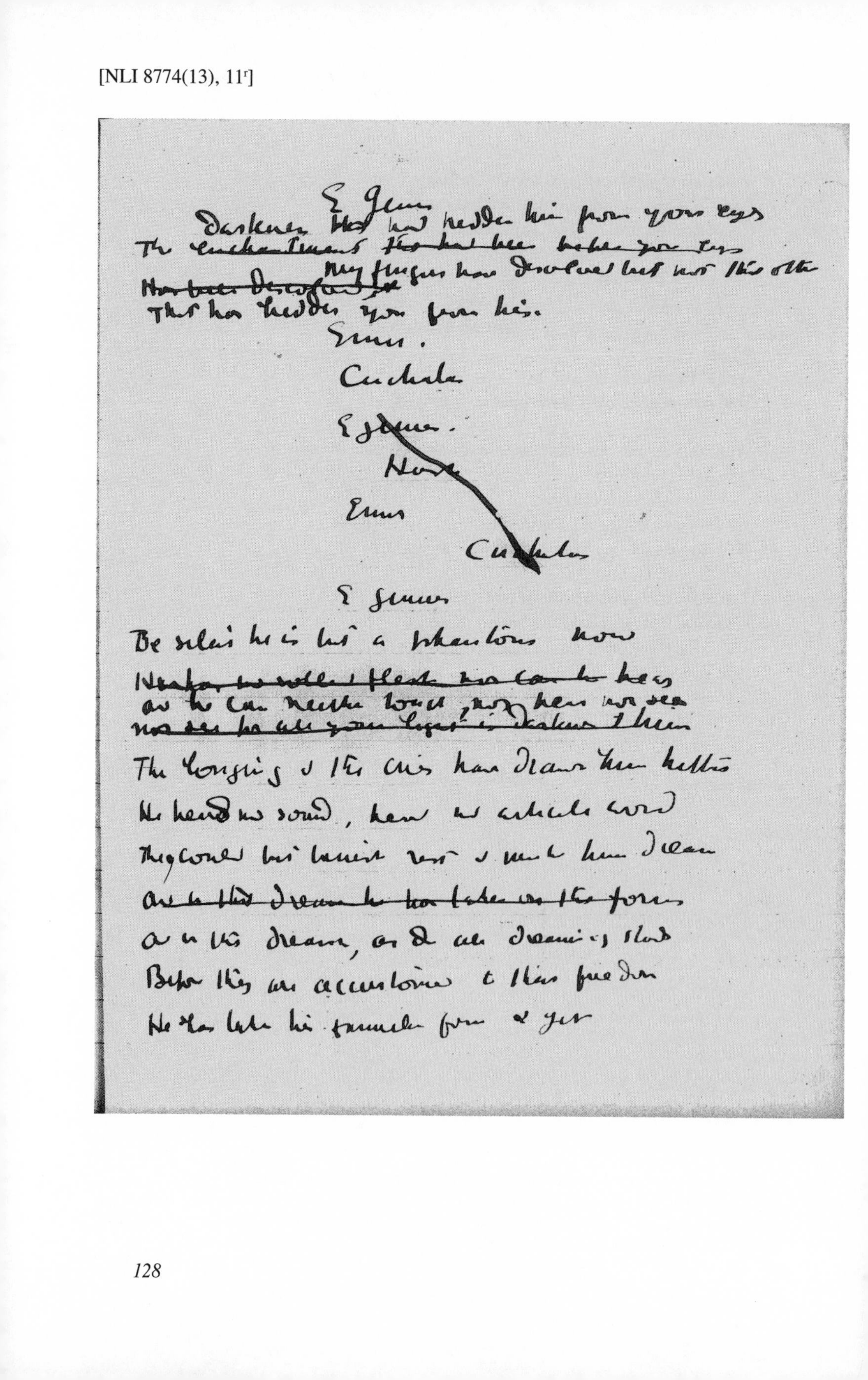

[NLI 8774(13), 11r]

[NLI 8774(13), 11^{r}]

E Genius
darkness that had hidden him from your eyes
1 The ~~enchantment that had been before your eyes~~
My fingers have dissolved but not that other
2 ~~Has been dissolved, &~~
3 That has hidden you from him.
Emer.
Cuchulain
E Genius
Hush
Emer
Cuchulain
E Genius
4 Be silent he is but a phantom now
5 ~~He has no sollid flesh nor can be hear~~
6 And he can neither touch, nor hear nor see
7 ~~Nor see for all your light is darkness to him~~
8 The longing & the cries have drawn him hither
9 He heard no sound, heard no articulate word
10 They could but banish rest & make him dream
11 ~~And in that dream he has taken on the form~~
12 And in this dream, as do all dreaming shades
13 Before they are accustomed to their freedom
14 He has taken his familiar form & yet

12^{r}, ll. 10–14 Bjersy, *Interpretation*, p. 152 n., prints a glossing passage from Yeats's letters to the spirit Leo Africanus: "In all alike you see, as Henry More has written, the gods or the dead fighting for men with dreams."

[NLI 8774(13), 12r]

[NLI 8774(13), 12r]

He crouches there not knowing where he is
Or at whose side, or what he would do or think
Emer
Who is that woman.
Evil Genius
From country under wave
She has come & dreamed herself into that shape
~~From country under wave~~
~~She has run hither & has dreamed herself~~
Into that shape to lead him hence
~~In that shape that he may follow her.~~
To country under wave
~~Whither she choose~~ – The Sidhe are fishers too
They fish for men with dreams upon the hook
Into where
^~~To~~ that shape to lead him she she will
He'll glitter in the basket for ~~sidhe~~ the Sidhe
Are fishers also, & they fish for men
With dreams upon the hook.
Emer. and so
She has hid herself in that disguise & made
Herself into a lie

Or at whose side he is crowded.

Emer.

Who is that woman

E. Inne

She has hurried ~~come~~ from the country under wave

And dreamed herself into these shapes that he

May glitter in her basket; for the Sidhe

Are fishers also & they fish for men

With dreams upon the hook

Emer.

I knew her now

The

[NLI 8774(13), 11v]

1 Or at whose side he is crouched.
Emer.
Who is that woman
E Genius
hurried the
2 She has ~~come~~ ^ from ^ country under wave
3 And dreamed herself into that shape that he
4 May glitter in her basket; for the Sidhe
5 Are fishers also & they fish for men
6 with dreams upon the hook
Emer

[NLI 8774(13), 12v]

1 I know her sort
2 The

11v Replaces canceled passage on facing 12r.

12v Yeats wrote these words as a reminder to himself to expand the dialogue on facing 13r; see MS K, 11r below.

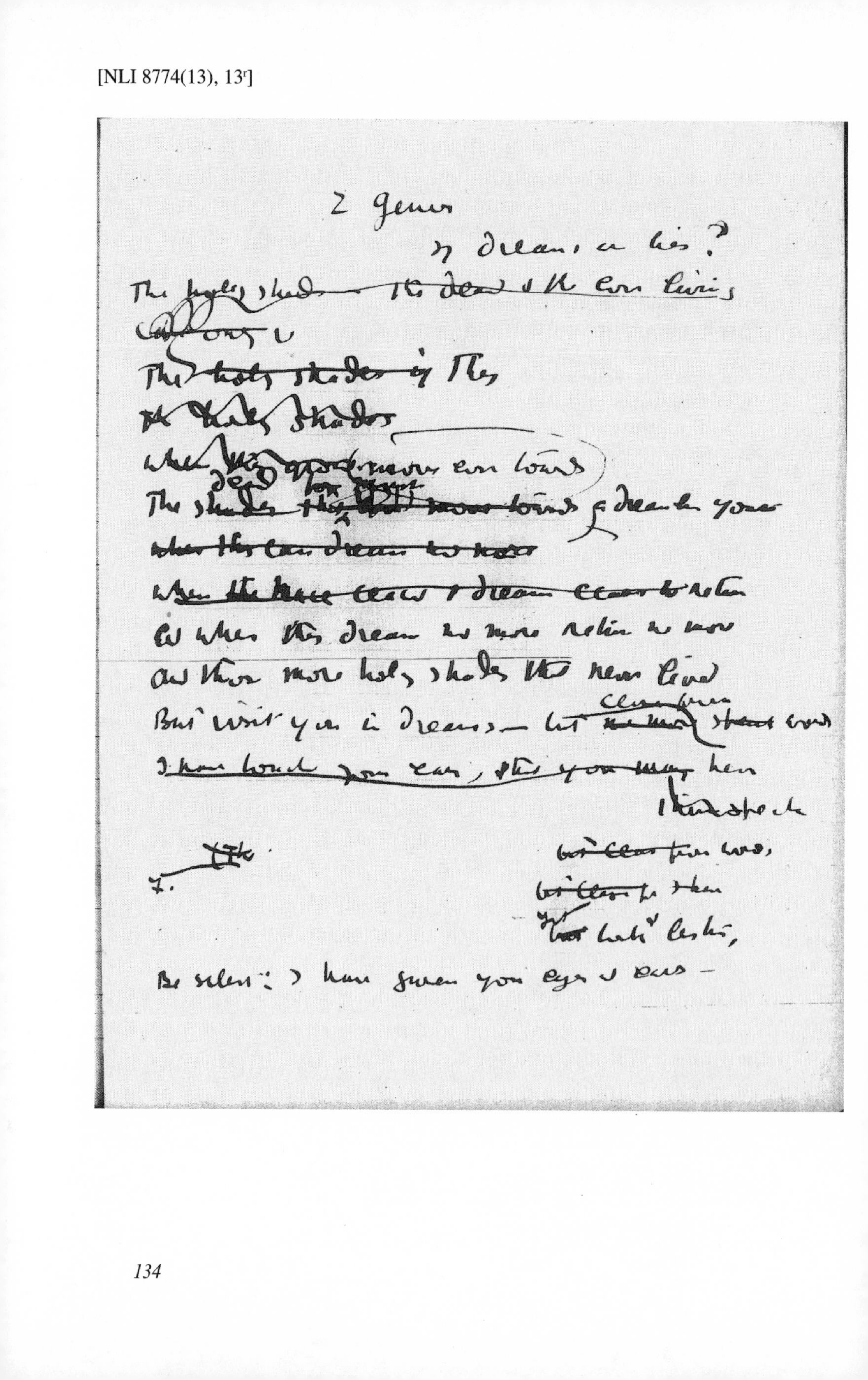

[NLI 8774(13), 13r]

[NLI 8774(13), 13r]

E Genius

1 If dreams are lies?
2 ~~The holy shades – the dead & the ever living~~
3 ~~Can only in~~
4 ~~The holy shades if they~~
5 ~~The holy shades~~
6 ~~When they grow~~ (move ever towards)
dead ~~live~~ must
7 The ~~shades~~ that^ ~~lived move towards~~^ a dreamless youth
8 ~~When they can dream no more~~
9 ~~When they have ceased to dream cease to return~~
10 And when they dream no more return no more
11 And those more holy shades that never lived
~~cease from~~
12 But visit you in dreams – ~~but no more~~ ~~speak~~ words
13 ~~I have touched your ears, that you may hear~~
~~them~~ ~~speak~~
~~(The~~ ~~but cease from words~~
~~F[?]~~ ~~but cease for I have~~
yet &
~~but~~ look listen,
Be silent : I have given you eyes & ears –

13r This passage clarified and expanded on MS K, 11r : "A dream is body."

9 The ideas of reincarnation later developed in *A Vision* are added to the text on MS C, 9r above; see also MS C, 2r, ll. 1b-4.

12 Cf. "Introduction" to *Essays and Introductions*, p. viii: "I have met with ancient myth in my dreams, brightly lit; and I think it allied to the wisdom or instinct that guides a migratory bird."

[NLI 8774(13), 14r]

(The woman of the sidhe moves
slowly round Cuchulain in a dance of the
manner of the chorus & he slowly awakens

Cuchulain

Why do you turn about me like a woman
Turning & smiling, & shaking, as you turn
Faint light out of your limbs & hair — ~~[illegible]~~ days
~~[illegible]~~
sang

In my young days I met you at a well
under bare thorn tree on a mountain side
When you had unsmiling eyes & a hawks wing?
Where have dropped your quills?

Woman of Sidhe

Look well — look well
And judge if I be friend or enemy

Cuchulain

What is your name & country?

Woman of Sidhe

Since you were born

[NLI 8774(13), 14^{r}]

(The woman of the Sidhe moves
slowly round Cuchulain in a dance to the
music of the chorus. He slowly awakens

Cuchulain

1 Why do you turn about me like a moon
2 Turning & smiling, & shaking as you turn
3 Faint light out of your limbs & hair – ~~In my young days~~
~~Yes – yes~~
Surely

In
4 ~~I in~~ my young days I met you at a well
5 Under bare thorn trees on a mountain side
6 When you had unsmiling eyes & a hawks wing?
7 Where have dropped your quills?

Woman of Sidhe

Look well – look well
8 And judge if I be friend or enemy

Cuchulain

9 What is your name & country

W of Sidhe

Since you were born

14^{r} The opening stage direction was not found in MS F. The text from here to the end of MS G is a revision of MS F, a draft which Yeats had written on previous pages of the notebook in which MSS E, F, and G are located.

6 Cf. MS F, 1^{r}, l. 8 above: "that woman that I followed once/ At the Hawks well." Yeats has added description here that refers back directly to the language of *At the Hawk's Well* (1917).

7 For "have" read "have you."

[NLI 8774(13), 15r]

[NLI 8774(13), 15r]

I have been close at hand – now dim now bright
According as your eyes were turned upon me
Or turned away.
Cuchulain
O beautiful woman
How could you gather up my light like a moon
When but for that brief dance at the well side
I never met you like this moment
W of S
And yet
There was a day when we had but one being
Nor had I ∈ claws & feathers on that day
Cuchulain
One loves & one forgets but not such beauty
W of S
Have you not heard that man before his birth
Is two in one – the yoke & the white of the egg
And that one half is born in ~~the~~ wretchedness
While the other half remains amid the ~~sh~~ Sidhe
Cuchulain
I have heard the learned say so

15r, l. 6 See MS G, 14r, l. 6 and note.

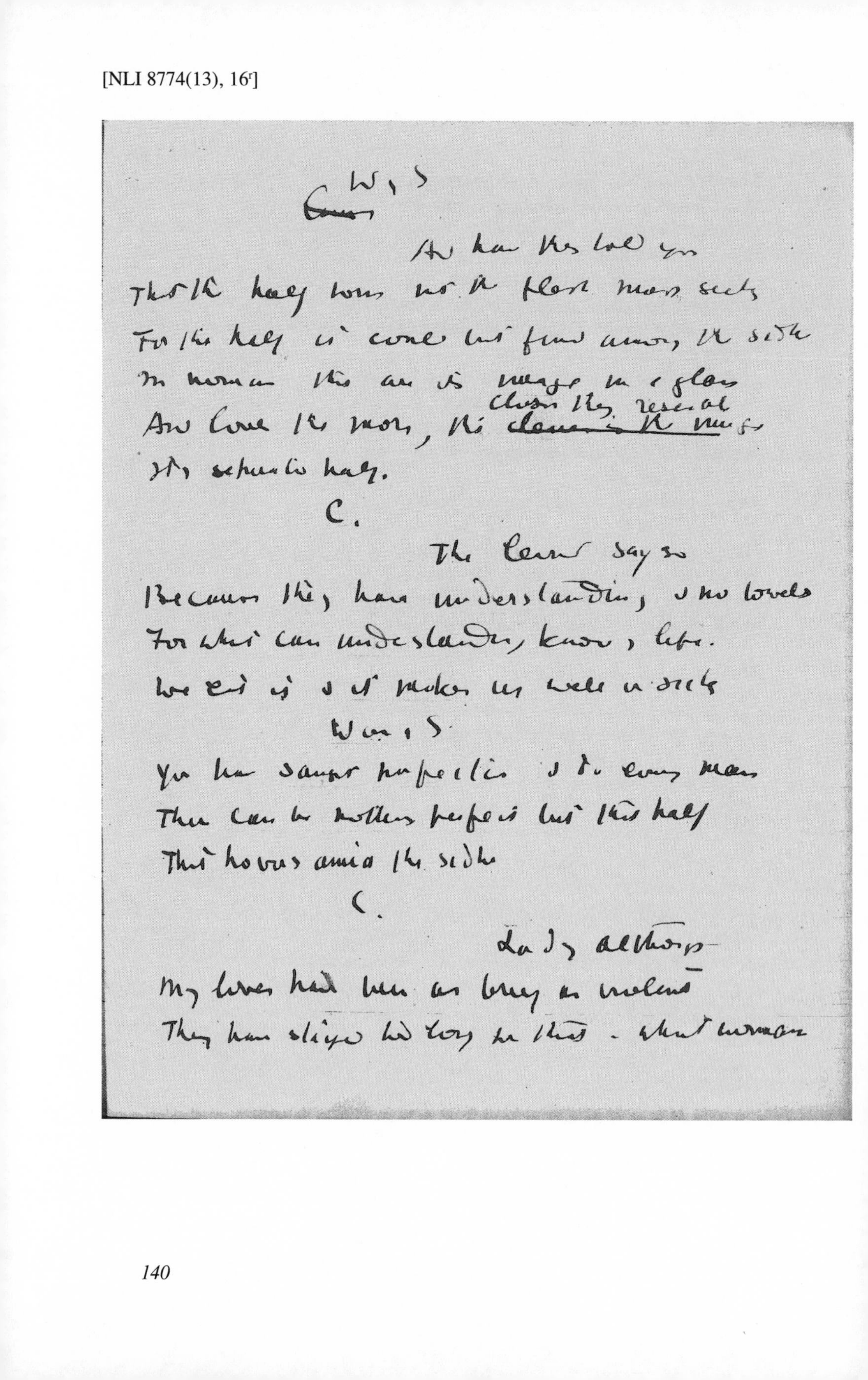

[NLI 8774(13), 16r]

[NLI 8774(13), 16r]

W of S
~~Cuchulain~~
1 And have they told you
2 That the half born into the flesh must seek
3 For the half it could but find among the sidhe
4 In women that are its image in a glass
closer they resemble
5 And love the more, the ~~clearer is the image~~
6 Its separated half.
C.
The learned say so
7 Because they have understanding & no bowels
8 For what can understanding know of life.
9 We eat it & it makes us well or sick
Woman of S.
10 You have sought perfection & to every man
11 There can be nothing perfect but that half
12 That hovers amid the sidhe
C.
Lady although
13 My loves have been as brief as violets
14 They have stayed too long for that – what woman

[NLI 8774(13), 17r]

Could satisfy this thirst till the sun set
It may be so my friend, yours I have loved so
But no such love has drawn eyes of God,
And kept me in this darkness until my head
Bowed on my knees

Wis Sith

But you love beauty

C

I have loved it and forgotten it many times
For it is nothing when it but a hand
That leads us always to its opposite
You never can have loved unless you know
It is the imperfect that we love — man loves
Some weakness he protects, or the moon lantern
Upon the table in the fisher's house
Protects the candle flame.

W y S

Is love not pity

C

I think it pity that is driven to frenzy.

[NLI 8774(13), 17^{r}]

1 Could satisfy that thirst till the sunset
2 It may be in my first youth I have loved so
3 But no such love has doubled up my body
                in this darkness
4 And kept me ~~with my he~~ with my head
5 Bowed on my knees
            W of Sidhe
                        But you love beauty
            C
6 I have loved it & begotten it many times
7 For it is nothing when its but a hand
8 That leads us almost to its opposite
9 You never can have loved unless you know
10 It's the imperfect that we love – man loves
11 Some weakness he protects as the horn lanthorn
12 Upon the table in the fishers house
13 Protects the candle flame.
            W of S
                        Is love but pity
            C
14 I think it pity that is driven to frenzy.

17^{r}, l. 8 opposite] Replaces the rather cumbersome "antithesis" of MS F, 4^{v} above.

11 Yeats described a horn lanthorn in a letter of August 22, 1925, to Professor Shotaro Oshima: " . . . it is a form of lanthorn no longer in use . . . One hangs in my hall at this moment . . . it is a cylinder with little squares of horn instead of glass to let the light through" (Shotaro Oshima, *W.B. Yeats and Japan* [Tokyo, 1965], p. 3).

[NLI 8774(13), 18r]

Woman Sidhe

You love this pale faced, ~~[illegible]~~ grey whose hunted eyes

[illegible] the passion shaken [illegible]

C

I have loved her

In battles I loved her like before

But this woman whose sleep ~~[illegible]~~ can be

~~weaker, than weakness~~.

weaker, than weakness says

Woman, Sidhe

has your lips

C

She has been patient kind & generous

And [illegible] I would [illegible] & [illegible]

The shelling hours

Woman, Sidhe

Cuchulain I have come

To bring, you who men love & yet are happy

To love the flame because we are the hour

Or love the hour because we are the flame

[NLI 8774(13), 18^{r}]

W of Sidhe

girl

1 You love that pale faced ~~woman~~ whose troubled eyes
2 Display the passion shaken heart

C

I have loved her

3 In bitterness & loved her like before
4 But there's woman in whom strength ~~because~~ can be
5 ~~Weaker, than weakness~~
6 Weaker, than weakness self

Woman of Sidhe

~~her~~ Your wife

C

7 She has been patient kind & generous
8 And for this I would love her again & be
9 The sheltering horn

Woman of Sidhe

Cuchulain I have come

10 To bring you where men love & yet are happy
11 To love the flame because we are the horn
12 Or love the horn because we are the flame

18^{r}, ll. 1–2 pale faced girl] The mistress. Yeats eliminates the dialogue on MS F, 6 above revolving around the word "pity."

4 For "woman" read "a woman."

6 For "self" read "itself."

7 On MS F, 7 above, Cuchulain had praised her "generosity and strength."

12 Yeats has dropped the line on MS F, 7^{r}, in which Cuchulain defines man's own weakness: "He but a candle in need of sheltering horn" (l. 12). Thus the line "Or love the horn because we are the flame" has lost its impact in this draft.

[NLI 8774(13), 18v]

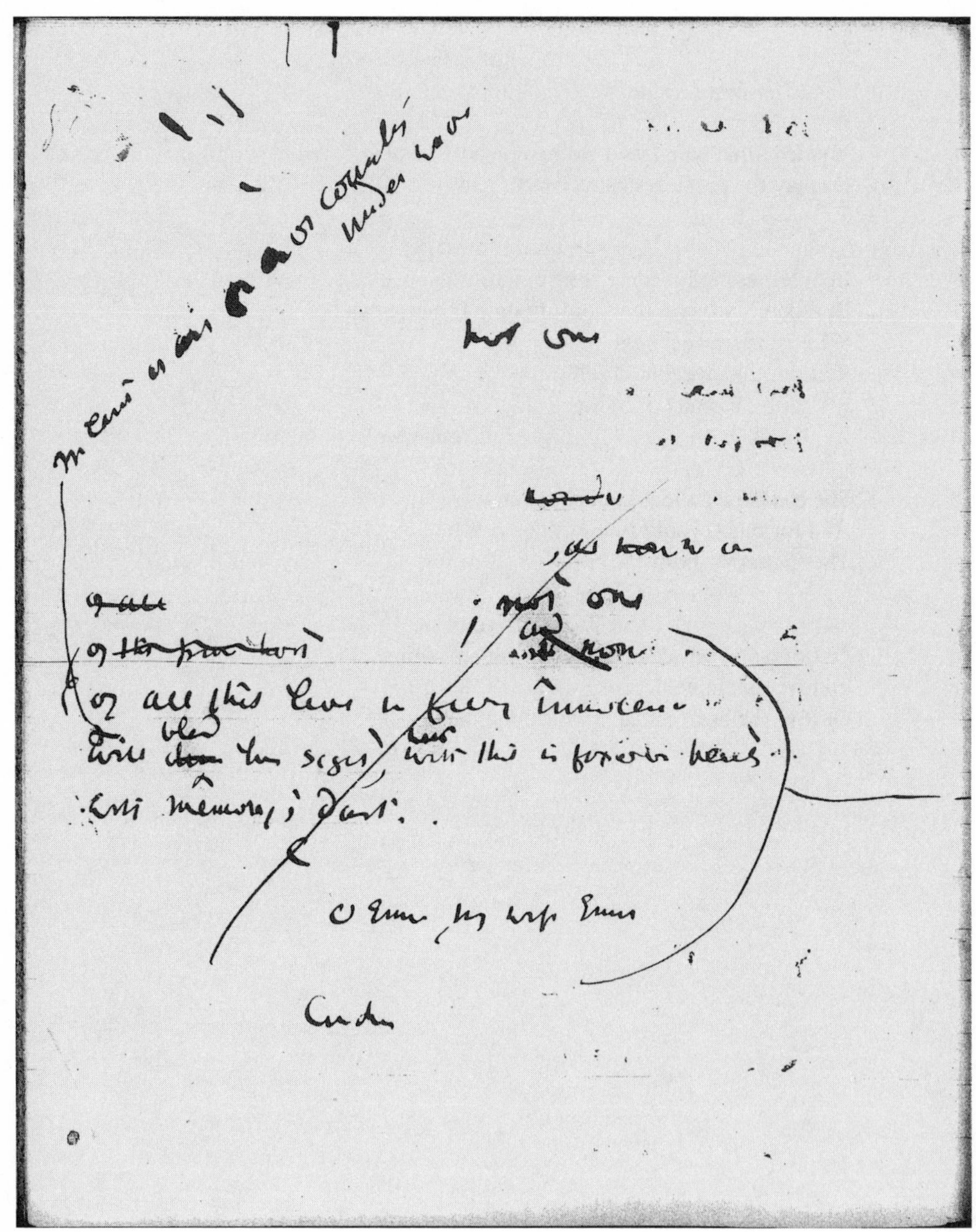

[NLI 8774(13), 18v]

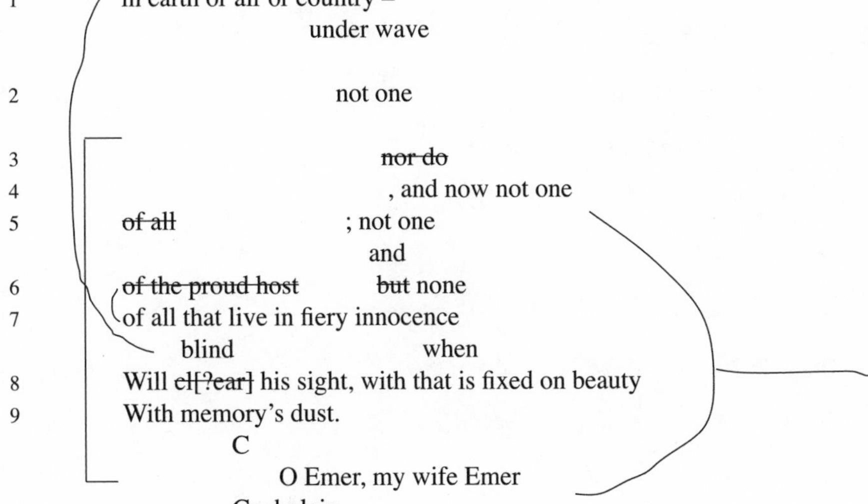

1 in earth or air or country –
under wave

2 not one

3 ~~nor do~~
4 , and now not one
5 ~~of all~~ ; not one
and
6 ~~of the proud host~~ ~~but~~ none
7 of all that live in fiery innocence
blind when
8 Will ~~el[?ear]~~ his sight, with that is fixed on beauty
9 With memory's dust.
C
O Emer, my wife Emer
Cuchulain

18v Arrowed to follow l. 10 on facing 19r. Both passages were then canceled.

[NLI 8774(13), 19r]

[NLI 8774(13), 19[r]]

Is to lie always on the fishers table
And shake against the wind, to be but loved
To our own tragedy or to anothers
Cuchulain
Men love in tragedy or not at all
And how should I love whose living flesh
Has got no mortal taint, & in whose mind
There is no needy frailty.
W of S.
The Sidhe
not nor
Do ‸ ask pity, & anything at all
they are given
But the desire of men, & ~~when they~~
In laughter at the dances end.
Cuchulain
O Emer
W of Sidhe
You left, when you lived, for other women Stet

See ~~foot~~ ~~of~~ other side of page

Cuchulain
I left her
~~You right~~ & I should leave the world behind
For that's irrecoverable but my mind
Is but the past because the past has made it

19[r], l. 5 For "love" read "love one" or "love her."
6–7 in whose mind . . . needy frailty] Cf. MS F, 8[r], ll. 7–8, above: "~~you~~ that are so high / Above my pity."
11 For "left" read "left her." Yeats reinstated this line after canceling the passage.
12 For "You right" read "You are right."

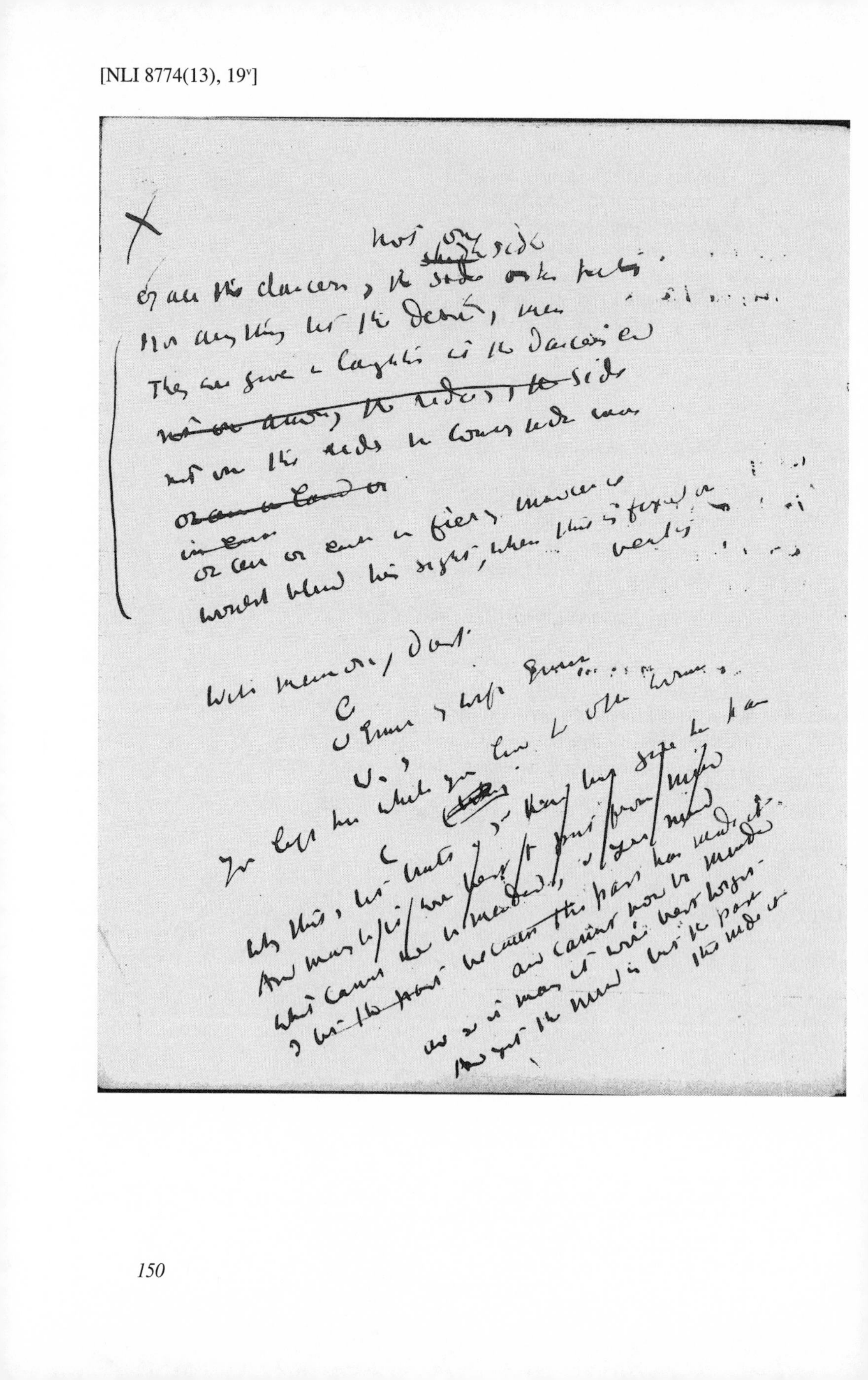

[NLI 8774(13), 19^{v}]

[NLI 8774(13), 19^{v}]

X Not one
~~shigh~~ sidhe
1 Of all the dancers of the ~~side~~ asks pity
2 Nor anything but the desire of men
3 They are given in laughter at the dances end
4 ~~Not one among the riders of the sidhe~~
5 Not one that rides in country under wave
6 ~~Or air or land or~~
7 ~~in earth~~
8 or air or earth in fiery innocence
9 would blind his sight, when that is fixed on
beauty
10 with memorys dust
C
O Emer my wife Emer
W of S
11 You left her while you lived for other women
C (~~rising~~
12 why that is but truth. I have but given her pain
13 And maybe it were best to put from mind
14 what cannot now be mended, & yet mind
15 ~~Is but the past because the~~ past has made it
And cannot now be mended
16 And so it may it were best forgot
17 And yet the mind is but the past
that made it

19^{v}, ll. 1–9 Keyed to replace lines on 19^{r}.
16 For "may" read "may be."

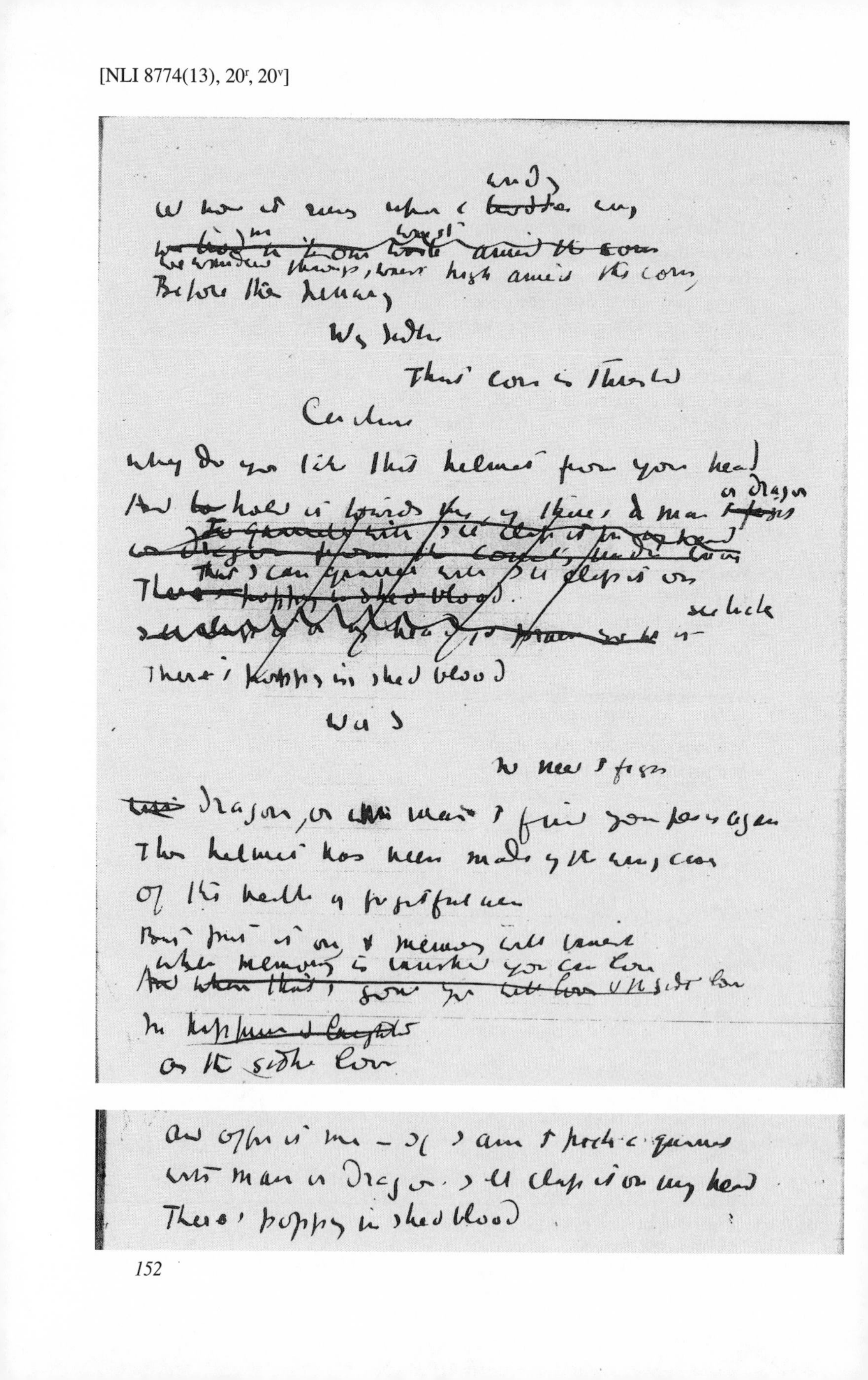

[NLI 8774(13), 20^{r}]

windy
1 And now it runs upon a ~~trodden~~ way
~~an~~ ~~waist~~
~~We trod a hour waste amid the corn~~
2 We wandered through, waist high amid the corn,
3 Before the harvesting
W of Sidhe
That corn is threshed
Cuchulain
4 Why do you take that helmet from your head
or dragon
5 And ~~to~~ hold it towards me, if there's ~~a~~ man ~~to fight~~
~~To quarrel with I'll clap it on my head~~
6 ~~Or dragon from the country under wave~~
That I can quarrel with I'll clap it on
7 ~~There's poppy in shed blood~~ see back
8 ~~I'll clap it on my head, & praise you for it~~
9 There's poppy in shed blood
W of S
No need to fight
10 ~~With~~ dragon, or ~~with~~ man to find your peace again
11 The helmet has been made of the wing case
12 Of the beetle of forgetfulness
13 But put it on, & memory will vanish
When memory is vanished you can love
14 ~~And when that's gone you will love as the sidhe love~~
15 ~~In happiness & laughter~~
16 As the sidhe love

[NLI 8774(13), 20^{v}]

1 And offer it me – If I am to pick a quarrel
2 With man or dragon I'll clap it on my head
3 There's poppy in shed blood

20^{r}, l. 7 "see back" refers to the three lines entered on the verso.
3b–4 Cf. MS F, 10^{r} above: "Could you live again / You would forsake her for some younger woman."

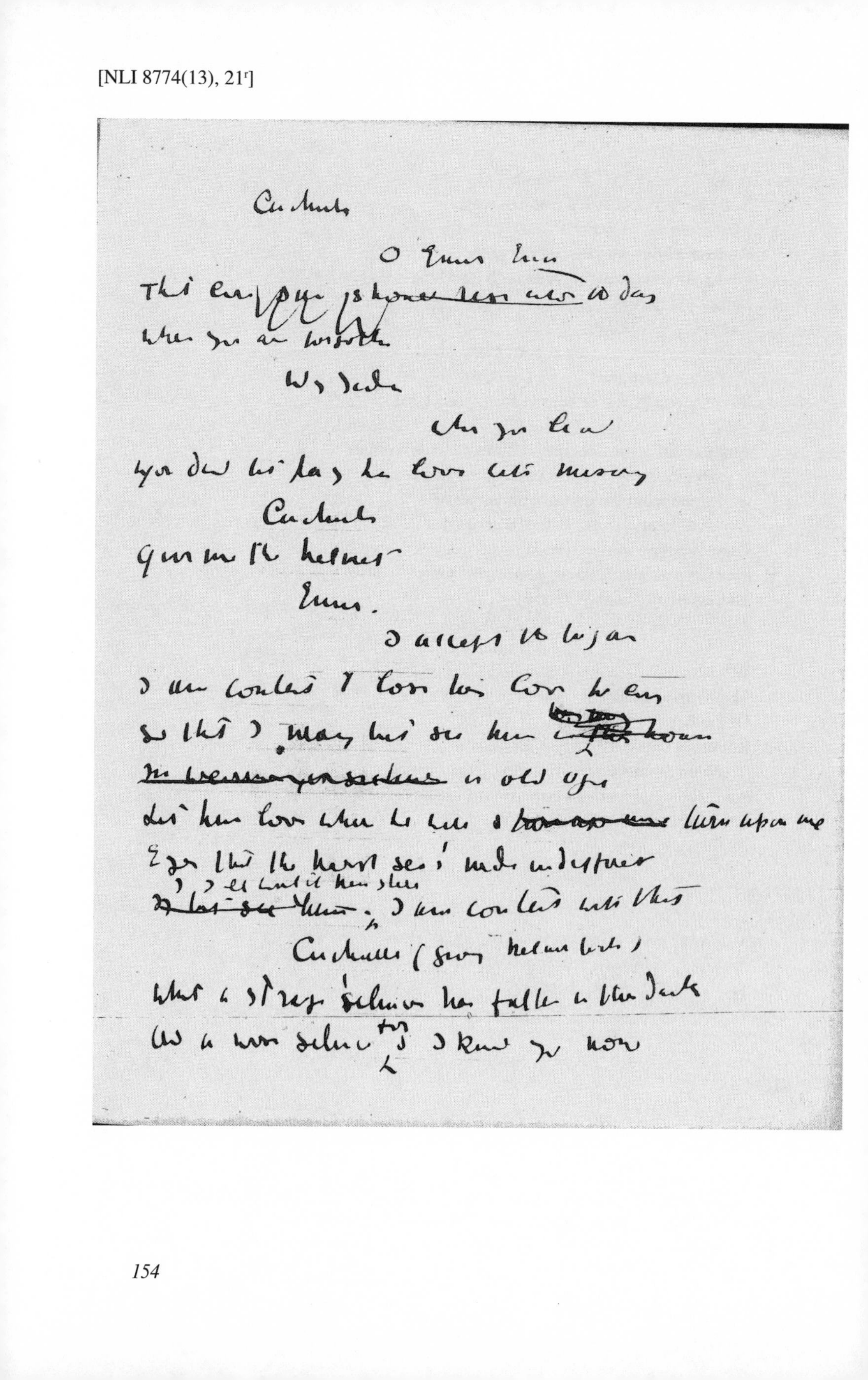

[NLI 8774(13), 21r]

[NLI 8774(13), 21r]

Cuchulain
O Emer Emer
That last sun should rise upon the day
When you are forgotten
W of Sidhe
When you lived
You did but pay her love with misery
Cuchulain
Give me the helmet
Emer.
I accept the bargain
I am content to lose his love for ever
~~in my~~
So that I may but see him ~~in~~^ ~~this~~ ~~house~~
~~In weariness, or sickness~~ or old age
Let him love where he will & ~~turn upon me~~ turn upon me
Eyes that the harsh sea's made indifferent
I I'll watch him still
~~If but see him,~~^ I am content with that
Cuchulain (giving helmet back)
What a strange silence has fallen in this dark
for
And a wise silence^ I know you now

21r, l. 5b Cf. MS F, 11r: "I will pay the price."

[NLI 8774(13), 22r]

[NLI 8774(13), 22r]

In all your ignorance
~~And know that you are ignorant~~ what dread has love
So great as to forget the least poor straw
Once seen in the incredible clear light
She ~~sa~~ cast about her some forlorn lost day.
That face though fair enough is a fools face
For not a wind has blown out of the north
So ~~bitt~~ bitter as the words that you have spoken
the
And there's a folly in^deathless Sidhe
Beyond the reach of man
W of Sidhe
you
I ~~taught~~ told^to forget
After my fashion – you will none of it
you
And so can forget in a man's fashion
~~I give you back your life. You are not dead~~
Go to the king of country under wave
Demand your life of him – you are not dead
I am ashamed that being of the shades
I chose a man whom memory made impure
(C goes)
to Evil Genius

22r, ll. 8–9 These lines were not on MS F, 12r.

[NLI 8774(13), 22^{v}]

[NLI 8774(13), 22^{v}]

To take Cuchulains place & play his part
And wear his image till satiety
Had set me free from a mans bitter love;
And that you chose to work for your own hand.
Some curse that you had laid on him & his
Was more to you than my good will & now

~~and a blight~~
and but a ~~blight~~ vapour
That can rise up & blot the changing moon

22^{v}, ll. 1–6 Lines replace those canceled on 23^{r}.

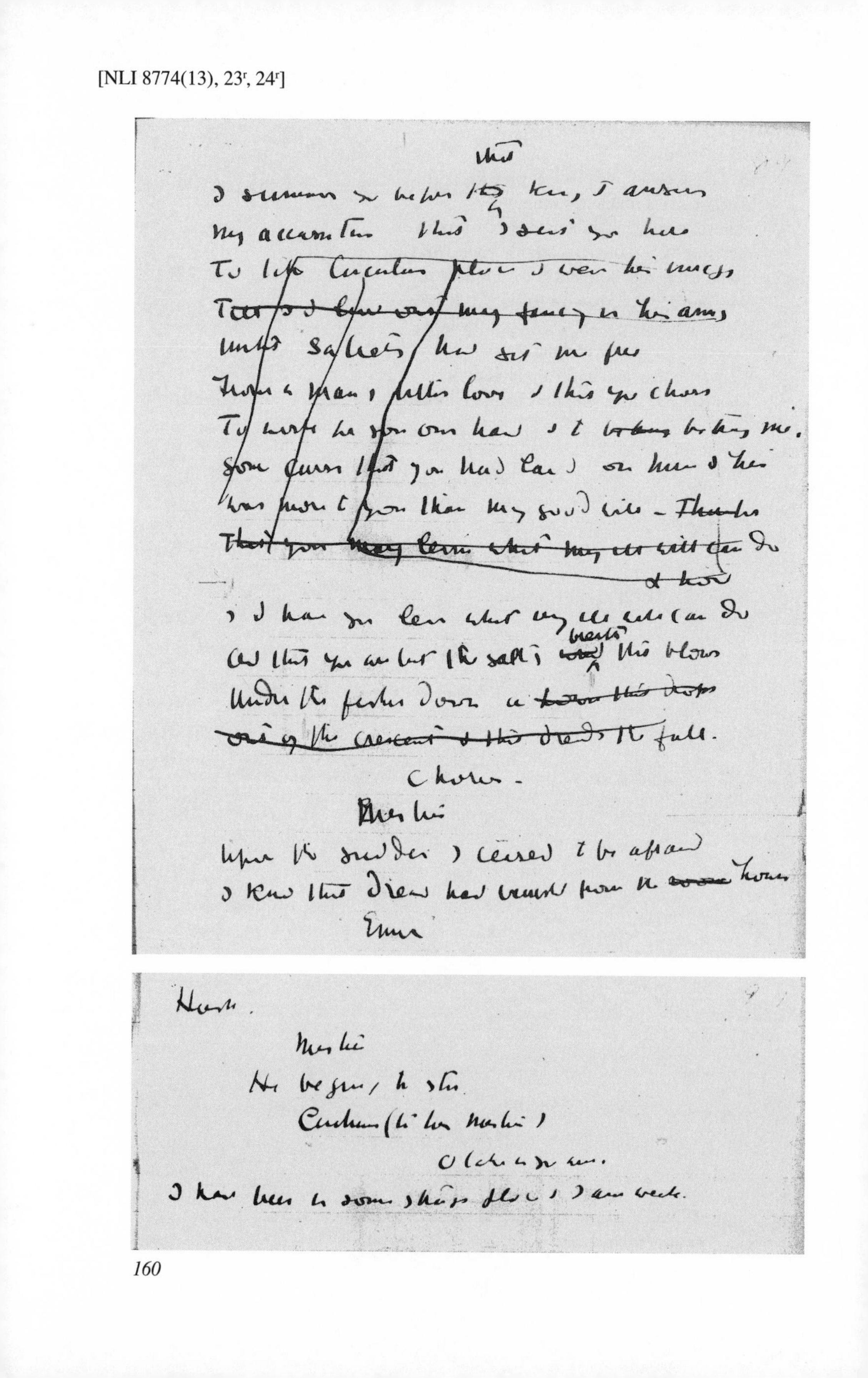

[NLI 8774(13), 23^r, 24^r]

[NLI 8774(13)23^{r}]

that
1 I summon you before ~~this~~ king to an^swer
2 My accusation that I sent you here
3 To take Cuchulains place & wear his image
4 ~~Till I I lived out my fancy in his arms~~
5 Until satiety had set me free
6 From a mans bitter love & that you chose
7 To work for your own hand & to ~~betray~~ betray me.
8 Some curse that you had laid on him & his
9 Was more to you than my good will – ~~Therefore~~
10 ~~That you may learn what my ill will can do~~
~~& how~~
11 I'd have you learn what my ill will can do
breath
12 And that you are but the salty ~~wind~~^ that blows
13 Under the fishers door ~~a power that drops~~
14 ~~Out of the crescent & that dreads the full.~~
Chorus –
Mistress
15 Upon the sudden I ceased to be afraid
16 I knew that dread had vanished from the ~~room~~ house
Emer

[NLI 8774(13), 24^{r}]

1 Hush.
Mistress
He begins to stir
Cuchulain (to his mistress)
O take me in your arms
2 I have been in some strange place & I am weak.

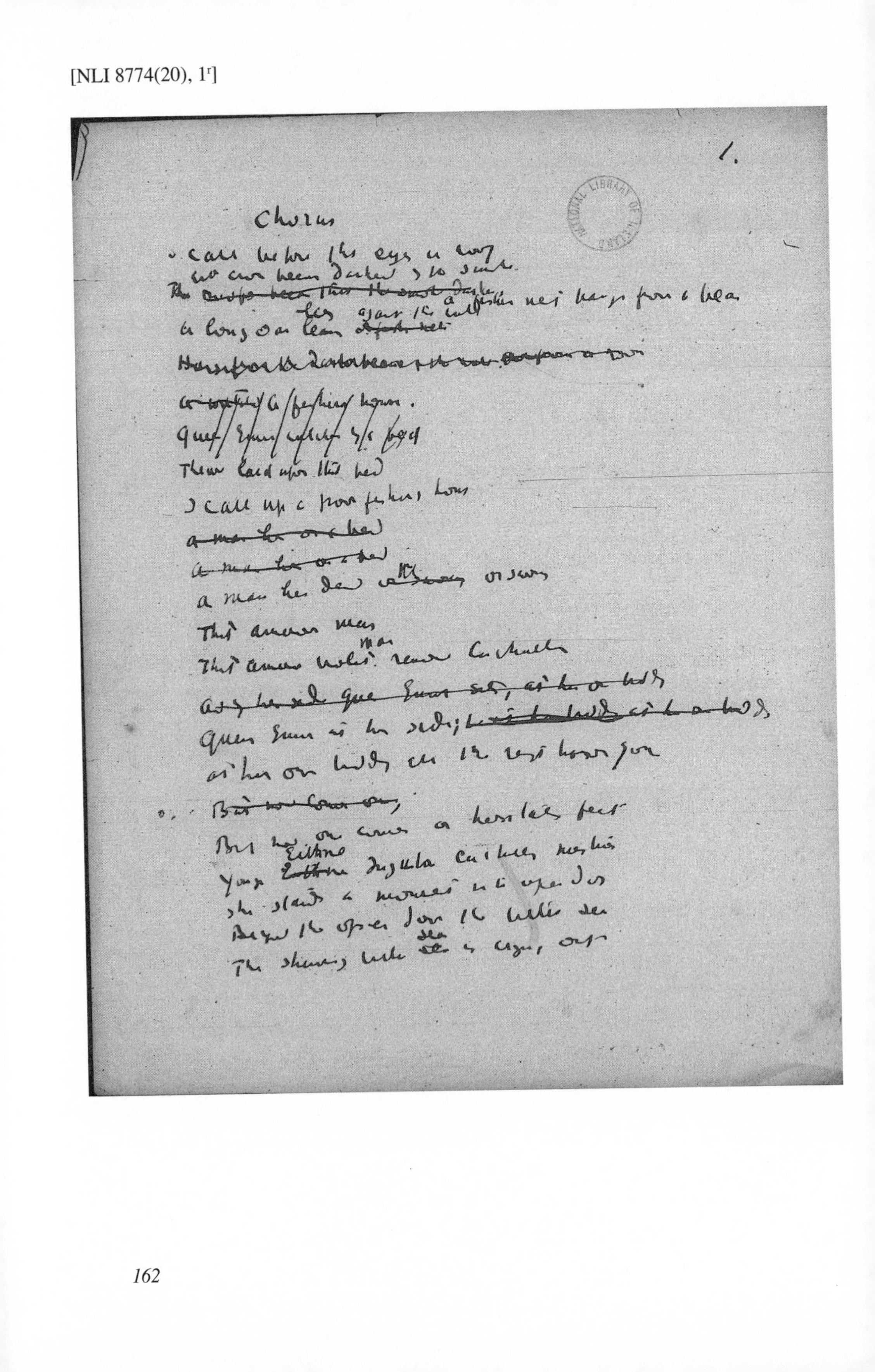

[NLI 8774(20), 1r]

[NLI 8774(20), 1r]

1.

Chorus

1 I call before the eyes a roof
With cross beams darkened by the smoke
2 ~~The roofs beams that the smoke darkens~~
a fishers net hangs from a beam
lies against the wall
3 A long oar ~~leans & fishers nets~~
4 ~~Hang from the dark beams & the wall. And from a room~~
5 ~~A wretched~~ A fishers house.
6 Queen Emer watches by a bed
7 There laid upon that bed
8 I call up a poor fishers house
9 ~~A man lies on a bed~~
10 ~~A man lies on a bed~~
~~for~~
11 A man lies dead ~~or swooning~~ or swooning
12 That amorous man
man
13 That amorous violent renowned Cuchullain
14 ~~And by his side Queen Emer sits, at her own bidding~~
15 Queen Emer at his side; ~~for at her bidding at her own bidding~~
16 At her own bidding all the rest have gone
17 ~~But now comes one~~,
18 But now one comes on hesitating feet
Eithne
19 Young ~~Eathne~~ Inguba Cuchullains mistress
20 She stands a moment in the open door
21 Beyond the open door the bitter sea
sea
22 The shining bitter ~~see~~ is crying out

1r Cf. MS G, 1r above. The new title "Queen Emer" in ll. 6 (canceled) and 15 increases Emer's stature and sets her further apart from Eithne Inguba; similarly Eithne approaches Emer more hesitantly than in previous drafts.

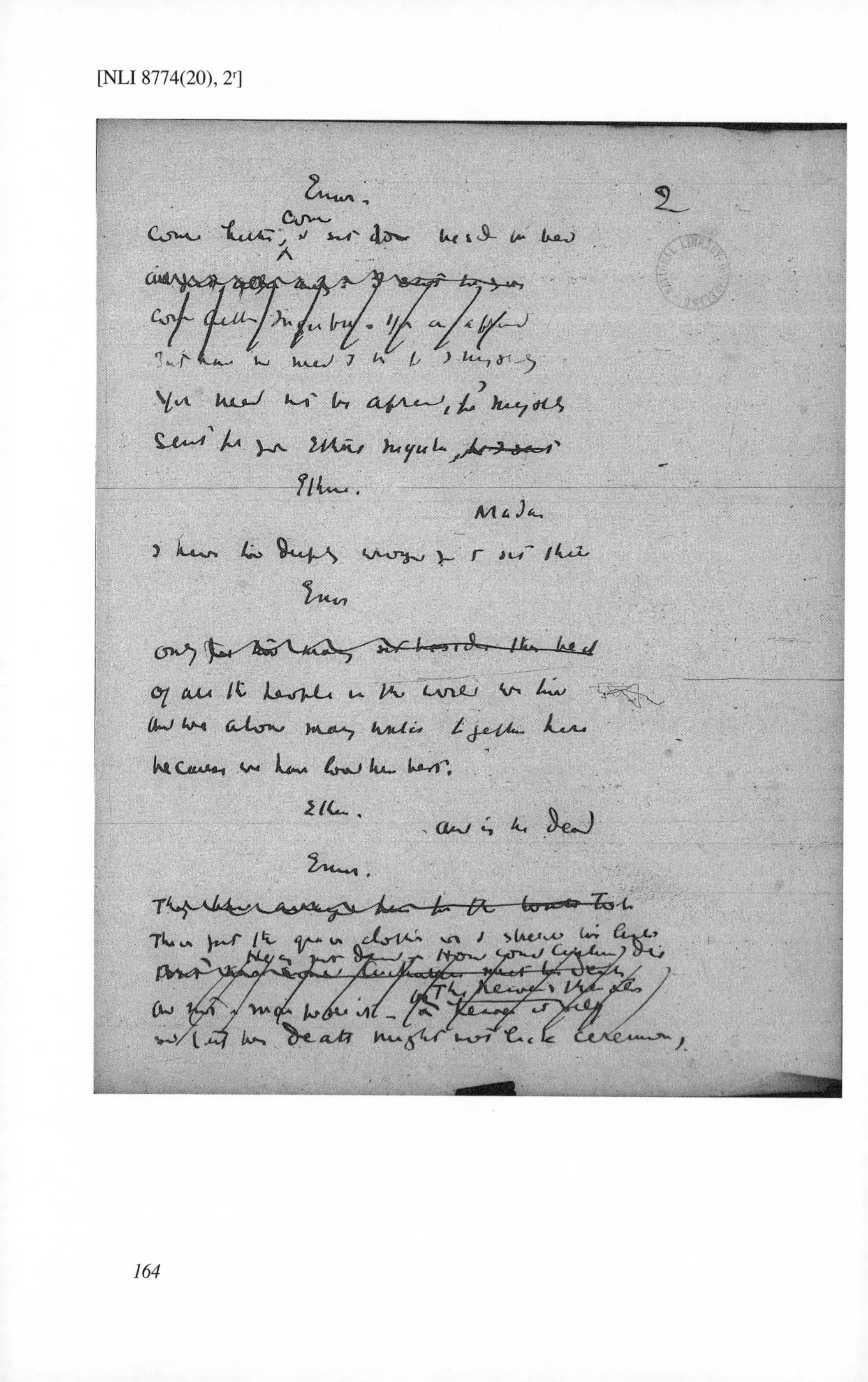

[NLI 8774(20), 2r]

[NLI 8774(20), 2r]

2

Emer.
come
Come hither,^ & sit down beside the bed
~~And put all away : I sent for you~~
Come Eithne Inguba. You are afraid
But have no need to be I myself
I
You need not be afraid, for myself
Sent for you Eithne Inguba, ~~for I sent~~
Eithne
Madam
I have too deeply wronged you to sit there
Emer
~~Only we two may sit beside this bed~~
Of all the people in the world we two
And we alone may watch together here
Because we have loved him best.
Eithne.
And is he dead
Emer.
~~They have arranged him for the tomb to be~~
They've put the grave clothes on & stretched his limbs
He is not dead – How could Cuchullain die
~~But never could Cuchullain meet his death~~
~~As~~ The heavens themselves
And not a man foresee it – ~~& heaven itself~~
So that his death might not lack ceremony

2r, l. 2 For "put all away" read "put all fear away."

13 grave clothes] There may be an echo here of the story of Lazarus. See John 11:44, "And he that was dead came forth, bound hand and foot with grave-clothes."

3

~~[illegible] throw out fires & [illegible]~~

And stretched his limbs Cuchulain is not dead
~~[illegible]~~
The very heavens when that day is at hand
So that his death may not lack ceremony,
Will throw out fires & ~~[illegible]~~ [illegible]
There shall not be a scullion but has known
Like the world end.

Eithne.
~~[illegible]~~
~~[illegible]~~

~~[illegible]~~ How did ~~[illegible]~~ he come to this

Emer.
Towards noon in the assembly of the king
He met with one who seemed a while most dear.
The kings stood round, some quarrel was blown up
He drove him out & killed him on the shore
At Baile's Tree & he who was so killed
Was his own son begot on some wild woman
When he was young or so I have heard it said
And thinking that he knew what man he had killed
And being mad with sorrow he ran out
And to his middle in the sea & while
[illegible] stood before him, his great sword in hand
Fought with the shapeless foam. The kings look on
~~[illegible]~~
And not a ~~[illegible]~~ a king dare stretch an arm, or even
~~[illegible]~~ call, his name, [illegible] from this [illegible]
After the death [illegible] sea, but all stood there
[illegible] dumb [illegible] like cattle in ~~[illegible]~~ a gale.

[NLI 8774(20), 3^r]

3

~~Would throw out fires & marvels~~
And stretched his limbs Cuchullain is not dead
~~The very heavens when that day is at hand~~
So that his death may not lack ~~cele~~ ceremony
Will throw out fires & ~~marvels~~ prodigies
There shall not be a scullion but foreknows it
Like the worlds end.
Eithne
~~You laid~~ on ~~him on this bed~~.
~~What laid him in this swoon~~
~~Emer~~ How did ~~the swoon~~ he come to this
Emer.
Towards noon in the assembly of the kings
He met with one who seemed a while most dear.
The kings stood round, some quarrel was blown up
He drove him out and killed him on the shore
At Baile's Tree & he who was so killed
Was his own son begot on some wild woman
When he was young or so I have heard it said
And there upon knowing what man he had killed
And being mad with sorrow he ran out
And to him middle in the sea a while
With ~~sword~~ shield before him, his great sword in hand
Fought with the shapeless foam. The kings look on
~~And not a man dared speak above his breath~~
And not a ~~man king~~ a king dared stretch an arm, or even
out
~~Or even~~ call ^ his name, to turn him from that war
Upon the deadly sea, but all stood there
In a dumb stupor like cattle in ~~the frost~~ a gale.

3^r, l. 4 For "cele" read "celebration"?
3^r, l. 19 For "look" read "looked."

[NLI 8774(20), 4r]

[NLI 8774(20), 4^{r}]

6 ~~6~~

1 He cannot help but listen.
~~Aeth~~ Eithne.
He loves me me ~~now~~ best
2 Being his newest love but in the end
3 He'll love the woman best, that loved him first
4 And served him through the years when love seemed lost
5 Women like me, when the violent hour's over
flung into some
6 Are ~~thrown into the~~ corner like an old nut shell.
7 Cuchulain listen.
Emer.
No not yet for first
8 I'll cover up that face & hide the sea
9 It's from the sea that the enchantment comes
(covers face)
10 Call to him now.
Eithne
Cuchulain
Emer.
~~Come~~ bend over him
11 Call out dear secrets till you have touched his heart
12 If he lies there, & if he is not there
13 Till you have made him jelous
~~Eath~~ Eithne
Cuchulain listen.

4^{r} Revision of MS G, 5^{r} above; paginated "6" as an indication that it should follow material at the top of MS G, 5, which Yeats had paginated "5." He then altered the pagination of MS G, 6^{r} from "6" to "6b."

6 like an old nut shell] Replaces the image on MS G, 5^{r}: "the foam upon the sailor's beard."

[NLI 8774(15)1v]

[NLI 8774(15)1^{v}]

Do you not know me Cuchulain
C
I saw you once beside a well in my youth
But then you were feathered like a hawk &
fierce to look at now you are gentle,
such a beauty
W
I have come to save you from memory
C.
Then you will set me free from all that binds me.
W
You have ~~for~~ but to kiss my lips
C.
Will nothing remain of all that has made
me wretched. Must I get even those that I
loved in my youth.
W.
When you have kissed my lips, when memory is fled
That's you've won my love for ever & I am all a flame.
C
She that I loved had me a flame
How can men love the perfect.
W.
Here take my head between your hands & kiss me & you shall
be as the gods are

1^{v} Revision of MS G, 14^{r} above. Woman of the Sidhe speaks first.

9 For "get" read "forget."

12 For "that's" read "that's when." The "condition of flame" which spirits achieve when their round of incarnations is complete; see *Per Amica Silentia Lunae* in *Mythologies*.

[NLI 8774(15), 2v]

[NLI 8774(15), 2v]

1 All life shall become still, ~~st~~ perfect & still
C
2 O Emer my wife Emer
W
3 When you lived you were unfaithful to her
4 If you should live you would be unfaithful once more.
5 Never on earth can she or any other woman keep your ~~lit~~ love.
C

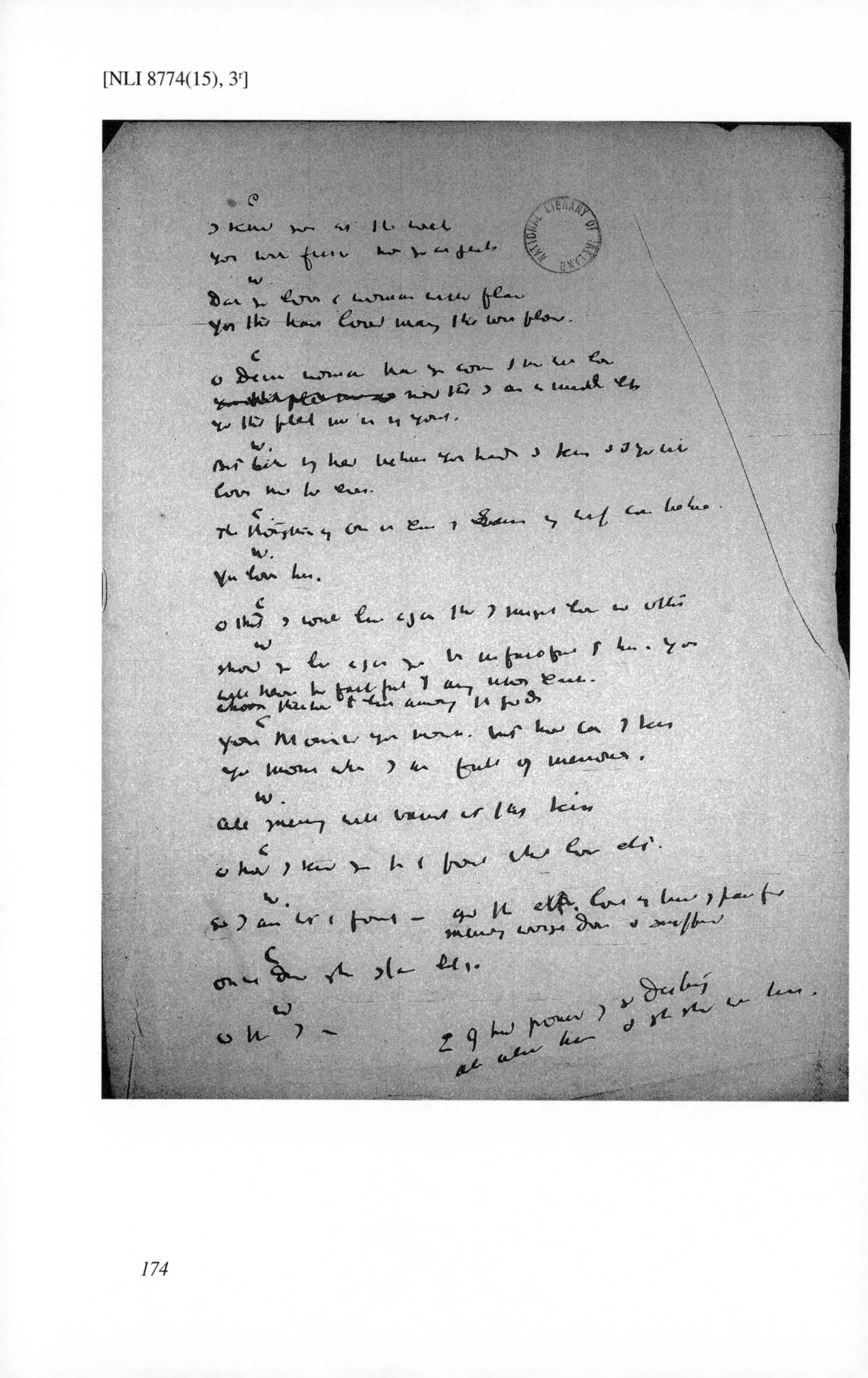

[NLI 8774(15), 3r]

[NLI 8774(15), 3^{r}]

C
I knew you at the well
You were fierce now you are gentle
W.
Dare you love a woman without flaw
You that have loved many that were flawed
C
O Demon woman have you come to me with love
~~You that fled me in~~ Now that I am in middle life
You that fled me in my youth.
W.
But take my head between your hands & kiss me & you will
love me for ever.
C.
The thoughts of one I love of Emer my wife come between
W.
You love her.
C
O that I might live again that I might love no other
W
Should you live again you would be unfaithful to her. You
will never be faithful to any upon earth.
Choose therefore to love among the gods.
C
Your mouth your mouth. But how can I kiss
your mouth when I am full of memories.
W.
All memory will vanish at that kiss
C
O now I know you for a fool what love etc.
W.
So I am but a fool – yet the ~~etc~~. love is but a painful
C memory wrongs done & suffered
Once did she stand etc.
W
O that I –
E G had power of so dealing
all about him & she [?stood with] him

3^{r}, ll. 1–24 Revision of MS I, 1^{r} above.
19 "etc." refers to MS G, 16^{r}, 17^{r} above.
20 For "yet the" read "yet that."
21 "etc." refers to MS G, 19^{r}.

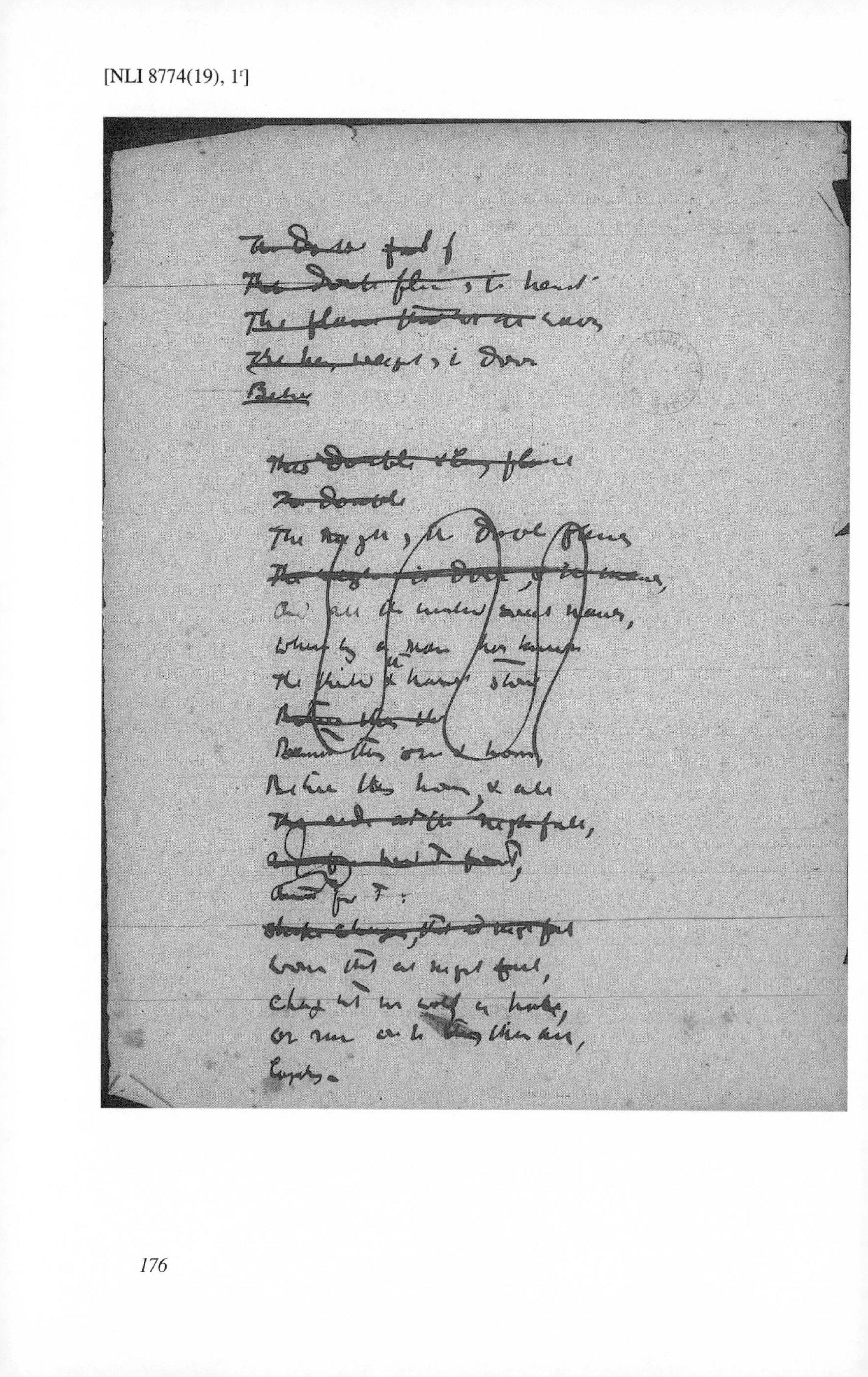

[NLI 8774(19), 1r]

[NLI 8774(19), 1^{r}]

~~The double fal f~~
~~The double flame of the~~ heart
~~The flame that we are~~ weaving
~~The heavy weight~~ of the door
~~Between~~

~~This double & living flame~~
~~This double~~
The height of the double flames
~~The weight of the door, & the names~~,
And all the hundred sweet names,
Where by a man has known
The thick & harsh stone
~~Between this [?]~~
Between this [?house] & home,
Between this house, & all
~~That ride at the nightfall~~,
~~Armed from head to feet~~,
~~Armed~~ for to:
~~Shape changers, that at nightfall~~
Women that at night fall,
Change into the wolf or hawk,
Or run on the ~~thin~~ thin air,
Laughing

[NLI 8774(19), 2r]

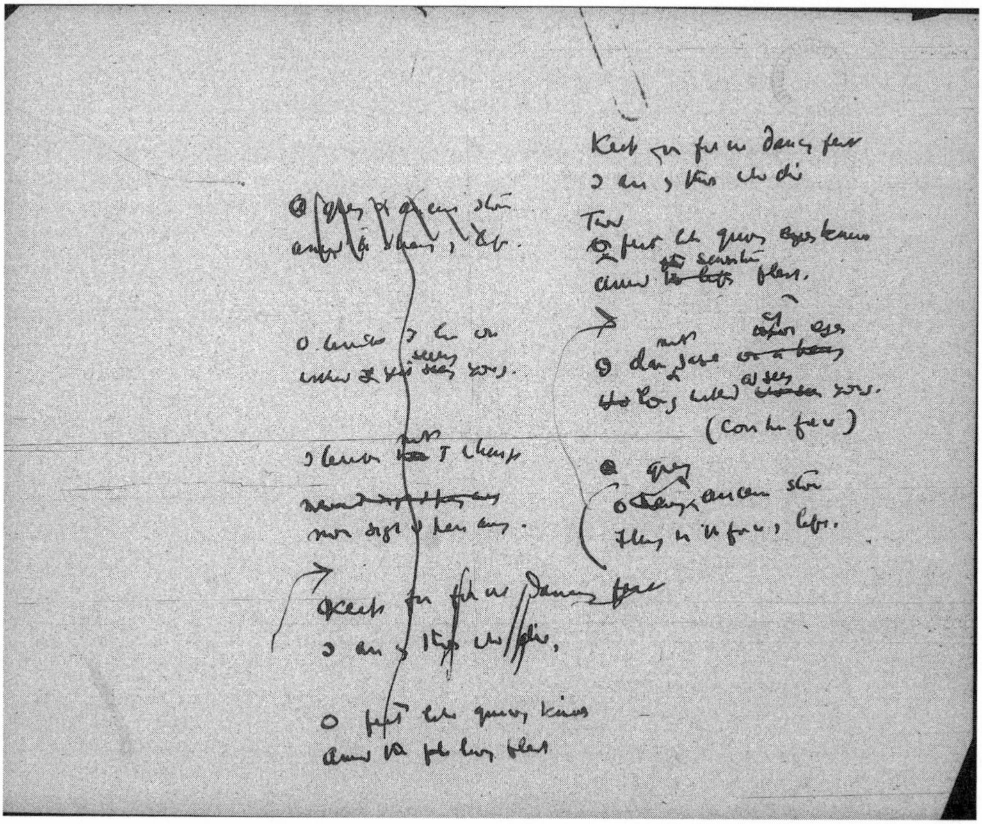

[NLI 8774(19), 2r]

Keep far from me dancing feet
I am of those who die

Two
~~O~~ feet like quivering ~~eyes~~ knives
^~~the~~ sensitive
Amid ~~the life~~ flesh

at
not ~~upon~~ eyes
I dare gaze ~~on a beauty~~
^
and seeming
~~Which~~ long withered ~~which seem~~ young.
(covers his face)
~~O~~ grey
O^heavy ancient stone
Flung in the face of life,

O grey & ancient stone
Amid the striving of life

O terrible to live on
seeming
Withered & yet ~~seem~~ young

not
O terrible ~~never~~ to change
~~Never to sigh & pain away~~
Nor sigh & pain away.

Keep far from me dancing feet
I am of those who die,

O feet like quivering knives
Amid the ~~flesh~~ living flesh

Yeats seems to have begun on the right and continued on the left.

4 For "life" read "life of."

7, 9 grey] The gray hawk of the Sidhe made her first appearance in Yeats's work in the story "The Wisdom of the King," where the witches of the spiritual order, clad in gray, came from "the grey hawk" (from *The Secret Rose* [London: Lawrence & Bullen, 1897]; repr. in *Mythologies* [London, 1959], p. 165). In *At the Hawk's Well*, the Woman of the Sidhe was a "great grey hawk" and her well of immortality was found "among grey boulders" (Alspach, *Variorum Plays*, pp. 406 and 404). Yeats confirmed the hawk's link with the spiritual, subjective order in his 1921 note to *Calvary*: "Certain birds, especially as I see things, such lonely birds as the heron, hawk, eagle, and swan, are the natural symbols of subjectivity" (ibid., p. 789).

[NLI 8774(8), 1r]

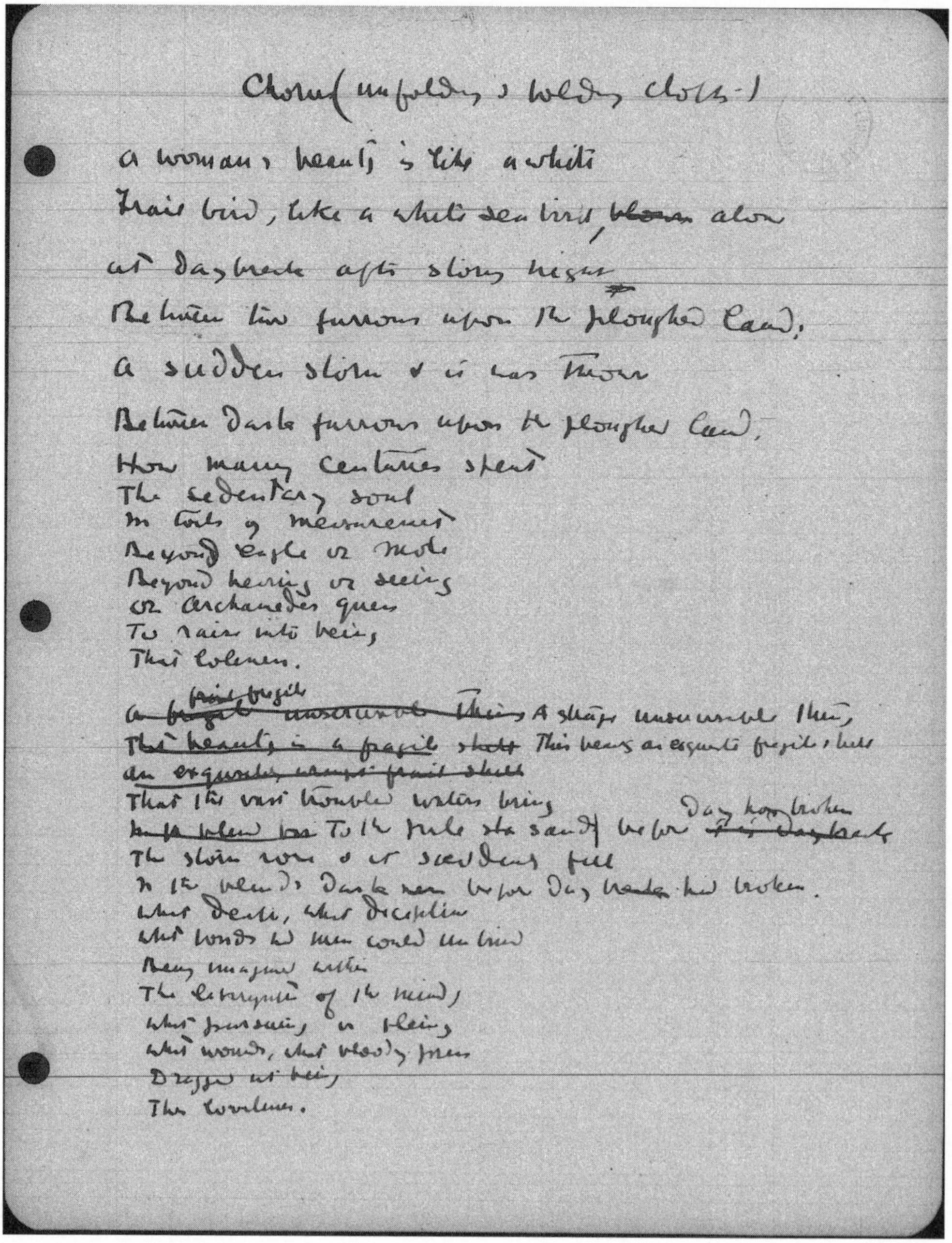

Chorus (unfolding & folding cloth)

A woman's beauty is like a white
Frail bird, like a white sea bird, ~~blown~~ alone
At daybreak after stormy night
Between two furrows upon the ploughed land;
A sudden storm & it was thrown
Between dark furrows upon the ploughed land.
How many centuries spent
The sedentary soul
In toils of measurement
Beyond eagle or mole
Beyond hearing or seeing
Or Archimedes' guess
To raise into being
That loveliness.

~~An fragile unserviceable thing~~ A strange unserviceable thing,
~~The beauty is a fragile shell~~ This beauty is an exquisite fragile shell
~~an exquisite ... frail shell~~
That the vast troubled waters bring
~~...~~ To the pale sea sand before ~~the daybreak~~ Day has broken
The storm rose & it suddenly fell
In the blind dark night before Day had broken.
What death, what discipline
What bonds no man could unbind
Being imagined within
The labyrinth of the mind,
What pursuing or fleeing
What wounds, what bloody press
Dragged into being
This loveliness.

[NLI 8774(8). 1^{r}]

Chorus (unfolding & folding cloth)

A womans beauty is like a white
Frail bird, like a white sea bird, ~~blown~~ alone
At daybreak after stormy night~~,~~
Between two furrows upon the ploughed land:
A sudden storm & it was thrown
Between dark furrows upon the ploughed land.
How many centuries spent
The sedentary soul
In toils of measurement
Beyond eagle or mole
Beyond hearing or seeing
Or Archimedes guess
To raise into being
That loveliness.
~~frail~~ fragile
~~A fragile unserviceable thing~~ A strange unserviceable thing
~~That beauty is a fragile shell~~ This beauty an exquisite fragile
~~An exquisitely wrought frail shell~~
That the vast troubled waters bring
day has broken
~~In the blind dar~~ To the pale sand~~s~~ before ~~it is daybreak~~
The storm rose & it suddenly fell
In the blind darkness before day ~~break~~ had broken
What death, what discipline
What bonds no man could unbind
Being imagined within
The labyrinth of the mind,
What pursuing or fleeing
What wounds, what bloody press
Dragged into being
This loveliness.

MS K, presented here as a continuous recension of several manuscripts, was originally a single set of pages, rearranged and heavily worked over by Yeats. As he continued to revise, MS K was pulled apart and the pieces incorporated with others or laid aside. Much later, the pieces were dispersed to two different archives, the National Library of Ireland and Houghton Library at Harvard University. See pp. xlii above for an outline of the composition of MS K. In what follows, the NLI manuscripts, archived in several folders, are found on pp. 179–181 and 208–247, the Harvard manuscript on pages 182–207 and 248–263.

[Harvard, 1r]

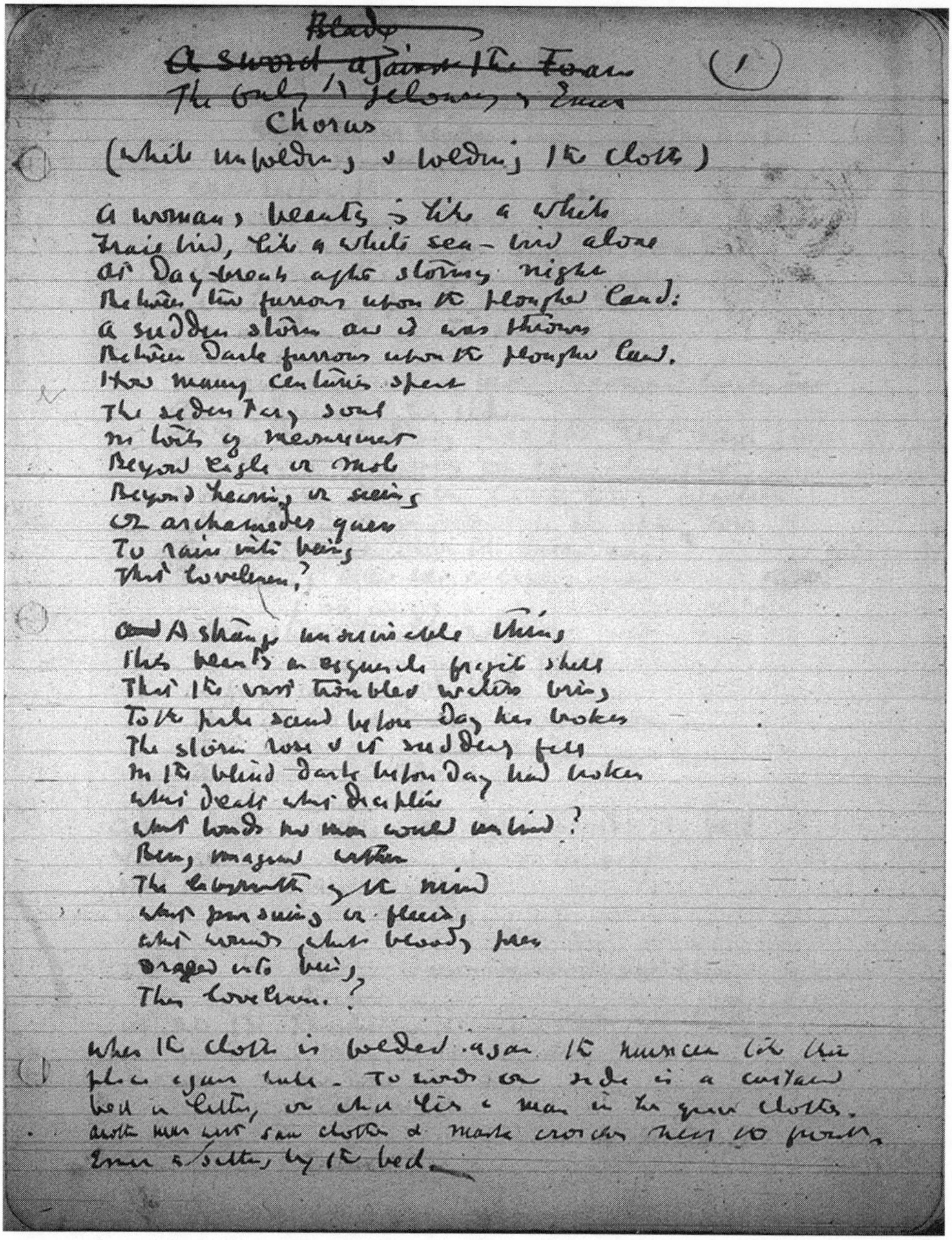

Line numbers in the transcription of Harvard are continuous to reveal the final revised state of this manuscript. Canceled lines, therefore, are not numbered unless they are immediately replaced, an exception to the general practice in this volume. The sequence continues through 12r on p. 207 and picks up again with 28r on pp. 248–249 below.

[Harvard, 1[r]]

~~Blade~~
~~A sword~~^ ~~against the Foam~~ (1)
The Only Jelousy of Emer
Chorus
(while unfolding & folding the cloth)

A woman s beauty is like a white
Frail bird, like a white sea-bird alone
At day-break after stormy night
Between two furrows upon the ploughed land:
A sudden storm and it was thrown
Between dark furrows upon the ploughed land.
How many centuries spent
The sedentary soul
In toils of measurement
Beyond eagle or mole
Beyond hearing or seeing
Or archamedes quest
To raise into being
That loveliness?

~~And~~ A strange unservisable thing
This beauty an exquisite fragile shell
That the vast troubled waters bring
To the pale sand before day has broken
The storm rose & it suddenly fell
In the blind dark before day had broken
What dealt what dicipline
What words no man could unbind?
Being imagined within
The labyrinth of the mind
What pursuing or fleeing
What wounds what bloody press
Dragged into being
This loveliness?

When the cloth is folded again the musicia[?n] take their
place against wall. Towards one side is a curtained
bed or litter, on which lies a man in his grave clothes.
Another man with same clothes & mask crouches near the front.
Emer is sitting by the bed.

1[r] Revision of NLI 8774(8). The deleted first title foreshadows the title Yeats would much later give to the prose version of this play: *Fighting the Waves*. The stage directions at the foot were not found in previous manuscripts.

[Harvard, 2r]

(2

~~Cho~~ Chorus leader
(speaking)
I call before the eyes a roof
With cross-beams darkened by smoke
A fisher's net hangs from a beam
A long oar lies against the wall
I call up a poor fisher's house
A man lies dead or swooning,
That amorous man
That amorous violent man renowned Cuchulain
Queen Emer at his side
At her own bidding all the rest have gone
But now one comes on hesitating feet
Young Eithne Inguba Cuchulain's mistress
She stands a moment in the open door
Beyond the open door the bitter sea
The shining bitter sea is crying out.
(singing)
White shell, white wing
I will not choose for my friend
A frail unserviceable thing
That drifts & dreams, & but knows
That waters are without end
And that wind blows.

Emer
Come hither. come & sit down beside the bed
You need not be afraid for I myself
sent for you Eithne Inguba.

Eithne Inguba.
Madam
I have too deeply wronged you to sit there.

Emer
Of all the people in the world we two
And we alone may watch together here
Because we have loved him best.

Eithne Inguba.
And is he dead

Emer.

[Harvard, 2r]

2

~~Cho~~ Chorus leader
(Speaking)

I call before the eyes a roof
With cross-beams darked by smoke
A fishers net hangs from a beam
A long oar lies against the wall
I call up a poor fishers house
A man lies dead or swooning
That amerous man
That amerous violent man renowned Cuchulain
Queen Emer at his side
At her own bidding all the rest have gone
But now one comes on hesitating feet
Young Eithne Injuba Cuchulain s mistress
She stands a moment in the open door
Beyond the open door the bitter sea
The shining bitter sea is crying out,

(singing)

White shell, white wing
I will not choose for my friend
A frail unserviceable thing
That drifts & dreams & but knows
That waters are without end
And that wind blows.

Emer

Come hither, come & sit down beside the bed
You need not be afraid for I myself
Sent for you Eithne Injuba.

Eithne Injuba.

Madam
I have too deeply wronged you to sit there.

Emer

Of all the people in the world we two
And we alone may watch together here
Because we have loved him best.

Eithne Injuba.

And is he dead

Emer.

28/29 Chorus leader] Cf. Harvard, 1r, above.
44–49 This song was not found in previous manuscripts.

3

Although they have dressed him out in his grave clothes
And stretched his limbs Cuchulain is not dead
The very heavens, when that day's at hand
~~with their own fires, & the earth prodigies~~
So that his death may not lack ceremony
With their own fires, & the earth ~~prodigies~~ grow red with blood
There shall not be a scullion but who knows or
[illegible] the words end.

Eithne Inguba
How did he come to this

Emer
Towards noon in the assembly of the kings
He met with one who seemed a while most dear.
The kings stood round, some quarrel was blown up
He drove him out & killed him on the shore
At Baile's Tree, & he who was so killed
Was his own son begot on some wild woman
When he was young, or so I have heard it said,
And thereupon knowing what man he had killed
And being mad with sorrow he ran out
And to his middle in the sea a while
With shield before him & great sword in hand
Fought with the shapeless foam. The kings looked on
And not a king dared stretch an arm or even
Call out his name to turn him from this war
Upon the deathless sea but all stood there
In a dumb stupor like cattle in a ~~grey~~ gale
Until at last fixing his eyes as though
On a new enemy he waded out
Until the water had swept over him,
But the waves washed his senseless image up
And laid it at this door.

Eithne Inguba
How pale he looks.

Emer
~~He Cuchulain is not dead~~
He is not dead.

Eithne Inguba

[Harvard, 3r]

3

57 Although they have dressed him out in his grave clothes
58 And stretched his limbs Cuchulain is not dead
59 The very heavens when that day's at hand
~~Will throw out fires, & the earth [?prodegies]~~
60 So that his death may not lack ceremony
61 Will throw out fires, & the earth ~~prodigies~~ grow red with blood
62 There shall not be a scullion but foreknows it
63 Like the worlds end.

Eithne Injuba

How did he come to this

Emer

64 Towards noon in the assembly of the Kings
65 He met with one who seemed a while most dear.
66 The kings stood round, some quarrel was blown up
67 He drove him out and killed him on the shore
68 At Bailes Tree and he who was so killed
son ~~child~~
69 Was his own ^~~son~~ begot on some wild woman
70 When he was young, or so I have heard it said,
71 And there upon knowing what man he had killed
72 And being mad with sorrow he ran out
73 And to his middle in the sea a while
74 With shield before him his great sword in hand
75 Faught with the shapeless foam. The Kings looked on
76 And not a king dared stretch an arm or even
77 Call out his name to turn him from that war
78 Upon the deathles sea but all stood there
79 In a dumb stupor like Cattle in a [?~~gag~~] gale
80 Until at last fixing his eyes as though
81 On a new enemy he waded out
82 Until the water had swept over him.
83 But the waves washed his senseless image up
84 And laid it at this door.

Eithne Injuba

How pale he looks.

Emer

~~He Cuchulain is not dead~~
85a He is not dead.

Eithne Injuba

84a Cf. MS G, 4r above: "He is unchanged but pale."

[Harvard, 4r, 3v]

[Harvard, 4r]

89 Or some stark horseman grown to old to ride
90 Among the troops of Mananan son of the Sidhe 4

85b You have not kissed his lips
86 Nor laid his head upon your breast.
Emer.
It may be
87 An image has been put into his place
88 A seaborn log bewitched but his likenes
89 ~~Or some strange phantom grown too old to drive~~
90 ~~The holy flocks in [?coverts]~~ under wave
91 Now that its joints are stiff.
Eithne.
Cry out his name
~~He may be close at hand & should he hear~~
~~He might being angry drive the changling o~~ut.
~~Emer~~.
92 All that are taken from our sight, they say,
93 Loiter amid the scenery of their lives
94 For certain hours or days ~~but it is~~ hard
~~To make them hear or see amid their darkness~~
~~And it is long since I could call him home~~
, ^ And should he hear
95 He might being angry drive the changeling out.
Emer
96 It is hard to make them hear amid their darkness
97 And it is long since I could call him home
98 I am but his wife, but if you cry aloud
99 With that sweet voice that is so dear to him
100 He cannot help but listen.
Eithne Injuba.
He loves me best
101 ~~But in the~~ Being his newest love but in the end
102 Hell love the woman best that loved him first
103 And loved him through the years when love seemd lost
Emer
104 I have that hope & the hope that some day & some where
105 We'll sit together at the hearth again.
Eithne Injuba
106 Women like me when the violent hour is over
107 Are flung into some corner like old nut shells
108 Cuchulain listen.
Emer
No not yet for first
109 Ill cover up his face to ~~see~~ hide it [?so],

89–90 Two lines are inscribed on 3v (shown opposite) with an arrow pointing towards the deleted ll. 89–90: "Or some stark horseman grows old to ride / Among the troops of Mananan son of the sea" (for "old" read "too old").

91b The reference to Cuchulain's being "the first champion in the world" on MS G, 4r above has been dropped.

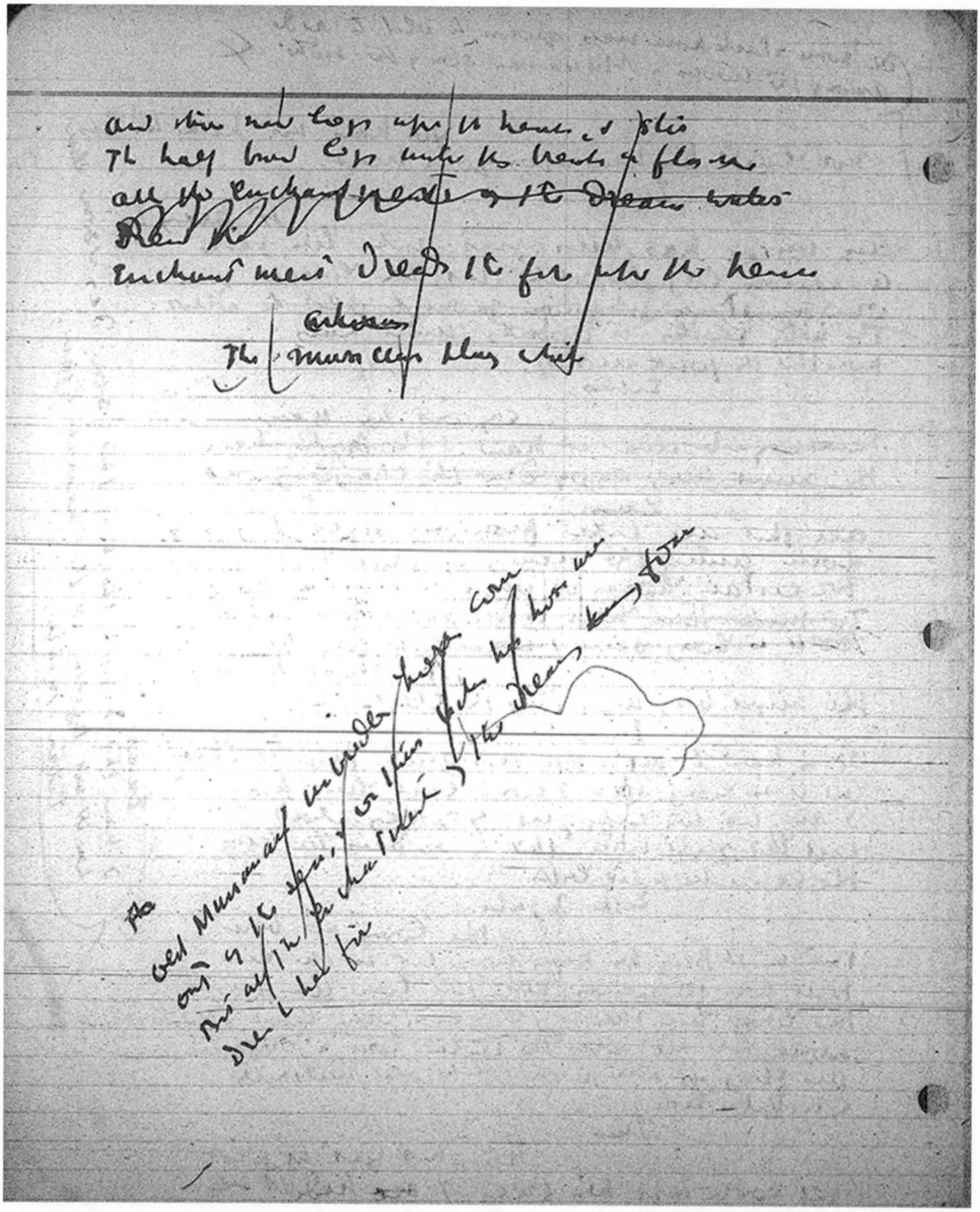

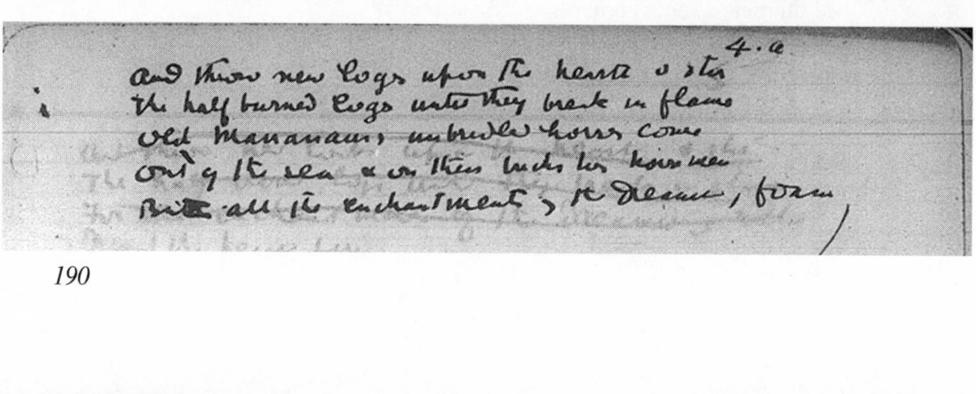

[Harvard, 4^v, 5^r]

[Harvard, 4^{v}]

And throw new logs upon the fire, & stir
 The half burned logs until they break in flame
~~All the enchantments of the dreaming water~~
 [?~~Rend the~~]
Enchantment dreads the fire when the [?heavens]

~~Chorus~~
The musicians play while

[?~~The~~]
Old Mananan unbridled horses come
Out of the sea, & on their backs his horsemen
But all the enchantments of the dreaming [~~?~~] foam
[?Drea th hea fire]

[Harvard, 5^{r}]

4.a

And throw new logs upon the hearth & stir
The half burned logs until they break in flame
Old Mananans unbridled horses come
Out of the sea & on their backs his horsemen
But[~~?~~] all the enchantments of the dreaming foam

4^{v} Enchantment dreads the fire] There was no such mention of fire in Manuscript H. Cf. Lady Wilde, *Ancient Legends*, I, p. 71: "Fire is a great preventative against fairy magic, for fire is the most sacred of all created things, and man alone has power over it. . . . And the spirit of the fire is certain to destroy all fairy magic, if it exist."

[Harvard, 6^{r}]

The order of composition of the next few pages is complex. Yeats wrote the entire page 6^{r}. Then he revised this and the next line on 4^{v}, writing in his light, "tentative" hand diagonally across the page. Then he wrote his final revision on the facing 3^{v} and again at the top of 5^{r} for insertion into the text. But he had earlier transcribed 7^{r} (paginated "6") following 5^{r} (paginated "4"). He then revised the first lines of 7^{r} on the facing verso, 5^{v}, altered these revisions, and then inserted his final version on a clean sheet 6^{r} (paginated "4a") between 5^{r} and 7^{r}.

[Harvard, 6r]

5

~~And throw new logs upon the fire & stir~~
~~The half burned logs until they break in flame~~
~~For all enchantments of the dreaming water~~
115 Dread the hearth fire.

(She goes to one side of platform & moves her hands as ~~though~~ though putting logs on a fire and stirring it to a blaze. While she makes these movements the musicians ~~accomanying~~ play, marking the movements with drums & flute ~~[?&] Having f~~ perhaps. Having finished she stands beside the imaginary fire at a little distance from Cuchulain & Eithne Injuba)

~~Call to him now~~ Call on Cuchulain now

~~Eithne In~~

Eithne Injuba.

116 Can you not hear my voice.

Emer.

Bend over him
117 Call out dear secrets till you have touched his heart
118 If he lies there; and if he is not there
119 Till you have made him jelous.

Eithne Injuba

Cuchulain listen

Emer.

120 You speak too timidly: to be afraid
121 Because his wife is but three paces off
122 When there is so great a need were but to prove
123 The man that chose you made but a poor choice.
124 We're but two women struggling with the sea.

Eithne Injuba.

125 O my beloved pardon me that I
126 Have been ashamed & you in so great need
127 I have never sent a message or called out
128 Scarce had a longing for your company
129 But you have known & come; & if indeed
130 You are lying there stretch out your arms & speak
131 Open your mouth & speak for to this hour
132 My company has made you talkative.

119b Last line of MS H, 4r above. Emer's following speech was not in MS G.
128 Cf. MS G, 6r above.

[Harvard, 6v]

[Harvard, 6v]

Emer

~~When~~
What do come for & from where?

F C.

I have come
From Mananans Court upon a bridleless horse.

Emer

What one among the Sidhe has dared to lie
Upon Cuchulains bed & take his image

F C.

~~Bri~~ I am named Bricriu – not the man, that Bricriu
Maker of discord among gods & men
Called Bricriu of the Sidhe

Emer.

Come for what purpose.?

6v contains revision work done after the manuscript was first written. Yeats revised the preceding canceled passage on 7r on the facing verso, 6v, then rewrote his revisions on the interpolated clean sheet 8r (which he paginated "6a").

Bricriu was the Irish version of the Greek Até. He tried to stir up discord between Cuchulain and the men of Ulster in the story "Bricriu's Feast," source of *The Green Helmet*. This reappearance of an adversary of Cuchulain from an earlier play in the cycle suggests a deliberate link, for in Irish mythology there is no "Bricriu of the Sidhe."

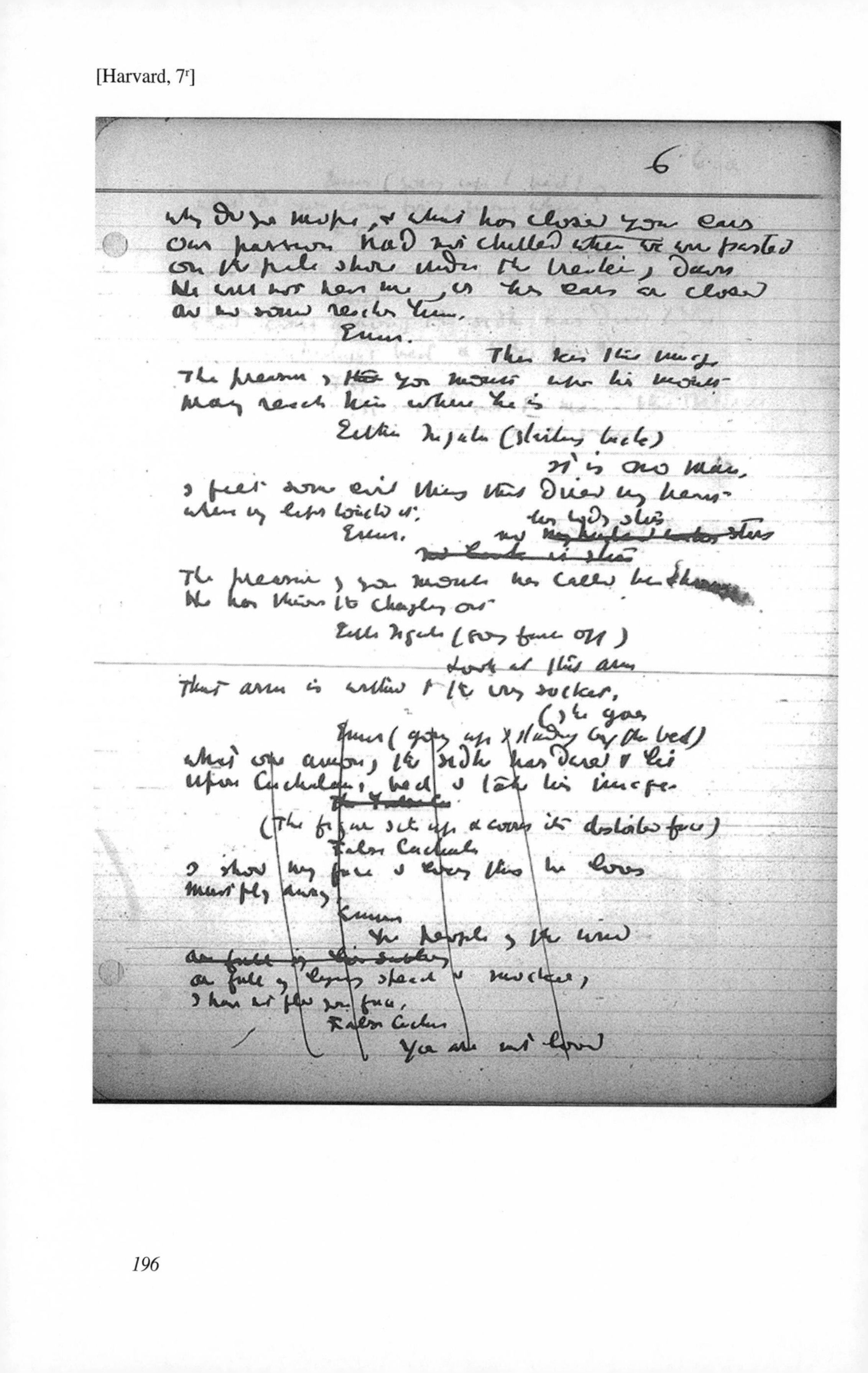

[Harvard, 7r]

[Harvard, 7^{r}]

6

133 Why do you mope, & what has closed your ears
134 Our passion had not chilled when we were parted
135 On the pale shore under the breaking dawn
136 He will not hear me, or his ears are closed
137 And no sound reaches him.

Emer

Then kiss that image

138 The pressure of ~~that~~ your mouth upon his mouth
139 May reach him where he is

Eithne Injuba (starting back)

It is no man,

140 I felt some evil thing that dried my heart
141 When my lips touched it.

his body stirs

Emer . no ~~my husband wakes~~ ~~st~~irs

~~No look it stirs~~

142 The pressure of your mouth has called him [?home]
143 He has thrown the changling out

Eithne Injuba (going further off)

Look at that arm

144 That arm is withered to the very socket.

(she goes

Emer (going up and standing by the bed)

What one among the Sidhe has dared to lie
Upon Cuchulains bed & take his image.

~~The False Cu~~

(The figure sits up & covers its distorted face)

False Cuchulain

I show my face & every thing he loves
Must fly away.

Emer

You people of the wind

~~Are full of this [?subtlety]~~
Are full of lying speach and mockery
I have not fled your face.

False Cuchulain

You are not loved

---

135 This line adds detail to MS G, 6^{r}, "When we were parted at the dawn of day"; it also recalls the imagery of the opening song.

143b Detail not found in MS G.

144*sd* (The figure . . . face)] Stage direction not in MS G.

Emer's canceled final speech not in MS G.

[Harvard, 8r]

[Harvard, 8r]

6 a

Emer (going up to bed)
145 What do you come for & from where?
F C.
I have come
146 From Mananaun s court upon a bridleless horse
Emer
147 What one among the Sidhe has dared to lie
148 Upon Cuchulain s bed & take his image?
F C.
149 I am named Bricriu – not the man – the Bricriu
150 Maker of discord among gods & men
151 Called Bricriu of the Sidhe.
Emer.
Come for what purpose
(figure sits up & shows its distorted face)
FC
152 I show my face and everything he loves
153 Must fly away
Emer
You people of the wind
154 Are full of lying speach & mockery
155 I have not fled your face
FC.
You are not loved.

151–155 These lines replace the canceled passage on 7r, an action probably indicated by the curved line in the right margin.

151*sd* Corrects the canceled stage direction of 7r: "covers."

[Harvard, 9r]

[Harvard, 9^{r}]

~~5~~ 7

Emer.

156 And therefore has no dread to meet your eyes
157 And to demand him of you.

False Cuchulain.

For that I have come
158 You have but to pay the price & he is free

Emer

159 Do the Sidhe bargain?

False Cuculain

When they set free a captive
160 They take in ransom ~~some~~ a less valued thing.
161 The fisher when some knowledgable man
162 Restores to him his wife or son or ~~daug~~ daughter
163 Knows he must ~~love~~ lose a boat or net, or it may be
164 The cow that gives his children milk & some
165 Have offered their own lives. I do not ask
166 Your life or any valulable thing.
167 You spoke but now of the mere chance that someday day
hearth
168 You 'd sit together by the [?~~heart~~] again.
169 Renounce that chance, that miserable hope
170 And he shall live again.

Emer.

~~On me alone~~
~~[?] You have of all that he gave love to us that love him~~
I do not question loves
171 But you have brought ill luck on all ~~he has loved~~ he ~~loves~~
~~[?] And now because you have~~ no
172 And now, because I am beyond your power
173 Unless your words are lies you come to bargain

False Cuchulain.

174 ~~You~~ You loved your power when but newly married
175 And I love mine although I am old & withered;
that
176 You have but to put your self into [?~~its~~] power
^
177 And he shall live again.

Emer.

Never never

False Cuchulain

178 You dare not be accursed yet he has dared

---

163 Cf. MS G, 8^{r} above: "pot"; a net is more precious.

174–175 These two lines were not in MS G.

177 Drops the unnecessary preceding line of MS G, 9^{r} above: "Of your own will & in that matter only."

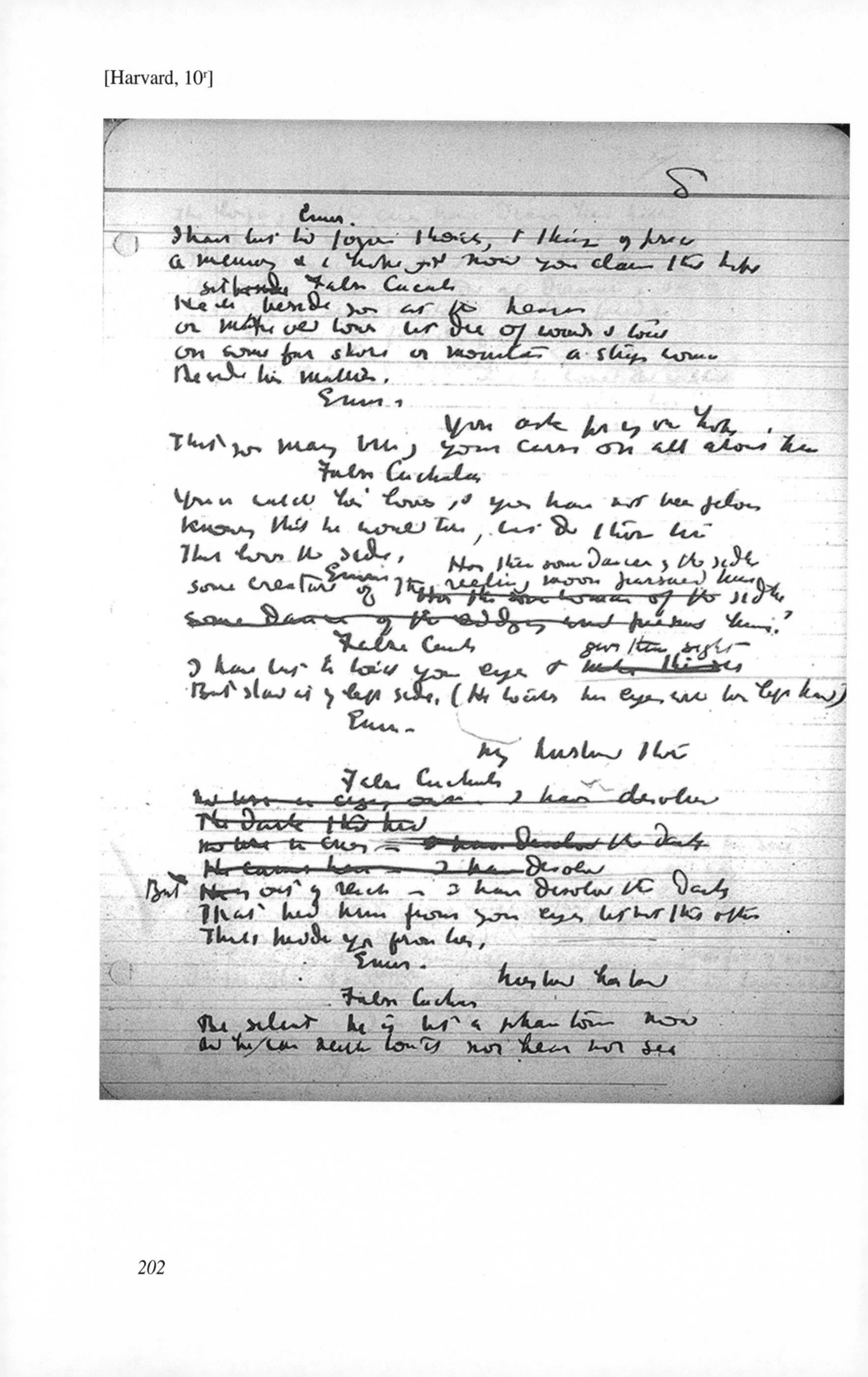

[Harvard, 10r]

[Harvard, 10[r]]

8

Emer.
179 I have but two joyous thoughts, t things I prize
180 A memory & a hope yet now you claim that hope
False Cuchulain
sit ~~beside~~
181 He ll ^ beside you at the hearth
182 Or make old bones but die of wounds & toil
183 On some far shore or mountain a strange woman
184 Beside his mattress.
Emer
You ask for my one hope
185 That you may bring your curse on all about him
False Cuchulain
186 Youve watched his loves, & you have not been jelous
187 Knowing that he would tire, but do those tire
188 That love the Sidhe.
Has then some dancer of the Sidhe
Emer
189 Some creature of the reeling moon pursued him
~~Has then some woman of the~~ Sidhe,
~~Some dancer of the eddying wind pursued~~ him?
False Cuchulain
give them sight
190 I have but to touch your eyes & ~~make them see~~
191 But stand at my left side. (He touches her eyes with his left hand)
Emer.
My husband there
False Cuchulain
~~No use in [? cryying] out – I have dissolved~~
~~The dark that hid~~
~~No use in cries – I have dissolved~~
~~He cannot hear – I have dissolved~~
192 But ~~He~~ is out of reach – I have dissolved the dark
193 That hid him from your eyes but not that other
194 Thats hidden you from him.
Emer.
Husband husband
False Cuchulain
195 Be silent he is but a phantom now
196 And he can neither touch nor hear nor see

179–180 Condenses the "two joyous thoughts" of MS G, 9[r], 10[r].
188b–189 Lines not in MS G; Yeats continues to add lunar imagery.

[Harvard, 11^{r}]

Notes to transcription on facing page:

215b Expansion of MS G, 12^{v} above: "I know her sort."

222 This knife was not found in previous manuscripts; in the sources Emer threatened Fand with a knife.

223*sd* Presumably Yeats added this stage direction after he had finished MS K, as a comparison seems intended here with the closing song.

[Harvard, 11r]

9

197 The longing and the cries have drawn him hither
198 He heard no sound, heard no articulate sound
199 They could banish rest, & make him dream
200 And in that dream as do all dreaming shades
201 Before they are accustomed to their freedom
202 He has taken his familiar form & yet
203 He crouches there no knowing where he is
whose he is crouched
204 Or at ~~whose~~ side, ~~or what he would do if that~~
(The Woman of the Sidhe has
entered & stands a little inside the door)
~~Emer~~ Emer
~~Who is this woman~~ Who is this woman?
False Cuchulain
205 She has hurried from the Country under wave
206 And dreamed herself into that shape that he
207 May glitter in her basket; for the Sidhe
208 Are fishers also and they fish for men
209 With dreams upon the hook.
Emer
And so that woman
210 Has had herself in this disguise & made
211 Herself into [?~~into~~] a lie.
False Cuchulain
A dream is body
212 The dead move ever toward a dreamless youth
213 And when they dream no more return no more
214 And those more holy shades that never lived
215 But visit you in dreams
Emer
[?~~Our men awake~~] I know her sort
216 They find our men a sleep, weary with war
217 Or weary with the chase & kiss their lips
drop their hair upon them
218 ~~hide~~/ And ~~[?flood] them with their hair~~, & from the hour
219 Our men, who yet know nothing of it all, we press
220 Are lonely, & when ~~we fold them in our arms~~^ at fall of night^
upon
221 ~~And press~~ Their hands^ on our ~~those hearts are cold~~ hearts those hearts are cold
False Cuchulain (leaving)
222 And so you think to wound her with a knife
~~Shes un[?bridelike]~~ = look & listen
223 She has an airy body

[Harvard, 12^{r}]

Lines of the canceled passage, [2]–[16], partly reinstated in later versions of the play, are numbered for ease of reference.

[1] The line does not appear on MS G, 13^{r} above; though it is uncanceled here, Yeats did not carry it over to the finally revised version.

[4] Why do you turn] Cf. MS G, 14^{r} above.

[Harvard, 12r]

10

Her mask & clothes must suggest gold or
bronze or brass or silver, so that she seems more
an idol than a human being. This suggestion may
be repeated in her movement. Her hair must keep the metal suggestion.

224 I have not given you eyes & ears for nothing

Emer

~~I may learn how to [?thwart] her yet~~

[1] I may learn how to [?thwart] her if I am patient

(The woman of the Sidhe moves ~~slowly~~
round Cuchulain in a dance that grows
gradually quicker, as he [?sho] slowly awakes.
~~She may~~ act at moments she may drop his
hair upon her for head, but she does not kiss
him. She is accompanied by string & flute & drum.
~~Her mask~~ ~~may be of gold, or of some~~

Cuchulain.

[2] ~~[?or] [?] but must keep a distance from life.~~

[3] The ~~[?hair] [?here] must have a certain strageness~~

Cuchulain

[4] Why do you turn about me like that ~~wind~~ moon

[5] ~~That makes the stars & dust whirl on the road~~

[6] Turning & smiling, & shaking as you turn

[7] Faint light out of your limbs & hair

[?sunny]

[8] In my young days I met you at a well

[9] Under [?] thorn trees on a mountain side

[10] When your unsmiling eyes & a hawkes wing

[11] Where have you dropped your quills

Woman of Sidhe

Look well – look well

[12] And judge if I be friend or enemy

Cuchlain

[13] What is your name & country

Woman of Sidhe

Since you were born

[14] I have been close at hand now dim now bright

[15] According as your eyes were turned upon me

[16] Or turned away.

Cuchulain

O Beautiful woman

See the notes on the facing page.

[NLI 8774(14), 13[r]]

[NLI 8774(14), 13r]

11

How could you gather up my light like a moon
When but for that brief dance at the well side
I have never met you like this moment.

Woman of Sidhe

And yet
There was a day when we had but one being
Nor had I ~~Cuchulain~~ claws & feather on that day

Cuchulain

One loves & one forgets but not such beauty

Woman of Sidhe

Have you not heard that man before his birth
Is two in one: the yoke & the white of the egg
And that one half is born in wretchedness
While the other half remains amid the sidhe

Cuchulain

I have heard the learned say so

Woman of Sidhe

And have they told you
That the half born into the flesh must seek
For the half it could but find among the sidhe
In ~~Of~~ Woman that are its image in a glass
~~And loves the more, the more the image seems~~
And loves the more the closer they resemble
Its separated half.

Cuchulain

The learned say so
Because they have understanding & no bowels
For what can understanding know of life.
We eat it & it makes us sick or well.

Woman of the Sidhe

You have sought perfection & to every man
There can be nothing perfect but that half
That hovers amid the sidhe.

Cuchulain

Lady although
My loves have been as brief as violets
They have stayed too long for that. What woman
Could satisfy that thirst beyond a day.

---

1 Cf. MS G, 15r above.

5 "Cuchulain" was entered first as a speaker tag, then canceled and the line written around it.

14 For "Woman" read "women."

[NLI 8774(14), 14r]

[NLI 8774(14), 14r]

12

that
It may be^in my first youth I loved so
But no such love has doubled up my body
And kept me in this darkness with my head
Bowed on my knees.
Woman of the Sidhe
~~have you not~~
And yet ~~But you^loved beauty~~ X
you have loved beauty
Cuchulain
~~I have~~
I have loved it, & begotten it many times
For it is nothing when its but a hand
That leads us almost to its opposite.
You never can have loved unless you know
It's the imperfect that we love. Man loves
Some weakness he protects as the horn lanthorn
Upon the table in the fishers house
Protects the candle flame.
Woman of Sidhe
Is love but pity?
Cuchulain
It think it pity that is driven to frenzy
Woman of Sidhe
You love that pale faced girl whose troubled eyes
Display the passion shaken heart.
Cuchulain
I have loved her
In bitterness & loved her like before
But theres a woman in whom strength can be
Weaker than weakness itself.
Woman of Sidhe (with a shrinking movement)
Your ~~fi~~ wife?
Cuchulain
O that I would but live again & be
The sheltering horn.
Woman of Sidhe
Cuchulain I have come
To bring you where men love & yet are happy
To love the flame because we are the horn
Or love the horn because we are the flame

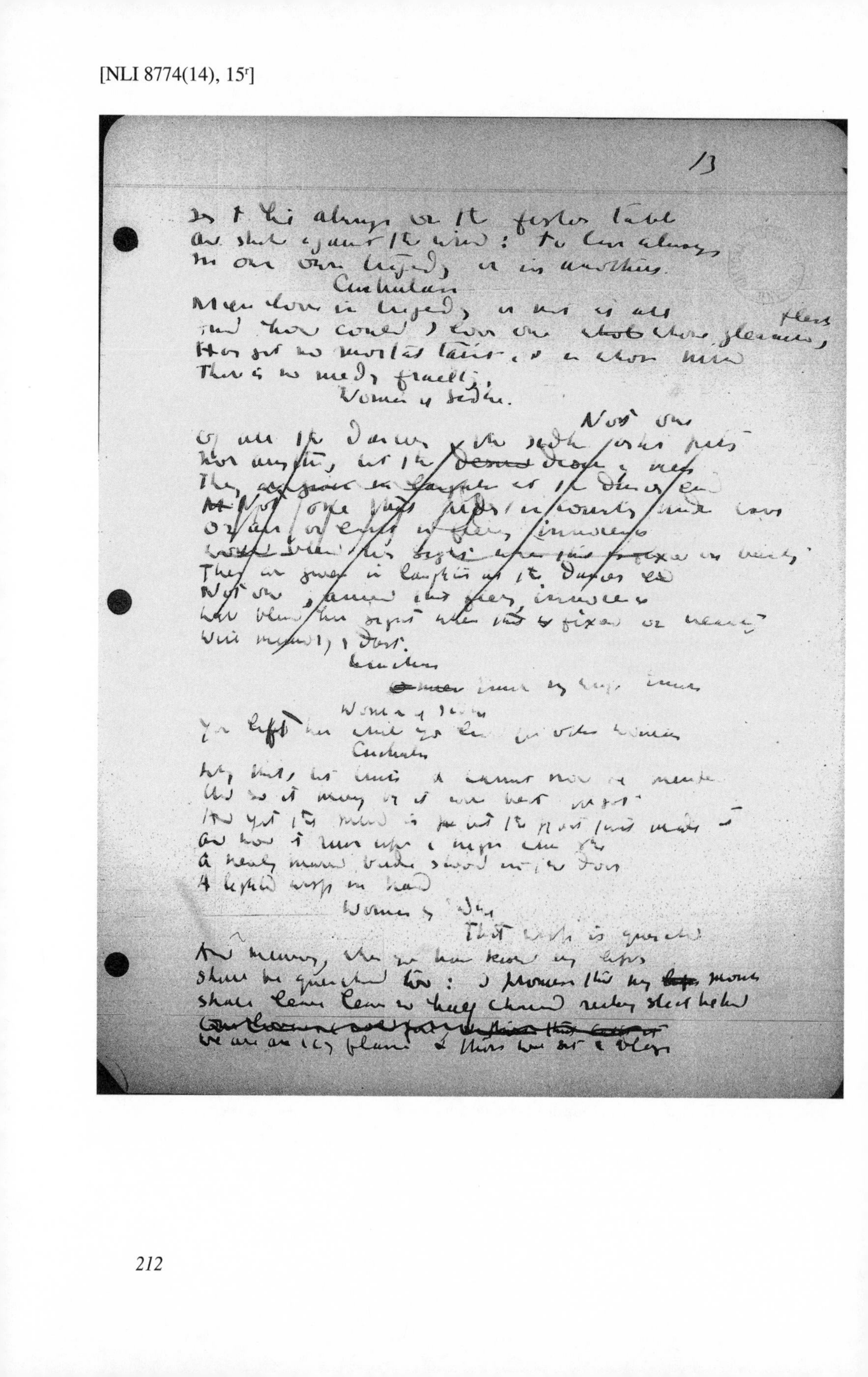

[NLI 8774(14), 15r]

[NLI 8774(14). 15r]

13

Is to lie always on the fishers table
And shake against the wind : to live always
In our own tragedy or in anothers.

Cuchulain

Men love in tragedy or not at all   flesh
But how could I love one ~~whole~~ whose gleaming
Has got no mortal taint, & in whose mind
There is no needy frailty.

Woman of Sidhe

Not one
Of all the dancers of the sidhe asks pity
Nor anything but the ~~desired~~ desire of men
They ~~are given in laughter~~ at the dances end
~~N~~ Not one that rides in country under wave
Or air or earth in fiery innocence
Would blind his ~~sight when that is fixed~~ on beauty
They are given in laughter at the dances end
Not one amid that fiery innocence
Will blind his sight when that is fixed on beauty
With memorys dust.

Cuchulain

~~O Emer~~ Emer my wife Emer

Woman of Sidhe

You left her while you lived for other women

Cuchulain

Why that but truth & cannot now be mended
And so it may be it were best forgot
And yet the mind is ~~from~~ but the past that made it
And now it runs upon a night when she
A newly married bride stood in the door
A lighted wisp in hand

Woman of Sidhe

That wisp is quenched
And memory, when you have kissed my lips
Shall be quenched too: I promise that my ~~lips~~ mouth
Shall leave no half charred raking stick behind
~~Our love is a cold fire, & those that catch it~~
We are an icy flame & those we set a blaze

---

5 With "gleaming" cf. "living" in MS G, 19r above; the new reading suggests the unreal light cast by the Woman.

25a lighted wisp in hand] Replaces the memory of the walk in the cornfields on MS G, 20r above. This lovely image of bridal innocence serves a structural function: the warm, clear, domestic, tranquil light of Emer's burning wisp is set against the Woman's cold flame.

30 flame] An image of Unity of Being; cf. MS I, 1v, l. 12 and note.

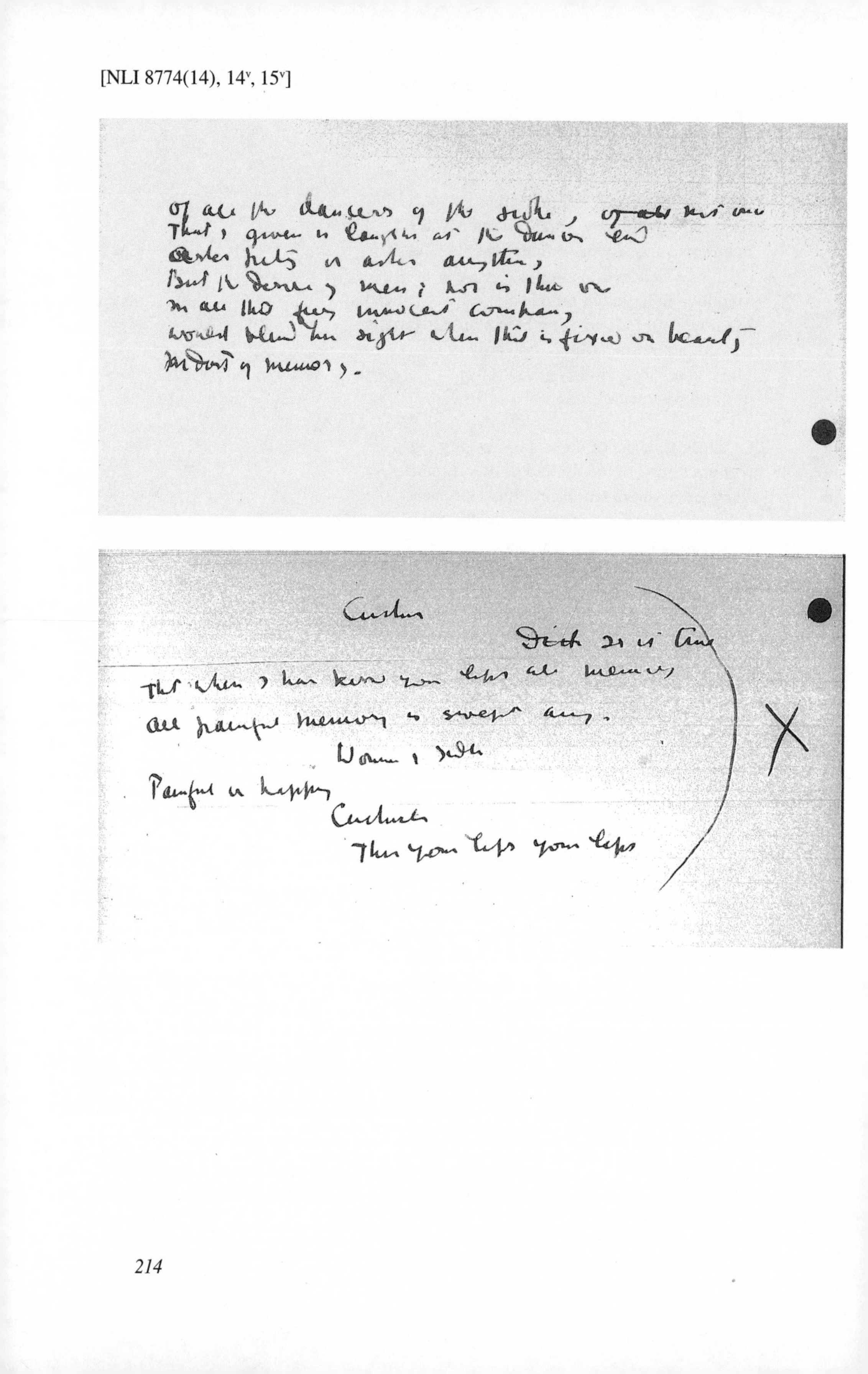

[NLI 8774(14), 14^{v}]

Of all the dancers of the sidhe, ~~of all~~ not one
That's given in laughter at the dances end
Asks pity or asks anything
But the desire of men nor is there one
In all that fiery innocent company
Would blind his sight when that is fixed on beauty
In dust of memory.

[NLI 8774(14), 15^{v}]

Cuchulain
~~Do the~~ is it true
That when I have kissed your lips all memory
All painful memory is swept away.
Woman of Sidhe
Painful or happy
Cuchulain
Then your lips your lips

[NLI 8774(14), 16r]

[NLI 8774(14), 16ʳ]

1 Have neither past nor future
Cuchulain
Emer
2 The ~~warm~~ warm bright smoking wisp in your hand.
Woman Sidhe
3 You would not love her if you lived again
4 But all would be as it has been.
Cuchulain
see ╳ Your lips, your lips
~~(He puts his hands~~
(She bends over him & he puts his hand upon
her shoulders & is about to draw her to him.~~)~~
5 Then as Emer speaks he turns away raising one
6 hand to his head, as if bewildered)
Emer
7 ~~I make this bargain, & give up that hope~~
8 I am content to lose his love for ever
9 ~~So that I can but see him in the flesh~~
10 Let him love where he will & turn upon me
11 ~~Eyes that the moon, or~~
12 Eyes that the cold moon or the harsh sea
13 Or what I know not has made indifferent
14 ~~So that I watch him still I am content.~~ stet
Cuchulain
15 What a strange silence has fallen in this dark
for
16 And a wise silence, for I know you now
17 In all your ignorance
(Woman of Sidhe ~~moves a~~ straightens herself up)
What dread has love
18 So great as to forget the least poor straw
19 Or blade of grass, or crack upon a door
20 Once seen in the incredible clear light
21 She cast about her some forlorn lost day
22 That face though fair enough is a fools face
23 And theres a folly in the deathless sidhe
24 Beyond the reach of man. ~~(He rises)~~

4 The canceled passage is replaced by the revision on 4ʳ.
19 These new details, not found on MS G, 22ʳ, add to the poignancy of the image.

[NLI 8774(14), 17^{r}]

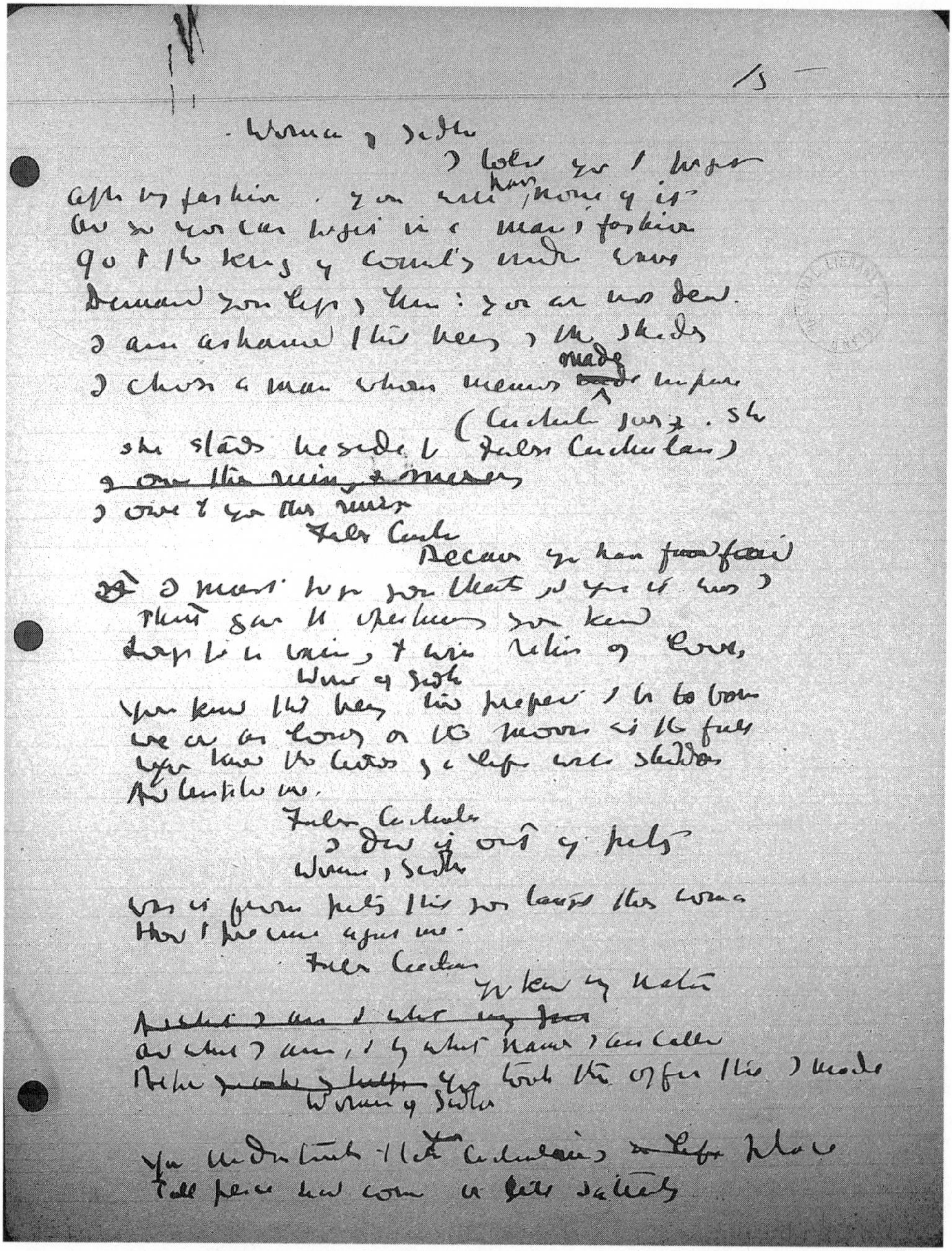

10–11 On 16^{v}, Yeats entered these two lines:
I must forgo your thanks, ~~& yet was you~~
~~That bid me make~~ ~~Your thanks that bid me~~

14 The first explicit equivalence in these drafts of the Woman and what would later be Phase 15 (Complete Subjectivity) in *A Vision*.

[NLI 8774(14), 17r]

15

Woman of Sidhe

1 I told you to forget
have
2 After my fashion. You will^ none of it
3 And so you can forget in a mans fashion
4 Go to the king of country under wave
5 Demand your life of him: you are not dead.
6 I am ashamed that being of the shades
made
7 I chose a man whom memory ~~made~~ impure
(Cuchulain^goes~~)~~. She
she stands beside the False Cuchulain)
8 ~~I owe this run, & misery~~
9 I owe to you this ruin

False Cuchulain

Because you have ~~failed~~ failed
10 ~~It~~ I must forgo your thanks, & yet it was I
11 That gave the opportunity your kind
12 Longs for in vain, to win the kiss of love.

Woman of Sidhe

13 You knew that being too perfect to be ~~be~~ born
14 We are as lonely as the moon at the full
15 ~~Who~~ You knew the tortures of a life with shaddows
16 And tempted me.

False Cuchulain

16b I did it out of pity

Woman of the Sidhe

17 Was it from pity that you taught this woman
18 How to prevail against me.

False Cuchulain

You knew my nature
19 ~~And what I am & what my fame~~
20 And what I am, & by what name I am called
21 Before ~~you asked my help~~ you took the offer that I made

Woman of Sidhe

~~Y~~
22 You undertook to take Cuchulain's ~~life~~ place
23 Till peace had come or till satiety

16b A twisted echo of Cuchulain's theory of love. Since the evil spirit is the evocation of irrational evil, his declaration must be taken with a large grain of salt. Perhaps in its own way absolute ugliness might love absolute beauty, forever out of its reach.

[NLI 8774(14), 18r, 17v]

[NLI 8774(14), 18r]

1 Had set me free from a mans bitter love
2 But chose to work for your own hand now instead
3 Some curse that you laid on him & his
4 Was more to you than my good will & now
5 I'd have you know what my ill will can do
6 I summon you to country under wave
7 To answer before its ~~kind~~ king

~~E G~~ False Cuchulain

He knows my heart

8 And that his own salt sea has made it cold. (He falls back ~~)~~
& turns his face away)

Woman of Sidhe

9 That's false for the sea lives & you have dropped
10 ~~Out of leprous dwindling~~
11 Out of a last leprous cresent when no fish
12 Could leap for all the calm nor dead rise up.

(She goes. There is music of drum & flute & then Eithne Inguba enters.

Eithne Inguba

13 All in a moment I ceased to be afriad.

Emer (bends over Cuchulain)

14 ~~Hush~~

Cuchulain wakens. ~~Eithne Inguba~~

~~He begins to stir~~

~~Emer~~ Cuchulain (To Eithne Inguba)

~~O~~ Take me in your arms

15 I have been in some strange place & I am weak.

The chorus stand up & slowly unfold their cloth until it hides the players & the bed. When they ~~unfold~~ fold it again these have left the room. While doing so the chorus sing.

[NLI 8774(14), 17v]

1 I lay you under word upon the instant
2 To stand before our king & face the charge
3 And take the punishment.

18r, ll. 11–12 In *A Vision*, Phases 26 to 28, wherein complete objectivity and an increasingly irrational evil are achieved.

13 A simplification of the rather literary "Upon the sudden" of MS G, 23r above.

[NLI 8774(16), 19^{r}]

The protracted philosophical dialogue between Cuchulain and the Woman of the Sidhe had clearly been giving Yeats many problems, as he had revised it many times. The major difficulty was that the debate was too abstract, too "talky." Yeats now drafted a new solution to the problem of integrating philosophy and drama: he united the Woman's dance with a dialogue in rhyming couplets founded on his lunar philosophy.

[NLI 8774(16), 19[r]]

Woman of Sidhe
~~If [?] ever woman pleased your sight~~
Now ~~that my beauty has brought you light~~
~~Why are~~
~~Why do you hide your face from~~ sight
~~Why do you cl[?]er you that kill so light~~
it
Why is stands before me there
~~Like the full moon when heavens are bare~~
And like the moon, when heavens are bare
~~Sheds from her own limbs faded light~~
~~Climbing [?through]~~
~~Flaming upon the fifteenth night~~
Flaming upon the fifteenth night
from her
Loving ~~on in~~ extreme delight:
full
Like the ~~new~~ moon, when heavens are bare
~~And so she hangs like a silver gong~~
And she ~~hangs like an an~~ hangs like an eastern gong
~~That That at a mans touch~~
That shakes, when touched by man in song
And all her lonely fifteenth night

~~Such~~ Shedding such light from limbs & hair
sheds
As the moon complete at last
As ~~the new only the fif fifteenth moon can cast~~
~~When all la~~
~~When every lonely crescent is past~~
When every crescent toil is past
And lonely with ex
~~And And all the toil of~~
When every toiling crescent is past
~~And in the extremity of delight~~ And lonely in her extreme delight
She flings out on the fifteenth night

1–5 Revision of ll. [4]–[11] on 12[r] above, beginning "Why do you turn about me like that ~~wind~~ moon."

5 For "cl[?]er" read "cower"?

6 Cuchulain speaks (Yeats omitted the speaker tag). For "Why is" read "Who is it." In the speech that follows, Yeats develops 13[r] (beginning "How could you gather up my light like a moon," l. 1) and 17[r] (beginning "We are as lonely as the moon at the full," l. 14).

19 For "all" read "all on."

22 For "la" read "laboring."

25 For "ex" read "extreme"?

[NLI 8774(16), 19v]

[NLI 8774(16), 19^{v}]

I must forgo your thanks, & yet it was you
Who bid me make him miserable & why he
might turn to each love
                                        I that took pity
~~Upon your love, & listened~~
~~Upon your hopeless love~~
Upon your love, & carried out your plan
To tangle all his life & make it ~~nothing~~ nothing
That he might turn to you.
            E G
                                                Was it from pity
            S
You taught that woman to prevail against me
            E G
You know my nature – by what name I am called
            S
Was it pity that you hid the truth
That men are bound to women by the wrongs
They do or suffer.
            E G
              You know what being I am.
            S

1–8 Spoken by Evil Genius.
2 For "why he" read "who hoped he"?
8b For "E G" read "Woman of the Sidhe."
11 For "Was it" read "Was it from."

[NLI 8774(16), 20r]

[NLI 8774(16), 20^{r}]

~~Woman of the Sidhe~~
Cuchulain
Who is it stands before me there
~~And~~ shedding such light from limb & hair
As the moon sheds complete at last
When every labouring crescent past
~~She flings out on the fifteenth n~~
And lonely with extreme delight
She flings out on the fifteenth night.
Woman of Sidhe
Because I long I am not complete.
What's pulled your hands about your feet
And your head down also upon your knees
And hid your face
~~False~~ Cuchulain
O memories
A dying boy with handsome face
Upturned upon a beaten place
A sacred yew tree on a strand
A woman that holds with steady hand
A burning wisp beside a door
Any many a round or crescent more
O memories o memories
Have pulled my head upon my knees.
Woman of Sidhe
Could you that have loved many a woman
That did not reach beyond the human
Being a whole day from the full
Love one that still can play the fool
Though lacking but an hour or so
Cuchulain
I know you now for long ago
I met you on a mountain side
~~Among old thorn trees by a well~~
By dried thorn trees & a dry well
Where yet the water rose & fell
And always there the grey hawk flew
I held out wrist & hand but you

17 For "Any" read "And."
22 Up to now, women of Phase 14 (like Eithne) have been Cuchulain's limit.
23 one] The Woman of the Sidhe herself.
28–29 Cf. MS I, 1^{r} above; the description of the Hawk's Well now vividly conjures up the earlier play.

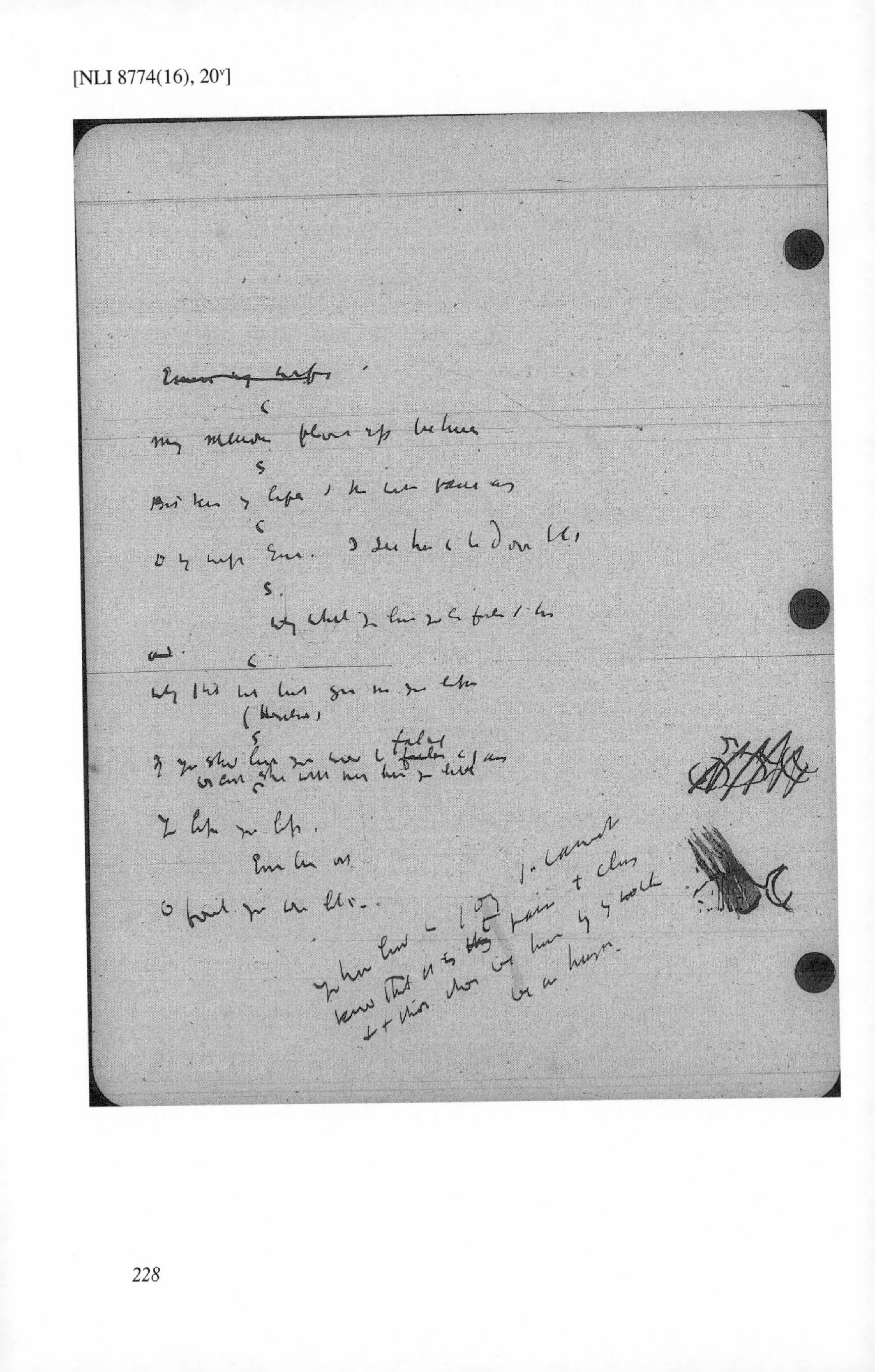

[NLI 8774(16), 20v]

[NLI 8774(16), 20v]

1 ~~Emer my wife~~

C

2 My memories flood up between

S

3 But kiss my lips & they will fade away

C

4 O my wife Emer. I see her at the door etc

S.

5 ~~Why~~ While you lived you lived false to her

6 And

C

7 Why thats but true give me your lips

([?Hesitates])

S

false

8 If you should live you would be ~~false~~ again

9 or even she will never have you back

C

10 Your lips your lips

Evil Genius on

11 O fool you were like

You have lived in joy & cannot

to

12 know that it is ~~they~~ pain to cling

to to those whom we turn by by ~~too~~ when

we are [?hurt]

13

14

15

The placement of this leaf can only be approximate. It is written in the light, "tentative" hand that Yeats used to outline his ideas. Here, he sketches material that appears on 21r to 23v.

4 etc] From MS. K 15r, ll. 23–25; developed on 22r.

9 For "or" read "And."

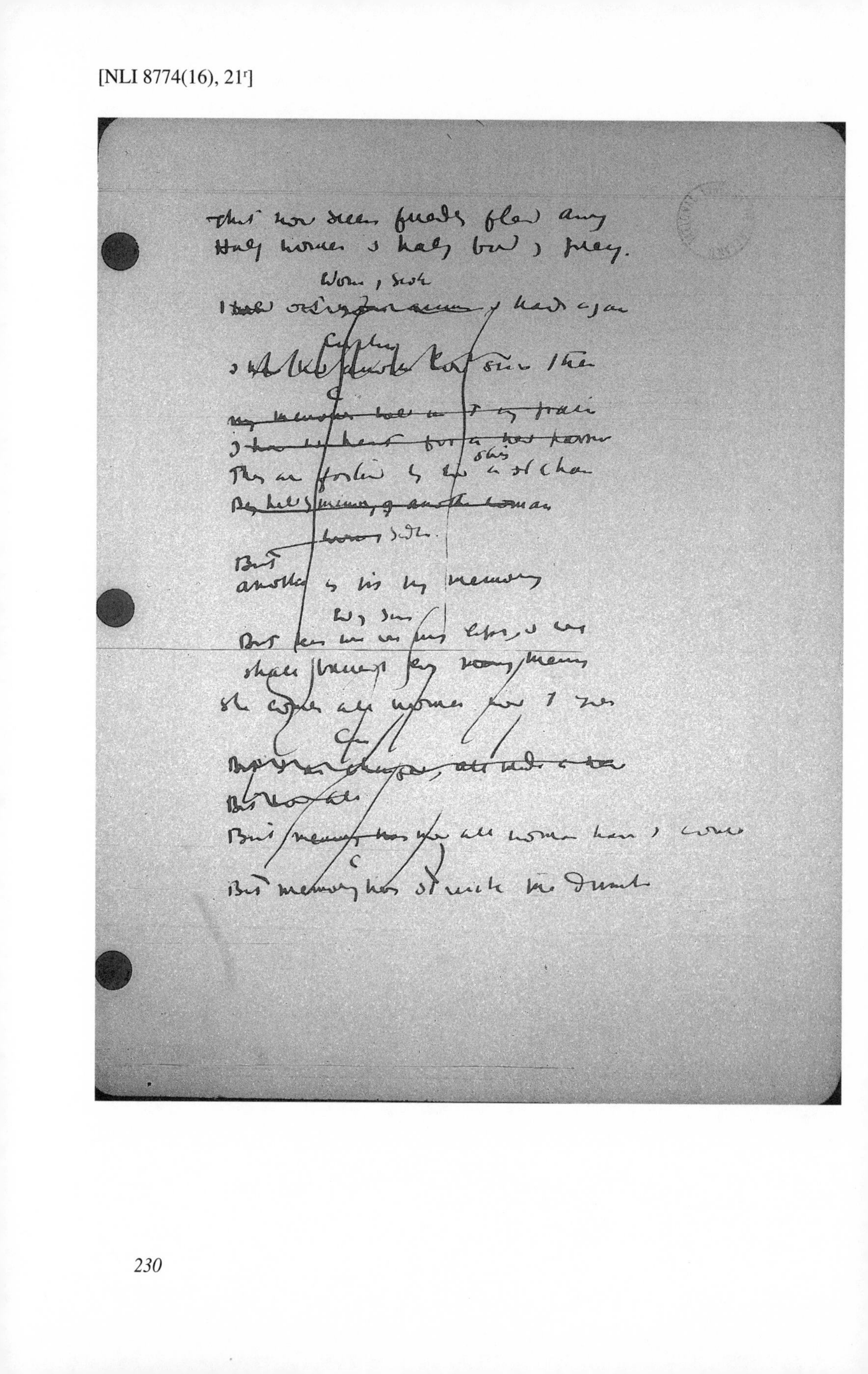

[NLI 8774(16), 21r]

[NLI 8774(16), 21^{r}]

1 That now seem friendly flew away
2 Half woman & half bird of prey.
Woman of Sidhe
3 ~~Hold out your arms &hands again~~
Cuchulain
4 I have had another love since then
C
5 ~~My memories hold me to my pain~~
6 ~~I have no heart for a new passion~~
strong
7 They are fastened by love in ~~st~~ chain
8 ~~Being held by memory of another woman~~
~~Woman of Sidhe~~
~~But~~
9 Another is ties my memory
W of Sidhe
10 But kiss me on my lips, & we
11 shall banish every ~~memory~~ memory
12 She comes all woman now to you
Cuchulain
13 ~~But I am changed, all made a new~~
14 ~~But new all~~
15 But ~~memory has~~ now all woman have I come
C
16 But memory has struck me dumb

---

7 For "in" read "in a."

9 For "Another is" read "Another it is."

12/ For "Cuchulain" read "Woman of Sidhe?

[NLI 8774(16), 21v]

[NLI 8774(16), 21v]

1 ~~All my round shall be complete~~
Time
2 ‸~~Even~~ shall seem to take his course
3 For when your mouth & my mouth mouth meet
4 All my move shall be complete
circles
5 ~~As though~~ ~~and dead~~ imagining all its ~~circles~~ run
6 As though there were oblivion
7 Even to slake Cuchullains thirst
8 And this shall be oblivion
9 Even to slake Cuchullains drouth
10 And quench his heart.
C.
Your mouth your mouth
~~O never,~~
11 O Emer, Emer.
S W
~~She then it is she~~
12 ~~Who has made you blind with memory~~
~~Is it for st~~ so then it is she
13 Made you impure with ~~memory~~ memory
Cuchulain
14 Still in my dream I see you stand
15 A burning wisp in your right hand
16 To wait my coming to the house
17 As when our parents married us
Shi

4 For "move" read "move round."

7–11 A sketch, perhaps of the stage, was entered first and the text around it.

[NLI 8774(16), 22r]

[NLI 8774(16), 22^{r}]

1 Hold out your hands arms again
2 ~~Am I less beautiful than then~~
now
3 ~~But that all woman I have come~~
4 You were not so dumbfounded when
5 I was that bird of prey & yet
6 I am all woman now
Cuchulain
I am not
young
7 I am not the young man that I was
8 And though those strange high looks surpass
9 All women else – My memories
10 Weigh down my hands, about my eyes
11 Another ~~woman holds my love~~
12 ~~Who is not~~
~~Shi Shi~~ Sidhe
my mouth
13 Then kiss ~~lips~~ – though memory
14 Be beautys bitterest enemy
my
15 I have no dread for at ~~kiss~~ kiss
16 ~~All but their passion vanishes~~
~~C.~~
17 All kind of memory vanishes
18 And only beauty will remain
C
19 And I shall never know again
20 Vain regret long lived remorse
Sidhe
21 Even time shall stay his course
22 As though he had been laid to rest
23 Long long ago upon my breast
24 So still, still.
C.
Your mouth ~~to kiss~~. Your mouth

1 For "hands arms" read "hands and arms."

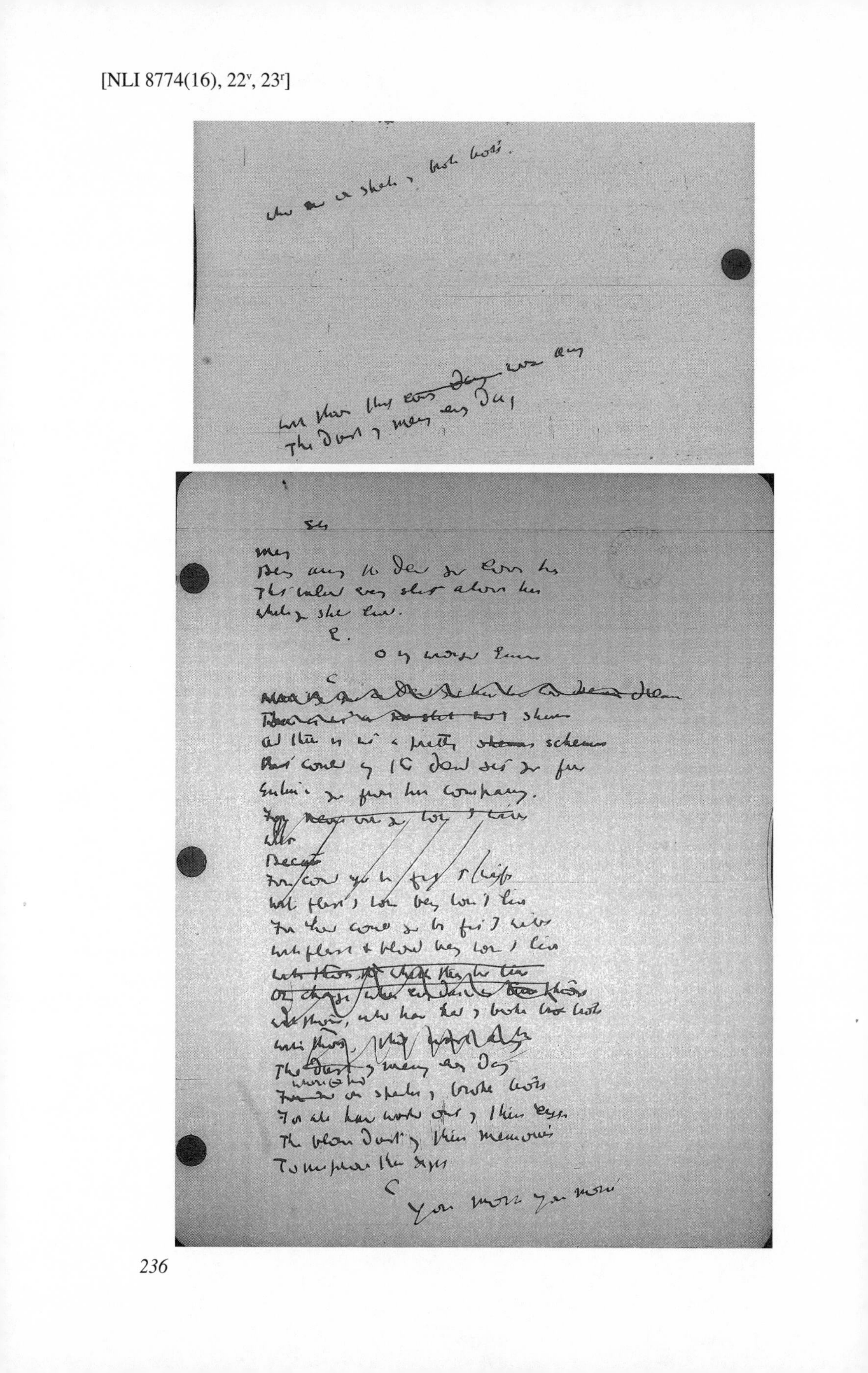

[NLI 8774(16), 22^{v}, 23^{r}]

[NLI 8774(16), 22v]

Where no one speaks of broken troth

With those, that ~~every day~~ wash away
The dust of memory every day

[NLI 8774(16), 23r]

Sh
Men
Being among the dead you love her
That valued every slut above her
While you still lived.
C.
O my wronged Emer.
C
~~Now that you are dead you will but love dream dream~~
~~There is not a no slut but I~~ shemer
And there is not a pretty ~~shemer~~ schemer
But could if the dead set you free
Entrance you from her company.
For ~~never were you born to wive~~
~~With~~
~~Because~~
For could you be fit to wife
With flesh & born being born to live
For how could you be fit to wive
With flesh & blood being born to live
~~With these, that whether there be time~~
~~Or change when every dance is true through~~
With those , who have lied & broken ~~tro~~ troth
With those, that wash away
The dust of memory every day
Where ~~o~~ no
~~For no~~ one speaks of broken troth
For all have washed out of their eyes
The blown dust of their memories
To improve their sight.
C
Your mouth your mouth

5ff. Spoken by Woman of Sidhe, not by Cuchulain. In l. 5, for "love" read "love a."
13 For "could" read "how could" and for "wife" read "wive."
14 For "flesh & born" read "flesh & blood."
19 For "have lied" read "have not lied."

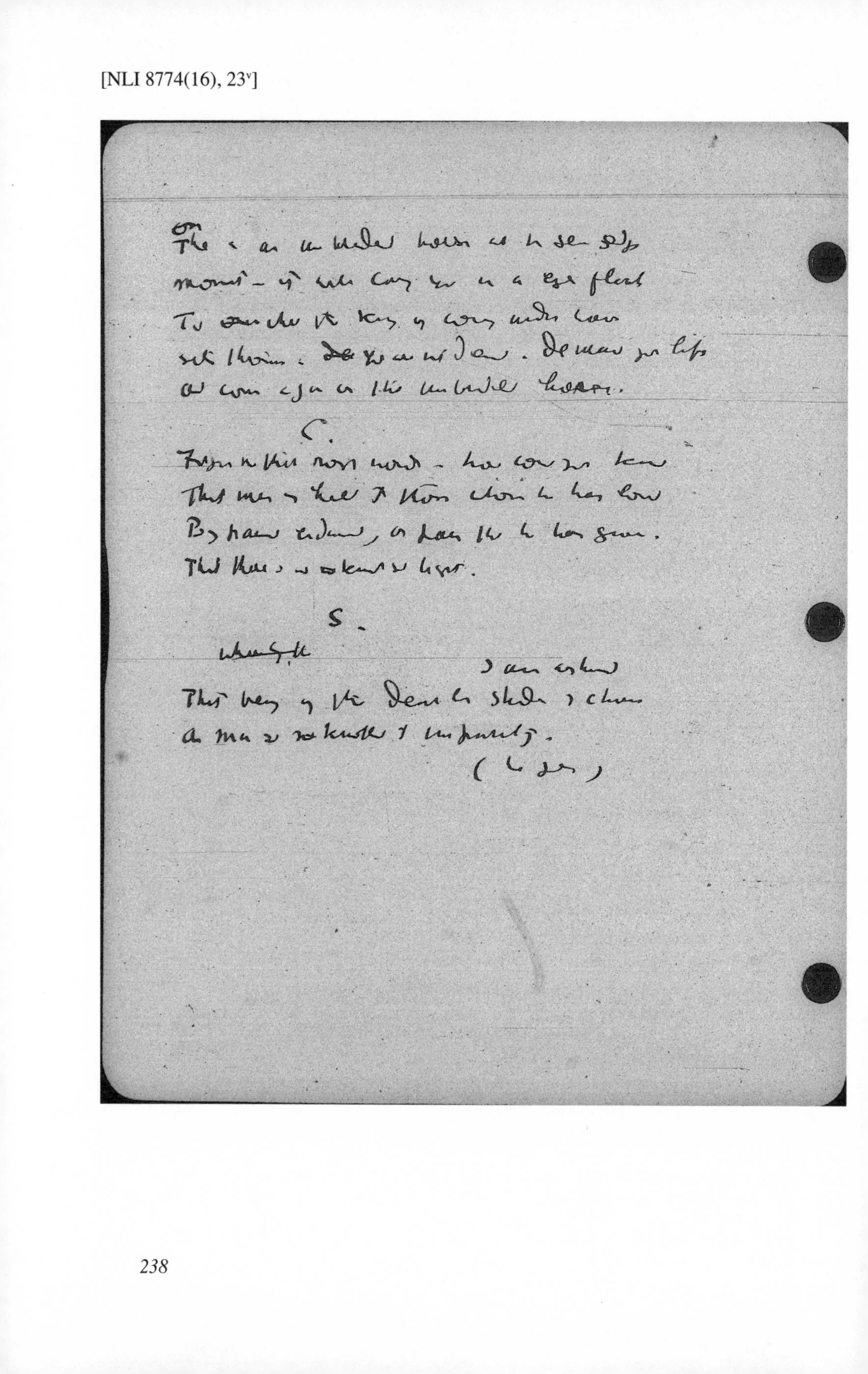

[NLI 8774(16), 23v]

[NLI 8774(16), 23^{v}]

On
1 Theres an unbridled horse at the seas edge
2 Mount – it will carry you in an eye flash
3 To ~~our~~ where the king of country under wave
4 Sits throned. ~~De~~ You are not dead. Demand your life
5 And come again on the unbridled horse.
C.
6 Forgive me those rough words – how could you know
7 That man is held to those whom he has loved
8 By pain endured, or pain that he has given,
9 That there's no ~~w~~ knot so tight.
S.
~~Where by the~~ I am ashamed
10 That being of the deathless shades I chose
11 A man so ~~n~~ knotted to impurity.
(he goes)

---

1 Yeats continued on the facing verso because, presumably, he had run out of paper; 25^{r} is lined, 24^{r} is unlined.
horse at the seas edge] The sea-horses were not mentioned in previous drafts. They were the horses of Manannan, god of the sea; the waves were their manes. Lady Gregory's chapter "Sea Stories" in *Visions and Beliefs* contains many vivid sightings of these horses by the Aran Islanders.

6 Revives passage on MS E, 5^{r} above: "Pardon woman of the sidhe."

9a This idea of spirits reliving their sufferings, and the sufferings they have caused others, is a familiar one in Yeats's plays; cf. *The Words Upon the Window-Pane* and *Purgatory*.

9b Canceled words echo l. 12 on 24^{r}: "Where by the heart of love – is riven & rent."

[NLI 8774(16), 24^r, 24^v]

[NLI 8774(16), 24^{r}]

If but
~~So that~~ he live I am content
If but the dead will set him free
~~I am content if I but see him near~~
That I may speak with at whiles,
~~Or see him for a moment I can content~~
I can content that he shall turn on me
Eyes the cold moon or the harsh sea
Or what I know not's made indifferent.
Cuchulain
What a strange silence has fallen in this dark
And a wise silence for I know you now
In all your ignorance. Of all the dreads
riven
Where by the heart of love – is ~~torn~~ & rent
What dread so great as that it should forget
~~The least poor blade of grass,~~
~~Or least chance word, or scratch or mark~~
The least chance sight or sound, a scratch a mark
On an old door, or birds cry heard or seen
In the incredible clear light she cast
All round about her some forlorn lost day
That face though fine enough is a fool's face
And there a folly in the deathless sidhe
Beyond the reach of man.
Sidhe
I told you to forget
After my fashion – you will have none of it
So now you may forget in a mans fashion

[NLI 8774(16), 24^{v}]

Sidhe.
I loved you

24^{r}, l. 4 For "with" read "with him."
5, 6 for "I can" read "I am."
21 For "there" read "there's."
24^{v} This scrap presumably relates to MS K, 25^{r}.

[NLI 8774(16), 25r]

[NLI 8774(16), 25[r]]

I summon you etc.
E G.
He know me & who I am
W of Sidhe
I'll tell you who you are – a foul creature
Fallen from a dwindling leprous ~~eres~~ cycle
No creature of the light
(he goes)

---

1 Spoken by the Woman of the Sidhe; cf. 18[r], l. 6. On 25[r], Yeats rapidly outlined the dialogue between the Woman and the Evil Genius, returning to it on subsequent pages.

2 For "He" read "You."

[NLI 8774(16), 26r]

[NLI 8774(16), 26^{r}]

W
1 It was that under
2 You that ~~me this advice;~~ You who tried ruin him
E G
3 I brought you here at your own will to your
4 speak with lies & with lies love it may
5 And had made love [?lie] a scene, was for so [?]d
6 ~~As else you had made do~~
W of Sidhe
7 ~~You knew in what great loneliness we live~~
8 You knew, that we are as lonely as the moon at full
9 Who grow too perfect for a human body
10 ~~You knew that being too~~ lonely
11 ~~And tempted me~~, knew that we live with shadows, you
12 Knew the burning of that longing
13 And tempted me.
E Gen
It was but my pity
Woman of Sidhe
14 Was it from pity that you taught this woman
15 How to prevail against me.
E Genius
16 You know me who I am & who I was
17 Before I asked my help
W of Sidhe
You have worked for your own hand
18 Some curse was more to you than my good will

---

1 For "was that under" read "was you that undertook."
2 For "that me" read "that gave me" and for "tried ruin" read "tried to ruin."
3 For "your" read "your image"?
4 Perhaps "spoke with lies & with love it may be."
6 For "made" read "made me"?
17 For "I asked" read "you asked."

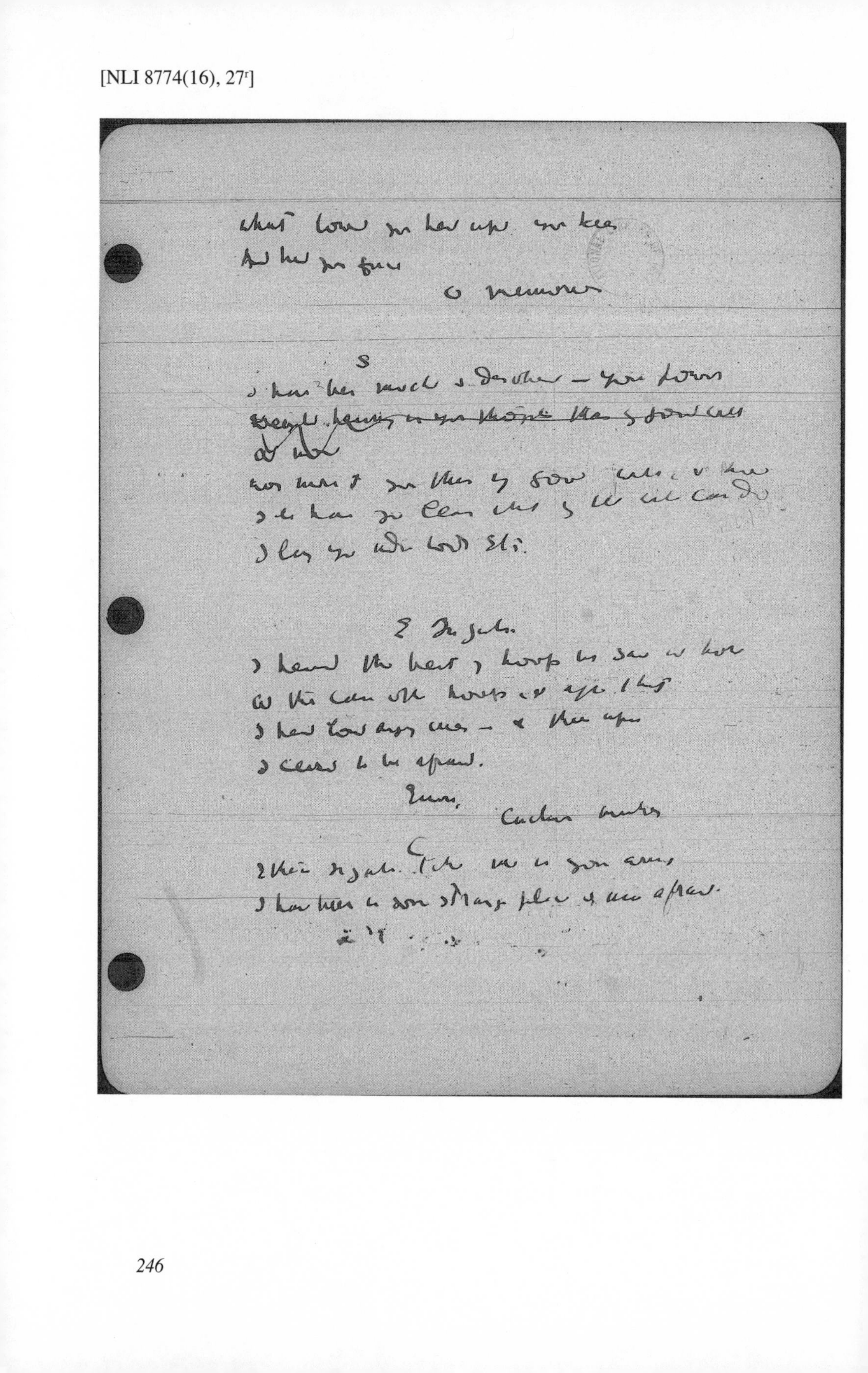

[NLI 8774(16), 27r]

[NLI 8774(16), 27^{r}]

What bowed your head upon your knees
And hid your face
O memories

S
I have been mocked & disobeyed – your power
Weighed heavily in your thoughts than my good will
And now
Was more to you than my good will & now
I'll have you learn what my ill will can do
I lay you under word etc.

E Inguba
I heard the beat of hoofs but saw no horse
And then came other hoofs, & after than
I heard low angry cries – & there upon
I ceased to be afraid.
Emer.
Cuchulain awakes
C
Eithne Inguba take me in your arms
I have been in some strange place & am afraid.

1–2 Yeats used the top of what would later be 27^{r} for rough work here for 20^{r}, ll. 8–11; later he used the rest of 27^{r} (ll. 3–14) to follow 26^{r}.

4–8 See 17^{v} above.

4 For "Weighed heavily" read "Weighed more heavily."

14 afraid] An effective replacement for "weak" in previous manuscripts.

[Harvard, 28r]

11

Cuchulain

Who is it stands before me there
shedding such light from limb & hair
As when the moon complete at last,
With every labouring crescent past
And lonely with extreme delight
Flings out on the fifteenth night.

Woman of Sidhe

Because I long I am not complete.
What pulled your hands about your feet
And your head down upon your knees
And hid your face,

Cuchulain

O memories
A dying boy with [illegible] face
Upturned upon a heather place
A [illegible] on a strand
A woman that held in steady hand
In all the happiness of her youth
Before her man had broken troth
A burning wisp to light the door;
And many a [illegible] or crescent more;
Dead men & women, memories
Have pulled my head upon my knees

Woman Sidhe

Could you that have loved many a woman
That did not reach beyond the human
Lacking a whole day from the full,

[Harvard, 28ʳ]

11

Cuchulain

Who is it stands before me there
Shedding such light from limbs & hair
when the
As ~~the~~^ moon ~~stands~~ complete at last,
[?] With ~~When~~
With long labouring crescent past
And lonely with extreme delight
Flings out on the fifteenth night.

Woman of Sidhe

Because I long I am not complete.
What pulled your hands about your feet
And your head down upon your knees
And hid your face.

Cuchulain

O memories
A dying boy with handsome face
Upturned upon a beaten place
A sacred yew tree on a strand
A woman that hold in steady hand
In all the happiness of her youth
Before her man had broken troth
A burning wisp to light the door
And many a round or crescent more
Dead men and women, memories
Have pulled my head upon my knees

Woman of Sidhe

Could you that have loved many a woman
That did not reach beyond the human
Being a whole day from the fall,

Revision of 19ʳ to 27ʳ, to follow the stage direction added to the margins of 12ʳ. Line numbering continues from the foot of 12ʳ to show the state of the revised Houghton MS.

239–240 This couplet was not on 20ʳ.

242 Cf. 20ʳ: "O memories o memories."

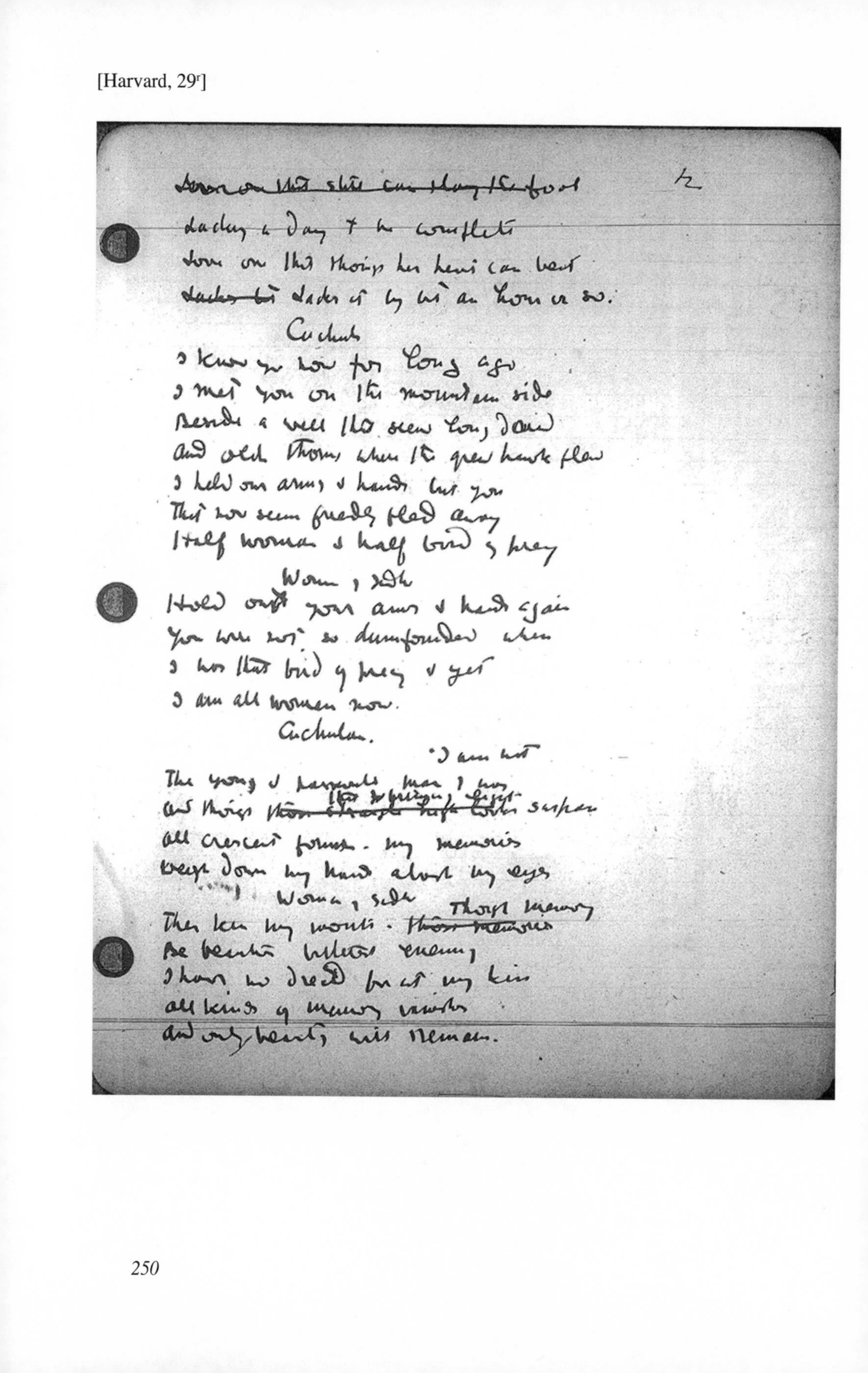

[Harvard, 29r]

[Harvard, 29r]

12

~~Love one that still can play the fool~~
247 Lacking a day to be complete
248 Love one that though her heart can beat
249 ~~Lacks but~~ Lacks it by but an hour or so.
Cuchulain
250 I know you now for long ago
251 I met you on the mountain side
252 Beside a well that seemed long dried
253 And old thorns where the great hawk flew
254 I held our arms and hands but you
255 That now seem friendly fled away
256 Half woman & half bird of prey
Woman of Sidhe
{t
257 Hold ou{r your arms & hands again
258 You were not so dumbfounded when
259 I was that bird of prey & yet
260 I am all woman now.
Cuchulain.
I am not
261 The young & passionate man I was
that [?] [?brilliant] light
262 And though ~~those strange high looks~~ surpass
263 All crescent forms, my memories
264 Weigh down my hands abash my eyes
Woman of Sidhe
Though memory
265 Then kiss my mouth. ~~Those memories~~
266 Be beauties bitterest enemy
267 I have no dread for at my kiss
268 All kinds of memory vanishes
269 And only beauty will remain.

247–248 Couplet not on 20r.
263 Cf. 22r: "All women else"; Yeats adds yet more lunar imagery.

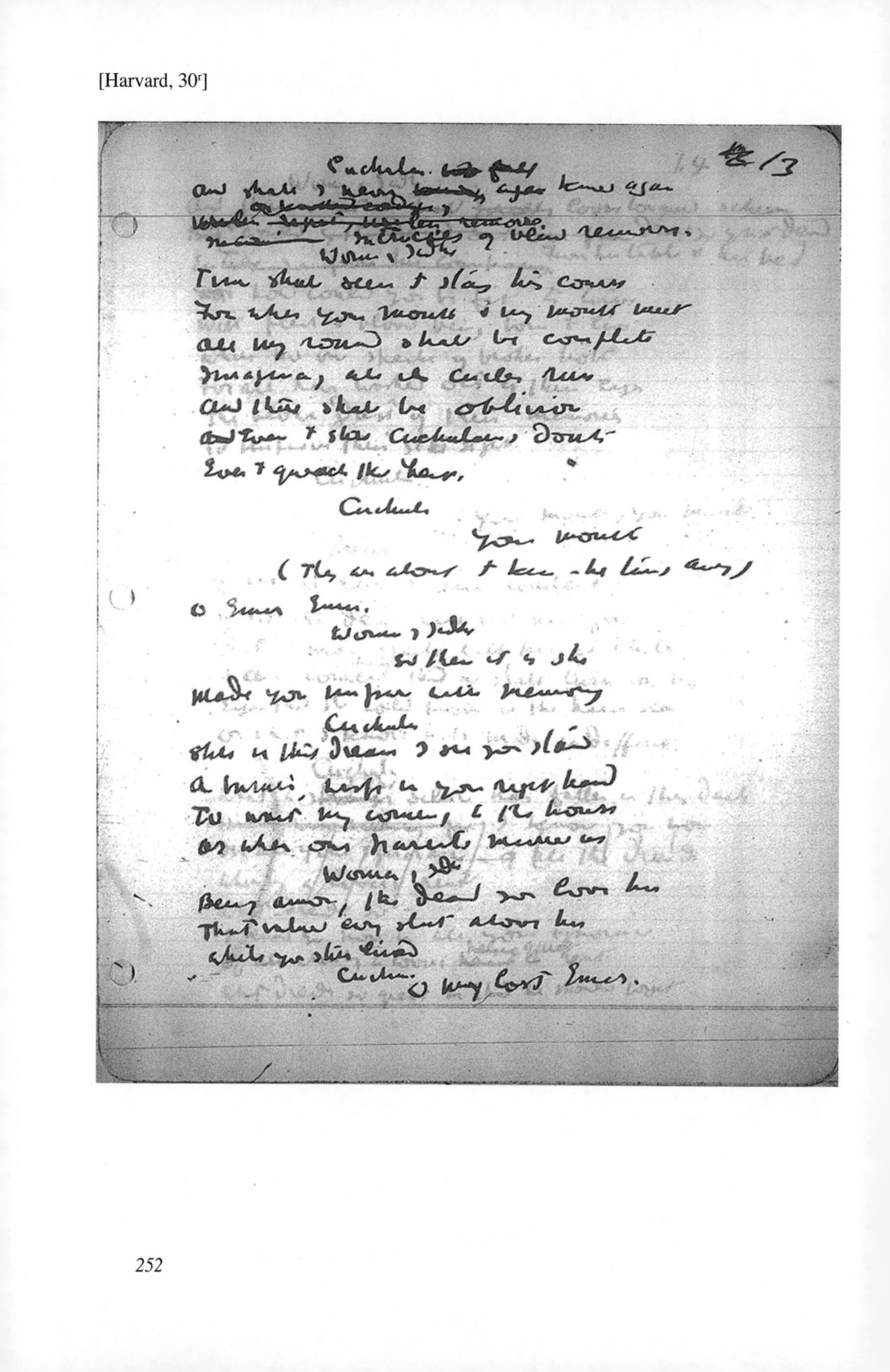

[Harvard, 30^{r}]

[Harvard, 30r]

~~12~~ 13

Cuchulain

[?~~bid~~] ~~feel~~

270 And shall I never [?~~know~~] ~~again~~ know again

~~on [? knowledge]~~ of

271 ~~Useless regret, useless remorse~~

[?~~Intricicies~~] Intricacies of blind remorse.

Woman of Sidhe

272 Time shall seem to stay his course
273 For when your mouth & my mouth meet
274 All my round shall be complete
275 Imagining all its circles run
276 And there shall be oblivion
277 ~~And~~ Even to still Cuchulain s doubts
278 Even to quench that heart.

Cuchulain

Your mouth

(They are about to kiss – he turns away)

279 O Emer Emer.

Woman of the Sidhe

So then it is she

280 Made you impure with memory

Cuchulain

281 Still in that dream I see you stand
282 A burning wisp in your right hand
283 To wait my coming to the house
284 As when our parents married us

Woman of Sidhe

285 Being among the dead you love her
286 That valued every slut above her
287 While you still lived

Cuchulain.

O my lost Emer.

---

277 Cf. 21v: "Even to slake Cuchullain's drouth."

278*sd* Stage direction not on 21v.

287b With "lost" compare 23r: "wronged."

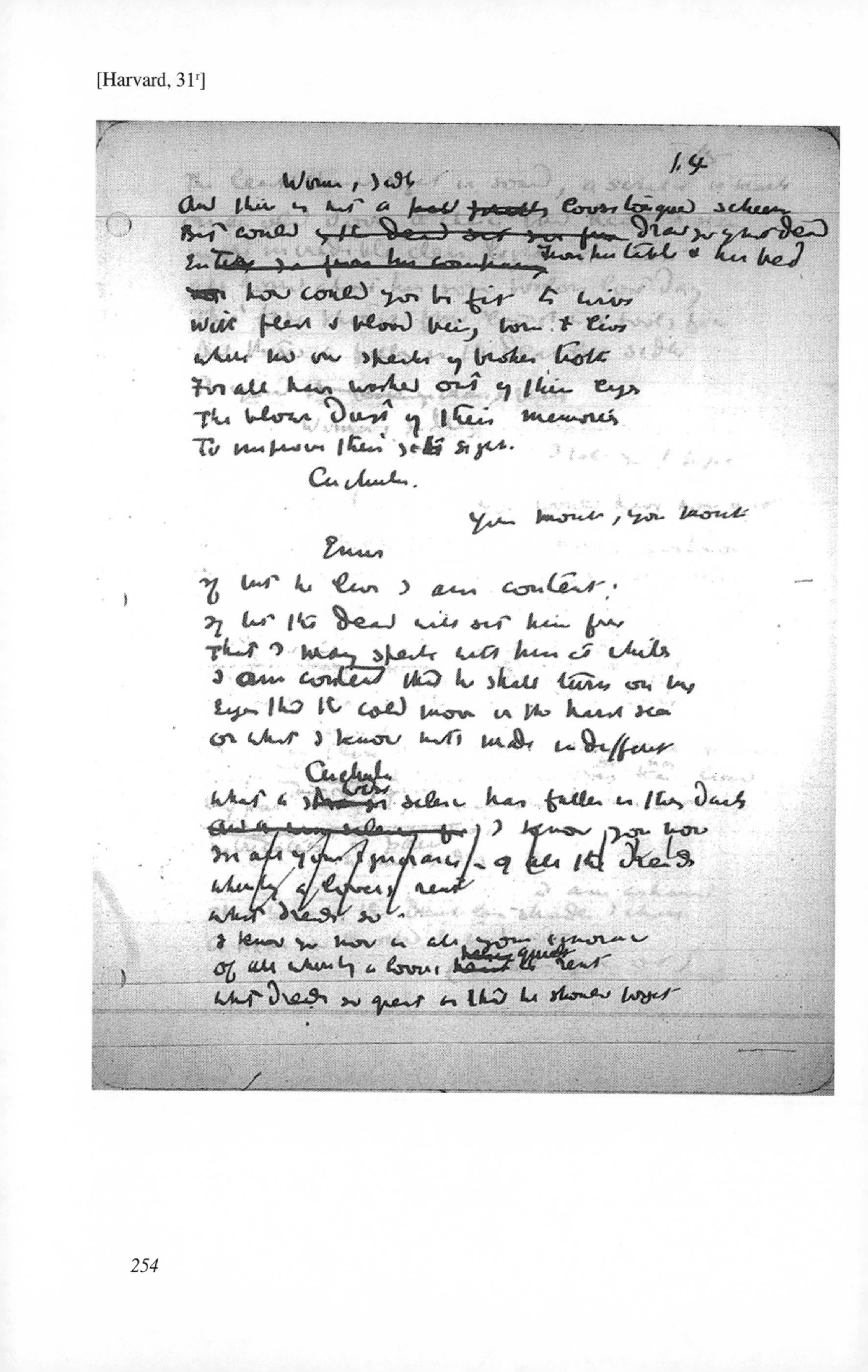

[Harvard, 31^{r}]

14

Woman of Sidhe

288 And there is not a ~~pale pretty~~ loose tongued schemer
289 But could ~~if the dead set you free~~ draw you if not dead
290 From her table & her bed
~~Entire [?] from her company~~ ^
291 [~~?~~] how could you be fit to wive
292 With flesh and blood being born to live
293 Where no one speaks of broken troth
294 For all have washed out of their eyes
295 The blown dust of their memories
296 To improve their ~~siht~~ sight.

Cuchulain.

Your mouth your mouth

Emer

297 If but he lives I am content:
298 If but the dead will set him free
299 That I may speak with him at whiles
300 I am content that he shall turn on me
301 Eyes that the cold moon or the harsh sea
302 Or what I know not made indifferent

Cuchulain

wise
303 What a ~~strange~~ silence has fallen in this dark
~~And a wise silence for~~ I know you now
In all your ignorance – of all the dreads
Whereby a lovers rent
What dreads so –
304 I know you now in all your ignorance
~~peace~~ quiet
305 Of all whereby a lovers ~~heart~~ is rent
306 What dread so great as that he should forget

[Harvard, 32r]

[Harvard, 32r]

15

307 The least chance sight or sound, a scratch or mark
308 On an old door, a chance bird heard & seen
309 In the incredible clear light she cast
310 All round about her some forlorn lost day
311 That face though fine enough is a fool s face
312 And theres a folly in the deathless Sidhe
313 Beyond ~~the reach of~~ mans reach
Woman of Sihe
I told you to forget
314 After my fashion – you would have none of it
315 So now you may forget in a man s fashion
316 There s an unbridled horse at the seas edge
317 Mount – it will carry you in an eye s flash
318 To where the King of Country under wave
319 Old Mananan nods & moves above the board
~~Old Mananan dreams. Demand your~~ life of him
320 His chessmen in a dream. Demand your life
321 And come again on the unbridled horse
Cuchulain
322 Forgive me those rough words. How could you know
{at man is he has
323 Th{ey ~~are~~ held to those whom ~~they have~~ loved
that they give
324 By pain ~~endured~~, or pain that he has given
~~That there so wind so strong~~
325 Intricacies of pain
Woman of Sidhe
I am ashamed
326 That being of the deathless shades I chose
327 A Man so knotted to inpurity
(Cuchulain goes out)

---

319 On 23v above, Manannan "sits throned." Cuchulain, who is among the spirits "dreaming back", is one of the chessmen moved by Manannan, the god of the dead.

325 The line echoes Yeats's revision on 30r, "Intricacies of blind remorse."

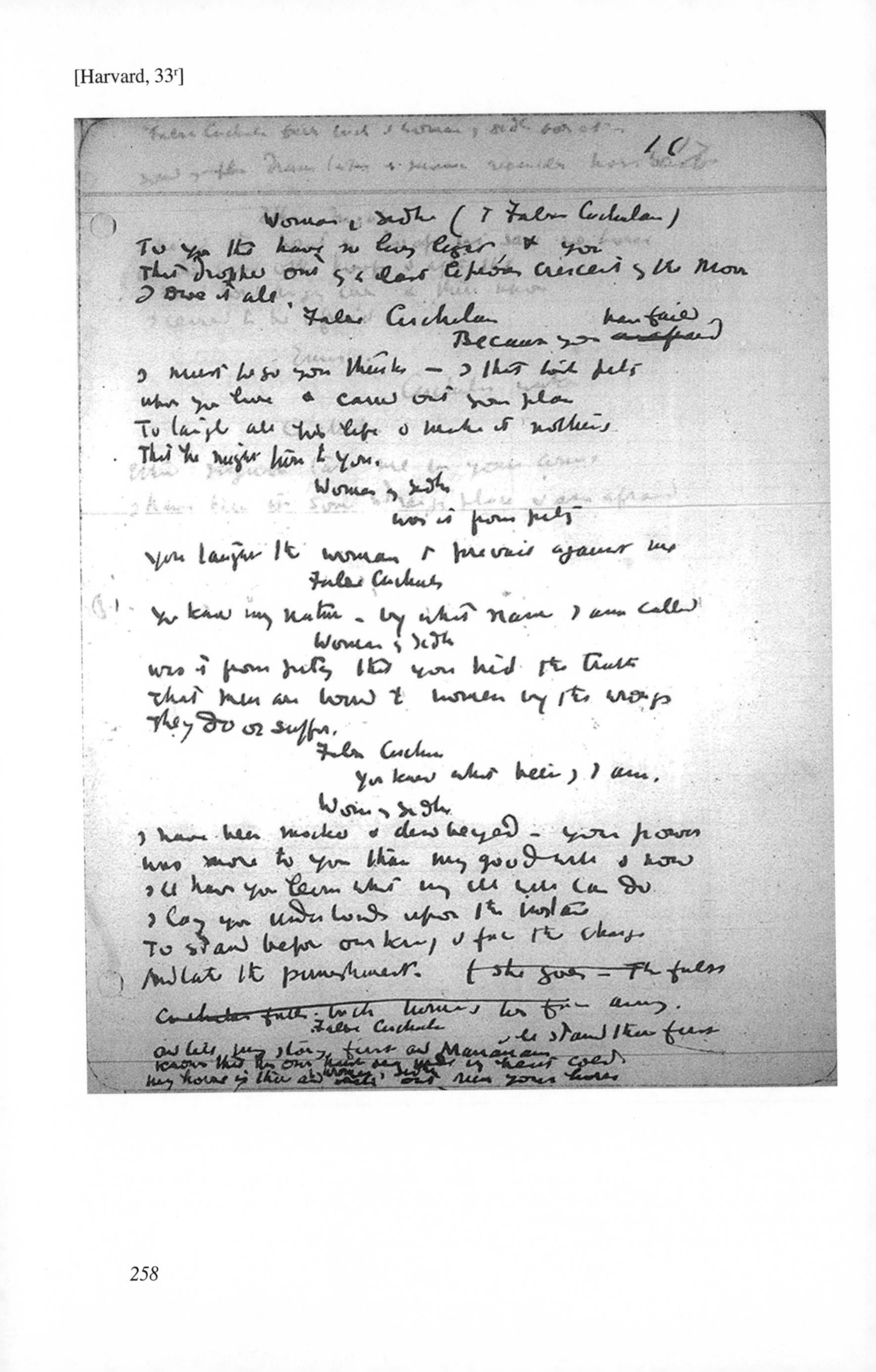

[Harvard, 33r]

[Harvard, 33[r]]

16

Woman of Sidhe (to False Cuchulain)

328 To you that have no living light, & you
329 That dropped out of a last leprous crescent of the Moon
330 I owe it all.

False Cuchulain

have failed
Because you ~~are afraid~~
331 I must forgo your thanks – I that took pity
332 Upon your love & carried out your plan
333 To tangle all his life & make it nothing
334 That he might turn to you.

Woman of Sidhe

Was it from pity
335 You taught the woman to prevail against me

False Cuchulain

336 You know my nature – by what name I am called

Woman of Sidhe

337 Was it from pity that you hid the truth
338 That men are bound to women by the wrongs
339 They do or suffer.

False Cuchulain

You know what being I am.

Woman of Sidhe

340 I have been mocked & disobeyed – your power
341 Was more to you than my good-will & now
342 I'll have you learn what my ill will can do
343 I lay you under bonds upon the instant
344 To stand before our King and face the charge
345 And take the punishment. ~~(she goes – T~~he false
~~Cuchulain falls back turning his face~~ away.

False Cuchulain

I'll stand there first
346 And tell my story first and Mananan
347 Knows that his own harsh sea made my heart cold.

Woman of Sidhe

348 My horse is there and shall out run your horse

---

331 Revision of 19[v]. Since this "pity" no longer echoes Cuchulain's speech on the nature of love in earlier manuscripts, the word has lost its bite.

340 Revision of 27[r].

343 Yeats had written "I lay you under word etc." on 27[r]; so, here he had to go back to 17[v] for his text, which he altered slightly, changing "word" to "bonds."

348 First appearance in the manuscripts of this "horse race."

[Harvard, 34r]

[illegible] Cuchulain [illegible]

[illegible]

Ethna Inguba.
I heard the beat of hoofs but saw no horse
And then came other hoofs & after that
I heard low angry cries & thereupon
I ceased to be afraid

Emer.

Cuchulain wakes

Cuchulain
Ethna Inguba take me in your arms
I have been in some strange place & am afraid.

[Harvard, 34r]

False Cuchulain falls back & Woman of Sidhe goes out –

17

Sound of the drum taps – music resembles horse hoofs

Eithne Injuba.
349 I heard the beat of hoofs but saw no horse
350 And then came other hoofs & after that
351 I heard low angry cries & there upon
352 I ceased to be afraid

Emer.

Cuchulain wakes

Cuchulain
353 Eithne Injuba take me in your arma
354 I have been in some strange place & am afraid.

348*sd* Stage direction not in previous drafts

349 Yeats now returns to 27r for his text.

354 Yeats halted halfway down the page.

On the following page is the first full version of the closing song, depicting the contrasting but similar positions of the Woman of the Sidhe and Emer. The first verse emphasizes the impossible nature of the woman's love for Cuchulain: a man can love ideal beauty, but, should he possess his prize, will in the end reject it as alien. The second verse of the song presents an equally limited option, the narrow world of domestic love, implacably opposed to the absolute. The burden of the refrain is that both the woman and Emer receive a "bitter reward" for their love, since both lose Cuchulain. Yeats altered his sources in *The Only Jealousy of Emer* to make Cuchulain choose a middle course (passion) which, though an action, is an inconclusive solution to the dilemma of conflicting opposites. Cuchulain, too, has a "bitter reward."

18

~~Cover chorus~~ 1C
(~~whole unfolding & folding, cloth~~)

How may this woman find
Being born to all lands as it seems
And groping her way blind
In labyrinths of her dreams,
A little friendship and love;
For all the delights of the chase
~~A passionate man, though~~ A lover his comradeship done
~~When the first [illegible]~~ has weary of her, of the alien lines on her brow

O little reward!
O of many a tragic tomb!
And we thought astonished and dumb
And gave but a look and a word
A passing word.

And how could I dream that this wife,
Burnt and her heartstone
And a mere part of our life,
Could speak with a gentle tongue
And give her the hand of a friend?
Could she not see in [illegible] eyes that
That she must endure to the end
Remorse and jealousy?

O little reward!
O many a tragic tomb!
And we thought astonished and dumb
Or gave but a look & a word
A passing word.

For all the charm and the jest & tears
Passion soon has enough
Of an alien thing on its brow.

[Harvard, 35r]

~~17~~ 18

~~Chorus~~

~~Corus~~ the

~~(while unfolding & folding ^ cloth)~~

355 How may that woman find
356 Being born to ill luck as it seems
half
357 And groping her way blind
358 In labyrinths of her dreams
359 A little friendship and love;
For all the delight of the chase
[?A] passionate mans enough
~~When he finds her not of his race~~

A lover his courtship done
will weary likely enough
of the alien thing he has won

363 O bitter reward!
364 O Of many a tragic tomb!
365 And we though astonished are dumb
Or
366 And give but a look and a word
367 A passing word.

368 And how could I dream that this wife,
369 Bowed at her hearth stone
370 And a mere part of our life,
371 Could speak with a gentle tongue
372 And give her the hand of a friend?
373 Could she not see in ~~her~~ eye that /
374 it / That ~~she~~ must endure to the end
375 Reproach & Jealousy?

376 O bitter reward!
377 O many a tragic tomb!
378 And we though astonished are dumb
379 Or give but a look & a word
380 A passing word.

360 For all the chase & its zest [?~~zeast~~]
361 Passion soon has enough
362 Of an alien thing on its breast.

First paginated "17" to follow 18r (paginated "16"); repaginated "18" to follow 34r (paginated "17").

[Quinn (14), 4v]

[Quinn (14), 4^{v}]

1 What could there be but those & these
~~Memories upon memories~~
2 To Have bowed my head upon my knees.
3 A dying boy with handsome ~~fa~~ face
4 Upturned upon a beaten place,
~~The s[? ?]~~
5 A sacred yew tree on a strand
~~A woman that with steady hand~~
~~Carries a~~
6 A woman [~~?~~] that holds in steady hand
7 A burning wisp beside a door
8 And many & many a woman more
~~And not another thought than these~~
10 Have bowed my head upon my knees.

9 Memories upon memories

~~sorrowfull~~
~~Sorry f~~

Cf. MS K, p 249 above, ll. 234b–244. The draft of Cuchulain's speech to the Woman of the Sidhe was first transcribed by Stephen Parrish in *The Wild Swans at Coole: Manuscript Materials*, Cornell Yeats (Ithaca, 1994), p. 419. The speech, with no speaker identified, is mixed in with lyrics Yeats included in his Cuala Press volume, *The Wild Swans at Coole, Other Verses and a Play in Verse* (1917).

Part II

The Only Jealousy of Emer: First Typescript and First Publication (1919)

Facsimiles of MS L (NLI 8774[21]) are faced by a transcription of the text in *Poetry* (1919), each with a collation below of related texts. In MS L, Yeats made quite legible ink corrections and additions to the typist's errors and omissions, as he prepared the typescript for the next typing. Most of these entries require no comment. Where the facsimile is obscured by extensive ink revisions or there is some doubt whether the typed text is an error or an earlier reading, transcriptions are provided below the facsimile.

The lines of dialogue in the two texts are numbered consecutively, but independently. The *Poetry* text loses a line in the count when Yeats collapses two lines (MS L, ll. 77–78) into one (*Poetry*, l. 77). From that point, the numbering of corresponding lines in the facing texts are out by one digit through l. 128, where Yeats inserted a new line in MS L, bringing the line count back into accord to the end of MS L. The *Poetry* text then presents a revised closing song that includes another thirteen lines, a version of which was first drafted in MS M (see pp. 311–326 below) and introduced into the text in NLI 30,873(C).

[MS L: NLI 8774(21), 1r]

THE ONLY JEALOUSY OF EMER.

(ENTER CHORUS, who are dressed as in the earlier play;
(They have the same musical instruments, which can
(either be already upon the stage or be brought in by
(the LEADER of the CHORUS before he stands in the
(CENTRE with the cloth between his hands.
(The Stage as before can be against the wall of any room.

CHORUS (During the unfolding and folding of the cloth.):-

A woman's beauty is like a white
Frail bird, like a white sea-bird, alone
At daybreak after stormy night
Between two furrows upon the ploughed land:
A sudden storm and it was thrown
Between dark furrows upon the ploughed land.
How many centuries spent
The sedentary soul
In toils of measurement
Beyond eagle or mole,
Between hearing or seeing,
Or Archimedes guess,
To raise into being
That loveliness?

A strange unserviceable thing
~~Exquisitely wrought~~ a fragile, exquisite, pale shell,
~~This beauty an exquisite, fragile shell~~
~~a fragile, exquisite, pale shell,~~
That the vast troubled waters bring
To the ~~pale sand~~ loud sands before day has broken.
The storm ~~rose~~ arose up and ~~it~~ suddenly fell
~~In~~ amid the ~~blind~~ dark night before day had broken.

---

found in NLI 8774(21), the earliest typescript *shown above and below on the left*
NLI 30,873(A) and (C)
inserted beside title corrected *NLI 30,873(A)* In this copy stage directions are corrected *NLI 30,873(C)*

An image of this page of typescript is repeated on p. 270, where ll. 15–20 are transcribed beneath it.

[*Poetry* (Chicago), 13, no. 4 (January 1919): 175]

THE ONLY JEALOUSY OF EMER

ENTER Musicians, with musical instruments. The First musician pauses at the centre and stands with a cloth between his hands. The stage can be against the wall of any room.

***First Musician* [*during the unfolding and folding of the cloth*]:**

A woman's beauty is like a white
Frail bird, like a white sea-bird alone
At daybreak after stormy night
Between two furrows upon the ploughed land:
A sudden storm and it was thrown
Between dark furrows upon the ploughed land.
How many centuries spent
The sedentary soul
In toils of measurement

---

found in Chicago (*Poetry* proofs)
NLI 30,007
Emory
published in *Poetry* (1919) *transcribed above and below on the right*
sd Enter Musicians, who are dressed as in the earlier play. They have the same musical instruments which can either be already upon the stage or be brought in by the First Musician before he stands in the centre with the cloth between his hands, or by a player when the cloth is unfolded. The stage as before can be against the wall of any room. *Chicago, but rev to text of Poetry*

Chicago sd earlier play] *The Dreaming of the Bones* preceded this play in *Two Plays for Dancers* (1919). Or perhaps this is a reference to *At the Hawk's Well*, the preceding dance play in the Cuchulain cycle. This stage direction was not in MS K.

[MS L: NLI 8774(21), 1r (foot)]

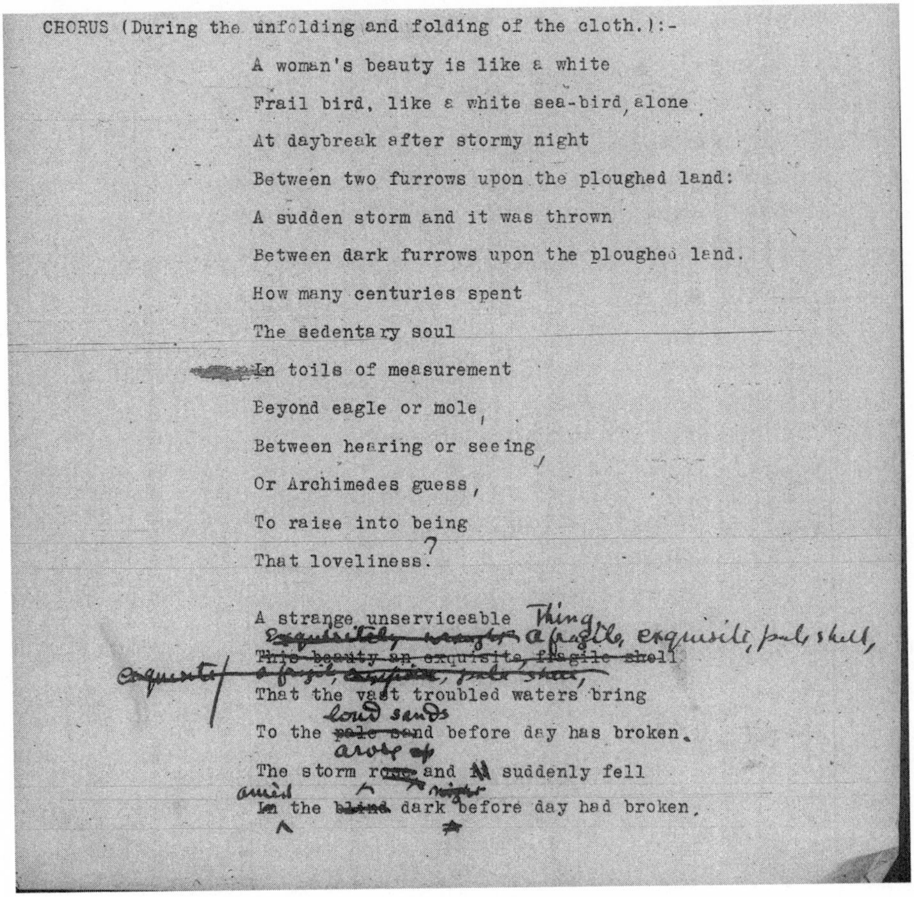

CHORUS (During the unfolding and folding of the cloth.):-

A woman's beauty is like a white
Frail bird, like a white sea-bird, alone
At daybreak after stormy night
Between two furrows upon the ploughed land:
A sudden storm and it was thrown
Between dark furrows upon the ploughed land.
How many centuries spent
The sedentary soul
In toils of measurement
Beyond eagle or mole,
Between hearing or seeing,
Or Archimedes guess,
To raise into being
That loveliness?

A strange unserviceable thing
~~This beauty an exquisite, fragile shell~~
That the vast troubled waters bring
To the ~~pale sand~~ before day has broken.
The storm ~~rose~~ and ~~it~~ suddenly fell
~~In~~ the ~~blind~~ dark before day had broken.

15–20 *typed lines at foot rev to*

A strange unserviceable thing
~~Exquisitely wrought~~ A fragile, exquisite, pale shell
~~This beauty an exquisite~~ , ~~fragile shell~~
exquisite ~~A fragile, exquisite, pale shell~~
That the vast troubled waters bring
loud sands
To the ~~pale sand~~ before day has broken.
arose ~~up~~
The storm ~~rose~~ and ~~it~~ suddenly fell
Amid ~~night~~
~~In~~ the ~~blind~~ dark before day had broken. *NLI 8774(21)*

[*Poetry* (Chicago), 13, no. 4 (January 1919): 176]

Beyond eagle or mole,
Beyond hearing or seeing,
Or Archimedes guess,
To raise into being
That loveliness?

A strange unserviceable thing,
A fragile, exquisite, pale shell.
That the vast troubled waters bring
To the loud sands before day has broken.
The storm arose up and suddenly fell
Amid the dark before day had broken.

---

11 Beyond *rev from* Between *Chicago*

[MS L: NLI 8774(21), 2r]

(2)

What death what discipline
What bonds no man could unbind ?
Being imagined within
The labyrinth of the mind ?
What pursuing or fleeing ?
What wounds, what bloody press ?
Dragged into being
This loveliness ?

(When the cloth is folded again the (MUSICIANS take their place against (wall. The folding of the cloth (shows ~~on~~ one side of the stage (the curtained bed or litter, on (which lies a man in his grave (clothes. He wears an heroic mask, (Another man in the same clothes and (mask crouches near the front. (EMER is sitting beside the bed.

LEADER of CHORUS (Speaking):-

I call before the eyes a roof
With cross-beams dark~~ed~~ened by smoke
A fisher's net hangs from a beam
A long oar lies against the wall;
I call up a poor fisher's house,
A man lies dead or swooning,
That amorous man,
That amorous violent man ~~=~~ renowned Cuchulain
Queen Emer at his side.
At her own bidding all the rest have gone
But now one comes on hesitating feet;
Young Eithne Injuba, Cuchulain's mistress

[*Poetry* (Chicago), 13, no. 4 (January 1919): 176, continued]

What death? what discipline?
What bonds no man could unbind
Being imagined within
The labyrinth of the mind?
What pursuing or fleeing?
What wounds, what bloody press?
Dragged into being
This loveliness.

[When the cloth is folded again the Musicians take their place against the wall. The folding of the cloth shows on one side of the stage the curtained bed or litter on which lies a man in his grave-clothes. He wears an heroic mask. Another man in the same clothes and mask crouches near the front. Emer is sitting beside the bed.]

***First Musician* [*speaking*]: I call before the eyes a roof**
With the cross-beams darkened by smoke.

[*Poetry* (Chicago), 13, no. 4 (January 1919): 177]

A fisher's net hangs from a beam,
A long oar lies against the wall.
I call up a poor fisher's house.
A man lied dead or swooning—
That amorous man,
That amorous, violent man, renowned Chuchlain—
Queen Emer at his side.
At her own bidding all the rest have gone.
But now one comes on hesitating feet,
Young Eithne Inguba, Cuchulain's mistress.

40ff. Injuba *rev to* Inguba *here and throughout Chicago*

[MS L: NLI 8774(21), 3r]

(3)

She stands a moment in the open door,
Beyond the open door the bitter sea,
The shining, bitter sea is crying out,

(Singing):- White shell, white wing
I will not choose for my friend
A frail unserviceable thing
That drifts and dreams, and but knows
That waters are without end
And that wind blows.

EMER (Speaking):- Come hither, come and sit down beside the bed
You need not be afraid, for I myself
Sent for you, Eithne Injuba.

EITHNE INJUBA :- No Madam,
I have too deeply wronged you to sit there

EMER :- Of all the people in the world we two,
And we alone, may watch together here,
Because we have loved him best.

EITHNE INJUBA :- And is he dead ?

EMER :- Although they have dressed him out in his grave clothes
And stretched his limbs, Cuchulain is not dead;
The very heavens when that day's at hand,
So that his death may not lack ceremony,
Will throw out fires, and the earth grow red with blood,
There shall not be a scullion but foreknows it
Like the world's end.

[*Poetry* (Chicago), 13, no. 4 (January 1919): 177, continued]

She stands a moment in the open door.
Beyond the open door the bitter sea,
The shining, bitter sea is crying out,
[*singing*] White shell, white wing,
I will not choose for my friend
A frail unserviceable thing
That drifts and dreams, and but knows
That waters are without end
And that wind blows.
***Emer* [*speaking*]: Come hither, come sit down beside the bed**
You need not be afraid, for I myself
Sent for you, Eithne Inguba.
Eithne Inguba: **No, Madam,**
I have too deeply wronged you to sit there.
Emer: **Of all the people in the world we two,**
And we alone, may watch together here,
Because we have loved him best.
Eithne Inguba: **And is he dead?**

[*Poetry* (Chicago), 13, no. 4 (January 1919): 178]

Emer: **Although they have dressed him out in his grave-clothes**
And stretched his limbs, Cuchulain is not dead.
The very heavens when that day's at hand,
So that his death may not lack ceremony,
Will throw out fires, and the earth grow red with blood.
There shall not be a scullion but foreknows it
Like the world's end.

---

58 dead. *rev from* dead; *Chicago*

[MS L: NLI 8774(21), 4r]

(4)

63b EITHNE INJUBA:- How did he come to this ?

64 EMER :- Towards noon in the assembly of the kings
65 He met with one who seemed a while most dear.
66 The kings stood round; some quarrel was blown up;
67 He drove him out and killed him on the shore
68 At Baile's tree, and he who was so killed
69 Was his own son begot on some wild woman
70 When he was young, or so I have heard it said,
71 And there upon, knowing what man he had killed,
72 And being mad with sorrow he ran out;
73 And [after] to his middle in the sea ~~awhile~~
74 [shd ~~Great~~] ~~With~~ shield before him, [and] ~~his great~~ [and with] sword in hand,
75 ~~Fought with~~ [He fought] the shapeless ~~forms~~ [foam]. The kings looked on
76 And not a king dared stretch an arm, or even
77 [~~Dared~~] Call ~~out~~ his name to ~~turn him from that war~~
78 ~~Upon the deathless sea~~, but all stood ~~there~~ [wondering]
79 In ~~a~~ [that] dumb stupor like cattle in a gale
80 Until at last, ~~fixing his eyes~~ as though [he had fixed his eyes]
81 On a new enemy, he waded out
82 Until the water had swept over him;
83 But the waves washed his senseless image up
84 And laid it at this door.

EITHNE INJUBA :- How pale he looks!

85 EMER :- He is not dead.

---

73 sea *rev to* foam *NLI 30,873(A), (C)*

74 With . . . him his great sword in hand *rev to* Great . . . him, and great sword in hand, *rev to* With . . . him, and with sword in hand, *NLI 8774(21)*

75 Fought with the shapeless forms *rev to* He fought the shapeless foam *NLI 8774(21)* shapeless foam *rev to* deathless sea *NLI 30,873(A), (C)*

76–79 *NLI 30,873(A), (C) rev as NLI 8774(21)*

81 out *rev to* on *then* out *restored NLI 30,873(A)*

[*Poetry* (Chicago), 13, no. 4 (January 1919): 178, continued]

63b **_Eithne Inguba:_ How did he come to this?**
64 **_Emer:_ Towards noon in the assembly of the kings**
65 **He met with one who seemed a while most dear.**
66 **The kings stood round; some quarrel was blown up;**
67 **He drove him out and killed him on the shore**
68 **At Baile's tree. And he who was so killed**
69 **Was his own son begot on some wild woman**
70 **When he was young, or so I have heard it said.**
71 **And thereupon, knowing what man he had killed,**
72 **And being mad with sorrow, he ran out;**
73 **And after to his middle in the foam,**
74 **With shield before him and with sword in hand,**
75 **He fought the deathless sea. The kings looked on**
76 **And not a king dared stretch an arm, or even**
77 **Dared call his name, but all stood wondering**
78 **In that dumb stupor like cattle in a gale;**
79 **Until at last, as though he had fixed his eyes**
80 **On a new enemy, he waded out**
81 **Until the water had swept over him.**
82 **But the waves washed his senseless image up**

[*Poetry* (Chicago), 13, no. 4 (January 1919): 179]

83 **And laid it at this door.**
Eithne Inguba: How pale he looks!
84 **_Emer:_ He is not dead.**

---

70 said. *rev from* said; *Chicago*
81 him. *rev from* him; *Chicago*

[MS L: NLI 8774(21), 3^{r}]

(5)

EITHNE INJUBA :- You have not kissed his lips
Nor laid his head upon your breast.

EMER :- It may be
An image has been put into his place
A sea-born log bewitched into his likeness,
Or some stark horseman grown too old to ride
Among the troops of Mananan, son of the ~~wave~~ sea
Now that ~~its~~ his joints are stiff.

EITHNE INJUBA :- Cry out his name.
All that are taken from our sight, they say,
Loiter amid the scenery of their lives
For certain hours or days, and should he hear
He might, being angry, drive the changeling out.

EMER :- ~~[illegible]~~ It is hard to make them hear amid their darkness,
And it is long since I could call him home;
I am but his wife, but if you cry aloud
With that sweet voice that is so dear to him
He cannot help but listen.

EITHNE INJUBA :- He loves me best
Being his newest love but in the end
Will love the woman best who loved him first
And loved him through the years when love seemed lost.

EMER :- I have that hope, the hope that some day and some where
We'll sit together at the hearth again.

[*Poetry* (Chicago), 13, no. 4 (January 1919): 179, continued]

Eithne Inguba: You have not kissed his lips
Nor laid his head upon your breast.
Emer: It may be
An image has been put into his place,
A sea-born log bewitched into his likeness,
Or some stark horseman grown too old to ride
Among the troops of Mananan, Son of the Sea,
Now that his joints are stiff.
Eithne Inguba: Cry out his name.
All that are taken from our sight, they say,
Loiter amid the scenery of their lives
For certain hours or days; and should he hear
He might, being angry, drive the changeling out.
Emer: It is hard to make them hear amid their darkness,
And it is long since I could call him home;
I am but his wife, but if you cry aloud
With that sweet voice that is so dear to him
He cannot help but listen.
Eithne Inguba: He loves me best
Being his newest love, but in the end
Will love the woman best who loved him first
And loved him through the years when love seemed lost.
Emer: I have that hope, the hope that some day and somewhere
We'll sit together at the hearth again.

86 place, *rev from* place *Chicago*
91 say, *rev from* say; *Chicago*
100 love, *rev from* love *Chicago*

[MS L: NLI 8774(21), 6[r]]

(6)

EITHNE INJUBA :- Women like me when the ~~worst~~ violent hour is over
Are flung into some corner like old nut shells,
Cuchulain, listen.

EMER :- No, not yet for first
I'll cover up his face to hide the sea
And throw new logs upon the hearth and stir
The half burned logs until they break in flame.
~~Old Manannan's unbridled horses come~~
Out of the sea and on their backs his horsemen
But all the enchantments of the dreaming foam
Dread the hearth fire. (She goes to one side of plat-
(form and moves her hands as
(though putting logs on a fire and stir-
(ring it to a blaze. While she makes
(these movements the MUSICIANS play,
(~~mocking~~ marking the movements with drums and
(flute perhaps.
(Having finished she stands beside the
(imaginary fire at a little distance
(from CUCHULAIN and ~~EITHNE INJUBA~~.
(She ~~has~~ pulls the curtains of the bed
(so as to hide CUCHULAIN'S face.

Call on Cuchulain now.

EITHNE INJUBA :- Can you not hear my voice

EMER :- Bend over him.
Call out dear secrets till you have touched his heart
If he lies there; and if he is not there
Till you have made him jealous.

EITHNE INJUBA :- Cuchulain, listen

EMER :- You speak too timidly; to be afraid
Because his wife is but three paces off
~~There~~ When there is so great a need were but to prove

116a, sd, l. 12 CUCHULAIN'S face *rev to* the sick man's face that the actor may change his mask unseen *NLI 30,873(C)*

[*Poetry* (Chicago), 13, no. 4 (January 1919): 180]

Eithne Inguba: Women like me when the violent hour is over
Are flung into some corner like old nut-shells.
Cuchulain, listen.
Emer: No, not yet—for first
I'll cover up his face to hide the sea;
And throw new logs upon the hearth, and stir
The half burnt logs until they break in flame.
Old Mananan's unbridled horses come
Out of the sea, and on their backs his horsemen;
But all the enchantments of the dreaming foam
Dread the hearth fire.

[She pulls the curtains of the bed so as to hide the sick man's face, that the actor may change his mask unseen. She goes to one side of platform and moves her hand as though putting logs on a fire and stirring it into a blaze. While she makes these movements the Musicians play, marking the movements with drum and flute perhaps. Having finished, she stands beside the imaginary fire at a distance from Cuchulain and Eithne Inguba.]

Call on Cuchulain now.
Eithne Inguba: Can you not hear my voice?
Emer: Bend over him
Call out dear secrets till you have touched his heart
If he lies there; and if he is not there
Till you have made him jealous.
Eithne Inguba: Cuchulain, listen.

[*Poetry* (Chicago), 13, no. 4 (January 1919): 181]

Emer: You speak too timidly; to be afraid
Because his wife is but three paces off,
When there is so great a need, were but to prove

107b yet— *rev from* yet *Chicago*
120 off, *rev from* off *Chicago*

[MS L: NLI 8774(21), 7^{r}]

The man that chose you made but a poor choice.
We're but two women struggling with the sea.

EITHNE INJUBA :- O my beloved pardon me, that I
Have been ashamed and you in so great need;
I have never sent a message or called out
Scarce had a longing for your company
But you have known and come; and if indeed
You are lying there stretch out your arms and speak;
Open your mouth and speak for, to this hour
My company has made you talkative.
Why do you mope, and what has ~~closed~~ closed your ears.
Our passion had not chilled when we were parted
On the pale shore under the breaking dawn.
He will not hear me; or his ears are closed
And no sound reaches him.

EMER :- Then kiss ~~this~~ that image
The pressure of your mouth upon his mouth
May reach him where he is.

EITHNE INJUBA
(starting back):- It is no man,
I felt some evil thing that dried my heart
When my lips touched it.

EMER :- No, his ~~hide~~ body stirs,
The pressure of your mouth has called him home;
He has thrown the changeling out.

EITHNE INJUBA
(going further off) - Look at ~~this~~ that arm
That arm is withered to the very socket.

128/129 *typist's omission?*

[*Poetry* (Chicago), 13, no. 4 (January 1919): 181, continued]

122 **The man that chose you made but a poor choice.**
123 **We're but two women struggling with the sea.**
124 ***Eithne Inguba:* O my beloved, pardon me, that I**
125 **Have been ashamed and you in so great need.**
126 **I have never sent a message or called out,**
127 **Scarce had a longing for your company,**
128 **But you have known and come. And if indeed**
129 **You are lying there stretch out your arms and speak;**
130 **Open your mouth and speak, for to this hour**
131 **My company has made you talkative.**
132 **Why do you mope, and what has closed your ears?**
133 **Our passion had not chilled when we were parted**
134 **On the pale shore under the breaking dawn.**
135 **He will not hear me: or his ears are closed**
136 **And no sound reaches him.**
Emer: **Then kiss that image:**
137 **The pressure of your mouth upon his mouth**
138 **May reach him where he is.**
***Eithne Inguba* [*starting back*]: It is no man.**
139 **I felt some evil thing that dried my heart**
140 **When my lips touched it.**
Emer: **No, his body stirs;**
141 **The pressure of your mouth has called him home;**
142 **He has thrown the changeling out.**
***Eithne Inguba* [*going further off*]: Look at that arm—**

[*Poetry* (Chicago), 13, no. 4 (January 1919): 182]

143 **That arm is withered to the very socket.**

---

122 choice. *rev from* choice, *Chicago*
125 need. *rev from* need; *Chicago*

[MS L: NLI 8774(21), 8r]

(8)

EMER (going up to the bed):-

144 What do you come for and from where ?

FIGURE of CUCHULAIN):- I have come

145 From Mananan's ~~xxxxx~~ court upon a bridl~~ed~~ ^less horse.

146 EMER :- What one among the sidhe has dared to lie

147 Upon Cuchulain's bed and take his image ?

148 FIGURE of CUCHULAIN :- I am named Bricriu - not the man - that Bricriu,

149 Maker of discord among gods and men,

150 Called Bricriu of the Sidhe.

EMER :- Come for what purpose?

FIGURE (sits up and shows
(its disturbed face ~~):-~~. Ethna Inguba goes out)

151 I show my face and everything he loves

152 Must fly away.

EMER :- You people of the wind

153 Are full of lying speech and mockery

154 I have not fled your face.

FIGURE - You are not loved.

155 EMER :- And therefore have no dread to meet your eyes

156 And ^to ~~I~~ demand him of you.

FIGURE :- For that I have come,

157 You have but to pay the prace and he is free.

158 EMER :- Do the Sidhe bargain ?

145 bridled *rev to* bridless [*sic* for bridleless] *NLI 8774(21)*
150sd disturbed *rev to* distorted *NLI 30,873(A), (C)*

[*Poetry* (Chicago), 13, no. 4 (January 1919): 182, continued]

Emer [going up to the bed]:
144 **What do you come for, and from where?**
Figure of Cuchulain: **I have come**
145 **From Mananan's court upon a bridleless horse.**
146 ***Emer:*** **What one among the Sidhe has dared to lie**
147 **Upon Cuchulain's bed and take his image?**
Figure of Cuchulain:
148 **I am named Bricriu—not the man—that Bricriu,**
149 **Maker of discord among gods and men,**
150 **Called Bricriu of the Sidhe.**
Emer: **Come for what purpose?**
Figure of Cuchulain: [sitting up and showing its distorted face, while Eithne Inguba goes out]:
151 **I show my face and everything he loves**
152 **Must fly away.**
Emer: **You people of the wind**
153 **Are full of lying speech and mockery.**
154 **I have not fled your face.**
Figure of Cuchulain: **You are not loved.**
155 ***Emer:*** **And therefore have no dread to meet your eyes**
156 **And to demand him of you.**
Figure of Cuchulain: **For that I have come.**
157 **You have but to pay the price and he is free.**
158 ***Emer:*** **Do the Sidhe bargain?**

150sd while *inserted Chicago*
153 mockery. *rev from* mockery *Chicago*
156b come. *rev from* come *Chicago*

(9)

FIGURE :- When they set free a ~~captain~~ captive
They take in ransom a less valued thing.
The fisher when some knowledgable man
Restores to him his wife, or son, or daughter,
Knows he must lose a boat or net, or it may be
The cow that gives his children milk; and some
Have offered their own lives. I do not ask
Your life, or any valuable thing;
~~You spoke but now of the mere chance that some day~~
You'd sit together by the hearth again:
Renounce that chance, that miserable hour
And he shall live again.

EMER :- I do not question
But you have brought ill luck on all he loves
And now, because I am thrown beyond your power,
Unless your words are lies, you come to bargain.

FIGURE :- You loved your power when but newly married
And I love mine although I am old and withered;
You have but to put your self out of that ~~hope~~ power
And he shall live again.

EMER :- No, Never, never.

FALSE CUCHULAIN: You dare not be accursed yet he has dared

EMER :- I have but two joyous thoughts, ~~and~~ Two things ~~of price~~ I prize
A hope, A memory ~~and a hope~~, and now you claim that hope.

FALSE CUCHULAIN:- He'll never sit beside you at the hearth
Or make old ~~love~~ bones, but die of wounds and ~~want~~ toil

177–221 FALSE CUCHULAIN] FIGURE OF CUCHULAIN *NLI 30,873(A)*
178 of price *rev to* I prize *NLI 30,873(A), (C)*

[*Poetry* (Chicago), 13, no. 4 (January 1919): 182, continued]

Figure of Cuchulain: **When they set free a captive**
They take in ransom a less valued thing.
The fisher, when some knowledgeable man

[*Poetry* (Chicago), 13, no. 4 (January 1919): 183]

Restores to him his wife, or son, or daughter,
Knows he must lose a boat or net, or it may be
The cow that gives his children milk; and some
Have offered their own lives. I do not ask
Your life, or any valuable thing.
You spoke but now of the mere chance that some day
You'd sit together by the hearth again:
Renounce that chance, that miserable hour,
And he shall live again.
Emer: **I do not question**
But you have brought ill luck on all he loves;
And now, because I am thrown beyond your power
Unless your words are lies, you come to bargain.
Figure of Cuchulain: **You loved your power when but newly married,**
And I love mine although I am old and withered.
You have but to put yourself into that power
And he shall live again.
Emer: **No, never, never!**
Figure of Chuchulain: **You dare not be accursed, yet he has dared.**
Emer: **I have but two joyous thoughts, two things I prize—**
A hope, a memory; and now you claim that hope.
Figure of Cuchulain: **He'll never sit beside you at the hearth**
Or make old bones, but die of wounds and toil

---

168 hour, *rev from* hour *Chicago*
174 withered. *rev from* withered; *Chicago*
176b never! *rev from* never, *Chicago*
178 thoughts. To things I prize *rev to* thoughts, two things I prize, *Chicago*

[MS L: NLI 8774(21), 10r]

(10)

(Continued):- On some far shore or mountain a strange woman
Beside his mattress.

EMER :- You ask for my one hope
That you may bring your curse on all about him.

FALSE CUCHULAIN: You've watched his loves and you have not been jealous
Knowing that he would tire, but do those tire
That love the Sidhe.

EMER :- [What dancer of the Sidhe?]
~~Has then some dancer of the Sidhe~~
~~Some~~ [What] creature of the reeling moon [has] pursued him ?

FALSE CUCHULAIN:- I have but to touch your eyes and give them sight,
But stand at my left side. (He touches her eyes with
(his left hand, [the right being withered)]

EMER :- My husband there,

FALSE CUCHULAIN:- But out of reach - I have disolved the dark
That hid him from your eyes but not that other
That's hidden you from his.

EMER :- Husband, husband !

FALSE CUCHULAIN:- Be silent, he is but a phantom now
And he can neither touch, nor hear, nor see;
The longing and the [cries] have drawn him hither,
He heard no sound, heard no articulate sound
They could [but] banish rest, and make him dream,
And in that dream as do all dreaming shades
Before they are accustomed to their freedom
He has taken his familiar form, and ~~[illegible]~~ [yet]

[*Poetry* (Chicago), 13, no. 4 (January 1919): 183, continued]

182 **On some far shore or mountain, a strange woman**
183 **Beside his mattress.**

[*Poetry* (Chicago), 13, no. 4 (January 1919): 184]

Emer: **You ask for my one hope**
184 **That you may bring your curse on all about him.**
185 ***Figure of Chuchulain:*** **You've watched his loves and you have not been jealous**
186 **Knowing that he would tire, but do those tire**
187 **That love the Sidhe?**
Emer: **What dancer of the Sidhe,**
188 **What creature of the reeling moon has pursued him?**
189 ***Figure of Cuchulain:*** **I have but to touch your eyes and give them sight;**
190 **But stand at my left side.**

[*He touches her eyes with his left hand, the right being withered.*]

Emer: **My husband there.**
191 ***Figure of Cuchulain:*** **But out of reach—I have dissolved the dark.**
192 **That hid him from your eyes, but not that other**
193 **That's hidden you from his.**
Emer: **Husband, husband!**
194 ***Figure of Cuchulain:*** **Be silent, he is but a phantom now,**
195 **And he can neither touch, nor hear, nor see.**
196 **The longing and the cries have drawn him hither.**
197 **He heard no sound, heard no articulate sound;**
198 **They could but banish rest, and make him dream,**
199 **And in that dream, as do all dreaming shades**
200 **Before they are accustomed to their freedom,**
201 **He has taken his familiar form, and yet**

190b *rev to* Emer seeing the crouching Ghost of Cuchulain My husband is there. *NLI 30,007*

[MS L: NLI 8774(21), 11r]

(11)

(continued):-

He crouches there ~~me~~ not knowing where he is
Or at whose side he is crouched.

(The WOMAN of the SIDHE has ENTERED
(and stands a little inside the door

EMER :- Who is this woman ?

FALSE CUCHULAIN:- She has hurried from the Country-Under-Wave
And dreamed herself into the shape that he
May glitter in her basket; for the Sidhe
Are fishers also and they fish for men
With dreams upon the hook.

EMER :- And so that woman
Has hid herself in this disguise and made
Herself into a lie.

FALSE CUCHULAIN: A dream is body.
~~[illegible]~~ The dead move ever towards a dreamless youth
And when they dream no more return no more
And those more ~~lowly~~ holy shades that never lived
But ~~went~~ visit you in dreams.

EMER :- I know her sort.
They find our men asleep, weary with war,
Or weary with the chase and kiss their lips
And drop their hair upon them, from that hour
Our men, who yet knew nothing of it all,
Are lonely, and when, at fall of night we press
Their hearts upon our hearts their hearts are cold.
(She draws a knife from her side.)

FALSE CUCHULAIN:- And so you think to wound her with a knife

[*Poetry* (Chicago), 13, no. 4 (January 1919): 185]

202 **He crouches there not knowing where he is**
203 **Or at whose side he is crouched.**

[A Woman of the Sidhe has entered, and stands a little inside the door.]

Emer: **Who is this woman?**
204 ***Figure of Cuchulain:*** **She has hurried from the Country-Under-Wave,**
205 **And dreamed herself into that shape that he**
206 **May glitter in her basket; for the Sidhe**
207 **Are fishers also and they fish for men**
208 **With dreams upon the hook.**
Emer: **And so that woman**
209 **Has hid herself in this disguise and made**
210 **Herself into a lie.**
Figure of Cuchulain: **A dream is body;**
211 **The dead move ever towards a dreamless youth**
212 **And when they dream no more return no more;**
213 **And those more holy shades that never lived**
214 **But visit you in dreams.**
Emer: **I know her sort.**
215 **They find our men asleep, weary with war,**
216 **Or weary with the chase, and kiss their lips**
217 **And drop their hair upon them. From that hour**
218 **Our men, who yet knew nothing of it all,**
219 **Are lonely, and when at fall of night we press**
220 **Their hearts upon our hearts their hearts are cold.**

[*She draws a knife from her girdle.*]

[*Poetry* (Chicago), 13, no. 4 (January 1919): 186]

221 ***Figure of Cuchulain:*** **And so you think to wound her with a knife.**

---

209 hid *rev from* had *Chicago*
221–222 No knife can wound that body of air. Be silent; listen; *NLI 30,007*

(12)

(continued):-

She has an airy body. Look and listen
I have not given you eyes and ears for nothing.

(The WOMAN of the SIDHE moves round CUCHULAIN in a dance that grows gradually quicker, as he slowly ~~wakens~~ awakes. At moments she may drop her hair upon his head but she does not kiss him. She is accompanied by string and flute and drum. Her mask and clothes must suggest gold, or bronze or brass or silver, so that she seems more an idol than a human being. This suggestion may be repeated in her movements. Her hair too must keep the metallic suggestion.

CUCHULAIN :-

Who is it stands before me there
Shedding such light from limb and hair
As when the moon complete at last
With every labouring crescent past,
And ~~comely~~ Lonely with extreme delight,
Flings out on upon the fifteenth night. ?

WOMAN OF THE SIDHE

Because I long I am not complete.
What pulled your hands about your feet
And your head down upon your knees,
And hid your face?

CUCHULAIN.

O memories:
A dying boy, with handsome face
Upturned upon a beaten place;
A sacred yew-tree ~~there~~ on a strand;
A woman ~~there~~ that held in steady hand

223sd CUCHULAIN *rev to* the crouching figure toward the front of the stage *NLI 30,873(C)* or bronze or brass or silver so that *omitted then inserted NLI 30,873(A), (C)*

224, 233 *in speaker tags* Ghost of *inserted before* CUCHULAIN *NLI 30,873(C)*

---

229 In NLI 8774(21) Yeats revised "out on" to "out on upon" without canceling "on."

[*Poetry* (Chicago), 13, no. 4 (January 1919): 186, continued]

222 **She has an airy body. Look and listen—**
223 **I have not given you eyes and ears for nothing.**

[*The Woman of the Sidhe moves round the crouching Ghost of Cuchulain at front of stage in a dance that grows gradually quicker, as he slowly awakes. At moments she may drop her hair upon his head, but she does not kiss him. She is accompanied by string and flute and drum. Her mask and clothes must suggest gold or bronze or brass or silver, so that she seems more an idol than a human being. This suggestion may be repeated in her movements. Her hair too must keep the metallic suggestion.*]

224 ***Ghost of Cuchulain:*** **Who is it stands before me there,**
225 **Shedding such light from limb and hair**
226 **As when the moon, complete at last**
227 **With every laboring crescent past,**
228 **And lonely with extreme delight,**
229 **Flings out upon the fifteenth night?**
230 ***Woman of the Sidhe:*** **Because I long I am not complete.**
231 **What pulled your hands about your feet,**
232 **And your head down upon your knees,**
233 **And hid your face?**
Ghost of Cuchulain: **Old Memories:**
234 **A dying boy, with handsome face**
235 **Upturned upon a beaten place;**
236 **A sacred yew-tree on a strand;**

[*Poetry* (Chicago), 13, no. 4 (January 1919): 187]

237 **A woman that held in steady hand**

---

222 listen— *rev from* listen; *Chicago*
227 laboring *rev from* labouring *Chicago*
231 *rev to* What pulled down your head upon your knees *NLI 30,007*

[MS L: NLI 8774(21), 13r]

(13)

Continued):-

In all the happiness of her youth
Before her man had broken troth,
A burning torch to light the door;
And many a round or crescent more;
Dead men and women, memories
Hve pulled my head upon my knees

WOMAN OF THE SIDHE

Could you that have loved many a woman
That did not reach beyond the human,
Lacking a day to be complete,
Love one that though her heart can beat,
Lacks it by but an hour or so.

CUCHULAIN

I know you now for long ago
I met you on the mountain side,
Beside a well that seemed long dried,
Beside old thorns where the hawk flew.
I held out arms and hands but you,
That now seem friendly, fled away
Half woman and half bird of prey.

WOMAN OF THE SIDHE.

Hold out your arms and hands again
You were not so dumbfounded when

---

246 Being a whole day from the [?end *rev to* full] *all del and replaced by l. 247 NLI 8774(21)*
249 by but *rev to* but by *NLI 30,873(A)*
250 *in speaker tag* Ghost of *inserted before* CUCHULAIN *NLI 30,873(C)*

[*Poetry* (Chicago), 13, no. 4 (January 1919): 187, continued]

238 **In all the happiness of her youth**
239 **Before her man had broken troth,**
240 **A burning wisp to light the door;**
241 **And many a round or crescent more;**
242 **Dead men and women. Memories**
243 **Have pulled my head upon my knees.**
244 *Woman of the Sidhe:* **Could you that have loved many a woman**
245 **That did not reach beyond the human,**
246 **Lacking a day to be complete,**
247 **Love one that, though her heart can beat,**
248 **Lacks it but by an hour or so?**
249 *Ghost of Cuchulain:* **I know you now, for long ago**
250 **I met you on the mountain side,**
251 **Beside a well that seemed long dry,**
252 **Beside old thorns where the hawk flew.**
253 **I held out arms and hands, but you,**
254 **That now seem friendly, fled away**
255 **Half woman and half bird of prey.**
256 *Woman of the Sidhe:* **Hold out your arms and hands again.**
257 **You were not so dumbfounded when**

---

251 *rev to* A woman danced and a hawk flew *NLI 30,007*

[MS L: NLI 8774(21), 14r]

(14)

(Continued):-

I was that bird of prey and yet
I am all woman now.

CUCHULAIN.

I am not
The young and passionate man I was
And though that brilliant light ~~upon~~ surpass
All crescent forms - my memories
Weigh down my hands ~~about~~ abash my eyes.

WOMAN OF THE SIDHE.

Then kiss my mouth. Though memory
Be ~~beauties~~ beauty's bitterest enemy
I have no dread for ~~with~~ at my kiss
~~All kinds of memory vanishes~~ Memory on the ~~instant~~ moment vanishes:
~~And only~~ nothing but beauty ~~will~~ can remain.

CUCHULAIN.

And shall I never know again
Intricacies of blind remorse.

WOMAN OF THE SIDHE

Time shall seem to stay his course
For when your mouth and my mouth meet
All my round shall be complete
~~Imaginary all~~ Imagining all its circles run;
And there shall be oblivion
Even to ~~start~~ quench Cuchulain's ~~doubt~~ drouth,
Even to ~~quench~~ still that heart.

261, 270 *in speaker tags* Ghost of *inserted before* CUCHULAIN *NLI 30,873(C)*

268 All kinds of memory vanishes *rev to* no memory but vanishes *rev to* Memory on the ~~instant~~ moment vanishes *NLI 8774(21)*

[*Poetry* (Chicago), 13, no. 4 (January 1919): 187, continued]

I was that bird of prey, and yet
I am all woman now.
Ghost of Cuchulain: **I am not**
The young and passionate man I was,
And though that brilliant light surpass
All crescent forms, my memories

[*Poetry* (Chicago), 13, no. 4 (January 1919): 188]

Weigh down my hands, abash my eyes.
Woman of the Sidhe: **Then kiss my mouth. Though memory**
Be beauty's bitterest enemy
I have no dread, for at my kiss
Memory on the moment vanishes:
Nothing but beauty can remain.
Ghost of Cuchulain: **And shall I never know again**
Intricacies of blind remorse?
Woman of the Sidhe: **Time shall seem to stay his course,**
For when your mouth and my mouth meet
All my round shall be complete
Imagining all its circles run;
And there shall be oblivion
Even to quench Cuchulain's drouth,
Even to still that heart.

(15)

CUCHULAIN.

Your mouth

(They are about to kiss, he turns
(away.

O Emer, Emer.

WOMAN OF THE SIDHE.

So then it is she
Made you impure with memory!

CUCHULAIN.

Still in that dream I see you stand,
A burning wisp in your right hand,
To wait my coming to the house,
As when our parents married us.

WOMAN OF THE SIDHE.

Being among the dead you love her
That ~~when~~ valued every slut above her
While you still lived.

CUCHULAIN.

O my lost Emer,

WOMAN OF THE SIDHE

And there is not a loose-tongued schemer
But could draw you, if not dead,
From her table and her bed.
How could you be fit to wive
With flesh and blood, being born to ~~live~~ live
Where no one speaks of broken troth
For all have washed out of their eyes
Wind blown dirt of their memories
To improve their sight?

278b, 281 *in speaker tags* Ghost of *inserted before* CUCHULAIN *NLI 30,873(C)*

295 Wind blown dirt *rev from* The blown dust *NLI 8774(21), NLI 30,873(A), (C)*

[*Poetry* (Chicago), 13, no. 4 (January 1919): 188, continued]

277b **_Ghost of Cuchulain:_ Your mouth.**
[_They are about to kiss, he turns away._]
278 **O Emer, Emer!**
Woman of the Sidhe: So then it is she
279 **Made you impure with memory.**
280 **_Ghost of Cuchulain:_ Still in that dream I see you stand,**
281 **A burning wisp in your right hand,**
282 **To wait my coming to the house—**
283 **As when our parents married us.**
284 **_Woman of the Sidhe:_ Being among the dead you love her,**
285 **That valued every slut above her**
286 **While you still lived.**

[*Poetry* (Chicago), 13, no. 4 (January 1919): 189]

Ghost of Cuchulain: O my lost Emer!
287 **_Woman of the Sidhe:_ And there is not a loose-tongued schemer**
288 **But could draw you if not dead,**
289 **From her table and her bed.**
290 **How could you be fit to wive**
291 **With flesh and blood, being born to live**
292 **Where no one speaks of broken troth—**
293 **For all have washed out of their eyes**
294 **Wind-blown dirt of their memories**
295 **To improve their sight?**

---

287 loose-tongued *rev from* loose tongued *Chicago*
290 *rev to* But what could make you fit to wive *Emory*
292 troth— *rev from* troth *Chicago*

[MS L: NLI 8774(21), 16r]

(16)

CUCHULAIN.

296b Your mouth, your mouth.

(~~Nothing but~~ (Their lips approach but Cuchulain turns away as Emer speaks)

EMER.

297 If but he ~~loves~~ lives I am content,
298 If but the dead will set him free
299 That I may speak with him at whiles,
300 ~~I am~~ content that he shall turn on me,
301 Eyes that the cold moon or the ~~hard~~ harsh sea
302 Or what I know not 's made indifferent.

CUCHULAIN.

303 What a wise silence has fallen in this dark.
304 I know you now in all your ignorance
305 Of all whereby a lover's quiet is ~~most~~ rent.
306 What dread so great is that he should forget'
307 ~~The least chance sight or sound, or scratch or mark~~
308 On an old door, a chance bird herd and seen
309 In the incredible clear light she cast
310 All round about ~~his~~ her ~~soon~~ some forlorn lost day ?
311 ~~This~~ That face, though fine enough, is a fool's face
312 And there's a folly in the deathless sidhe
313 Beyond man's reach

WOMAN OF THE SIDHE

I told you to forget
314 After my fashion; you would have none of it;
315 So now you may forget in a man's fashion.
316 There's an unbridled horse at the sea's edge
317 Mount - it will carry you in an eye's ~~flash~~ wink

~~Exeunt~~

---

296 *in speaker tag* Ghost of *inserted before* CUCHULAIN *NLI 30,873(C)*
306 is *rev to* as *NLI 30,873(A), (C)*
308 a chance *rev to* or frail *NLI 30,873(A), (C)*
309 she cast *rev to* love cast *NLI 30,873(A), (C)*
310 soon *rev to* some *NLI 30,873(A), (C)*

---

300 The revised line is arrowed to follow l. 297 in NLI 8774(21) and NLI 30,873(A).

[*Poetry* (Chicago), 13, no. 4 (January 1919): 189, continued]

295b **_Ghost of Cuchulain:_ Your mouth, your mouth.**
[*Their lips approach but Cuchulain turns away as Emer speaks.*]
296 **_Emer:_ If he may live I am content,**
297 **Content that he shall turn on me—**
298 **If but the dead will set him free**
299 **That I may speak with him at whiles—**
300 **Eyes that the cold moon or the harsh sea**
301 **Or what I know not's made indifferent.**
302 **_Ghost of Cuchulain:_ What a wise silence has fallen in this dark!**
303 **I know you now in all your ignorance**
304 **Of all whereby a lover's quiet is rent.**
305 **What dread so great as that he should forget**
306 **The least chance sight or sound, or scratch or mark**
307 **On an old door, or frail bird heard and seen**
308 **In the incredible clear light love cast**

[*Poetry* (Chicago), 13, no. 4 (January 1919): 190]

309 **All round about her some forlorn lost day?**
310 **That face, though fine enough, is a fool's face**
311 **And there's a folly in the deathless Sidhe**
312 **Beyond a man's reach.**
Woman of the Sidhe: I told you to forget
313 **After my fashion; you would have none of it;**
314 **So now you may forget in a man's fashion.**
315 **There's an unbridled horse at the sea's edge.**
316 **Mount—it will carry you in an eye's wink**

---

297 me— *rev from* me, *Chicago*
302 dark! *rev from* dark *Chicago*
316 Mount— *rev from* Mount; *Chicago*

(17)

(continued):-

To where the King of Country-Under-Wave
Old Mananan, nods above the board and moves
His chessmen in a dream. Demand your life
And come again on the unbridled horse.

CUCHULAIN

Forgive me those rough words. How could you know
That man is held to those whom he has loved
By pain that they give, or pain that he has given
Intricacies of pain.

WOMAN OF THE SIDHE

I am ashamed
That being of the deathless shades I chose
A man so knotted to impurity.

(CUCHULAIN GOES OUT)

WOMAN OF THE SIDHE (to FALSE CUCHULAIN)

To you that have no living light ~~and~~ to you
That dropped out of a last leprous crescent of the moon
I owe it all

~~FALSE~~ Figure of CUCHULAIN

Because you have failed
I must ~~longer~~ forego your thanks, I that took pity
Upon your love and carried out your plan
To tangle all his life and make it nothing
That he might turn to you.

WOMAN OF THE SIDHE

Was it from pity
You taught the woman to prevail against me.

---

322 *in speaker tag* Ghost of *inserted before* CUCHULAIN *NLI 30,873(C)*
324 that they give *rev to* they gave *NLI 30,873(A), (C)*
327sd The Ghost of *inserted before* CUCHULAIN goes out *NLI 30,873(C)*
328sd (to FALSE CUCHULAIN)] (to FIGURE OF CUCHULAIN) *NLI 30,873(A)*
328 to you *rev to* but dropped *NLI 30,873(A)*
329 That dropped out of *rev to* From *NLI 30,873(A)*

[*Poetry* (Chicago), 13, no. 4 (January 1919): 190, continued]

To where the King of Country-Under-wave,
Old Mananan, nods above the board and moves
His chessmen in a dream. Demand your life,
And come again on the unbridled horse.
***Ghost of Cuchulain:* Forgive me those rough words. How could you know**
That man is held to those whom he has loved
By pain they gave, or pain that he has given—
Intricacies of pain.
***Woman of the Sidhe:* I am ashamed**
That being of the deathless shades I chose
A man so knotted to impurity.
[*The Ghost of Cuchulain goes out.*]
***Woman of the Sidhe* [*to figure of Cuchulain*]: To you that have no living light, but dropped**
From a last leprous crescent of the moon
I owe it all.
***Figure of Cuchulain:* Because you have failed**
I must forego your thanks, I that took pity

[*Poetry* (Chicago), 13, no. 4 (January 1919): 191]

Upon your love and carried our your plan
To tangle all his life and make it nothing
That he might turn to you.
***Woman of the Sidhe:* Was it from pity**
You taught the woman to prevail against me?

321 Cuchulain] Cuchulian *Poetry*
328 moon *rev to* moon, *Chicago*

(18)

Figure of ~~FALSE~~ CUCHULAIN.

You know my nature - by what name I am called

WOMAN OF THE SIDHE.

Was it from pity that you hid the truth
That men are bound to women by the wrongs
They do or suffer.

Figure of ~~FALSE~~ CUCHULAIN.

You know what being I am

WOMAN OF THE SIDHE.

I have been mocked and disobeyed - your power
Was more to you than my good-will, and now
I'll have you learn what my ill-will can do;
I lay you under bonds upon the instant
To stand before our king and face the charge
And take the punishment.

Figure of ~~FALSE~~ CUCHULAIN.

I'll stand there first
And tell my story first, and Manannan
Knows that his own harsh sea made my heart cold
~~Myxhsrsxxisxthsxs~~

WOMAN OF THE SIDHE

My horse is there and shall out run your horse.

(The figure of ~~FALSE~~ CUCHULAIN falls back, the
(WOMAN of the SIDHE GOES OUT)
(Drum taps, music resembles horse
(hoofs.

EITHNE INJUBA (entering, quickly)

I heard the beat of hoofs, but saw no horse,
And then came other hoofs and after that

[*Poetry* (Chicago), 13, no. 4 (January 1919): 191, continued]

335 ***Figure of Cuchulain:*** **You know my nature—by what name I am called.**
336 ***Woman of the Sidhe:*** **Was it from pity that you hid the truth**
337 **That men are bound to women by the wrongs**
338 **They do or suffer?**
Figure of Cuchulain: **You know what being I am.**
339 ***Woman of the Sidhe:*** **I have been mocked and disobeyed—your power**
340 **Was more to you than my good-will, and now**
341 **I'll have you learn what my ill-will can do:**
342 **I lay you under bonds upon the instant**
343 **To stand before our King and face the charge**
344 **And take the punishment.**
Figure of Cuchulain: **I'll stand there first,**
345 **And tell my story first; and Mananan**
346 **Knows that his own harsh sea made my heart cold.**
347 ***Woman of the Sidhe:*** **My horse is there and shall outrun your horse.**
[*The Figure of Cuchulain falls back, the Woman of the Sidhe goes out. Drum taps, music resembling horse hoofs.*]
348 ***Eithne Inguba*** **[*entering quickly*]: I heard the beat of hoofs, but saw no horse;**

[*Poetry* (Chicago), 13, no. 4 (January 1919): 192]

349 **And then came other hoofs, and after that**

341 do: *rev from* do; *Chicago*

[MS L: NLI 8774(21), 19r]

(Continued):-

(19)

351 I heard low angry cries and there upon

352 I ceased to be afraid.

EMER.

Cuchulain wakes

CUCHULAIN.

353 Eithne Injuba take me in your arms

354 I have been in some strange place and am afraid.

The ~~chor~~ leader of chorus comes to the front of stage, the others from each side & unfold the curtain singing

351b wakes] wakes. (The Figure turns round. It once more wears the heroic mask.) *NLI 30,873(C)*

354sd The ~~chor~~ leader of chorus comes to the front / of stage, the others from each side & unfold / the curtain singing *NLI 8774(21)* curtain singing *rev to* cloth singing:— *NLI 30,873(A), (C)*

[*Poetry* (Chicago), 13, no. 4 (January 1919): 192, continued]

I heard low angry cries, and thereupon
I ceased to be afraid.
***Emer:* Cuchulain wakes.**

[The figure turns round. It once more wears the heroic mask.]

***Cuchulain:* Eithne Inguba, take me in your arms—**
I have been in some strange place and am afraid.

[The First Musician comes to the front of the stage, the others from each side. They unfold the cloth, singing.]

---

350 cries, *rev from* cries *Chicago*
353sd each side and unfold *rev to* each side. They unfold *Chicago*

(20)

How may that woman find,
Being born to ill-luck as it seems
And groping her way half blind
In labyrinths of her dreams,
A little friendship and love;
For all the chase and its zest
Passion soon has enough
Of an alien thing on its breast.

O bitter reward !
Of many a tragic tomb !
And we though astonished are dumb
Or give but a look and a word,
A passing word.

And how could I dream that this wife,
Bowed at her hearth-stone
And a mere part of our life,
Could speak with a gentle tongue
And give her the hand of a friend ?
Could she not see in that eye
That it must endure to the end,
Reproach and jealousy.

O bitter reward !
O many a tragic tomb !
And we though astonished are dumb
Or give but a look and a word
A passing word.

When the Curtain is folded again the stage is bare.

355–380 *Below is a transcription of the thirty-nine-line revision of the song added in Yeats's ink in NLI 30,873(C), similar to text of closing song in* Poetry *(1919), facing. For drafts leading to this revision, see pp. 312–325 below.*

What makes her heart beat thus,
Plain to be understood
I have met in a mans house
A statue of solitude
Moving there and walking;
Its strange heart beating fast
For all our talking.
O still that heart at last

O bitter reward
Of many a tragic tomb
And we though astonished are dumb
And give but a sigh & a word
A passing word.

[*Poetry* (Chicago), 13, no. 4 (January 1919): 192, continued]

The Musicians:

What makes her heart beat thus,
Plain to be understood?
I have met in a man's house
A statue of solitude,
Moving there and walking;
Its strange heart beating fast
For all our talking.
Oh, still that heart at last!

O bitter reward!
Of many a tragic tomb!
And we though astonished are dumb
And give but a sigh and a word,
A passing word.

Although the door be shut
And all seem well enough,

[*Poetry* (Chicago), 13, no. 4 (January 1919): 193]

Although wide world hold not
A man but will give you his love
The moment he has looked at you,
He that has loved the best
May turn from a statue
His too human breast.

O bitter reward!
Of many a tragic tomb!
And we though astonished are dumb
Or give but a sigh and a word,
A passing word.

[*stanza break*]
Although the door be shut
And all seem well enough
Although wide world hold not
A man but will give you his love
The moment he has looked at you
He that has loved the best
May turn from a statue
His too human breast.

O bitter reward
Of many a tragic tomb
And we though astonished are dumb
Or
~~That~~ give but a sigh & a word
A passing word.

[*Poetry* (Chicago), 13, no. 4 (January 1919): 193, continued]

What makes your heart so beat?
Some one should stay at her side.
When beauty is complete
Her own thought will have died
And danger not be diminished;
Dimmed at three-quarter light,
When moon's round is finished
The stars are out of sight.

O bitter reward!
Of many a tragic tomb!
And we though astonished are dumb
Or give but a sigh and a word,
A passing word.

[*When the cloth is folded again the stage is bare.*]

William Butler Yeats

[*stanza break*]
What makes your heart so beat
Some one should stay at her side
When beauty is complete
Her own thoughts will have died
And danger not be diminished
Danced at [?three] quarter light
When moon's round is finished
The stars are out of sight.

O bitter reward
Of many a tragic tomb
And we though astonished are dumb
Or give but a sigh & a word
A passing word. *NLI 30,873(C)*

Revisions of the Closing Song in *The Only Jealousy of Emer*

Drafts of the closing song for *The Only Jealousy of Emer* are found in MS M, a collection of five loose leaves arranged here in their probable order, which is not their folder order. Indeed, two of the leaves, 4 and 5, were moved to another manuscript that is now the Harvard manuscript of the play (Houghton Library, Eng Ms 338.7; see the note to 4^r below).

See the collation of NLI 30,873(C) and the text of *Poetry* (1919) for further revisions to the song (pp. 308–310 above).

[NLI 8774(22), 1r]

[NLI 8774(22), 1^{r}]

O Being of solitude
Who are but the same
~~Death by death it grows~~
All things burn away

Like the stars which groan

Being born of loving moon

~~O beauty~~
O what but solitudes
Fire made your heart beat
Born of a loving mood
An image to walk the street

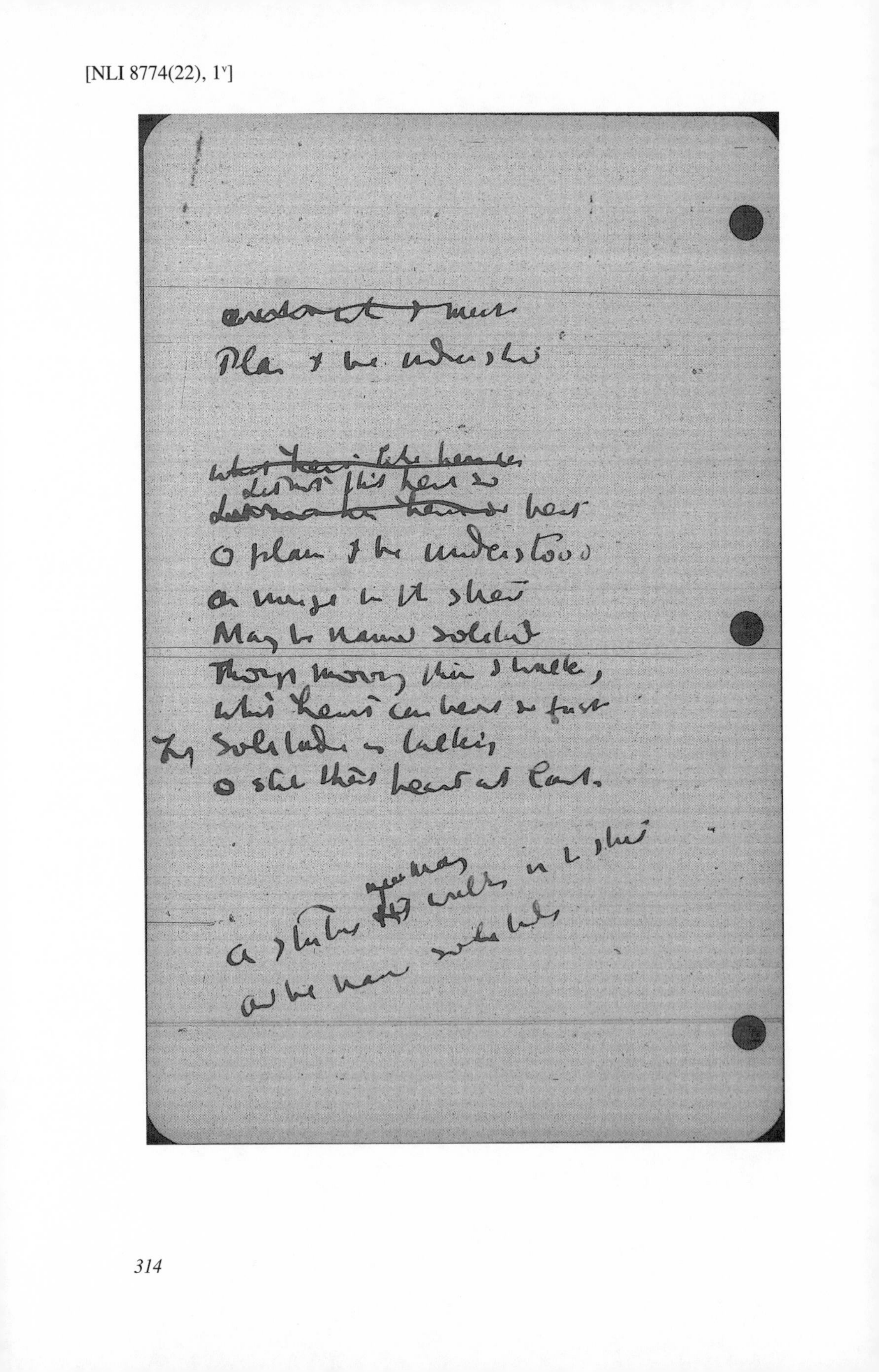

[NLI 8774(22), 1^{v}]

[NLI 8774(22), 1v]

~~And still when I meet~~
Plain to be understood

~~what heart like hers can~~
    Let not that heart so
~~Let not her heart so~~ beat
O plain to be understood
An image in the street
May be named solitude
Though moving there & walking
What heart can beat so fast
for Solitude is talking
O still that heart at last.

    now may
A statue ~~that~~ walks in the street
And be named solitude

12–13 The angled entry of these lines is a sign they were inserted later.

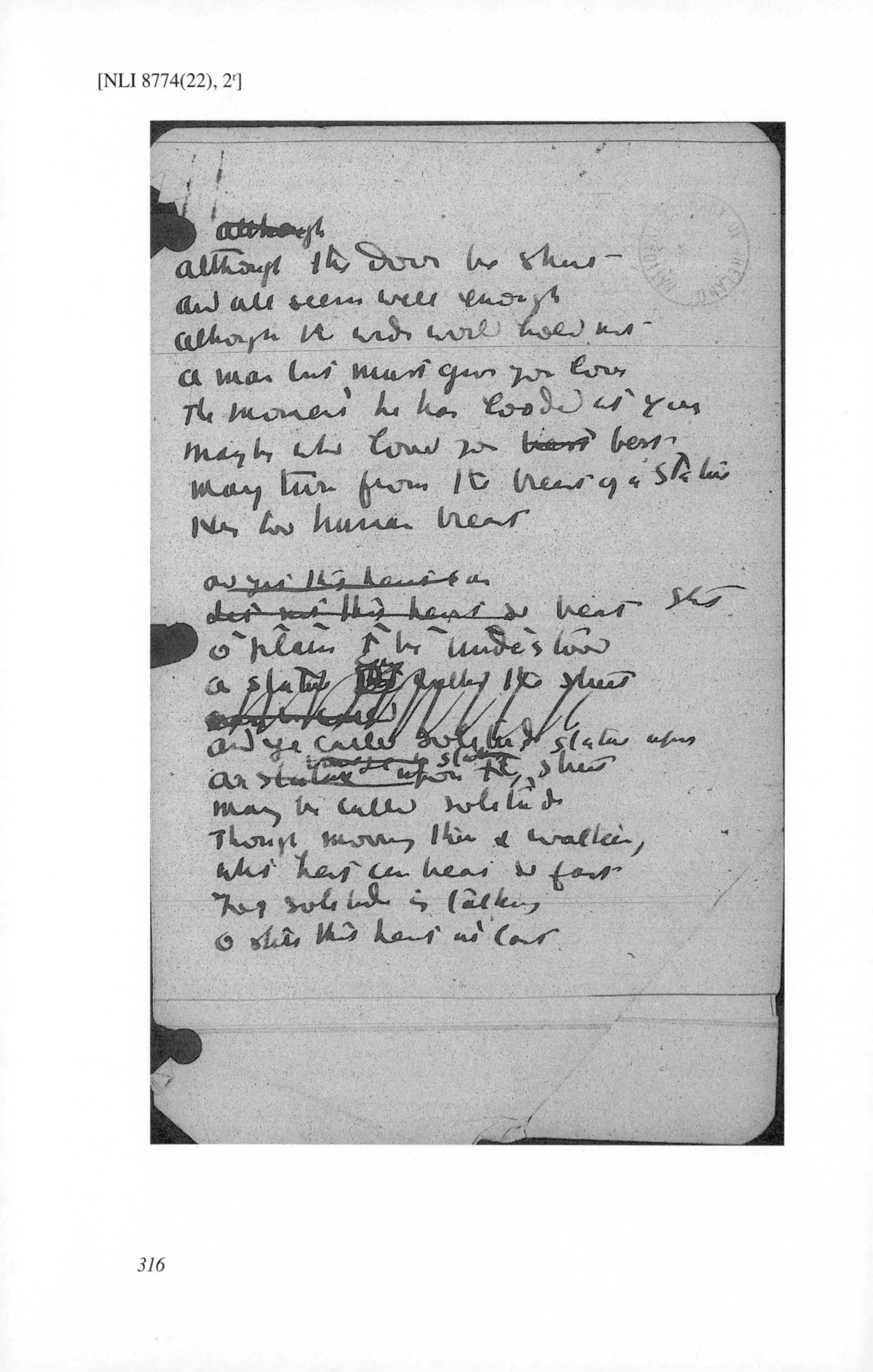

[NLI 8774(22), 2r]

[NLI 8774(22), 2^r]

~~Although~~
Although the door be shut
And all seem well enough
Although the wide world hold not
A man but must give you love
The moment he has looked at you
May be who loved you ~~breast~~ best
May turn from the breast of a statue
His too human breast

~~And yet that heart can~~
~~Let not that heart so~~ beat stet
O plain to be understood
can
A statue ~~that~~ walked the street
~~May be called~~
And yet called solitude
~~image to~~ ~~statue~~ statue upon
A ~~statue upon~~ the ^ street
May be called solitude
Though moving there & walking
What heart can beat so fast
For solitude is talking
O still that heart at last

[NLI 8774(22), 3r]

[NLI 8774(22), 3r]

~~How should she win his love~~
What ground for her life has she
Than beauty

That head from harm to keep
Who will be standing by
When beauty climbs the steep
Her own dear thoughts must die
As stars light must diminish
From Moon that gathers light
When the moons round is finished
                    had
The star light ~~has~~ diminished
When the moon hid half her light
And when that round is finished
Theres not a star in sight.

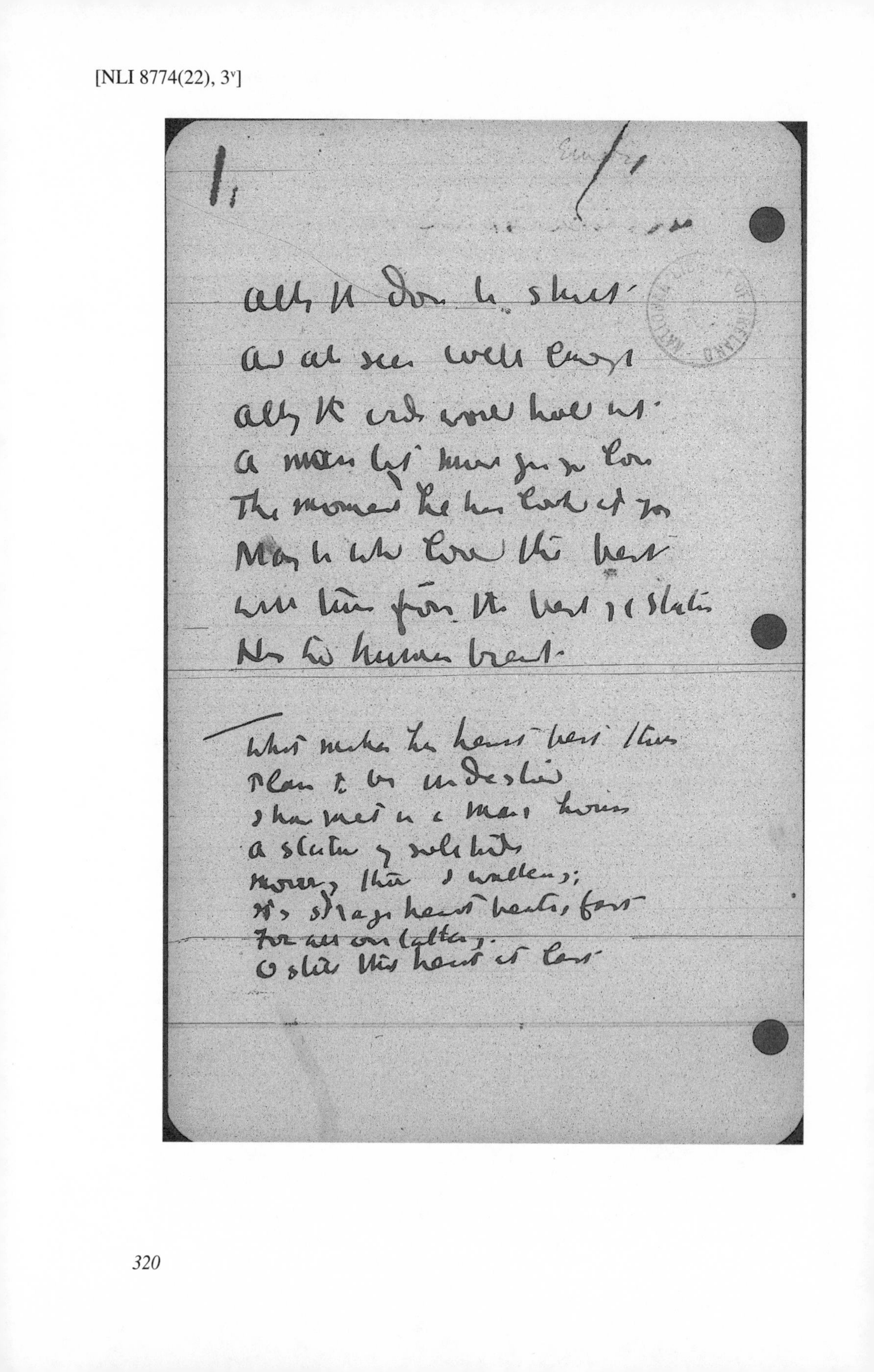

[NLI 8774(22), 3v]

[NLI 8774(22), 3^{v}]

Although the door be shut
And all seem well enough
Although the wide world hold not
A man but must give you love
The moment he has looked at you
May be who loved the best
Will turn from the breast of a statue
His too human breast.

What makes her heart beat thus
Plain to be understood
I have met in a mans house
A statue of solitude
Moving there & walking;
Its strange heart beating fast
For all our talking.
O still that heart at last

[Harvard, 4r]

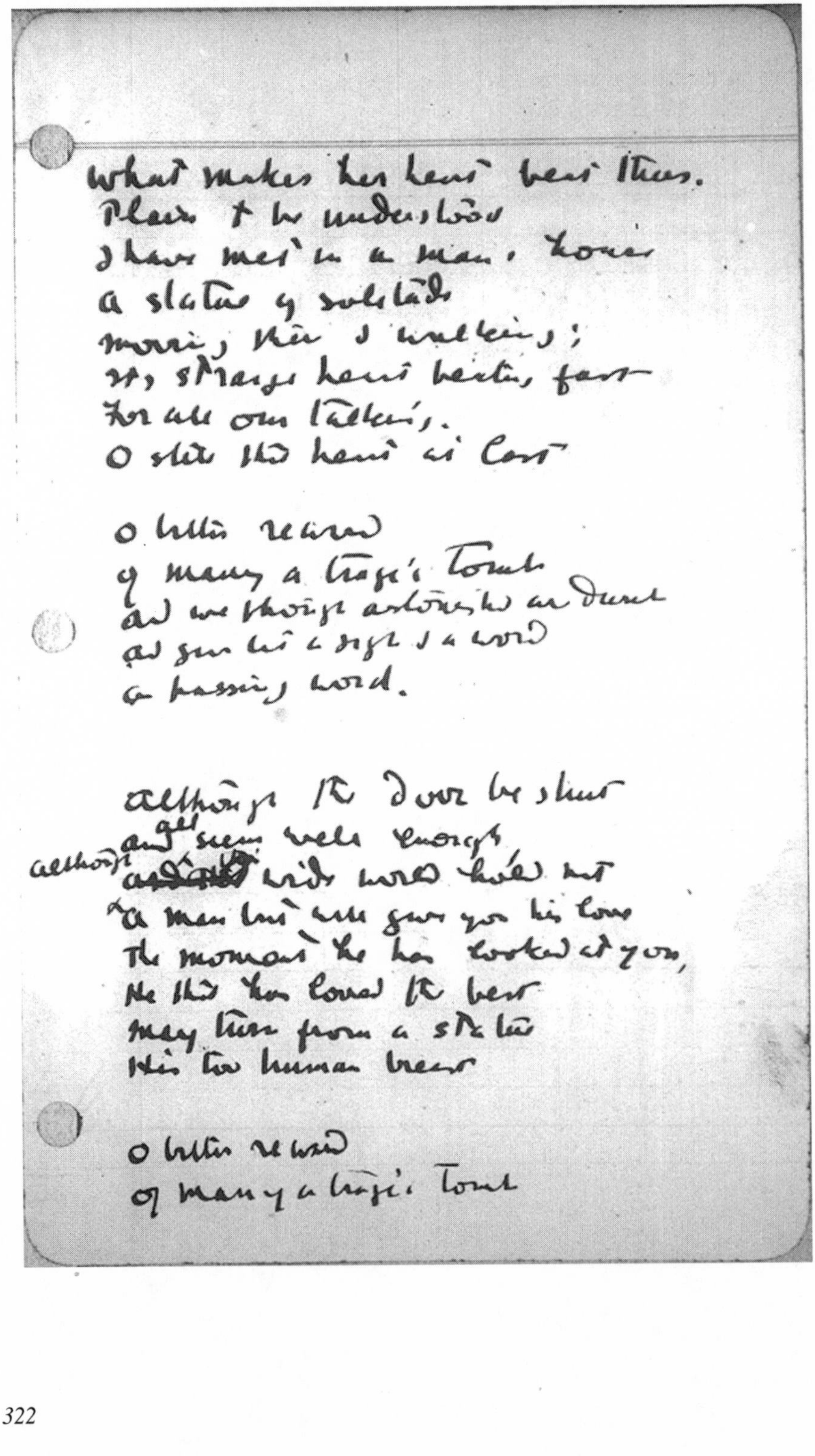
What makes her heart beat thus.
Plain to be understood
I have met in a man's house
a statue of solitude
moving, there I walking;
it, strange heart beating fast
For all our talking.
O still that heart at last

O bitter reward
of many a tragic tomb
And we though astonished are dumb
And gave but a sigh & a word
a passing word.

Although the door be shut
and all seem well enough
although wide words hold not
a man but will give you his love
The moment he has looked at you,
He that has loved the best
May turn from a statue
His too human breast

O bitter reward
of many a tragic tomb

[Harvard, 4^{r}]

1 What makes her heart beat thus.
2 Plain to be understood
3 I have met in a man's house
4 A statue of solitude
5 Moving there & walking;
6 Its strange heart beating fast
7 For all our talking.
8 O still that heart at last

9 O bitter reward
10 Of many a tragic tomb
11 And we though astonished are dumb
12 And give but a sigh & a word
13 A passing word.

14 Although the door he shut
all
15 And ^ seem well enough
Although ~~that~~
16 ^ ~~And that~~ wide world hold not
17 A man but will give you his love
18 The moment he has looked at you,
19 He that has loved the best
20 May turn from a statue
21 His too human breast

22 O bitter reward
23 Of many a tragic tomb

4^{r}, 5^{r} Revision of 1^{r} to 3^{v} above, now with refrain. Folios 4^{r} and 5^{r} were later added to the Harvard manuscript, presumably to make it complete for sale.

12 sigh & a word] Cf. the note to MS L (NLI 8774[21]), 20^{r}, l. 379, "look and a word"; the new phrase in MS M gives an even greater feeling of powerlessness.

and we though astonished are dumb
or give but a sigh and a word,
a passing word.

What makes ~~her~~ [your] heart so beat.
Some one should stay at her side
When beauty is complete
Her own thoughts will have died
and danger be [not] ~~not~~ diminished.
[When] ~~Dimmed~~ at their quarter light
~~The~~ Moon's round ~~once~~ [is] finished
The stars are out of sight

O letters record
Of many a tragic tomb
and we though astonished are dumb
Or give but a sigh and a word
a passing word.

[Harvard, 5r]

And we though astonished are dumb
Or give but a sigh and a word
A passing word.
            your
What makes ~~her~~ heart so beat
Some one should stay at her side
When beauty is complete
Her own thought will have died

          not
And danger^ be ~~not~~ diminished.
Dimmed at three quarter light
When ~~When~~ {M   is is
~~When~~^ {moon's round^ ~~once~~ finished
The stars are out of sight

O bitter reward
Of many a tragic tomb
And we though astonished are dumb
Or give but a sigh and a word
A passing word.

Part III

Fighting the Waves (1934) and Late Revisions of *The Only Jealousy of Emer*

Revisions toward *Fighting the Waves* (1934)

The drafts of *Fighting the Waves* are much less complicated than those of *The Only Jealousy of Emer*; there are but two typescripts.[1] The 1934 revisions to the verse play show the clear influence of the prose one, and are therefore included here as an outgrowth of that labor, rather than with the *Emer* papers.

Manuscript N: First Typescript Draft

The hallmark of the first draft of *Fighting the Waves* (found in NLI 8774[5] and still called *The Only Jealousy of Emer*) was simplification—simplification of action, character, and language. Miss de Valois had asked Yeats for a nonspeaking role for the Woman of the Sidhe; this enabled Yeats to dispense at a stroke with the complex philosophical dialogue between Cuchulain and the Woman of the Sidhe which had given him so many problems in the writing of *The Only Jealousy of Emer*. The general elimination of esoteric doctrine resulted in the prose play whose simplicity of language and situation recalled the mythological sources from which Yeats had begun so long before. The details of the changes to *The Only Jealousy* made in Manuscript N are discussed in the notes to the transcriptions.

The typescript contains Yeats's corrections in both pencil and ink. Internal evidence shows that the ink corrections preceded the pencil ones. The notes indicate which changes are made in pencil; all others are in ink. Some of the cancellations seem to have been made by Mrs. Yeats as she typed at Yeats's dictation; they are in broader pencil strokes (as one would make correcting a sheet still in the typewriter). In addition, they break off in the middle of a sentence. All of these cancellations are listed in the notes below.

---

[1]The National Library of Ireland collection also includes many manuscripts and typescripts of Yeats's "Introduction" to *Fighting the Waves*; a selection of these is transcribed in Appendix III below.

[NLI 8774(5)]

[1^r]

The best man to gain the love of a woman.

Only Jealousy.

house,

1st M. **I call before your eyes some poor fisherman's ^ dark with smoke, nets hanging from the rafters, here and there an oar perhaps, and in the midst upon a bed a man dead or swooning. ~~The fisherman have brought him here~~ It that famous man, Cuchu- -ullain, the best man with every sort of weapon, ~~the best man to defeat an enemy~~ , his wife Queen Emer is at his side; there is no one with her for she has sent everyone away, but yonder at the door someone stands and hesitates, wishes to come into the room and is afraid to do so, it young Eithne Inguba, Cuch- -ullain's mistress.~~there in the open door~~, ~~beyond the door the open sea~~.**

Beyond her through the open door the stormy sea.

(Song "white shell")

Emer **Come hither, come sit beside the bed, do not be afraid it was I that sent for you –**

Eithne I. **No madam I have wronged you too deeply to sit there.**

Emer **We two alone of all the people in the world have the right to watch together here because we have loved him best**

E I (**<u>coming nearer</u>**) **Is he dead?**

Emer **The fishermen think him dead it was they that put**

1^r, title Yeats called his play by both titles while it was being written and rehearsed. Thus he wrote to Lady Gregory on April 10, 1929, "I heard some of George Antheil's music for *The Only Jealousy* the other day" (Wade, *Letters*, p. 761).

4–5 "The . . . here": canceled in pencil.

7 "the . . . enemy": canceled in pencil. Yeats replaces an unnecessary repetition praising Cuchulain the warrior with praise of Cuchulain the lover. The Chorus in the verse play did not speak such praises of Cuchulain. A public audience, however, could not be expected to know the sources.

11–13 With the holograph additions, cf. *Only Jealousy*, "shining, bitter," adjectives that suggest the reflection of the moonlight in the cold sea. This esoteric lunar imagery has been eliminated from the prose play.

11 For "it" read "it is."

12–13 "beyond . . . sea": canceled in pencil.

the grave clothes upon him,) ~~but though there is no~~
~~E.I/~~ **~~breath no sound of the beating heart they say that he~~**
~~lives, how should he die and I not know it?~~

such things
E.I. **I have heard of ~~men like that~~, the very heart**
stop~~peds~~ and yet they ~~have~~ lived after. What happened?
& killed an **unknown man, and found after**
Emer **He fought ~~with ^ someone, killed him, and he that he~~**
~~killed they say~~ that it was his own son, ~~found when he~~
~~had killed the man~~ that he had killed
E.I. (~~going~~ feeling the body) He is cold. There is no breath
upon his lips.
Emer ^Those who win the terrible friendship of gods sometimes
lie a long time as if dead.

[2r]

E.I. **A son of yours and his?**

Emer **So that is your first thought – his son and mine. (<u>she</u>**
<u>laughs</u>) Did you think that he belonged to you and me
alone, ~~that we could keep him to ourselves~~. ~~Do not~~
~~look so strangely,~~^ The man he killed was the son of
some woman he loved long ago, and I think he loved her
has / **better than he ^ loved you or me**
in those days
E.I **That is natural, he must have been ~~a very~~ young ~~man~~, ^**
and loved as you and I love.
I think he
Emer **~~He must have~~ loved her as no man e^ver loved ~~woman for~~**
~~when he learnt what man he had killed, that the dying~~
for/ **~~man spoke~~ ~~And~~ ^ when the dying man told ~~him~~ his name and**
his mother's name he ~~seemed ^ to go~~ out of his senses *went*/
utterly,. ~~for~~ He ran ~~out~~ into the sea and with shield
before him and sword in hand he fought the deathless sea.

1r, l. 25 Yeats eliminates the supernatural portents of *The Only Jealousy*; their Elizabethan language would have been unsuitable.

27 Cf. *Only Jealousy*: "How did he come to this?" Yeats makes Eithne's speech blunter, less "literary."

28–29 The first phrase from "-one" through "say" was canceled in pencil (shown by a wavy line), the second from "with" through "say" in ink. Perhaps for the sake of simplification, Yeats dropped detailed references to the events of *On Baile's Strand*.

2r, l. 1 Eithne asks a less obvious question in *The Only Jealousy*. Emer's next speech, unlike that in the verse play, suggests that she has been jealous of Cuchulain's women. Yeats presumably simplifies her character for the prose play.

4 "that . . . ourselves": canceled in pencil.

8 "man": canceled in pencil.

10–12 "woman . . . spoke": canceled in pencil by the typist.

[NLI 8774(5)]

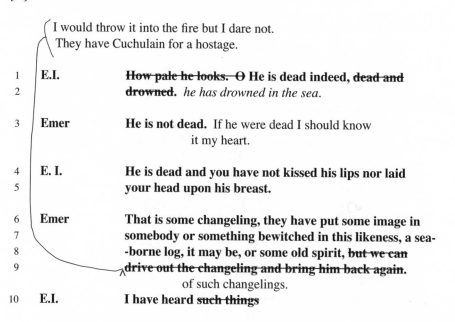

Of all the many men who had stood there to see the fight no one dared stop him or even call his name, they stood in a kind of stupor collected together in a bunch like cattle in the storm, until at last, fixing his eyes as it seemed upon some new enemy, he waded out further still and at last the waves swept over him.

He loved women before he heard our names, & he will love ~~women~~ women after he has forgotten us both.

[3r]

I would throw it into the fire but I dare not.
They have Cuchulain for a hostage.

E.I. **~~How pale he looks. O~~ He is dead indeed, ~~dead and drowned~~.** *he has drowned in the sea.*

Emer **He is not dead.** If he were dead I should know it my heart.

E. I. **He is dead and you have not kissed his lips nor laid your head upon his breast.**

Emer **That is some changeling, they have put some image in somebody or something bewitched in this likeness, a sea- -borne log, it may be, or some old spirit, ~~but we can~~ ^~~drive out the changeling and bring him back again~~.**

of such changelings.

E.I. **I have heard ~~such things~~**

19 "storm": Cf. *Only Jealousy*, "gale," a more "literary" word.

21 The typescript halts in the middle of the page, presumably for a break in the dictation; the text continues uninterrupted at the top of the next page. The penciled passage below this line is arrowed to replace that canceled in ll. 4–5 above.

3r, l. 1–2 "dead and drowned": canceled in pencil.

3 For "it my heart." read "in my heart."

6 For "image in" read "image of."

8 The phrase "some old spirit" simplifies *The Only Jealousy*: "Or some stark horseman grown too old to ride / Among the troops of Mananan, son of the sea" (*Poetry*, ll. 88–89).

8–9 The lines entered above l. 1, revising the canceled clause at ll. 8–9, propose the traditional folk solution for expelling a changeling from the possessed person's body; see Lady Wilde's *Ancient Legends*, I, pp. 119–124, and 170–172.

9 Yeats now drops Eithne's speech in *The Only Jealousy* on how the souls of the dead "Loiter amid the scenery of their lives."

Emer **Before you came I called his name again and again, I told him ~~how the land needs him~~, that Queen Maeve and all her Connaught men are marching north and east and that there is none but he to make stand against them, but he would not hear me, I am but his wife and a man grows tired of a wife. But if you call upon him with that sweet voice, that voice that is so dear to him he cannot help but listen.**

but

E.I. **I am but his newest love, ~~and~~ in the end he will turn to the woman ~~that he loved longest, to the woman who that~~ who has loved him longest, who has kept the house for him not matter where he strayed or to whom.**

Emer **I have indeed that hope – the hope that some day he and I will sit together at the fire as when we were first married.**

E.I. **Women like me awoke a violent love for a while and when the time is over are flung into some corner like some old eggshell. Cuchullain, listen.**

Emer **No, not yet, for first I must cover up his face, I must hid him from the sea, I must throw new logs upon the fire and stir the half burnt logs into a flame, the sea is full of enchantment, whatever lies there is from sea, for all enchantments dread the hearth fire.**

(put in stage direction from "Only Jealousy")

3r, ll. 11–15 Emer had not even tried to call Cuchulain back in *The Only Jealousy*, being "but his wife." Yeats has presumably added the Connaught armies here to simplify the characters' motivations.

20 "that he . . . who that": canceled in pencil by the typist; Yeats then dictated the revised reading.

21–22 Cf. *Only Jealousy*: "Will love the woman best who loved him first / And loved him through the years when love seemed lost" (*Poetry*, ll. 100–102). The emphasis in *Fighting the Waves* shifts from "love" to housewifely virtues; Emer's nobility is somewhat reduced.

32 For "from" read "from the."

[NLI 8774(5)]

[4^{r}]

Speak to it as though it were his very self

Emer **Call on Cuchullain now.**

E.I. **Can you hear my voice, Cuchullain?**

Emer **Bend over whatever thing lies there, call out dear secrets ~~to it, till~~ ~~have touched his heart and~~ ~~made him jealous of it.~~** ~~you have~~

E.I. **Cuchullain, listen.**

Emer when/ **Those are timid words. To be afraid because his wife is standing by ~~where~~ there is so great need but proves that he chose badly. Remember who you are and who he is, and that we are two women struggling with the sea.**

E.I. **O my beloved, pardon me, pardon me that I could be ashamed when you were in such need. Never did I send a message, never did I call your name, scarce had I a longing for your company but that you have known and come. If you are lying there stretch out your arms and speak, open your mouth and speak. Remember that never up to this hour have you been silent when I would have you speak, remember that I have always made you talkative. If you are not lying there, if that is some stranger, or someone or something bewitched into your likeness, drive it away, remember that for anyone to take your likeness from you is a great insult. He does not hear me ~~or else he cannot speak~~ no sound reaches him, or it reaches him and he cannot speak.**

4^{r}, ll. 3–5 Yeats simplifies Emer's speech from *The Only Jealousy*, which turns on two possible explanations for Cuchulain's state: if he lies there and if he is not there. He simply uses the second and makes it clearer for a public audience. He canceled "to it, till" and "made . . . it" in pencil. He also eliminated the word "jealousy" in Emer's later speech (4^{r}, l. 30). In *Fighting the Waves* jealousy plays a secondary role to fighting the gods; hence the change of title.

8 standing by] The more literary phrasing in *The Only Jealousy* is "but three paces off" (*Poetry*, l. 120).

23 Revives the original language of one of Emer's speeches in the *Emer* drafts: "Who are you / To dare to so affront this ancient house" (MS G, 7^{r} above).

24 "or . . . speak": canceled in pencil.

Emer **Then kiss that image, these things are a great mystery and maybe that his mouth will feel the pressure of your mouth upon that image.** ~~**I know little but of this I am certain, that if you can put the passion of your youth into a kiss he will know it whether in love or in jealousy no matter where he is.**~~ *Is it not so that we ~~approach~~ approach the gods?*

[left margin, vertical:] ~~But if he does not feel he will know by it~~ – if there is enough passion in the kiss –.

E.I. **(starting back) I felt it was some evil, devilish thing.**

Emer **No, his body stirs, the pressure of your mouth has called him.** He has thrown the changeling out.

E.I. **(going further off) Look at that arm! That arm is withered to the socket.** ~~(She (She goes~~

[5r]

Emer **(going up to the bed) What are you, what do you come for and from where?**

F. of C. **I am one of the spirits from the sea.**

Emer **What spirit from the sea dares lie upon Cuchulain's bed and take his image?**

F. of C. **I am called Bricriu, I am the maker of discord.**

Emer **Come for what purpose?**

(Exit E.I.)

F of C. **I show my face and everything he loves must fly away.**

Emer **I have not fled your face.**

F of C. **You are not loved.**

Emer **And therefore have no dread to meet your eyes and to demand my husband.**

4r, ll. 26–31 Revision simplifies *Only Jealousy*: "image, . . . may reach him where he is" (*Poetry*, ll. 136–138).

5r, l. 3 Simplifies *Only Jealousy*: "I have come / From Mananan's court upon a bridleless horse" (*Poetry*, ll. 144–145).

Renounce his love for ever

F of C. **And I have come to give him back to you but at a price.**

Emer **~~No~~, there is no price I will not pay.**

F of C. **You spoke but now of your hope that some day his love would return to you, that you would sit together by the hearth as when you were first married. Renounce that hope and he shall live again.**

Emer **Never, never will I renounce it.**

F of C. **What can you offer to the gods but your misery?**

hope

Emer **What ~~other happiness~~ have I but that ~~thought, that~~ hope?**

F of C. **~~Renounce~~ ~~Whether you renounce it or not he is lost to you, but~~ renounce it and he returns and leads your people against the hosts of Maeve.**

Emer **I will get him back without your help, that woman and I will call out upon him until he hears our voices.**

F of C. Your voices have reached him but as a vague trouble. He is here but bound by a dream.

EM My husband here.

[6r]

He is here – but a stronger than you, & a stronger even than his mistress keeps him from [?love]

F of C. **You think because he has so often strayed away after some adventure, some woman it may be, and come back to you again, but do those return that a goddess loves?**

Emer **That a goddess loves?**

5r, l. 13ff. Yeats deletes all the text from this point to the end of MS N as unnecessary; it corresponds to the passage in *The Only Jealousy* in which the Figure of Cuchulain tells Emer how the Sidhe bargain.

23 The first word is canceled in pencil, probably by the typist.

24–25 The evil spirit cannot understand love; he takes literally the arguments which Emer had merely used as an excuse on 3r above.

F of C. Stand at my left side that I may touch your eyes and give them second sight.

Emer ~~**What!**~~ ~~**My**~~ **husband,** ~~**is there**~~**! husband**

F of C. Yes, but out of your reach. I have made him visible to your eyes, I have not made you visible to his.

Emer Husband, husband!

~~She would summon him to the~~

F of C. Be silent. ~~**That goddess comes.**~~

~~king Mananan~~ the king.

p. 7

(Emer draws knife)

F of C And so you think to wound her with a knife. Put up that useless knife, she has an airy body. Look, I have not given you your eyes for nothing. She has come seeking his kiss. He half remembers you, or maybe that other woman, for your cries have called him hither, but if he kiss her he will no longer remember that you and she have lived, he will become as the gods who remember nothing.

Emer What would you have of me, what must I do?

F of C. Before he gives that kiss you must cry out "I renounce him, I renounce Cuchullain's love for ever."

Emer Never, never will I give that cry.

(dance)

G. of C. Your mouth, your mouth.

Emer I renounce Cuchullain's love, I renounce it for ever.

~~[?*Mananan*]~~

6ʳ, ll. 6–7 "A supposed power by which occurrences in the future or things at a distance are perceived as though they were actually present" (*OED*).

9–10 I have made him visible / to your eyes] A simpler locution than in *The Only Jealousy*: "I have dissolved / the dark" (*Poetry*, ll. 191–192). At this point, Yeats eliminates the passage in *Only Jealousy* describing how the "dreaming shades" at first resemble their earthly forms.

13 "p. 7" is a direction inserted in pencil, perhaps by the typist (the hand is not Yeats's), for the insertion of 7ʳ here. Yeats then canceled most of 5ʳ and all of 6ʳ and 7ʳ.

14–21 With this speech, Yeats eliminates from the prose play the complex dialogue between Cuchulain and the Woman of the Sidhe. The kiss of forgetfulness is here retained, but without the lunar explanations for its efficacy.

[NLI 8774(5)]

[7r]

F of C. **Your cries your love hold him here she comes to lure him away to her own country. Once he come there he is hers for ever, there is no returning, ~~she will offer him her mouth and withhold her mouth, leading him on~~ Cry out that you renounce his love and all her power is gone, you can do what you like with him then and she nothing, desire makes us weak, those who seek nothing command all.**

Emer **Never will I renounce that hope.**

(Dance)

F of C. **Renounce before it is too late.**

(goddess and ghost go out)

Emer **I will never set eyes upon him again.**

F of C **Quickly, quickly, they are not yet there. They still ride the bridleless horses of the sea.**

Emer **I renounce Cuchullain's love let him return and face the armies of Maeve. I am content.**

F of C. **I have won, I have won. She and I are in eternal enmity. I have thwarted her again, but I must hurry, I must hurry, she knows what I have done and will accuse me to Mananan, I must be there to defend myself, I too must find one of the horses of the sea, the bridleless horses. (<u>he falls back</u>)**

E I **(<u>enters</u>)**

7r, ll. 7–8 desire . . . command all] An idea not found in *The Only Jealousy*.

10 On this page Yeats dropped the kiss of forgetfulness in favor of seductive dance, thus doing away with the need for the Ghost of Cuchulain to say anything at all (cf. 6r, l. 27).

15 These horses will be replaced in the next draft by Fand's chariot. Perhaps Yeats was here adapting the "horse race" of *The Only Jealousy*.

18–19 In *The Only Jealousy*, their "eternal enmity" had been explained as the result of the opposition of Phases 1 and 15, an esoteric explanation unsuitable here (see the introduction, pp. xxxv–xxxvii above).

24 The draft halts two-thirds of the way down the page.

Manuscript Fragment of the Ending of *Fighting the Waves*

Yeats continued the process of simplifying the text in NLI 30,492, a holograph fragment of the ending of *Fighting the Waves* (cf. ll. 185–259 of the text published in *Wheels and Butterflies* reproduced below).

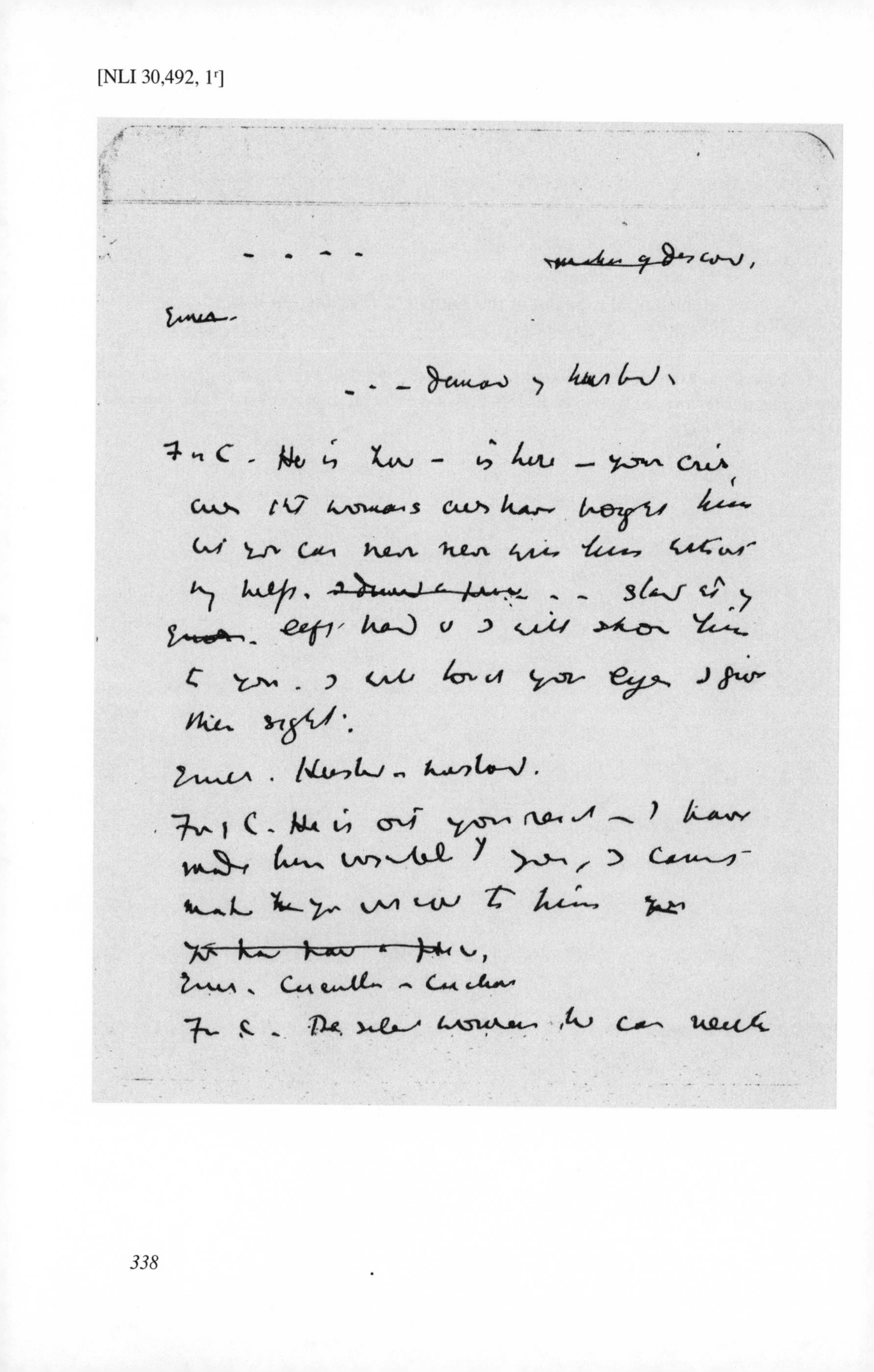

[NLI 30,492, 1r]

[NLI 30,492, 1^{r}]

– – – –   ~~[?spreader] of d~~iscord.

~~Emer~~.
– – – demand my husband.

Fig C. He is here – is here – your cries
and that womans curse have brought him
but you can never never win him without
my help. ~~I demand a prize~~ – – stand at my
~~Emer~~. left hand & I will show him
to you. I will touch your eyes & give
them sight.
Emer. Husband – husband.
Fig of C. He is out your reach – I have
made him visible to you, I cant
make you visible to him ~~you~~
~~you now have a face,~~
Emer. Cuchulain – Cuchulain!
Fig. C. Be silent, woman, he can neither

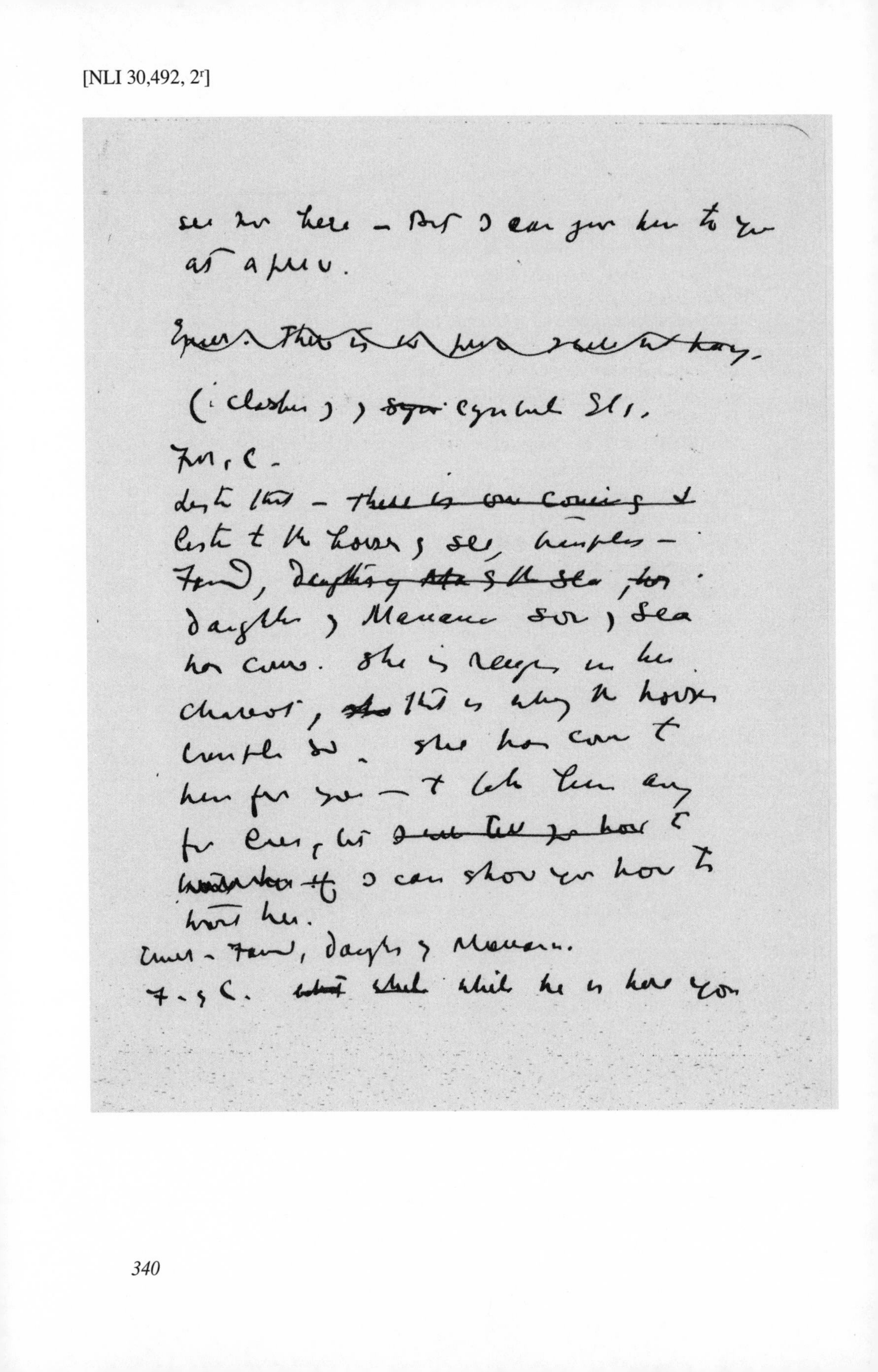

[NLI 30,492, 2r]

[NLI 30,492, 2^{r}]

1 see nor hear – But I can give him to you
2 at a price.

3 ~~Emer – There is no price I would not pay.~~
(: Clashing of ~~sym~~ cymbals Etc.
Fig of C.
4 Listen to that – ~~there is one coming &~~
5 Listen to the horses of the sea, trampling –
6 Fand, ~~daughter of Ma of the sea, has~~
7 daughter of Mananan, son of Sea
8 has come. She is reining in her
9 chariot, ~~th~~ that is why the horses
10 trample so. She has come to
11 [?him] for you — to take him away
12 for ever, but ~~I will tell you how~~ to
13 ~~thwart her if~~ I can show you how to
14 thwart her.
15 Emer – Fand, daughter of Mananan.
16 Fig. of C. ~~What Which~~ While he is here you

[NLI 30,492, 2v]

Those who love the daylight, & the sea
do not grow weary. The daughters of the
sea do not release their lovers.

[NLI 30,492, 2^{v}]

Those who love the daughter of the sea
do not grow weary. The daughters of the
sea do not release their loves.

For insertion on facing 3^{r}, l. 4.

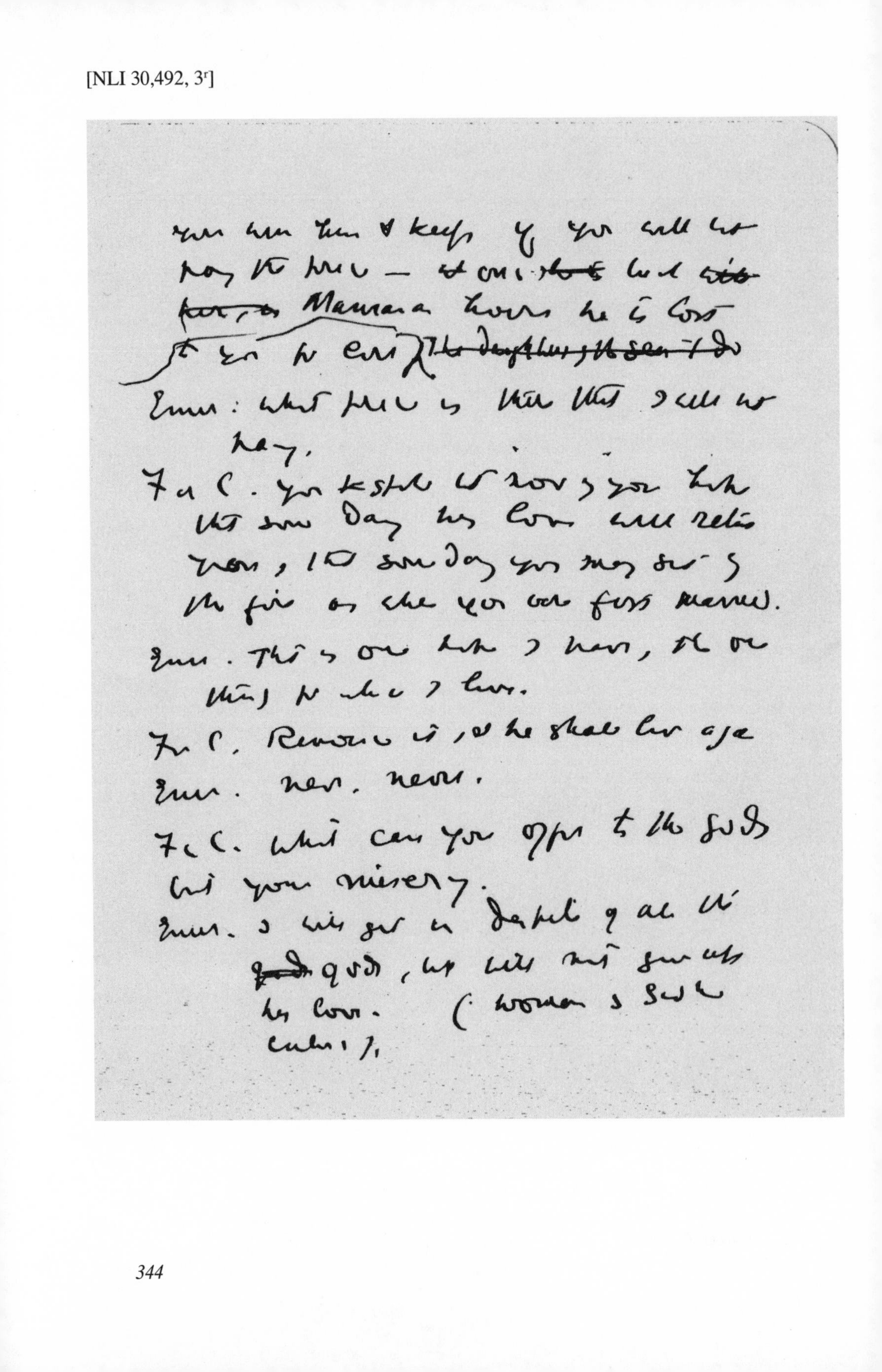

[NLI 30,492, 3r]

[NLI 30,492, 3^{r}]

you win him to keep if you will but
pay the price – ~~W~~ once ~~she is~~ back ~~with~~
~~her, in~~ Mananans house he is lost
to you for ever ~~The daughters of the sea [?] do~~
Emer: What price is there that I will not
pay.
F of C. You [?] spoke but now of your hope
that some day his love will return
you, that some day you may sit by
the fire as when you were first married.
Emer. That is one hope I have, the one
thing for which I live.
Fig C. Renounce it, and he shall live agai
Emer. Never, never.
F of C. What can you offer to the gods
but your misery.
Emer. I will get in despite of all the
~~gads~~ gods, but will not give up
her love. (Woman of Sidhe
enters).

[NLI 30,492, 4r]

[NLI 30,492, 4^{r}]

& so you think to wound her with a knif
she has an airy body — put down
that knife [?~~put~~] but watch — Remember
cries
that though your ~~dreams~~ have dragged him
hither, ~~once he stands in Mananans house~~
this shore
~~he~~ once he has left [?~~shape~~], once he has
passed through the bitter sea, once he stands
in Mananan's house, he will be as the gods
who remember nothing.
(They dance)
F. C.
Cry out, cry that you ~~a~~ renounce his love
cry that you renounce it for ever –
Emer. No no. never will I give that cry
~~never will I~~ ~~(Certain of dancer go out.)~~
Emer – I will never sit [?down with] him again.
never will I give him to such as she.
F of C – Fool, fool! I am Fands enemy,
I have come to tell you how to thwart her
& you do nothing.
Emer – I will not give him to such as she

1 For "knif" read "knife".
12sd "Certain" seems most likely, though the word may be "Curtain."

Fig. C — This is [illegible]. [illegible] I
— to the chariot — there Fig are [illegible]
on the shore — there wild & trembling
she has mounted up her chariot — but
Cuchulain is at feet below her (clothes)
Emer.
I remember Cuchulain['s] love — I almost
up to the end.
(E. I come to door — calling on Cuchullain
remembers her g love meeting — they were
together under — dawn — Fig heard the
cry of the waking birds upon the shore. She
sees the man stir up the bed. She
cries out that she has forgotten her bed
— her love has [illegible] — he is hers now
she has the right to keep him ever against
his wife. Emer strikes to her [illegible].
Cuchulain awakes & takes E. I in his
arms.

[NLI 30,492, 5r]

Fig. C – There is yet time. Listen to
to the chariot – There they are trampling
on the shore – their wild and trampling
she has mounted into her chariot – but
Cuchulain is not yet beside her (clashing)
Emer.
I renounce Cuchulains love – I renounce
it for ever.
(E. I comes to door – calling on Cuchullain
reminding him of last meeting – they were
together until – dawn – they heard the
cry of the waking birds upon the shore. She
sees the man stir upon the bed. She
cries out that she has brought him back
— her love has triumphed – he is hers now
she has the right to keep him ever against
his wife. Emer speaks to her fiercely.
Cuchulain awakes & takes E. I in his
arms.

Fighting the Waves (1934)

The reading text of *Fighting the Waves* is based on that published in *Wheels and Butterflies* (London: Macmillan, 1934). Appended to it are collations from NLI 30,602, NLI 8774(6), and LCP. For Yeats's work on versions of the introduction to *Fighting the Waves*, see Appendix III below.

FIGHTING THE WAVES

PROLOGUE

Musicians and speaker off stage. There is a curtain with a wave pattern. A man wearing the Cuchulain mask enters from one side with sword and shield. He dances a dance which represents a man fighting the waves. The waves may be represented by other dancers: in his frenzy he supposes the waves to be his enemies: gradually he sinks down as if overcome, then fixes his eyes with a cataleptic stare upon some imaginary distant object. The stage becomes dark, and when the light returns it is empty. The Musicians enter. Two stand one on either side of the curtain, singing.

FIRST MUSICIAN

A woman's beauty is like a white
Frail bird, like a white sea-bird alone

---

found in NLI 30,602
NLI 8774(6) (MS O)
LCP
published in *Wheels and Butterflies* (1934)

---

note in LCP: dedication page
For John Masefield, who made me a boat [boat *rev to* ship]
PROLOGUE

prologue:

Musicians and speaker . . . a wave pattern] When the curtain rises two musicians are seen, a flute player and a drummer They are at the two front corners. At the back there is a curtain with a wave pattern *NLI 30,602* When the curtain rises two musicians are seen crouching upon the stage, a flute player [*rev to* a singer] and a drummer. They are at the two front corners *LCP*

sword and shield] sword, or sword and shield, or no sword but a spear, according as the dancer prefers *NLI 30,602, NLI 8774(6), LCP*

The waves may be represented by other dancers *omitted but* dancers in waves? *inserted in margin NLI 30,602; omitted but* The waves may be represented by other dancers; *entered in margin NLI 8774(6); omitted LCP*

following "object": He goes out at one side *NLI 30,602, LCP*

The stage becomes dark . . . empty *omitted NLI 30,602, LCP; so NLI 8774(6) but entered in margin*

The Musicians enter . . . singing] Two persons enter dressed in costume similar to that of the musicians. They stand in the centre in the front of the wave pattern curtain and part it and pull it back *NLI 30,602, so LCP but all del* The Musicians enter. They stand on ~~one~~ either side of the curtain singing *inserted in ink NLI 8774(6)* Two persons enter dressed in costume similar to that of the musicians they stand in the centre in the front of the wave pattern curtain and part it and pull it back *all del LCP*

Typos, misspellings, errors of hyphenation and spacing, and most variants in stage directions are excluded from this record. All variants entered in the proofs, listed in the Census, are anticipated or duplicated in the manuscripts or are reported as printed variants in *The Variorum Edition of the Plays of W. B. Yeats,* ed. Russell K. Alspach (London: Macmillan, 1966).

At daybreak after stormy night
Between two furrows upon the ploughed land:
A sudden storm and it was thrown
Between dark furrows upon the ploughed land.
How many centuries spent
The sedentary soul
In toil of measurement
Beyond eagle or mole,
Beyond hearing or seeing,
Or Archimedes' guess,
To raise into being
That loveliness?

A strange, unserviceable thing,
A fragile, exquisite, pale shell,
That the vast troubled waters bring
To the loud sands before day has broken.
The storm arose and suddenly fell
Amid the dark before day had broken.
What death? What discipline?
What bonds no man could unbind,
Being imagined within
The labyrinth of the mind,
What pursuing or fleeing,
What wounds, what bloody press
Dragged into being
This loveliness?

[*When the curtain is drawn the Musicians take their place against the wall. One sees a bed with curtains: the man lying on the bed is Cuchulain; the part is taken, however, by a different actor, who has a mask similar to that of the dancer—the Cuchulain mask. Emer stands beside the bed. The Ghost of Cuchulain crouches near the foot of the bed.*]

FIRST MUSICIAN [*speaking*]. I call before your eyes some poor fisherman's house dark with smoke, nets hanging from the rafters, here and there an oar perhaps, and in the midst upon a bed a man dead or swooning. It is that famous man Cuchulain, the best man with every sort of weapon, the best man to gain the love of a woman; his wife Queen Emer is at his side; there is no one with her, for

9 toil] toils *NLI 30,602, NLI 8774(6), LCP*

she has sent everyone away, but yonder at the door someone stands and hesitates, wishes to come into the room and is afraid to do so; it is young Eithne Inguba, Cuchulain's mistress. Beyond her, through the open door, the stormy sea. Beyond the foot of the bed, dressed in grave-clothes, the ghost of Cuchulain is kneeling.

FIRST MUSICIAN [*singing*]

White shell, white wing!
I will not choose for my friend
A frail, unserviceable thing
That drifts and dreams, and but knows
That waters are without end
And that wind blows.

EMER. Come hither, come sit beside the bed; do not be afraid, it was I that sent for you.

EITHNE INGUBA. No, madam, I have wronged you too deeply to sit there.

EMER. We two alone of all the people in the world have the right to watch together here, because we have loved him best.

EITHNE INGUBA [*coming nearer*]. Is he dead?

EMER. The fishermen think him dead, it was they that put the grave-clothes upon him.

EITHNE INGUBA [*feeling the body*]. He is cold. There is no breath upon his lips.

EMER. Those who win the terrible friendship of the gods sometimes lie a long time as if dead.

EITHNE INGUBA. I have heard of such things; the very heart stops and yet they live after. What happened?

EMER. He fought and killed an unknown man, and found after that it was his own son that he had killed.

EITHNE INGUBA. A son of yours and his?

EMER. So that is your first thought! His son and mine. [*She laughs.*] Did you think that he belonged to you and me alone? He loved women

---

41–43 omitted *NLI 30,602* Beyond the foot . . . kneeling *converted into a stage direction NLI 8774(6), LCP with* the ghost of Cuchulain] his *NLI 8774(6) and* foot] head *LCP*

50 hither *rev from* nearer *NLI 30,602*

56 best *rev from* better *NLI 30,602*

before he heard our names, and he will love women after he has forgotten us both. The man he killed was the son of some woman he loved long ago, and I think he loved her better than he has loved you or me.

EITHNE INGUBA. That is natural, he must have been young in those days and loved as you and I love.

EMER. I think he loved her as no man ever loved, for when he heard the name of the man he had killed, and the name of that man's mother, he went out of his senses utterly. He ran into the sea, and with shield before him and sword in hand he fought the deathless sea. Of all the many men who had stood there to look at the fight not one dared stop him or even call his name; they stood in a kind of stupor, collected together in a bunch like cattle in a storm, until, fixing his eyes as it seemed upon some new enemy, he waded out further still and the waves swept over him.

EITHNE INGUBA. He is dead indeed, and he has been drowned in the sea.

EMER. He is not dead.

EITHNE INGUBA. He is dead, and you have not kissed his lips nor laid your head upon his breast.

EMER. That is some changeling they have put there, some image of somebody or something bewitched in his likeness, a sea-washed log, it may be, or some old spirit. I would throw it into the fire, but I dare not. They have Cuchulain for a hostage.

EITHNE INGUBA. I have heard of such changelings.

EMER. Before you came I called his name again and again. I told him that Queen Maeve and all her Connacht men are marching north and east, and that there is none but he to make a stand against them, but he would not hear me. I am

---

74 and *del NLI 8774(6), omitted NLI 30,602*

82–83 for . . . mother] for whom the dying man told his name and his mother's name *NLI 30,602, NLI 8774(6), LCP*

86–87 look at] see *NLI 30,602, LPC, rev from* see *NLI 8774(6)*

89 until] until at last *NLI 30,602, NLI 8774(6), LCP*

91 and] and at last *NLI 30,602, NLI 8774(6), LCP*

95 If he were dead I should know it in my heart *del NLI 30,602*

99 there *omitted NLI 30,602 omitted then inserted NLI 8774(6)*

100 sea-washed] sea-borne *NLI 30,602, LCP*

105 came I *inserted NLI 30,602*

but his wife, and a man grows tired of a wife. But if you call upon him with that sweet voice, that voice that is so dear to him, he cannot help but listen.

EITHNE INGUBA. I am but his newest love, and in the end he will turn to the woman who has loved him longest, who has kept the house for him no matter where he strayed or to whom.

EMER. I have indeed that hope, the hope that some day he and I will sit together at the fire as when we were first married.

EITHNE INGUBA. Women like me awake a violent love for a while, and when the time is over are flung into some corner like an old eggshell. Cuchulain, listen!

EMER. No, not yet; for first I must cover up his face, I must hide him from the sea. I must throw new logs upon the fire and stir the half-burnt logs into a flame. The sea is full of enchantment, whatever lies on that bed is from the sea, but all enchantments dread the hearth-fire.

[*She pulls the curtains of the bed so as to hide the sick man's face, that the actor may change his mask unseen. She goes to one side of the stage and moves her hand as though putting logs on a fire and stirring it into a blaze. While she makes these movements the Musicians play, marking the movements with drum and flute perhaps. Having finished she stands beside the imaginary fire at a distance from Cuchulain and Eithne Inguba.*

Call on Cuchulain now.

EITHNE INGUBA. Can you hear my voice, Cuchulain?

EMER. Bend over whatever thing lies there, call out dear secrets and speak to it as though it were his very self.

EITHNE INGUBA. Cuchulain, listen!

EMER. Those are timid words. To be afraid because his wife is standing by when there is so great need but proves that he chose badly. Remember who you are and who he is, that we are two women struggling with the sea.

---

111 call *rev from* called *NLI 8774(6)* called *LCP*
129 on that bed] there
141 that] and that *NLI 30,602*

EITHNE INGUBA. O my beloved! Pardon me, pardon me that I could be ashamed when you were in such need. Never did I send a message, never did I call your name, scarce had I a longing for your company but that you have known and come. Remember that never up to this hour have you been silent when I would have you speak, remember that I have always made you talkative. If you are not lying there, if that is some stranger or someone or something bewitched into your likeness, drive it away, remember that for someone to take your likeness from you is a great insult. If you are lying there, stretch out your arms and speak, open your mouth and speak. [*She turns* to *Emer.*] He does not hear me, no sound reaches him, or it reaches him and he cannot speak.

EMER. Then kiss that image; these things are a great mystery, and maybe his mouth will feel the pressure of your mouth upon that image. Is it not so that we approach the gods ?

EITHNE INGUBA [*starting back*]. I felt it was some evil, devilish thing!

EMER. No, his body stirs, the pressure of your mouth has called him. He has thrown the changeling out.

EITHNE INGUBA [*going further off*]. Look at that hand! That hand is withered to the bone.

EMER [*going up* to *the bed*]. What are you, what do you come for, and from where?

FIGURE OF CUCHULAIN. I am one of the spirits from the sea.

EMER. What spirit from the sea dares lie upon Cuchulain's bed and take his image?

FIGURE OF CUCHULAIN. I am called Bricriu, I am the maker of discord.

EMER. Come for what purpose?

[*Exit Eithne Inguba.*

FIGURE OF CUCHULAIN. I show my face and everything he loves must fly.

EMER. I have not fled your face.

---

156 *sd omitted NLI 30,602, omitted then inserted LCP*
156–158 *sd written in margin NLI 30,602:* Short moves toward Emer & then takes a few
161 may be] may be that *NLI 30,602, NLI 8774(6), LCP*
168–169 hand . . . hand . . . bone] arm . . . arm . . . socket *NLI 30,602. LCP*
181 fly] fly away *NLI 30,602, LCP*
182 are *rev from* have *NLI 8774(6)*

FIGURE OF CUCHULAIN. You are not loved.

EMER. And therefore have no dread to meet your eyes and to demand my husband.

FIGURE OF CUCHULAIN. He is here, your lamentations and that woman's lamentations have brought him in a sort of dream, but you can never win him without my help. Come to my left hand and I will touch your eyes and give you sight.

EMER [*seeing the Ghost of Cuchulain*]. Husband! Husband!

FIGURE OF CUCHULAIN. He seems near, and yet is as much out of reach as though there were a world between. I have made him visible to you. I cannot make you visible to him.

EMER. Cuchulain! Cuchulain!

FIGURE OF CUCHULAIN. Be silent, woman! He can neither see nor hear. But I can give him to you at a price. [*Clashing of cymbals, etc.*] Listen to that. Listen to the horses of the sea trampling! Fand, daughter of Manannan, has come. She is reining in her chariot, that is why the horses trample so. She is come to take Cuchulain from you, to take him away for ever, but I am her enemy, and I can show you how to thwart her.

EMER. Fand, daughter of Manannan!

FIGURE OF CUCHULAIN. While he is still here you can keep him if you pay the price. Once back in Manannan's house he is lost to you for ever. Those who love the daughters of the sea do not grow weary, nor do the daughters of the sea release their lovers.

EMER. There is no price I will not pay.

FIGURE OF CUCHULAIN. You spoke but now of a hope that some day his love may return to you, that some day you may sit by the fire as when first married.

EMER. That is the one hope I have, the one thing that keeps me alive.

FIGURE OF CUCHULAIN. Renounce it, and he shall live again.

EMER. Never, never!

FIGURE OF CUCHULAIN. What else have you to

186–187 lamentations . . . lamentations] cries . . . cries *NLI 30,602, LCP*
189 Come to] Stand at *NLI 30,602, LCP*
191 the ghost of *omitted NLI 30,602, NLI 8774(6), LCP*
199 clashing cymbals *written in margin NLI 30,602*
201 is reining *rev to* has reined *NLI 30,602*
202 trampled *rev to* trample *NLI 30,602*

offer?

EMER. Why should the gods demand such a sacrifice?

FIGURE OF CUCHULAIN. The gods must serve those who living become like the dead.

EMER. I will get him in despite of all the gods.

[*Fand, the Woman of the Sidhe, enters. Emer draws a dagger and moves as if to strike her.*

FIGURE OF CUCHULAIN [*laughing*]. You think to wound her with a knife! She has an airy body, an invulnerable body. Remember that though your lamentations have dragged him hither, once he has left this shore, once he has passed the bitter sea, once he lands in Manannan's house, he will be as the gods who remember nothing.

[*The Woman of the Sidhe, Fand, moves round the crouching Ghost of Cuchulain at front of stage in a dance that grows gradually quicker as he awakes. At moments she may drop her hair upon his head, but she does not kiss him. She is accompanied by string and flute and drum. Her mask and clothes must suggest gold or bronze or brass and silver, so that she seems more an idol than a human being. This suggestion may be repeated in her movements. Her hair, too, must keep the metallic suggestion. The object of the dance is that having awakened Cuchulain he will follow Fand out; probably he will seek a kiss and the kiss will be withheld.*

FIGURE OF CUCHULAIN. Cry out that you renounce his love, cry that you renounce his love for ever.

[*Fand and Cuchulain go out.*

EMER. No, no, never will I give that cry.

FIGURE OF CUCHULAIN. Fool, fool! I am Fand's enemy. I come to tell you how to thwart her and you do nothing. There is yet time. Listen to the horses of the chariot, they are trampling the shore. They are wild and trampling. She has mounted into her chariot. Cuchulain is not yet beside her. Will you leave him to such as she? Renounce his

---

227–228 (almost as dance) *sd entered in margin NLI 30,602*

229 *after* knife! *sd inserted* (Emer drops knife) *followed by* Put down that knife but watch *NLI 30,602*

231 lamentations] cries *NLI 30,602, LCP*

sd 237/238 Fand and Cuchulain go out] Dancers go out *inserted NLI 30,602* The dancers go out *NLI 8774(6), LCP*

241 *sd* (The dancers go out) *NLI 30,602 del*

244–245 *sd written in margin* Music *NLI 30,602*

love, and all her power over him comes to an end.

EMER. I renounce Cuchulain's love. I renounce it for ever.

[*Figure of Cuchulain falls back upon the bed, drawing or partly drawing its curtain that he may change his mask.*

Eithne Inguba enters.

EITHNE INGUBA. Cuchulain, Cuchulain! Remember our last meeting. We lay all night among the sand-hills; dawn came; we heard the crying of the birds upon the shore. Come to me, beloved. [*The curtain of the bed moves.*] Look, look! He has come back, he is there in the bed, he has his own rightful form again. It is I who have won him. It is my love that has brought him back to life!

[*The figure in the bed pulls back the curtain. He wears the mask of Cuchulain.*

EMER. Cuchulain wakes!

CUCHULAIN. Your arms, your arms! O Eithne Inguba, I have been in some strange place and am afraid.

EPILOGUE

[*The Musicians, singing as follows, draw the wave-curtain until it masks the bed, Cuchulain, Eithne Inguba, and Emer.*

FIRST MUSICIAN

Why does your heart beat thus?
Plain to be understood,
I have met in a man's house
A statue of solitude,
Moving there and walking,

---

sd 248–249 (Figure of Cuchulain falls back upon the bed *with* (Changes mask) *added and* music *written in margin NLI 30,602* Figure of Cuchulain falls back upon the *bed NLI 8774(6) with* and changes mask.) *rev to* drawing or partly drawing the curtain that he may change his mask *NLI 8774(6)* (Figure of Cuchulain falls back and changes mask *LCP*

sd 253, 256/7 *omitted NLI 30,602, LCP, inserted in margin NLI 8774(6)*

EPILOGUE

sd 259/260 (The two Musicians, singer and speaker, advance from their place and pull over the inner curtain.) *NLI 30,602; NLI 8774(6) del; so LCP but* speaker] drummer *followed by* The leader of the Chorus and the man who sits opposite rise singing and draw the wave curtain until it masks the bed, Cuchulain, Eithne, and Emer. Singing they return to their original positions. *NLI 8774(6) as second portion of LCP with* leader of the chorus . . . and draw *rev to* The musicians rise singing *rev to* The musicians singing as follows

Its strange heart beating fast
For all our talking;
O still that heart at last.

O bitter reward
Of many a tragic tomb!
And we though astonished are dumb
And give but a sigh and a word,
A passing word.

Although the door be shut
And all seem well enough,
Although wide world hold not
A man but will give you his love
The moment he has looked at you,
He that has loved the best
May turn from a statue
His too human breast.

O bitter reward
Of many a tragic tomb!
And we though astonished are dumb
And give but a sigh and a word,
A passing word.

What makes your heart so beat?
Is there no man at your side?
When beauty is complete
Your own thought will have died
And danger not be diminished;
Dimmed at three-quarter light,
When moon's round is finished
The stars are out of sight.

O bitter reward
Of many a tragic tomb!
And we though astonished are dumb
And give but a sigh and a word,
A passing word.

---

280 breast *rev from* breath *NLI 8774(6)*
292 round] light *NLI 30,602, NLI 8774(6), LCP*

[*The Musicians return to their places, Fand, the Woman of the Sidhe, enters and dances a dance which expresses her despair for the loss of Cuchulain. As before there may be other dancers who represent the waves. It is called, in order to balance the first dance, 'Fand mourns among the waves.' It is essentially a dance which symbolises, like water in the fortune-telling books, bitterness. As she takes her final pose of despair the Curtain falls.*

---

sd 298 *NLI 30,602, NLI 8774(6) basically as text, with minor rearrangements, but all three add a "Note":* As in two places in the dramatic part of the play symbols are used to express the dashing of waves, some use of symbols should be made at any rate in the dance with which the play opens *NLI 30,602, LCP; so 8774(6) then del*

The 1934 Revisions of *The Only Jealousy of Emer*

Yeats's efforts at turning his verse play, *The Only Jealousy of Emer*, into a dance play for masks, *Fighting the Waves*, led him to return to the original play in an effort to simplify it. Evidence is found in MS P, which consists of a three-page holograph manuscript, NLI 8774(17), and a two-page typescript, NLI 8774(19).

[NLI 8774(17)]

[1r]

1 ~~The hearts are cold that beat upon beauty~~
2 ~~What st[?rike] would a shadow & draw a shadow~~ blood
~~What wound a shadow~~ dream
3 Or draw a shadows blood
Put up that knife
4 She [?lets] [?it]

[1v]

1 The following ~~h~~ rymed dialogue should be
2 sung – but if the ~~dancer cannot sing~~
3 ~~woman dancer~~ dancer cannot sing
4 as well as dance, ~~then it~~
5 they may be left out altogether – In which
6 case Cuchullain follows the ~~singer out at~~ the
7 woman of the sidhe out after the end
8 of the dance. I have never been clear
9 where the dance should, all at the beginning
10 or partly at the beginning & partly elsewhere
11 in the singing, for I have not yet at
12 ~~the opportunity~~ had the opportunity to experiment.
~~other~~ difficulty of finding
13 I do not know, & ~~probably the impossibility~~
14 of ~~combining~~ two such gifts as dancing & singing
15 in one person, will ~~probably make it~~ [?alright]
16 provi[?ding] a kind of dancing & singing can
17 be combined.

[2r]

1 mouth.
2 The Woman of the Sidhe goes out followed by Cuchullain.
3 Fig of C
make hast
4 Cry out that you renounce his love – ~~cry out~~

The entries on these holograph leaves do not seem to follow any particular order. They are arranged here in the folder order.

1r Figure of Cuchulain speaks. Cf. MS L, 11r, ll. 220–221; developed on MS P (NLI 8774[18]), 1r below.

1v Cf. the stage direction at l. 223, MS L, 12r above. This stage direction was not used in *Collected Plays*. It shows the influence of *Fighting the Waves*, where Yeats had simply dropped the dialogue.

9 For "should" read "should go."

11 For "at" read "had."

2r, l. 1 "mouth" is the last word spoken by Cuchulain. Cf. MS L, 15r, l. 278b above; the revision is based on the text in *Fighting the Waves*, see p. 359 above.

4 For "hast" read "haste."

[2^{r}, continued]

5 ~~Renounce his love forever~~ And cry that you renounce his love for
ever.

6 Emer.

No ~~No no~~

7 ^Never will I give that cry

8 The Fig of C.

Fool ~~f~~ Fool

9 I am Fand's enemy & come to wreck her will
10 And you stand gaping there – There is still time
11 Hear how the horses trample on the shore.
12 ~~The~~ How wild it tramples, she has mounted up
13 Cuchullain is not beside her in the chariot
14 There is still a moment left – cry out
15 Renounce him & her power is at an end.
16 Cuchullains foot on the chariot step
17 Cry –

[3^{r}]

1 Emer
2 I renounce Cuchullain's love for ever
3 Eithne
4 Come to me beloved – it is I
5 I Eithne Inguba – Look he is there –
6 He has come back & moved upon the bed
7 And it is that won him from the sea
8 That brought him back to life.
9 Emer
10 Cuchullain wakes.

[3^{v}]

I met you on a cloudy hill
Beside ~~an old~~ a lost old empty well
Beside

2^{r}, l. 12 For "it tramples" read "they trample" (that is, the horses).
16 For "foot" read "foot is."

3^{r}, l. 7 For "it is" read "it is I."

3^{v} These lines were scrapped and do not appear in *Collected Plays* (1934). Cf. MS L, 12^{r}, ll. [8–9] above.

[NLI 8774(18)]

[1^r]

"Only Jealousy of Emer." Page 369. Delete from "or weary with" to end of page and insert the following.

Lap them in cloudy hair or kiss their lips
Our men awake in ignorance of it all
But when we take them in our arms at night
We cannot break their solitude.
(She draws a knife from her girdle.)

No ~~kine~~ knife
Fig. of Cuch. ~~Look: listen.~~ ~~That body is~~ air
a that is air & cloud.
~~No knife~~ can would ~~that~~ body~~, look and listen~~.
~~I have not given you eyes and ears for nothing~~.
(Emer lets the knife fall)

[2^r]

Corrections to "The Only Jealousy of Emer"

When the Ghost of Cuchulain and the Woman of the Sidhe have gone out comes the following:

Figure of Cuchulain Cry out that you renounce his love; make haste
And cry that you renounce his love for ever.
Emer No, never will I give that cry.
Figure of Cuchulain Fool, fool!
I am Fand's enemy and come to thwart her will
And you stand gaping there. There is still time.
Hear how the horses trample oh the shore
Hear how they trample, she has mounted up,
Cuchullain's not beside her in the chariot
There is still a moment left; cry out
Renounce him, and her power is at an end,
Cuchullain's foot is on the chariot step,
Cry –
Emer I renounce Cuchullain's love for ever.
(The Figure of Cuchullain sinks back upon the bed, half drawing the curtain. Eithne Inguba

---

1^r, 2^r Typed sheets of passages selected for correction, with Yeats's holograph revisions; cf. MS L, 11^r above.

1^r, l. 1 Yeats's direction above the line is based on the text of MS L, 11^r, l. 216ff.

1^r, l. 3–4 Simpler than MS L, 11^r, ll. 219–220: "and when, at fall of night we press / Their hearts upon our hearts their hearts are cold."

2^r Cf. The holograph portion of MS P, 2^r–3^r above (NLI 8774[17]).

[2r, continued]

<u>comes in and kneels by bed</u>)

<u>Eithne Inguba</u> **Come to me, beloved, it is I/I Eithne Inguba.⌃—**
Look! He is there. –/He has come back and
moved upon the bed/ ⌃A a nd it is I that won him from
the sea,/ ⌃T t hat brought him back to life.

<u>Emer</u> **Cuchulain wakes.**

2r, ll. 13–16 Yeats converted the prose speech into verse by adding strokes and capital letters, in ink.

Appendixes

Appendix I

George Antheil and Yeats

Antheil had been working in Berlin in 1928, but a recurrence of his pneumonia sent him south to Rapallo, where he knew only Ezra Pound. The composer recounted his collaboration with Yeats in his autobiography, *Bad Boy of Music* (London, 1947), pp. 180–181.

> Ezra now introduced me to a number of persons who habitually sat at the only free table of Rapallo's only decent restaurant, the Hotel Rapallo café. Two of them were Nobel Prize winners, William Butler Yeats and Gerhart Hauptmann. I had never so much as met a Nobel Prize winner before, and now, every day, I could sit down with *two* of them and question them on all kinds of little mundane matters, such as what they were feeding their dogs on, had they read any good detective stories lately, etc.
>
> All of them, incidentally, were voracious detective story readers, including Ezra. When they eventually exhausted the local English lending library, I decided to write a detective story for them. I started it, and as it developed, chapter by chapter, almost every one of this august literary body took part in editing and correcting my grammar (which was hopeless). Eventually, through T. S. Eliot (then editor-in-chief of Faber and Faber) it was published under the title *Death in the Dark*, by "Stacey Bishop".
>
> It was a poorly written but honest-to-God detective story, and the criminal was apprehended by glandular methods, too. I can understand to-day why Faber and Faber purchased the manuscript. Being a "first" in glandular detective methods was not as interesting to them as the fact that the original manuscript was full of copious corrections and footnoting by T. S. Eliot, Yeats, Hauptmann, Pound and even [Franz] Werfel.
>
> I wish I could get that manuscript back!
>
> The two other literary habitués of the long table were Franz Werfel and Emil Ludwig. Franz Werfel never talked, but just sat there and looked and looked and looked, while Ludwig never looked, but just sat there and talked and talked.
>
> Yeats was always getting messages from spirits. He was also a veritable expert on seeing ghosts in broad daylight—a rather difficult feat, as I am told by those who are authorities on this subject.
>
> I saw quite a bit of Yeats now, because when he discovered that I was a composer whom Ezra had once written a book about, he conceived the gay idea of my writing incidental music to three of his thoroughly Irish plays (I did, finally, write music to one, *Fighting the Waves*, which he subsequently produced at the Abbey Theatre, Dublin).

> We would often sit together discussing our project, when suddenly he'd say: "Hallo, William," and he'd tip his soft felt sombrero.
>
> I'd follow his look and, seeing nobody within fifty feet of our table, I'd ask him, not without astonishment, where William was.
>
> "Right in the chair alongside of you; he's the ghost of my indigestion," Yeats would say.
>
> Yeats would sometimes talk quite a bit to William, and also other Irish spirits who had been kind enough to come all the way from Dublin to see him. Previously I had often visited Yeats at night, but now I developed the habit of seeing him exclusively in the daytime. Not being on such friendly relations with the spirits as Yeats, I hated the idea of walking home alone at night.
>
> But I think I wrote him a good enough background score for his play. He seemed well enough pleased with it, at least in the introduction to his group of plays, *Wheels and Butterflies*, published by the Macmillan Company. *Fighting the Waves* was played in Dublin with notable success, and raving Dublin critics from then on decided that I was really an Irishman, because the score (so they said) was so thoroughly Irish.
>
> As a matter of fact, the secret of my success in writing such true Irish music is contained in the fact that Yeats's play is entirely about Irish ghosts. With "William" sitting there alongside of me at the café every day, what else could have happened but that William soon became quite visible and even audible, giving me not only valuable tips on ancient Irish music, but also singing old Irish melodies (in a rather cracked voice, I admit) while I hastily wrote them down in my notebook.

Antheil's reminiscences of his collaboration with Yeats are similar to those he described in a letter to Yeats of June 27, 1934, giving Yeats permission to print his music for *Fighting the Waves* in *Wheels and Butterflies*:

> It is curious, but I was very happy writing this music. I am not Irish, but it seemed as if some spirit moved me, and spoke through me, and as I listened to the music that came from within I realized, almost as if it came from somewhere or someone else, that it was very Irish-heroic. It was mediumistic.[1]

Antheil's memory was somewhat faulty; it was Lennox Robinson, on meeting the musician in Paris in 1928, who suggested that he compose the music for Yeats's newly written ballet. However, during a longer stay in Rapallo in 1929, after meeting the Yeatses, Antheil began to write in earnest.[2]

---

[1] *Letters to Yeats*, p. 564.

[2] Saddlemyer, *Becoming George*, pp. 416–417.

Appendix II

Rhys's Account of Cuchulain and Fand

John Rhys's retelling of the story of Cuchulain and Fand (as found in *Celtic Heathendom*, pp. 460–464) begins with a celebration by the Ultonians (the men of Ulster) of the great festival which marked the Calends of winter, and the days immediately before and after. A flock of beautiful wild birds alighted on a nearby loch, and all the ladies of King Conchobar's court desired a pair. They appealed to Cuchulain's gallantry and, overcoming his initial distrust at the triviality of the errand, he brought down pairs of the birds for the women with his sling. However, he neglected to bring down a pair for his wife. He then saw two birds more beautiful than all the others, linked with a chain of gold. Cuchulain missed them with his sling, and had to bring them down with his spear. This made him woeful; he was not accustomed to failure. He rested against a stone and dreamed that two women, one in green and one in red, whipped him. He went to bed, saying nothing.

> This all took place on the eve of November, when the Celtic year begins with the ascendancy of the powers of darkness. When Cuchulain had lain in his bed, speaking to nobody, for nearly a year, and the Ultonian nobles and his wife happened to be around him, some on the bed and the others close by, they suddenly found a stranger seated on the side of the bed. He said he had come to speak to Cúchullain, and he sang a song in which he informed them that he had come from his sister Fand and his sister Liban to tell him that they would soon heal him if they were allowed. Fand, he said, had conceived great love for him, and would give him her hand if only he visited her land, and treat him to plenty of silver and gold, together with much wine to drink. She would, moreover, send her sister Liban on November-eve to heal him. After having added that his own name was Aengus, brother to Fand and Liban, he disappeared as mysteriously as he had come.
>
> Cúchullain then sat up in his bed and told his friends all about the dream which had made him ill: he was advised to go to the spot where it had occurred to him twelve months previously, for such are the requirements of the fairy reckoning of time. He did so, and he beheld the woman in green coming towards him: he reproached her for what she had done, and she explained that she and her sister had come, not to harm him, but to seek his love: Fand, she said, had been forsaken by Manannan mac Lir, and she had set her heart on hum, Cúchullain; moreover, she had a message now from her own husband, Labraid of the Swift Hand on the Sword, to the effect that he would give him Fand to wife for one day's assistance against his enemies.
>
> Cúchullain objected that he was not well enough to fight; but he was induced

to send Loeg his charioteer with Liban to see the mysterious land to which he was invited. Loeg, after conversing with Fand and Labraid of the Swift Hand on the Sword, returned with a glowing account of what he had seen. This revived the dropping spirits of his master, who passed his hand over his face and rapidly recovered his strength. Even then he would not go to Labraid's Isle on a woman's invitation, and Loeg had to visit it again and assure him that Labraid was impatiently expecting him for the war that was about to be waged. Then at length he went thither in his chariot and fought.

He abode there a month with Fand, and when he left her he made an appointment to meet her at *Ibar Cinn Tachta*, or the Yew at the Strand's End, the spot, according to O'Curry, where Newry now stands. This came to the ears of Emer, Cúchullain's wedded wife, and she, with the ladies of Ulster, repaired there, provided with sharp knives to slay Fand. A touching scene follows, in which Emer recovers Cúchullain's love, and Fand beholds herself about to be forsaken, whereupon she begins to bewail the happy days she had spent with her husband Manannan mac Lir in her bower at *Dun Inbir*, or the Fort of the Estuary. Nay, Fand's position in the unequal conflict with the ladies of Ulster became known to Manannan, the shape-shifting Son of the Sea, and he hastened over the plain to her rescue.

"What is that there?" inquired Cúchullain.

"That," said Loeg, "is Fand going away with Manannan mac Lir, because she was not pleasing to thee."

At those words Cúchullain went out of his mind, and leaped the three high leaps and the three southern leaps of Luachair. He seemed a long time without food and without drink, wandering on the mountains and sleeping nightly on the road of Midluachair. Emer went to consult the king about him, and it was resolved to send the poets, the professional men and the druids of Ulster, to seek him and bring him home to Emain. He would have slain them, but they chanted spells of Druidism against him, whereby they were enabled to lay hold of his arms and legs. When he had recovered his senses a little, he asked for drink, and they gave him a drink of forgetfulness, which made him forget Fand and all his adventures; as Emer was not in a much better state of mind, the same drink was also administered to her; and Manannan had shaken his cloak between Fand and Cúchullain that they might never meet again.

Appendix III

Yeats's Introductions to *Fighting the Waves* (1932–1934)

The principal concern of this volume has been with the manuscripts of the two plays, *The Only Jealousy of Emer* and *Fighting the Waves*. Among the *Waves* papers, however, is a substantial number of documents relating to the two versions of the Introduction, the first published in *Dublin Magazine*, April–June 1932, and the second in *Wheels and Butterflies* in 1934 (London: Macmillan). In general, the typescript and holograph drafts of these two texts are very similar to the published texts, and so need not be transcribed here in their entirety. Yet some materials among these papers were not included in the published texts, and in the interests of thoroughness (and in the hope that someone might find them useful) they are duly transcribed here.

The original form of the 1932 Introduction was slightly different from the published one. The text, a comprehensive scheme of "intellectual nationalism" for Ireland, was in seven sections:

(1) Yeats gives his reasons for rewriting his private play for the public stage, and for simplifying the play's language.

(2) He explains the place of *Fighting the Waves* in Yeats's cycle of plays on the Irish heroic age; the ideals of the founders of the Irish dramatic movement (Yeats, Synge, and Lady Gregory), which should have been the foundation of a new intellectual nationalism (something richer than mere flag-waving, street-fighting, or economic upheaval) contrasted with the new, realistic school of dramatists.

(3) He finds the contrast between Greek and Latin literature to be similar to that between Irish and English writing, proposes a scheme for the use of Greek and Irish in Irish schools, and makes a plea for the preservation of the Irish language (but not for the narrow-minded purposes of the Gaelic League and other such "patriotic" organizations), and likewise for the preservation of Ireland's historical heritage.

(4) Beyond these external matters, he sees the need for the Irish to change their "subconscious prepossessions," to find their true intellectual ancestry by aligning themselves with Berkeley rather than with Locke and modern scientific thought.

(5) He recommends the historical schemes of Swift and Vico to the Irish nationalists, presumably to make them see Ireland's place in history on something other than an immediate scale.

(6) Returning to the play, he invokes the theories of Castiglione on women's beauty to explain the opening song; presumably Yeats intended a belief in reincarnation to be part of his projected reorientation of the Irish national consciousness, away from scientism and back to tradition.

(7) He discusses the image of the sea in *Fighting the Waves*, and puts aside as meaningless the question of the play's "originality": being rooted in the sea, the play is firmly based

on an image of (for want of a better expression) absolute reality.

Yeats subsequently canceled sections (5) and (6), and, after some inconsequential reshuffling of its sentences, united section (4) with section (3). Most of the sections he kept are so close to the published text as not to require transcribing here.

Section (1): As this section is identical to the published text, it is not transcribed.

Section (2): Toward the end of this section there is a canceled passage that identifies the "Caesar" of the published text as the novelist Peadar O'Donnell, who was just beginning to attract attention at that time.

[NLI 8774(1), 5^{v}]

do
only a Caesar would^what I want ~~& as I find~~
that admirable novelist Mr Peadar O Donnell ~~is~~
~~credited with~~ has according to the Cellars & Garrets
selected himself for the post I write the remainder of
this essay for his ~~ear~~ ears
~~but they then as~~
but as the Cellars & Garretts may ~~find him one day~~
discover one, now that they have taken to communism
I write for Ceasars eyes

Section (3): Yeats returns to his attack on O'Donnell in this section while discussing the need for the National Museum of Ireland to have sufficient funds for its job of preserving Ireland's past. One presumes that O'Donnell was too small a target for Yeats to fire at with dignity and the passage was dropped.

[NLI 8774(1), 7^{v}]

Ceasar ~~double treble the Museum's wretched grant~~
Then let ~~Mr O'Donnell~~ ^ talk to the curates of the
museum; he will have the confidence I lack ~~For~~ for the
~~devout &~~
~~the charming heroine of his novel "The Knife" has~~
spoken of her deep regret that she had never been
associated however indirectly with the murder or strife

7^{v}, l. 3 "The Knife"] The heroine of this dreadful "IRA novel," published in 1930, is Nuala, a kind of scaled-down Cathleen Ni Houlihan. She spends much of her time inciting the men of her district to join the IRA and drive out the English. "The Knife" is the young IRA man she loves. She is an idealist, believing that "Ireland will be one big family of workers, living for each other, when we're free" (p. 112). She expresses her regret at not being a man to "The Knife" on p. 171.

Section (4): This section is virtually identical and is not transcribed.
Section (5): Yeats canceled this section, so it is here transcribed in full.

[NLI 8774(3), 4r]

~~**5**~~ V

not even at Ceasar's bidding
But nobody is going to deny his son ^ **the pride of under-**
standing the Latin tags in the <u>Irish Times</u> to create a nationality
better than a screech of bagpipes, nobody is going to substitute
philosophy for the popular science that is the opium of the sub-
urbs; nor can I see any situation in the near future when they
will for such things are accomplished when governing men, after
some great victory against an internal enemy, are full of
unexhausted energy. ~~**There are cruder and more violent means of**~~
~~**imposing a form upon the mirror-like masses.**~~
We contemplative men should discuss our impracticable
aims that such moments of energy may not lack ideas, ~~**and for**~~ Stet
~~**that discussion's sake I commend two great myths to Cellar**~~
(~~like Swift~~) Is as Swift thought
~~**Shall we**~~ ^ ~~**consider**~~ **civilisation or nation as moving** ^ **towards de-**
decrepitude and a proletarian dictatorship ~~might~~
~~**crepitude and gloom**~~ ^ **–** ~~**Swift would not have rejected the commun-**~~
– does it as
~~**ist diagnosis of a final capitalist tyranny.**~~ **- or** ~~**shall we think**~~
thought
~~**with**~~ **Vico** ~~**that it**~~ **lives a grub and dies a butterfly**~~:~~**?** ~~**though I**~~
– ~~shall we think with the~~
~~**think he would have rejected the conviction of the**~~ **Japanese Christ-**
& labour leader ~~in its final moments~~
ian, Kantian, socialist saint ^ **Kagawa** ~~**that the present moment of**~~
[-?-] our ~~freed from everything but itself~~
[-?-] ~~**ours when all has been outlived but**~~ ^ ~~**intellect**~~ ^ ~~**may illuminate the**~~
(thinks become the) (~~some~~ new) ~~succeeding~~
conscience of ~~**a**~~ ^ **civilisation yet to come.** ~~**Is the nation a self**~~
~~**imposed discipline, a deliberate limit,**~~ ~~**Must a nation always**~~
~~**regret its past spontaneity and always substitute a self**~~ **imposed**

NLI 8774(3), 4r, l. 12 "To Cellar" was canceled with x's by the typist.

18 Toyohiko Kagawa (1888–1960). He was born in Kobe and graduated from its Theological School; during this time he lived in the city's slums, preached the Gospel to the poor, and set up a free clinic there. He went to the United States in 1916 to study philosophy at Princeton. On returning, he devoted himself to social and evangelical works; he was a co-founder of the Japan Farmers' Union. Immediately after the great Tokyo earthquake of 1923, he went there to set up a settlement school. He toured Europe and America publishing more than fifty books, including novels and works on social issues like the Spiritual Movement and the Labor Movement. (Information from *Japan Biographical Encyclopaedia* and *Who's Who* [Tokyo, 3d ed., 1964–1965], p. 465.)

20–21 "Is the nation . . . limit" canceled by the typist.

[NLI 8774(3), 4^r, continued]

~~**discipline, a deliberate limit, or is the final spontaneity**~~ **the**
~~**greatest? If Vico is right, if there is some half truth in**~~
~~**Kagawa's dream, and if there is we must not put into authority**~~[8]
(as its final moment approaches with intellect freed from everything itself become as the)

Section (6): Yeats also canceled this section, which is built on his note to *The Only Jealousy of Emer* in *Four Plays for Dancers* (see Alspach, *Variorum Plays*, p. 566); it is here transcribed in full.

[NLI 8774(1), 6^r]

VI

"How many centuries spent the sed^entary soul . . . . . to
raise into being that loveliness." I remembered what Castiglione
if better than
had said about a woman's beauty, that it ~~**was**~~ **a mere promise of**
and "an easy way to get it" it was
pleasure^ ~~**or**~~ **"the spoil or monument of the victory of the soul,"**
and wondered, being as much a Platonist as the author of the
Courtier, how many hard or perilous lives went to the victory.
caught
If we do not admit those many lives we are ~~**soon tied up**~~
in some ~~**such**~~ **sophistry like that in which the wise and profound**
Von Hugel caught himself when he justified the exile of ~~**the**~~ **children**
that died in the cradle, neither heaven nor hell earned, to the
pleasant but inferior state called limbo, on the ground that it should
satisfy them as they knew no better. We should not explain
in their variety
everything, we should think of men's souls^ as the first inexplicable
{of
fact and {**as God as the final multitudinous perfection, that is yet**

NLI 8774(3), 4^r, ll. 25ff. The rest of the text is missing.

NLI 8774(1), 6^r, l. 4 *The Courtier*, Thomas Hoby, tr. (1561), in *Tudor Translations*, W. E. Henley, ed., vol. 23 (London, 1900), p. 350: "In conclusion this comelye and holye beawtie is a wondrous settinge out of everie thinge. And it may be said that Good and beawtifull be after a sort one selfe thinge, especiallie in the bodies of men: of the beawtie whereof the nighest cause (as I suppose) is the beawtie of the soule: the which as a partner of the right and heavenlye beawtie, maketh sightlye and beawtifull what ever she toucheth, and most of all, if the bodye, where she dwelleth, be not of so vile a matter, that she can not imprint in it her proprtye. Therfore Beawtie is the true monument and spoile of the victorye of the soule, when she with heavenlye influence beareth rule over materiall and grosse nature, and with her light overcometh the darkness of the bodye."

[NLI 8774(1), 6r, continued]

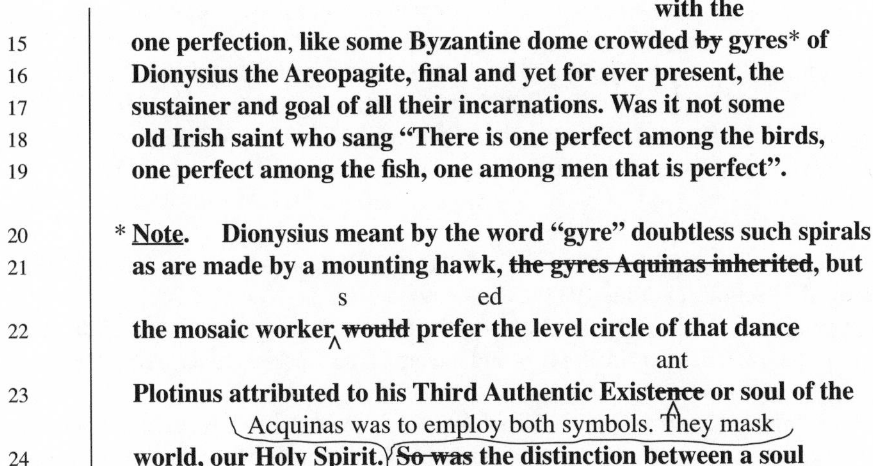

with the
one perfection, like some Byzantine dome crowded ~~by~~ gyres* of
Dionysius the Areopagite, final and yet for ever present, the
sustainer and goal of all their incarnations. Was it not some
old Irish saint who sang "There is one perfect among the birds,
one perfect among the fish, one among men that is perfect".

* **Note. Dionysius meant by the word "gyre" doubtless such spirals**
as are made by a mounting hawk, ~~the gyres Aquinas inherited~~, but
s ed
the mosaic worker^ ~~would~~ prefer the level circle of that dance
ant
Plotinus attributed to his Third Authentic Exist~~ence~~ or soul of the
Acquinas was to employ both symbols. They mask
world, our Holy Spirit.^ ~~So was~~ the distinction between a soul

[NLI 8774(1), 7r]

plunging into the immensity of God and the same soul in adoration,
or
between knowledge and love, ~~perhaps~~,^ seeing that of all things
love dreads a change of object. ^

Section (7): This section is virtually identical and is not transcribed here; this became section (5) in the 1932 text.

NLI 8774(1), 6r, l. 23 The first order of human beings lead purely materialistic lives; the second order lift themselves a little above the sensual realm but "fall back in virture." "But there is a third order—those godlike men who, in their mightier power, in the keenness of their sight, have clear vision of the splendour of the world above and rise to it from the fog and cloud of earth and There abide, looking beyond all here, delighted in that, their native region of Real Being, like one returning from wide wanderings to the well-ordered ways of his own land" (*Enneads* V, 9; Stephen MacKenna, tr., *The Essence of Plotinus*, compiled by Grace H. Turnbull [New York, 1934], p. 179).

NLI 8774(1), 7r The text halts at l. 3.

The 1934 Introduction

The 1932 version of the Introduction, besides touching on some aspects of Yeats's play, had also ranged far from that subject in Yeats's attempt to present an "intellectual nationalism" to the young men of the "Cellars and Garrets." Late in 1933, he began to rewrite this Introduction for *Wheels and Butterflies* (see pp. xxv and 375 above). His subject now was heroic art and its problems and possibilities in the modern age. His holograph draft containing his extensive revisions has survived, and shows that at this stage he planned an introduction in at least six sections:

(1) The opening section of the new material is headed "II," suggesting that Yeats planned to keep the section (1) of his 1932 text as it stood.

(2) In revising section (2) of the 1932 text on the history of heroic art in modern Ireland, he drops the reference to Greek plays and the attack on the Irish government, and adds an apposite quotation from Aristotle.

(3) In a development from the revised second section, Yeats shows how literary history is a series of complete reversals of mood, as in modern Ireland, where the political art of the late nineteenth century gave way after Parnell's fall to a romantic and legendary art, which in turn gave way to a satirical and realistic art. Here, Ireland is a mirror of the general changes that occur in European thought. In 1933, the works of writers like Joyce and Woolf are seen as hopeful signs of a change back to an aesthetic that will accept heroic art.

(4) He argues that even the support of the Cellars and Garretts, had it been forthcoming for heroic art, would have been insufficient; a general change in European thought was necessary. Yeats added this new section to section (3) on a new leaf.

(5) Professor Crookes's scientific presentation of spiritualistic phenomena is a sign of a revolution in European thought that will once more sustain heroic art. This art will be more deliberate than its ancient ancestors, but like them will present the true self-sacrifice. Yeats renumbered this section "IV."

(6) (But numbered "V.") Professor Richet's survey of psychical research presents further evidence of the fundamental change that must come in science, once it accepts the reality of the unseen.

In the published text, Yeats made the fifth section from the 1932 text serve as section (6), and provided a final brief paragraph (not present in this holograph draft) as section (7).

As in the case of the 1932 text, only those sections of the draft that differ markedly from the text published in 1934 have been transcribed, as the rest are identical or virtually identical to the published text.

Section (1): Not represented in the manuscript. Yeats reprints section (1) from 1932.

Section (2): In a partially canceled passage Yeats discusses the problem of language in heroic art (cf. the relevant pages in Alspach, *Variorum Plays*, pp. 569–570).

[NLI 13,567, 1r]

in later years she dwelt much upon the
saying of Aristotle "To think like a wise man but ~~th~~ to
think like the common people", & always her wise man was
heroic man. ~~Her task & O'Grady's task like the task~~
of Morris in ~~Seagurd~~ Seagurd the Volsung ~~was less difficult~~
was to find adequate modern speech for a heroic life that
must remain ancient & remote. My task was more difficult

[NLI 13,567, 2r]

~~that any representation upon the stage intelligible to a modern~~
~~audience would destroy its particular quality~~.

Section (3): Yeats sets out the changes that had been taking place in European literature; the canceled material in the manuscript includes a reference to James Joyce.

[NLI 13,567, 5r]

~~but characters so passive, that they need to steer their boat and~~
made passive that ~~more~~
self analysis might ~~steer their boat~~, or brutalized that we ~~might~~
~~we ourselves~~
satisfy their ambitions might reason ~~understand~~ ourselves
understand
described
When Stendhal ~~defined~~ a masterpiece as a mirror dawdling
down a lane, ~~he brought defined~~ he was swayed by the mechanistic
philosophy of the French eighteenth century; gradually literature
~~was~~ conformed to this ideal, Balzac became old fashioned
romanticism hold
~~romantic~~ became theatrical in its strain to ~~catch~~ the
by the principal characters in the most famous books had
public till ~~at~~ the end of the nineteenth century
~~passive buffeted hither & thither~~
~~came those everywhere books where the ^ principal character is was~~
~~several [?ways]~~
buffeted ~~hitherto, or then wholly occupied with the epoch~~
&
~~the impressions an analysis of his impressions~~. ~~Then with James~~

1r, l. 1 she] Lady Gregory.
2 For "man but" read "man is but."
7 For "difficult" read "difficult in."
5r, l. 9 In the revision, for "had" read "had been."
12 For "the" read "his."

[NLI 13,567, 5r, continued]

13 Joyce came a change, man was ~~as passive as be~~ still
14 passive but no longer a mirror, he became
15 a green jewel, where matter

some
16 But there are signs of change four years ~~go~~ ago
17 the Russian government silenced the mechanists because
18 socialist dialectic is impossible ~~does not~~ if matter is
19 not in itself active & living, & ~~our~~ certain characteristic
20 books Ulysses, Mrs Virginia Woolfs "Waves", Mr Ezra Pounds
21 Canto suggest a philosophy like that of ~~the Indian~~ Samkara
22 school of Indian thought, mental & physical objects alike
23 ~~material~~, material, ~~surges of intellectual & physical~~
24 ~~experience~~ a deluge of experience, ~~breaking over the passive mind~~

melting limits whether of line or tint
25 over us, ~~but in kind & dissolving & transforming~~ but in this

[NLI 13,567, 4v]

1 itself [?marching] is trundled about by
2 some limited measurable force

3 and self moving

by the dry sticks of the hedge
4 man no ~~bright hard mirror~~
5 ~~bright dawdling~~ mirror bright hard
6 dawdling, but a swimmer or rather
7 the waves themselves

[NLI 13,567, 6r]

1 new ~~announced foretold~~ announced perhaps
2 ~~kind~~ [of] literature, ~~announced perhaps for~~ by Balzac in Le Chef-

~~as~~
3 -d'oeuvre inconnu, ~~or in the old with its hard dry matter~~
4 ~~matter, both hard & dry, its bright brittle mirror~~

as an old
5 ~~man himself is nothing~~ ~~as in the old~~ man is in himself

nothing

5r, l. 14 For "be still" read "before still."

21 For "Canto" read "Cantos."

4v, ll. 1–2 Arrowed to be inserted in l. 18 of facing 5r.

3 Arrowed to be inserted in l. 23 of facing 5r.

4–5 Arrowed to be inserted in l. 25 of facing 5r.

Section (4): Yeats canceled this short section and added it in revised form to section (3) on a new leaf; the first entry is transcribed here.

[NLI 13,567, 7r]

IV
1 But ~~even we walk about the we~~ had there been so great
2 cause of bitterness & self contempt we could not long
considering
3 ~~have held the scene~~, every man every where is more
4 of his time than of his nation, ~~& praises science which has~~
5 ~~matter solid & improves the soil, had~~
6 ~~only a general change of philosophy could~~
7 ~~nothing could have made~~
scene, no not even with the whole support of
Garrets & Cellars
8 long have held the ~~scene~~, ^ only a general change ~~in the~~
~~he or us~~ make it possible
9 in European philosophy could ~~make possible~~.

Section (5): In a lengthy canceled passage, Yeats worked out his definition of the true self-sacrifice.

[NLI 13,567, 9r]

crumpled
1 Ireland we have come to think of self sacrifice as the ~~flung~~ gage of ~~the [?patriot]~~
2 ~~We have learned In Ireland self sacrifice is the same thing as~~
~~crumpled gage~~
3 ~~as the sacrificial [?offering] by the Abstract & made~~
4 ~~therefrom we have even begun to [?calculate] it, abstracted it~~
fixed so
for
flung with eye ~~to~~ calculation
5 ~~until it seems still & empty, we think of them as with a calculating~~ upon the future
or in rage
upon the
[?~~covering] glance of rage~~ present
6 ~~eye fixed upon the future or a raging eye upon the upon the~~
7 ~~present, we have abstracted it until we have simply killed it~~
8 ~~that we cannot speak of it without becoming shrill. The her[?oic]~~
as it descends through
9 The heroic act ~~as it has come down to us through~~

6r Text ends with l. 5; rest of page blank.

9r, l. 1 Read "In Ireland we."

[NLI 13,567, 9^{r} continued]

is
10 tradition, ~~is a sacrifice of the or something that a~~
because being himself
11 ~~man must do because~~ he is himself, a ~~sacrifice~~ ,
can
~~himself to himself because~~ he ~~will~~ ask nothing of
room
12 other ~~men~~ men, but ~~a~~ ~~place~~ amid remembered tragedies;
13 a sacrifice of himself to himself, almost, ~~so little~~ so little
14 may he bargain, of the moment to the moment.

Section (6): In this section (numbered "V"), Yeats canceled a passage at the beginning; the entire section is transcribed.

[NLI 13,567, 12^{r}]

V
~~our modern philosophy that~~ bear ~~always~~
1 Yet it may be that ~~science~~, our ~~science, rem remembering that its~~
~~those~~
17th
2 foundations laid at the close of the ~~seventeenth~~ century must go
3 should they attend to that slow-moving flower, that with
may go too
4 those foundations ^ all that seems to them most reasonable, most
5 orderly in our civilisation. ~~Then perhaps all will get~~
as Prof
6 ~~nothing~~ or it may ~~even~~ be as Richet suggests at

[NLI 13,567, 11^{v}]

1 our science, our modern philosophy
keep a subconscious knowledge
2 ~~useful raft~~ – ~~may remember~~ that
roped
3 their raft ~~was~~ ~~clamped~~ together at the end
must
4 of the 17th ~~might well~~ part, did but glance
5 at that slow moving flower, & abandon us
6 to that storm.

11^{v} Arrowed to replace ll. 1–5 on facing 12^{r}.

2 For "useful" read "a useful."

5 moving flower] William Crookes's account of the flower was published in 1874: "The hands and fingers (of materialization) do not always appear to me to be solid and life-like. Sometimes, indeed, they present more the

[NLI 13,567, 13r]

1 the end of his survey of ~~Res~~ Psychical research, from the
2 first experiments of Sir William Crookes to the
it is about after a steady scrutiny ~~the~~
3 present, that ~~we are about~~ to discover^the
intellect ~~&~~
4 poverty of the human ~~understanding~~ that we are
lost amid
5 ~~about to find our seves seles selves~~ amid^~~new~~
6 a ~~surrounding intellect surrounding intellect as~~
other intellects near but invisible and more
7 ~~incomprehensible~~ ~~among intellectual existences~~^~~as~~ incomprehensible
than ~~happen~~ ever happen
8 ~~as~~^the most distant stars. Should ~~that be so the~~
9 mass of men ~~like~~ lacking those customary convenient
10 explanations may plunge into the most indefensible
11 superstition.
we ~~might~~ may
~~should we~~^~~find~~
12 ~~or should science too long without its attesting~~, ~~convince men~~
~~its suddenly~~ lacking its ~~happy~~ convenient, happy
13 ~~find that those customary convenient~~ explanations ~~no longer~~

---

appearance of a nebulous cloud partly condensed into the form of a hand. This is not equally visible to all present. For instance, a flower or other small object is seen to move; one person present will see a luminous cloud hovering over it, another will detect a nebulous-looking hand, whilst others will see nothing at all but the moving flower. . . . [The hand] is not always a mere form, but sometimes appears perfectly life-like and graceful, the fingers moving and the flesh apparently as human as that of any in the room. At the wrist, or arm, it becomes hazy, and faces off into a luminous cloud. "To the touch, the hand sometimes appears icy cold and dead, at other times, warm and life-like, grasping my own with the firm pressure of an old friend." (*Crookes and the Spirit World*, p. 119).

13r, l. 4 Yeats, by canceling "understanding" and replacing it with "intellect," seems to be suggesting the contemporary scientific intellect, which he is attacking here. Richet, on the other hand, is cautioning the practitioners of the new discipline: "Metapsychics will then emerge from Occultism, as Chemistry emerged from Alchemy: and none can foresee its amazing career. But we must keep clear of illusions: the fragments of uncomprehended truth that the science of the occult offers to us reveal the poverty of the human understanding. The study of the heavens soon convinces an astronomer that man is an infinitesimally small object in the universe. Similarly in metapsychic science, when pale and fugitive gleams reveal intellectual worlds circling around us and in us, we feel that these worlds may perhaps ever remain as distant and incomprehensible as the far, incomprehensible starts in the depths of space." Charles Richet, *Thirty Years in Psychical Research*, tr. Stanley de Brath (London, 1923), pp. 625–626. Richet defines "metapsychics" as "a science dealing with mechanical or psychological phenomena due to forces that seem to be intelligent, or to unknown powers latent in human intelligence." Yeats probably received with ambivalent feelings Richet's attack on spiritualists' misuse of the work of Crookes and others: "They refused to see that metapsychic facts are of the present, not of the beyond, for perhaps there is no beyond. 'The beyond' has been their ruin, and they have lost themselves in puerile theology and theosophy" (pp. 6, 13).

[NLI 13,567, 13[r], continued]

as did
~~fall~~ ~~pour~~ plunge, ~~like~~ Rome in the fourth century ~~into~~
14 ~~may match their kno knowledge may return to their~~
according to some philosopher of that day into
15 ~~old suppositions, or new superstitions~~ " a fabulous formless darkness"
Rome
16 may burn like Europe, as ^ it did ~~aced~~ ^ according to
~~during Romes decay~~
17 a philosopher of that time, ~~little before the fall of Rome~~.

18 Should G. R. Wells aflict you
19 Put white-wash in a ~~pale~~ pail
20 Paint "science, opium of the subburbs"
21 On some waste wall

13[r], l. 18 For "G. R. Wells" read "H. G. Wells."